Howard Shreve Fisher

𝔉rancis 𝔓arkman's 𝔚orks.

NEW LIBRARY EDITION.

Vol. VIII.

FRANCIS PARKMAN'S WORKS.

New Library Edition.

Louis Joseph, Marquis de Montcalm — Gozon de Saint-Veran.

From the painting in the possession of the Marquis de Montcalm.

MONTCALM AND WOLFE, I., *Frontispiece.*

MONTCALM AND WOLFE.

FRANCE AND ENGLAND IN NORTH AMERICA.

PART SEVENTH.

BY

FRANCIS PARKMAN.

IN TWO VOLUMES.
VOL. I.

BOSTON:
LITTLE, BROWN, AND COMPANY.
1912.

𝔓rinters

S. J. Parkhill & Co., Boston, U. S. A.

TO

HARVARD COLLEGE,

THE ALMA MATER UNDER WHOSE INFLUENCE THE
PURPOSE OF WRITING IT WAS CONCEIVED,

THIS BOOK

IS AFFECTIONATELY INSCRIBED.

PREFACE.

THE names on the titlepage stand as representative of the two nations whose final contest for the control of North America is the subject of the book.

A very large amount of unpublished material has been used in its preparation, consisting for the most part of documents copied from the archives and libraries of France and England, especially from the Archives de la Marine et des Colonies, the Archives de la Guerre, and the Archives Nationales at Paris, and the Public Record Office and the British Museum at London. The papers copied for the present work in France alone exceed six thousand folio pages of manuscript, additional and supplementary to the "Paris Documents" procured for the State of New York under the agency of Mr. Brodhead. The copies made in England form ten volumes, besides many English documents consulted in

the original manuscript. Great numbers of
autograph letters, diaries, and other writings
of persons engaged in the war have also been
examined on this side of the Atlantic.

I owe to the kindness of the present Marquis
de Montcalm the permission to copy all the letters written by his ancestor, General Montcalm,
when in America, to members of his family in
France. General Montcalm, from his first arrival in Canada to a few days before his death,
also carried on an active correspondence with
one of his chief officers, Bourlamaque, with
whom he was on terms of intimacy. These
autograph letters are now preserved in a private
collection. I have examined them, and obtained
copies of the whole. They form an interesting
complement to the official correspondence of the
writer, and throw the most curious side-lights
on the persons and events of the time.

Besides manuscripts, the printed matter in the
form of books, pamphlets, contemporary newspapers, and other publications relating to the
American part of the Seven Years' War, is
varied and abundant; and I believe I may safely
say that nothing in it of much consequence has
escaped me. The liberality of some of the older
States of the Union, especially New York and

Pennsylvania, in printing the voluminous records of their colonial history, has saved me a deal of tedious labor.

The whole of this published and unpublished mass of evidence has been read and collated with extreme care, and more than common pains have been taken to secure accuracy of statement. The study of books and papers, however, could not alone answer the purpose. The plan of the work was formed in early youth; and though various causes have long delayed its execution, it has always been kept in view. Meanwhile, I have visited and examined every spot where events of any importance in connection with the contest took place, and have observed with attention such scenes and persons as might help to illustrate those I meant to describe. In short, the subject has been studied as much from life and in the open air as at the library table.

These two volumes are a departure from chronological sequence. The period between 1700 and 1748 has been passed over for a time. When this gap is filled, the series of "France and England in North America" will form a continuous history of the French occupation of the continent.

The portrait in the first volume is from a

photograph of the original picture in possession of the Marquis de Montcalm ; that in the second, from a photograph of the original picture in possession of Admiral Warde.

BOSTON, September 16, 1884.

CONTENTS.

———◆———

CHAPTER VI.

1754, 1755.

THE SIGNAL OF BATTLE.

CHAPTER VII.

1755.

BRADDOCK.

CHAPTER VIII.

1755.

REMOVAL OF THE ACADIANS.

CHAPTER IX

1755.

DIESKAU.

CHAPTER X.

1755, 1756.

SHIRLEY. — BORDER WAR.

CHAPTER XI.

1712–1756.

MONTCALM.

CHAPTER XII.

1756.

OSWEGO.

CHAPTER XIII.

1756, 1757.

PARTISAN WAR.

CHAPTER XIV.

1757.

MONTCALM AND VAUDREUIL.

CHAPTER XV.

1757.

FORT WILLIAM HENRY.

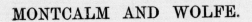

MONTCALM AND WOLFE.

BRITISH COLONIES
AND
NORTHERN NEW FRANCE
1750 – 1760.

LAKE SUPERIOR

Ojibwas

L.Nip

Sioux

Ft.Ste Marie

LAKE HURON

Michillimackinac

Ottigamics

Sacs
R.Wisconsin

Ft.La Baye

Winnebagoes

Menomonies

Ottawas

Ojibwas

Ft.Toront

Iowas

R.Mississippi

R. James

LAKE MICHIGAN

Wyandots

R. Des Moines

Pottawattamies

Detroit

LAKE ERIE

R.le Boeuf

Venang

R.Miami

R.Maumee

Wyandots

Logstown

R.Illinois

R.St Joseph

Delawares

Ft.Fort

Piekawillany

Shawanoes

R.Meskeet

Miamis

R.Maumee

Mingoes

R.Cuisi

R.Missouri

Vincennes

R.Kentucky

Kaskaskia

Fr.Cahokia

Fr.Chartres

R.Ohio

Chero

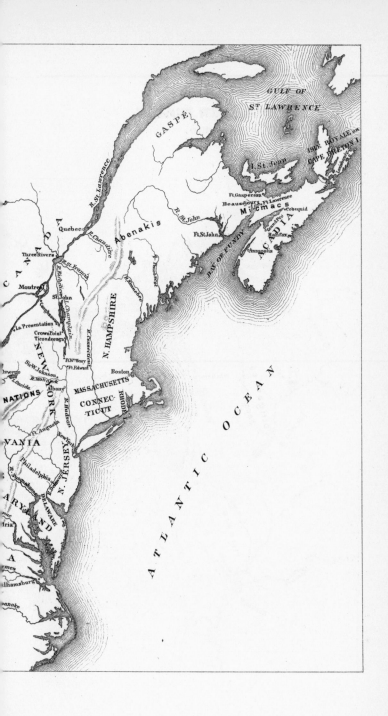

MONTCALM AND WOLFE.

INTRODUCTION.

IT is the nature of great events to obscure the great events that came before them. The Seven Years' War in Europe is seen but dimly through revolutionary convulsions and Napoleonic tempests; and the same contest in America is half lost to sight behind the storm-cloud of the War of Independence. Few at this day see the momentous issues involved in it, or the greatness of the danger that it averted. The strife that armed all the civilized world began here. "Such was the complication of political interests," says Voltaire, "that a cannon-shot fired in America could give the signal that set Europe in a blaze." Not quite. It was not a cannon-shot, but a volley from the hunting-pieces of a few backwoodsmen, commanded by a Virginian youth, George Washington.

To us of this day, the result of the American part of the war seems a foregone conclusion. It was far from being so; and very far from being so regarded by our forefathers. The numerical superiority of the British colonies was offset by organic weaknesses fatal to vigorous and united action. Nor at the outset did they, or the mother-country, aim at conquering Canada, but only at pushing back her boundaries. Canada — using the name in its restricted sense — was a position of great strength; and even when her dependencies were overcome, she could hold her own against forces far superior. Armies could reach her only by three routes, — the Lower St. Lawrence on the east, the Upper St. Lawrence on the west, and Lake Champlain on the south. The first access was guarded by a fortress almost impregnable by nature, and the second by a long chain of dangerous rapids; while the third offered a series of points easy to defend. During this same war, Frederic of Prussia held his ground triumphantly against greater odds, though his kingdom was open on all sides to attack.

It was the fatuity of Louis XV. and his Pompadour that made the conquest of Canada possible. Had they not broken the traditionary policy of France, allied themselves to Austria, her ancient enemy, and plunged needlessly into the European war, the whole force of the kingdom would have been turned, from the first, to the humbling of England and the defence of the French colonies. The French soldiers left dead on inglorious Continental battle-fields could have saved Canada, and perhaps made good her claim to the vast territories of the West.

But there were other contingencies. The possession of Canada was a question of diplomacy as well as of war. If England conquered her, she might

restore her, as she had lately restored Cape Breton.
She had an interest in keeping France alive on the
American continent. More than one clear eye saw,
at the middle of the last century, that the subjection
of Canada would lead to a revolt of the British
colonies. So long as an active and enterprising
enemy threatened their borders, they could not break
with the mother-country, because they needed her
help. And if the arms of France had prospered in
the other hemisphere; if she had gained in Europe
or Asia territories with which to buy back what she
had lost in America, then, in all likelihood, Canada
would have passed again into her hands.

The most momentous and far-reaching question
ever brought to issue on this continent was: Shall
France remain here, or shall she not? If, by diplomacy or war, she had preserved but the half, or less
than the half, of her American possessions, then a
barrier would have been set to the spread of the Eng-
lish-speaking races; there would have been no Revolutionary War; and for a long time, at least, no
independence. It was not a question of scanty popu-
lations strung along the banks of the St. Lawrence;
it was — or under a government of any worth it would
have been — a question of the armies and generals of
France. America owes much to the imbecility of
Louis XV. and the ambitious vanity and personal
dislikes of his mistress.

The Seven Years' War made England what she is.
It crippled the commerce of her rival, ruined France

in two continents, and blighted her as a colonial power. It gave England the control of the seas and the mastery of North America and India, made her the first of commercial nations, and prepared that vast colonial system that has planted new Englands in every quarter of the globe. And while it made England what she is, it supplied to the United States the indispensable condition of their greatness, if not of their national existence.

Before entering on the story of the great contest, we will look at the parties to it on both sides of the Atlantic.

CHAPTER I.

1745–1755.

THE COMBATANTS.

ENGLAND IN THE EIGHTEENTH CENTURY: HER POLITICAL AND
SOCIAL ASPECTS; HER MILITARY CONDITION. — FRANCE: HER
POWER AND IMPORTANCE. — SIGNS OF DECAY. — THE COURT,
THE NOBLES, THE CLERGY, THE PEOPLE. — THE KING AND
POMPADOUR. — THE PHILOSOPHERS. — GERMANY. — PRUSSIA. —
FREDERIC II. — RUSSIA. — STATE OF EUROPE. — WAR OF THE
AUSTRIAN SUCCESSION. — AMERICAN COLONIES OF FRANCE AND
ENGLAND. — CONTRASTED SYSTEMS AND THEIR RESULTS. —
CANADA: ITS STRONG MILITARY POSITION. — FRENCH CLAIMS
TO THE CONTINENT. — BRITISH COLONIES. — NEW ENGLAND.
— VIRGINIA. — PENNSYLVANIA. — NEW YORK. — JEALOUSIES,
DIVISIONS, INTERNAL DISPUTES. — MILITARY WEAKNESS.

THE latter half of the reign of George II. was one
of the most prosaic periods in English history. The
civil wars and the Restoration had had their enthusi-
asms, religion and liberty on one side, and loyalty
on the other; but the old fires declined when William
III. came to the throne, and died to ashes under the
House of Hanover. Loyalty lost half its inspiration
when it lost the tenet of the divine right of kings;
and nobody could now hold that tenet with any consistency except the defeated and despairing Jacobites.
Nor had anybody as yet proclaimed the rival dogma

of the divine right of the people. The reigning
monarch held his crown neither of God nor of the
nation, but of a parliament controlled by a ruling
class. The Whig aristocracy had done a priceless
service to English liberty. It was full of political
capacity, and by no means void of patriotism; but it
was only a part of the national life. Nor was it at
present moved by political emotions in any high
sense. It had done its great work when it expelled
the Stuarts and placed William of Orange on the
throne; its ascendency was now complete. The
Stuarts had received their death-blow at Culloden;
and nothing was left to the dominant party but to
dispute on subordinate questions, and contend for
office among themselves. The Tory squires sulked
in their country-houses, hunted foxes, and grumbled
against the reigning dynasty, yet hardly wished to
see the nation convulsed by a counter-revolution and
another return of the Stuarts.

If politics had run to commonplace, so had morals;
and so too had religion. Despondent writers of the
day even complained that British courage had died
out. There was little sign to the common eye that,
under a dull and languid surface, forces were at work
preparing a new life, material, moral, and intellectual. As yet, Whitefield and Wesley had not
wakened the drowsy conscience of the nation, nor
the voice of William Pitt roused it like a trumpet-
peal.

It was the unwashed and unsavory England of

Hogarth, Fielding, Smollett, and Sterne; of Tom Jones, Squire Western, Lady Bellaston, and Parson Adams; of the "Rake's Progress" and "Marriage à la Mode;" of the lords and ladies who yet live in the undying gossip of Horace Walpole, be-powdered, be-patched, and be-rouged, flirting at masked balls, playing cards till daylight, retailing scandal, and exchanging double meanings. Beau Nash reigned king over the gaming-tables of Bath; the ostrich-plumes of great ladies mingled with the peacock-feathers of courtesans in the rotunda at Ranelagh Gardens; and young lords in velvet suits and em-broidered ruffles played away their patrimony at White's Chocolate-House or Arthur's Club. Vice was bolder than to-day, and manners more courtly, perhaps, but far more coarse.

The humbler clergy were thought — sometimes with reason — to be no fit company for gentlemen, and country parsons drank their ale in the squire's kitchen. The passenger-wagon spent the better part of a fortnight in creeping from London to York. Travellers carried pistols against footpads and mounted highwaymen. Dick Turpin and Jack Sheppard were popular heroes. Tyburn counted its victims by scores; and as yet no Howard had ap-peared to reform the inhuman abominations of the prisons.

The middle class, though fast rising in importance, was feebly and imperfectly represented in Parliament. The boroughs were controlled by the nobility and

gentry, or by corporations open to influence or
bribery. Parliamentary corruption had been reduced
to a system; and offices, sinecures, pensions, and
gifts of money were freely used to keep ministers in
power. The great offices of State were held by men
sometimes of high ability, but of whom not a few
divided their lives among politics, cards, wine, horse-
racing, and women, till time and the gout sent them
to the waters of Bath. The dull, pompous, and
irascible old King had two ruling passions, — money,
and his Continental dominions of Hanover. His
elder son, the Prince of Wales, was a centre of opposition to him. His younger son, the Duke of Cumberland, a character far more pronounced and vigorous,
had won the day at Culloden, and lost it at Fontenoy;
but whether victor or vanquished, had shown the
same vehement bull-headed courage, of late a little
subdued by fast-growing corpulency. The Duke of
Newcastle, the head of the government, had gained
power and kept it by his rank and connections, his
wealth, his county influence, his control of boroughs,
and the extraordinary assiduity and devotion with
which he practised the arts of corruption. Henry
Fox, grasping, unscrupulous, with powerful talents,
a warm friend after his fashion, and a most indulgent
father; Carteret, with his strong, versatile intellect
and jovial intrepidity; the two Townshends, Mans-
field, Halifax, and Chesterfield, — were conspicuous
figures in the politics of the time. One man towered
above them all. Pitt had many enemies and many

critics. They called him ambitious, audacious, arrogant, theatrical, pompous, domineering; but what he has left for posterity is a loftiness of soul, undaunted courage, fiery and passionate eloquence, proud incorruptibility, domestic virtues rare in his day, unbounded faith in the cause for which he stood, and abilities which without wealth or strong connections were destined to place him on the height of power. The middle class, as yet almost voiceless, looked to him as its champion; but he was not the champion of a class. His patriotism was as comprehensive as it was haughty and unbending. He lived for England, loved her with intense devotion, knew her, believed in her, and made her greatness his own; or rather, he was himself England incarnate.

The nation was not then in fighting equipment. After the peace of Aix-la-Chapelle, the army within the three kingdoms had been reduced to about eighteen thousand men. Added to these were the garrisons of Minorca and Gibraltar, and six or seven independent companies in the American colonies. Of sailors, less than seventeen thousand were left in the Royal Navy. Such was the condition of England on the eve of one of the most formidable wars in which she was ever engaged.

Her rival across the Channel was drifting slowly and unconsciously towards the cataclysm of the Revolution; yet the old monarchy, full of the germs of decay, was still imposing and formidable. The

House of Bourbon held the three thrones of France,
Spain, and Naples; and their threatened union in a
family compact was the terror of European diplomacy.
At home France was the foremost of the Continental
nations; and she boasted herself second only to
Spain as a colonial power.   She disputed with England the mastery of India, owned the islands of
Bourbon and Mauritius, held important possessions
in the West Indies, and claimed all North America
except Mexico and a strip of sea-coast.   Her navy
was powerful, her army numerous and well appointed;
but she lacked the great commanders of the last reign.
Soubise, Maillebois, Contades, Broglie, and Clermont
were but weak successors of Condé, Turenne, Ven-
dôme, and Villars.   Marshal Richelieu was supreme
in the arts of gallantry, and more famous for con-
quests of love than of war.   The best generals of
Louis XV. were foreigners.   Lowendal sprang from
the royal house of Denmark; and Saxe, the best of
all, was one of the three hundred and fifty-four bas-
tards of Augustus the Strong, Elector of Saxony and
King of Poland.   He was now, 1750, dying at Cham-
bord, his iron constitution ruined by debaucheries.

The triumph of the Bourbon monarchy was complete.   The government had become one great ma-
chine of centralized administration, with a king for
its head; though a king who neither could nor would
direct it.   All strife was over between the Crown
and the nobles; feudalism was robbed of its vitality,
and left the mere image of its former self, with noth-

ing alive but its abuses, its caste privileges, its exactions, its pride and vanity, its power to vex and
oppress.   In England, the nobility were a living part
of the nation, and if they had privileges, they paid
for them by constant service to the State; in France,
they had no political life, and were separated from
the people by sharp lines of demarcation.   From
warrior chiefs, they had changed to courtiers.   Those
of them who could afford it, and many who could
not, left their estates to the mercy of stewards, and
gathered at Versailles to revolve about the throne as
glittering satellites, paid in pomp, empty distinctions,
or rich sinecures, for the power they had lost.   They
ruined their vassals to support the extravagance by
which they ruined themselves.   Such as stayed at
home were objects of pity and scorn.   "Out of your
Majesty's presence," said one of them, "we are not
only wretched, but ridiculous."

Versailles was like a vast and gorgeous theatre,
where all were actors and spectators at once; and all
played their parts to perfection.   Here swarmed by
thousands this silken nobility, whose ancestors rode
cased in iron.   Pageant followed pageant.   A picture
of the time preserves for us an evening in the great
hall of the Château, where the King, with piles of
louis d'or before him, sits at a large oval green table,
throwing the dice, among princes and princesses,
dukes and duchesses, ambassadors, marshals of
France, and a vast throng of courtiers, like an animated bed of tulips; for men and women alike wear

bright and varied colors. Above are the frescoes of
Le Brun; around are walls of sculptured and inlaid
marbles, with mirrors that reflect the restless splendors
of the scene and the blaze of chandeliers, sparkling
with crystal pendants. Pomp, magnificence, profusion, were a business and a duty at the Court.
Versailles was a gulf into which the labor of France
poured its earnings; and it was never full.

Here the graces and charms were a political power.
Women had prodigious influence, and the two sexes
were never more alike. Men not only dressed in
colors, but they wore patches and carried muffs.
The robust qualities of the old nobility still lingered
among the exiles of the provinces, while at Court
they had melted into refinements tainted with corruption. Yet if the butterflies of Versailles had lost
virility, they had not lost courage. They fought as
gayly as they danced. In the halls which they
haunted of yore, turned now into a historical picture-
gallery, one sees them still, on the canvas of Lenfant,
Lepaon, or Vernet, facing death with careless gallantry, in their small three-cornered hats, powdered
perukes, embroidered coats, and lace ruffles. Their
valets served them with ices in the trenches, under
the cannon of besieged towns. A troop of actors
formed part of the army-train of Marshal Saxe. At
night there was a comedy, a ballet, or a ball, and in
the morning a battle. Saxe, however, himself a
sturdy German, while he recognized their fighting
value, and knew well how to make the best of it,

sometimes complained that they were volatile, excitable, and difficult to manage.

The weight of the Court, with its pomps, luxuries, and wars, bore on the classes least able to support it. The poorest were taxed most; the richest not at all. The nobles, in the main, were free from imposts. The clergy, who had vast possessions, were wholly free, though they consented to make voluntary gifts to the Crown; and when, in a time of emergency, the minister Machault required them, in common with all others hitherto exempt, to contribute a twentieth of their revenues to the charges of government, they passionately refused, declaring that they would obey God rather than the King. The cultivators of the soil were ground to the earth by a threefold extortion, — the seigniorial dues, the tithes of the Church, and the multiplied exactions of the Crown, enforced with merciless rigor by the farmers of the revenue, who enriched themselves by wringing the peasant on the one hand, and cheating the King on the other. A few great cities shone with all that is most brilliant in society, intellect, and concentred wealth; while the country that paid the costs lay in ignorance and penury, crushed and despairing. On the inhabitants of towns, too, the demands of the tax-gatherer were extreme; but here the immense vitality of the French people bore up the burden. While agriculture languished, and intolerable oppression turned peasants into beggars or desperadoes; while the clergy were sapped by cor-

ruption, and the nobles enervated by luxury and
ruined by extravagance,— the middle class was growing in thrift and strength.   Arts and commerce prospered, and the seaports were alive with foreign trade.
Wealth tended from all sides towards the centre.
The King did not love his capital; but he and his
favorites amused themselves with adorning it.   Some
of the chief embellishments that make Paris what it
is to-day — the Place de la Concorde, the Champs
Élysées, and many of the palaces of the Faubourg
St. Germain — date from this reign.

One of the vicious conditions of the time was the
separation in sympathies and interests of the four
great classes of the nation, — clergy, nobles, burghers,
and peasants; and each of these, again, divided itself
into incoherent fragments.   France was an aggregate
of disjointed parts, held together by a meshwork of
arbitrary power, itself touched with decay.   A disastrous blow was struck at the national welfare when
the government of Louis XV. revived the odious
persecution of the Huguenots.   The attempt to scour
heresy out of France cost her the most industrious
and virtuous part of her population, and robbed her
of those most fit to resist the mocking scepticism and
turbid passions that burst out like a deluge with the
Revolution.

Her manifold ills were summed up in the King.
Since the Valois, she had had no monarch so worthless.   He did not want understanding, still less the
graces of person.   In his youth the people called him

the "Well-beloved;" but by the middle of the century they so detested him that he dared not pass
through Paris, lest the mob should execrate him.
He had not the vigor of the true tyrant; but his
languor, his hatred of all effort, his profound selfishness, his listless disregard of public duty, and his
effeminate libertinism, mixed with superstitious devotion, made him no less a national curse.   Louis XIII.
was equally unfit to govern; but he gave the reins to
the Great Cardinal.   Louis XV. abandoned them to
a frivolous mistress, content that she should rule on
condition of amusing him.   It was a hard task; yet
Madame de Pompadour accomplished it by methods
infamous to him and to her.   She gained and long
kept the power that she coveted: filled the Bastille
with her enemies; made and unmade ministers;
appointed and removed generals.   Great questions of
policy were at the mercy of her caprices.   Through
her frivolous vanity, her personal likes and dislikes,
all the great departments of government — army,
navy, war, foreign affairs, justice, finance — changed
from hand to hand incessantly, and this at a time of
crisis when the kingdom needed the steadiest and
surest guidance.   Few of the officers of State, except,
perhaps, D'Argenson, could venture to disregard
her.   She turned out Orry, the comptroller-general,
put her favorite, Machault, into his place, then made
him keeper of the seals, and at last minister of
marine.   The Marquis de Puysieux, in the ministry
of foreign affairs, and the Comte de Saint-Florentin,

charged with the affairs of the clergy, took their cue
from her. The King stinted her in nothing. First
and last, she is reckoned to have cost him thirty-
six million francs, — answering now to more than as
many dollars.

The prestige of the monarchy was declining with
the ideas that had given it life and strength. A
growing disrespect for king, ministry, and clergy
was beginning to prepare the catastrophe that was
still some forty years in the future. While the
valleys and low places of the kingdom were dark
with misery and squalor, its heights were bright with
a gay society, — elegant, fastidious, witty, — craving
the pleasures of the mind as well as of the senses,
criticising everything, analyzing everything, believing nothing. Voltaire was in the midst of it, hating,
with all his vehement soul, the abuses that swarmed
about him, and assailing them with the inexhaustible
shafts of his restless and piercing intellect. Montes-
quieu was showing to a despot-ridden age the principles of political freedom. Diderot and D'Alembert
were beginning their revolutionary Encyclopædia.
Rousseau was sounding the first notes of his mad
eloquence, — the wild revolt of a passionate and dis-
eased genius against a world of falsities and wrongs.
The *salons* of Paris, cloyed with other pleasures,
alive to all that was racy and new, welcomed the
pungent doctrines, and played with them as children
play with fire, thinking no danger; as time went on,
even embraced them in a genuine spirit of hope and

good-will for humanity. The Revolution began at the top, — in the world of fashion, birth, and intellect, — and propagated itself downwards. "We walked on a carpet of flowers," Count Ségur afterwards said, "unconscious that it covered an abyss;" till the gulf yawned at last, and swallowed them.

Eastward, beyond the Rhine, lay the heterogeneous patchwork of the Holy Roman, or Germanic, Empire. The sacred bonds that throughout the Middle Ages had held together its innumerable fragments had lost their strength. The empire decayed as a whole; but not so the parts that composed it. In the south the House of Austria reigned over a formidable assemblage of States; and in the north the House of Brandenburg, promoted to royalty half a century before, had raised Prussia into an importance far beyond her extent and population. In her dissevered rags of territory lay the destinies of Germany. It was the late King, that honest, thrifty, dogged, headstrong despot, Frederic William, who had made his kingdom what it was, trained it to the perfection of drill, and left it to his son, Frederic II., the best engine of war in Europe. Frederic himself had passed between the upper and nether millstones of paternal discipline. Never did prince undergo such an apprenticeship. His father set him to the work of an overseer, or steward, flung plates at his head in the family circle, thrashed him with his rattan in public, bullied him for submitting to such treatment, and imprisoned him for trying to run away from it. He came at last out of purgatory; and Europe felt him to her farthest bounds. This bookish, philosophizing, verse-making cynic and profligate was soon to approve himself the first warrior of his time, and one of the first of all time.

Another power had lately risen on the European world. Peter the Great, half hero, half savage, had roused the inert barbarism of Russia into a titanic life. His daughter Elizabeth had succeeded to his throne, — heiress of his sensuality, if not of his talents.

Over all the continent the aspect of the times was the same. Power had everywhere left the plains and the lower slopes, and gathered at the summits. Popular life was at a stand. No great idea stirred the nations to their depths. The religious convulsions of the sixteenth and seventeenth centuries were over, and the earthquake of the French Revolution had not begun. At the middle of the eighteenth century the history of Europe turned on the balance of power; the observance of treaties; inheritance and succession; rivalries of sovereign houses struggling to win power or keep it, encroach on neighbors, or prevent neighbors from encroaching; bargains, intrigue, force, diplomacy, and the musket, in the interest not of peoples but of rulers. Princes, great and small, brooded over some real or fancied wrong,

nursed some dubious claim born of a marriage, a will,
or an ancient covenant fished out of the abyss of
time, and watched their moment to make it good.
The general opportunity came when, in 1740, the
Emperor Charles VI. died and bequeathed his personal dominions of the House of Austria to his
daughter, Maria Theresa. The chief Powers of
Europe had been pledged in advance to sustain the
will; and pending the event, the veteran Prince
Eugene had said that two hundred thousand soldiers
would be worth all their guaranties together. The
two hundred thousand were not there, and not a sovereign kept his word. They flocked to share the
spoil, and parcel out the motley heritage of the
young Queen. Frederic of Prussia led the way,
invaded her province of Silesia, seized it, and kept
it. The Elector of Bavaria and the King of Spain
claimed their share, and the Elector of Saxony and
the King of Sardinia prepared to follow the example.
France took part with Bavaria, and intrigued to set
the imperial crown on the head of the Elector, thinking to ruin her old enemy, the House of Austria, and
rule Germany through an emperor too weak to dispense with her support. England, jealous of her
designs, trembling for the balance of power, and
anxious for the Hanoverian possessions of her King,
threw herself into the strife on the side of Austria.
It was now that, in the Diet at Presburg, the beautiful and distressed Queen, her infant in her arms,
made her memorable appeal to the wild chivalry of

her Hungarian nobles; and, clashing their swords,
they shouted with one voice: "Let us die for our
king, Maria Theresa;" *Moriamur pro rege nostro,
Mariâ Theresiâ*, — one of the most dramatic scenes in
history; not quite true, perhaps, but near the truth.
Then came that confusion worse confounded called
the war of the Austrian Succession, with its Mollwitz,
its Dettingen, its Fontenoy, and its Scotch episode
of Culloden. The peace of Aix-la-Chapelle closed
the strife in 1748. Europe had time to breathe; but
the germs of discord remained alive.

THE AMERICAN COMBATANTS.

The French claimed all America, from the Alleghanies to the Rocky Mountains, and from Mexico
and Florida to the North Pole, except only the ill-
defined possessions of the English on the borders of
Hudson Bay; and to these vast regions, with adjacent islands, they gave the general name of New
France. They controlled the highways of the continent, for they held its two great rivers. First, they
had seized the St. Lawrence, and then planted themselves at the mouth of the Mississippi. Canada at
the north, and Louisiana at the south, were the keys
of a boundless interior, rich with incalculable possi-
bilities. The English colonies, ranged along the
Atlantic coast, had no royal road to the great inland,
and were, in a manner, shut between the mountains
and the sea. At the middle of the century they

numbered in all, from Georgia to Maine, about eleven
hundred and sixty thousand white inhabitants. By
the census of 1754 Canada had but fifty-five thousand.[1] Add those of Louisiana and Acadia, and the
whole white population under the French flag might
be something more than eighty thousand. Here is
an enormous disparity; and hence it has been argued
that the success of the English colonies and the
failure of the French was not due to difference of
religious and political systems, but simply to numerical preponderance. But this preponderance itself
grew out of a difference of systems. We have said
before, and it cannot be said too often, that in making Canada a citadel of the State religion, — a holy
of holies of exclusive Roman Catholic orthodoxy, —
the clerical monitors of the Crown robbed their country of a transatlantic empire. New France could
not grow with a priest on guard at the gate to let in
none but such as pleased him. One of the ablest of
Canadian governors, La Galissonière, seeing the
feebleness of the colony compared with the vastness
of its claims, advised the King to send ten thousand
peasants to occupy the valley of the Ohio, and hold
back the British swarm that was just then pushing
its advance-guard over the Alleghanies. It needed
no effort of the King to people his waste domain,
not with ten thousand peasants, but with twenty

[1] *Censuses of Canada*, iv. 61. Rameau (*La France aux Colonies*,
ii. 81) estimates the Canadian population, in 1755, at sixty-six thousand, besides *voyageurs*, Indian traders, etc. Vaudreuil, in 1760,
places it at seventy thousand.

times ten thousand Frenchmen of every station, —
the most industrious, most instructed, most disciplined by adversity and capable of self-rule, that
the country could boast.   While La Galissonière was
asking for colonists, the agents of the Crown, set
on by priestly fanaticism, or designing selfishness
masked with fanaticism, were pouring volleys of
musketry into Huguenot congregations, imprisoning
for life those innocent of all but their faith, — the
men in the galleys, the women in the pestiferous
dungeons of Aigues Mortes, — hanging their ministers,
kidnapping their children, and reviving, in short,
the dragonnades.   Now, as in the past century, many
of the victims escaped to the British colonies, and
became a part of them.   The Huguenots would have
hailed as a boon the permission to emigrate under
the fleur-de-lis, and build up a Protestant France in
the valleys of the West.   It would have been a bane
of absolutism, but a national glory; would have set
bounds to English colonization, and changed the face
of the continent.   The opportunity was spurned.
The dominant Church clung to its policy of rule and
ruin.   France built its best colony on a principle of
exclusion, and failed; England reversed the system,
and succeeded.

I have shown elsewhere the aspects of Canada,
where a rigid scion of the old European tree was set
to grow in the wilderness.   The military governor,
holding his miniature court on the rock of Quebec;
the feudal proprietors, whose domains lined the

shores of the St. Lawrence; the peasant; the roving
bushranger; the half-tamed savage, with crucifix and
scalping-knife; priests; friars; nuns; and soldiers,
— mingled to form a society the most picturesque
on the continent. What distinguished it from the
France that produced it was a total absence of revolt
against the laws of its being, — an absolute conservatism, an unquestioning acceptance of Church and
King. The Canadian, ignorant of everything but
what the priest saw fit to teach him, had never heard
of Voltaire; and if he had known him, would have
thought him a devil. He had, it is true, a spirit of
insubordination born of the freedom of the forest;
but if his instincts rebelled, his mind and soul were
passively submissive. The unchecked control of a
hierarchy robbed him of the independence of intellect
and character, without which, under the conditions
of modern life, a people must resign itself to a position of inferiority. Yet Canada had a vigor of her
own. It was not in spiritual deference only that she
differed from the country of her birth. Whatever
she had caught of its corruptions, she had caught
nothing of its effeminacy. The mass of her people
lived in a rude poverty, — not abject, like the peasant
of old France, nor ground down by the tax-gatherer;
while those of the higher ranks — all more or less engaged in pursuits of war or adventure, and inured
to rough journeyings and forest exposures — were
rugged as their climate. Even the French regular
troops, sent out to defend the colony, caught its

hardy spirit, and set an example of stubborn fighting which their comrades at home did not always
emulate.

Canada lay ensconced behind rocks and forests.
All along her southern boundaries, between her and
her English foes, lay a broad tract of wilderness,
shaggy with primeval woods. Innumerable streams
gurgled beneath their shadows; innumerable lakes
gleamed in the fiery sunsets; innumerable mountains
bared their rocky foreheads to the wind. These
wastes were ranged by her savage allies, — Micmacs,
Etechémins, Abenakis, Caughnawagas; and no
enemy could steal upon her unawares. Through the
midst of them stretched Lake Champlain, pointing
straight to the heart of the British settlements, — a
watery thoroughfare of mutual attack, and the only
approach by which, without a long *détour* by wilderness or sea, a hostile army could come within striking
distance of the colony. The French advanced post
of Fort Frederic, called Crown Point by the English,
barred the narrows of the lake, which thence spread
northward to the portals of Canada guarded by Fort
St. Jean. Southwestward, some fourteen hundred
miles as a bird flies, and twice as far by the prac-
ticable routes of travel, was Louisiana, the second of
the two heads of New France; while between lay the
realms of solitude where the Mississippi rolled its
sullen tide, and the Ohio wound its belt of silver
through the verdant woodlands.

To whom belonged this world of prairies and

forests? France claimed it by right of discovery and occupation. It was her explorers who, after De Soto, first set foot on it. The question of right, it is true, mattered little; for, right or wrong, neither claimant would yield her pretensions so long as she had strength to uphold them; yet one point is worth a moment's notice. The French had established an excellent system in the distribution of their American lands. Whoever received a grant from the Crown was required to improve it, and this within reasonable time. If he did not, the land ceased to be his, and was given to another more able or industrious. An international extension of her own principle would have destroyed the pretensions of France to all the countries of the West. She had called them hers for three-fourths of a century, and they were still a howling waste, yielding nothing to civilization but beaver-skins, with here and there a fort, trading-post, or mission, and three or four puny hamlets by the Mississippi and the Detroit. We have seen how she might have made for herself an indisputable title, and peopled the solitudes with a host to maintain it. She would not; others were at hand who both would and could; and the late claimant, disinherited and forlorn, would soon be left to count the cost of her bigotry.

The thirteen British colonies were alike, insomuch as they all had representative governments, and a basis of English law. But the differences among

them were great. Some were purely English; others
were made up of various races, though the Anglo-
Saxon was always predominant. Some had one prevailing religious creed; others had many creeds.
Some had charters, and some had not. In most cases
the governor was appointed by the Crown; in Pennsylvania and Maryland he was appointed by a feudal
proprietor, and in Connecticut and Rhode Island he
was chosen by the people. The differences of disposition and character were still greater than those of
form.

The four northern colonies, known collectively as
New England, were an exception to the general rule
of diversity. The smallest, Rhode Island, had features all its own; but the rest were substantially one
in nature and origin. The principal among them,
Massachusetts, may serve as the type of all. It was
a mosaic of little village republics, firmly cemented
together, and formed into a single body politic through
representatives sent to the " General Court " at Boston.
Its government, originally theocratic, now tended to
democracy, ballasted as yet by strong traditions of
respect for established worth and ability, as well as
by the influence of certain families prominent in
affairs for generations. Yet there were no distinct
class-lines, and popular power, like popular education, was widely diffused. Practically Massachusetts
was almost independent of the mother-country. Its
people were purely English, of sound yeoman stock,
with an abundant leaven drawn from the best of the

Puritan gentry; but their original character had been somewhat modified by changed conditions of life. A harsh and exacting creed, with its stiff formalism and its prohibition of wholesome recreation; excess in the pursuit of gain, — the only resource left to energies robbed of their natural play; the struggle for existence on a hard and barren soil; and the isolation of a narrow village life, — joined to produce, in the meaner sort, qualities which were unpleasant, and sometimes repulsive. Puritanism was not an unmixed blessing. Its view of human nature was dark, and its attitude towards it one of repression. It strove to crush out not only what is evil, but much that is innocent and salutary. Human nature so treated will take its revenge, and for every vice that it loses find another instead. Nevertheless, while New England Puritanism bore its peculiar crop of faults, it produced also many good and sound fruits. An uncommon vigor, joined to the hardy virtues of a masculine race, marked the New England type. The sinews, it is true, were hardened at the expense of blood and flesh, — and this literally as well as figuratively; but the staple of character was a sturdy conscientiousness, an undespairing courage, patriotism, public spirit, sagacity, and a strong good sense. A great change, both for better and for worse, has since come over it, due largely to reaction against the unnatural rigors of the past. That mixture, which is now too common, of cool emotions with excitable brains, was then rarely seen. The New England colonies abounded in high examples of public and private virtue, though not always under the most prepossessing forms. They were conspicuous, moreover, for intellectual activity, and were by no means without intellectual eminence. Massachusetts had produced at least two men whose fame had crossed the sea, — Edwards, who out of the grim theology of Calvin mounted to sublime heights of mystical speculation; and Franklin, famous already by his discoveries in electricity. On the other hand, there were few genuine New Englanders who, however personally modest, could divest themselves of the notion that they belonged to a people in an especial manner the object of divine approval; and this self-righteousness, along with certain other traits, failed to commend the Puritan colonies to the favor of their fellows. Then, as now, New England was best known to her neighbors by her worst side.

In one point, however, she found general applause. She was regarded as the most military among the British colonies. This reputation was well founded, and is easily explained. More than all the rest, she lay open to attack. The long waving line of the New England border, with its lonely hamlets and scattered farms, extended from the Kennebec to beyond the Connecticut, and was everywhere vulnerable to the guns and tomahawks of the neighboring French and their savage allies. The colonies towards the south had thus far been safe from danger. New York alone was within striking distance of the Cana-

dian war-parties. That province then consisted of a
line of settlements up the Hudson and the Mohawk,
and was little exposed to attack except at its northern
end, which was guarded by the fortified town of
Albany, with its outlying posts, and by the friendly
and warlike Mohawks, whose "castles" were close
at hand. Thus New England had borne the heaviest
brunt of the preceding wars, not only by the forest,
but also by the sea; for the French of Acadia and
Cape Breton confronted her coast, and she was often at
blows with them. Fighting had been a necessity with
her, and she had met the emergency after a method
extremely defective, but the best that circumstances
would permit. Having no trained officers and no
disciplined soldiers, and being too poor to maintain
either, she borrowed her warriors from the workshop
and the plough, and officered them with lawyers,
merchants, mechanics, or farmers. To compare them
with good regular troops would be folly; but they
did, on the whole, better than could have been expected, and in the last war achieved the brilliant
success of the capture of Louisbourg. This exploit,
due partly to native hardihood and partly to good
luck, greatly enhanced the military repute of New
England, or rather was one of the chief sources of it.

The great colony of Virginia stood in strong contrast to New England. In both the population was
English; but the one was Puritan with Roundhead
traditions, and the other, so far as concerned its governing class, Anglican, with Cavalier traditions. In

the one, every man, woman, and child could read
and write; in the other, Sir William Berkeley once
thanked God that there were no free schools, and no
prospect of any for a century. The hope had found
fruition. The lower classes of Virginia were as un-
taught as the warmest friend of popular ignorance
could wish. New England had a native literature
more than respectable under the circumstances, while
Virginia had none; numerous industries, while
Virginia was all agriculture, with but a single crop;
a homogeneous society and a democratic spirit, while
her rival was an aristocracy. Virginian society was
distinctly stratified. On the lowest level were the
negro slaves, nearly as numerous as all the rest together; next, the indented servants and the poor
whites, of low origin, good-humored, but boisterous,
and sometimes vicious; next, the small and despised
class of tradesmen and mechanics; next, the farmers
and lesser planters, who were mainly of good English
stock, and who merged insensibly into the ruling
class of the great landowners. It was these last who
represented the colony and made the laws. They
may be described as English country squires trans-
planted to a warm climate and turned slave-masters.
They sustained their position by entails, and constantly undermined it by the reckless profusion which
ruined them at last. Many of them were well born,
with an immense pride of descent, increased by the
habit of domination. Indolent and energetic by
turns; rich in natural gifts and often poor in book-

learning, though some, in the lack of good teaching
at home, had been bred in the English universities;
high-spirited, generous to a fault; keeping open house
in their capacious mansions, among vast tobacco-fields
and toiling negroes, and living in a rude pomp where
the fashions of St. James were somewhat oddly
grafted on the roughness of the plantation, — what
they wanted in schooling was supplied by an education which books alone would have been impotent to
give, the education which came with the possession
and exercise of political power, and the sense of a
position to maintain, joined to a bold spirit of independence and a patriotic attachment to the Old
Dominion. They were few in number; they raced,
gambled, drank, and swore; they did everything that
in Puritan eyes was most reprehensible; and in the
day of need they gave the United Colonies a body of
statesmen and orators which had no equal on the
continent. A vigorous aristocracy favors the growth
of personal eminence, even in those who are not of
it, but only near it.

The essential antagonism of Virginia and New
England was afterwards to become, and to remain for
a century, an element of the first influence in American history. Each might have learned much from
the other; but neither did so till, at last, the strife
of their contending principles shook the continent.
Pennsylvania differed widely from both. She was a
conglomerate of creeds and races, — English, Irish,
Germans, Dutch, and Swedes; Quakers, Lutherans,

Presbyterians, Romanists, Moravians, and a variety
of nondescript sects. The Quakers prevailed in the
eastern districts; quiet, industrious, virtuous, and
serenely obstinate. The Germans were strongest
towards the centre of the colony, and were chiefly
peasants; successful farmers, but dull, ignorant, and
superstitious. Towards the west were the Irish, of
whom some were Celts, always quarrelling with their
German neighbors, who detested them; but the
greater part were Protestants of Scotch descent, from
Ulster; a vigorous border population. Virginia and
New England had each a strong distinctive character.
Pennsylvania, with her heterogeneous population,
had none but that which she owed to the sober
neutral tints of Quaker existence. A more thriving
colony there was not on the continent. Life, if
monotonous, was smooth and contented. Trade and
the arts grew. Philadelphia, next to Boston, was
the largest town in British America; and was, moreover, the intellectual centre of the middle and southern
colonies. Unfortunately, for her credit in the approaching war, the Quaker influence made Pennsylvania non-combatant. Politically, too, she was an
anomaly; for, though utterly unfeudal in disposition
and character, she was under feudal superiors in the
persons of the representatives of William Penn, the
original grantee.

New York had not as yet reached the relative
prominence which her geographical position and
inherent strength afterwards gave her. The English,

joined to the Dutch, the original settlers, were the
dominant population; but a half-score of other lan-
guages were spoken in the province, the chief among
them being that of the Huguenot French in the
southern parts, and that of the Germans on the
Mohawk. In religion, the province was divided
between the Anglican Church, with government
support and popular dislike, and numerous dissenting
sects, chiefly Lutherans, Independents, Presbyterians,
and members of the Dutch Reformed Church. The
little city of New York, like its great successor, was
the most cosmopolitan place on the continent, and
probably the gayest. It had, in abundance, balls,
concerts, theatricals, and evening clubs, with plenti-
ful dances and other amusements for the poorer
classes. Thither in the winter months came the
great hereditary proprietors on the Hudson; for the
old Dutch feudality still held its own, and the manors
of Van Rensselaer, Cortland, and Livingston, with
their seigniorial privileges, and the great estates and
numerous tenantry of the Schuylers and other leading
families, formed the basis of an aristocracy, some of
whose members had done good service to the province, and were destined to do more. Pennsylvania
was feudal in form, and not in spirit; Virginia in
spirit, and not in form; New England in neither;
and New York largely in both. This social crystal-
lization had, it is true, many opponents. In politics,
as in religion, there were sharp antagonisms and frequent quarrels. They centred in the city; for in the

well-stocked dwellings of the Dutch farmers along
the Hudson there reigned a tranquil and prosperous
routine; and the Dutch border town of Albany had
not its like in America for unruffled conservatism and
quaint picturesqueness.

Of the other colonies, the briefest mention will
suffice: New Jersey, with its wholesome population
of farmers; tobacco-growing Maryland, which, but
for its proprietary government and numerous Roman
Catholics, might pass for another Virginia, inferior in
growth, and less decisive in features; Delaware, a
modest appendage of Pennsylvania; wild and rude
North Carolina; and, farther on, South Carolina and
Georgia, too remote from the seat of war to take a
noteworthy part in it. The attitude of these various
colonies towards each other is hardly conceivable to
an American of the present time. They had no
political tie except a common allegiance to the British
Crown. Communication between them was difficult
and slow, by rough roads traced often through
primeval forests. Between some of them there was
less of sympathy than of jealousy kindled by con-
flicting interests or perpetual disputes concerning
boundaries. The patriotism of the colonist was
bounded by the lines of his government, except in
the compact and kindred colonies of New England,
which were socially united, though politically distinct. The country of the New Yorker was New
York, and the country of the Virginian was Virginia.
The New England colonies had once confederated;

but, kindred as they were, they had long ago dropped
apart. William Penn proposed a plan of colonial
union wholly fruitless. James II. tried to unite all
the northern colonies under one government; but the
attempt came to naught. Each stood aloof, jealously
independent. At rare intervals, under the pressure
of an emergency, some of them would try to act in
concert; and, except in New England, the results
had been most discouraging. Nor was it this segre-
gation only that unfitted them for war. They were
all subject to popular legislatures, through whom
alone money and men could be raised; and these
elective bodies were sometimes factious and selfish,
and not always either far-sighted or reasonable.
Moreover, they were in a state of ceaseless friction
with their governors, who represented the King, or,
what was worse, the feudal proprietary. These disputes, though varying in intensity, were found everywhere except in the two small colonies which chose
their own governors; and they were premonitions of
the movement towards independence which ended in
the war of Revolution. The occasion of difference
mattered little. Active or latent, the quarrel was
always present. In New York it turned on a question of the governor's salary; in Pennsylvania on the
taxation of the proprietary estates; in Virginia on a
fee exacted for the issue of land patents. It was
sure to arise whenever some public crisis gave the
representatives of the people an opportunity of extorting concessions from the representative of the Crown,

or gave the representative of the Crown an opportunity to gain a point for prerogative. That is to
say, the time when action was most needed was the
time chosen for obstructing it.

In Canada there was no popular legislature to
embarrass the central power. The people, like an
army, obeyed the word of command, — a military
advantage beyond all price.

Divided in government; divided in origin, feel-
ings, and principles; jealous of each other, jealous of
the Crown; the people at war with the executive,
and, by the fermentation of internal politics, blinded
to an outward danger that seemed remote and vague,
— such were the conditions under which the British
colonies drifted into a war that was to decide the fate
of the continent.

This war was the strife of a united and concentred
few against a divided and discordant many. It was
the strife, too, of the past against the future; of the
old against the new; of moral and intellectual torpor
against moral and intellectual life; of barren absolutism against a liberty, crude, incoherent, and chaotic,
yet full of prolific vitality.

CHAPTER II.

1749-1752.

CÉLORON DE BIENVILLE.

La Galissonière. — English Encroachment. — Mission of Céloron. — The Great West: its European Claimants; its Indian Population. — English Fur-Traders. — Céloron on the Alleghany: his Reception; his Difficulties. — Descent of the Ohio. — Covert Hostility. — Ascent of the Miami. — La Demoiselle. — Dark Prospects for France. — Christopher Gist, George Croghan: their Western Mission. — Pickawillany. — English Ascendency. — English Dissension and Rivalry. — The Key of the Great West.

WHEN the peace of Aix-la-Chapelle was signed, the Marquis de la Galissonière ruled over Canada. Like all the later Canadian governors, he was a naval officer; and, a few years after, he made himself famous by a victory, near Minorca, over the English admiral Byng, — an achievement now remembered chiefly by the fate of the defeated commander, judicially murdered as the scapegoat of an imbecile ministry. La Galissonière was a humpback; but his deformed person was animated by a bold spirit and a strong and penetrating intellect. He was the chief representative of the American policy of France. He felt that, cost what it might, she must hold fast to Canada, and link her to Louisiana by chains of forts

strong enough to hold back the British colonies, and
cramp their growth by confinement within narrow
limits; while French settlers, sent from the mother-
country, should spread and multiply in the broad
valleys of the interior. It is true, he said, that
Canada and her dependencies have always been a
burden; but they are necessary as a barrier against
English ambition; and to abandon them is to abandon
ourselves; for if we suffer our enemies to become
masters in America, their trade and naval power will
grow to vast proportions, and they will draw from
their colonies a wealth that will make them pre-
ponderant in Europe.[1]

The treaty had done nothing to settle the vexed
question of boundaries between France and her rival.
It had but staved off the inevitable conflict. Meanwhile, the English traders were crossing the mountains from Pennsylvania and Virginia, poaching on
the domain which France claimed as hers, ruining
the French fur-trade, seducing the Indian allies of
Canada, and stirring them up against her. Worse
still, English land speculators were beginning to
follow. Something must be done, and that promptly,
to drive back the intruders, and vindicate French
rights in the valley of the Ohio. To this end the
governor sent Céloron de Bienville thither in the
summer of 1749.

He was a chevalier de St. Louis and a captain in

[1] La Galissonière, *Mémoire sur les Colonies de la France dans
'Amérique septentrionale.*

the colony troops.   Under him went fourteen officers
and cadets, twenty soldiers, a hundred and eighty
Canadians, and a band of Indians, all in twenty-three
birch-bark canoes.   They left La Chine on the fifteenth of June, and pushed up the rapids of the St.
Lawrence, losing a man and damaging several canoes
on the way.   Ten days brought them to the mouth
of the Oswegatchie, where Ogdensburg now stands.
Here they found a Sulpitian priest, Abbé Piquet,
busy at building a fort, and lodging for the present
under a shed of bark like an Indian.   This enterprising father, ostensibly a missionary, was in reality a
zealous political agent, bent on winning over the red
allies of the English, retrieving French prestige, and
restoring French trade.   Thus far he had attracted
but two Iroquois to his new establishment; and these
he lent to Céloron.

Reaching Lake Ontario, the party stopped for a
time at the French fort of Frontenac, but avoided
the rival English post of Oswego, on the southern
shore, where a trade in beaver-skins, disastrous to
French interests, was carried on, and whither many
tribes, once faithful to Canada, now made resort.
On the sixth of July Céloron reached Niagara.   This,
the most important pass of all the western wilderness,
was guarded by a small fort of palisades on the point
where the river joins the lake.   Thence, the party
carried their canoes over the portage road by the
cataract, and launched them upon Lake Erie.   On
the fifteenth they landed on the lonely shore where

the town of Portland now stands; and for the next
seven days were busied in shouldering canoes and
baggage up and down the steep hills, through the
dense forest of beech, oak, ash, and elm, to the
waters of Chautauqua Lake, eight or nine miles distant.   Here they embarked again, steering southward
over the sunny waters, in the stillness and solitude of
the leafy hills, till they came to the outlet, and glided
down the peaceful current in the shade of the tall
forests that overarched it.   This prosperity was short.
The stream was low, in spite of heavy rains that
had drenched them on the carrying place.   Father
Bonnecamp, chaplain of the expedition, wrote in his
Journal: "In some places — and they were but too
frequent — the water was only two or three inches
deep; and we were reduced to the sad necessity of
dragging our canoes over the sharp pebbles, which,
with all our care and precaution, stripped off large
slivers of the bark.   At last, tired and worn, and
almost in despair of ever seeing La Belle Rivière, we
entered it at noon of the 29th."   The part of the
Ohio, or "La Belle Rivière," which they had thus
happily reached, is now called the Alleghany.   The
Great West lay outspread before them, a realm of
wild and waste fertility.

French America had two heads, — one among the
snows of Canada, and one among the canebrakes of
Louisiana; one communicating with the world through
the Gulf of St. Lawrence, and the other through the
Gulf of Mexico.   These vital points were feebly

connected by a chain of military posts, — slender,
and often interrupted, — circling through the wilderness nearly three thousand miles. Midway between
Canada and Louisiana lay the valley of the Ohio.
If the English should seize it, they would sever the
chain of posts, and cut French America asunder. If
the French held it, and intrenched themselves well
along its eastern limits, they would shut their rivals
between the Alleghanies and the sea, control all the
tribes of the West, and turn them, in case of war,
against the English borders, — a frightful and insupportable scourge.

The Indian population of the Ohio and its northern
tributaries was relatively considerable. The upper
or eastern half of the valley was occupied by mingled
hordes of Delawares, Shawanoes, Wyandots, and
Iroquois, or Indians of the Five Nations, who had
migrated thither from their ancestral abodes within
the present limits of the State of New York, and who
were called Mingoes by the English traders. Along
with them were a few wandering Abenakis, Nipissings,
and Ottawas. Farther west, on the waters of the
Miami, the Wabash, and other neighboring streams,
was the seat of a confederacy formed of the various
bands of the Miamis and their kindred or affiliated
tribes. Still farther west, towards the Mississippi,
were the remnants of the Illinois.

France had done but little to make good her claims
to this grand domain. East of the Miami she had
no military post whatever. Westward, on the

Maumee, there was a small wooden fort, another on the St. Joseph, and two on the Wabash. On the meadows of the Mississippi, in the Illinois country, stood Fort Chartres, — a much stronger work, and one of the chief links of the chain that connected Quebec with New Orleans. Its four stone bastions were impregnable to musketry; and, here in the depths of the wilderness, there was no fear that cannon would be brought against it. It was the centre and citadel of a curious little forest settlement, the only vestige of civilization through all this region. At Kaskaskia, extended along the borders of the stream, were seventy or eighty French houses; thirty or forty at Cahokia, opposite the site of St. Louis; and a few more at the intervening hamlets of St. Philippe and Prairie à la Roche, — a picturesque but thriftless population, mixed with Indians, totally ignorant, busied partly with the fur-trade, and partly with the raising of corn for the market of New Orleans. They communicated with it by means of a sort of row galley, of eighteen or twenty oars, which made the voyage twice a year, and usually spent ten weeks on the return up the river.[1]

The Pope and the Bourbons had claimed this wilderness for seventy years, and had done scarcely more for it than the Indians, its natural owners.

[1] Gordon, *Journal*, 1766, appended to Pownall, *Topographical Description*. In the Dépôt des Cartes de la Marine at Paris, C. 4,040, are two curious maps of the Illinois Colony, made a little after the middle of the century. In 1753 the Marquis Duquesne denounced the colonists as debauched and lazy.

On the next day they reached a village of Iroquois under a female chief, called Queen Alequippa by the English, to whom she was devoted. Both queen and subjects had fled; but among the deserted wigwams were six more Englishmen, whom Céloron warned off like the others, and who, like them, pretended to obey. At a neighboring town they found only two withered ancients, male and female, whose united ages, in the judgment of the chaplain, were full two centuries. They passed the site of the future Pittsburg; and some seventeen miles below approached Chiningué, called Logstown by the English, one of the chief places on the river.[1] Both English and French flags were flying over the town, and the inhabitants, lining the shore, greeted their visitors with a salute of musketry, — not wholly welcome, as the guns were charged with ball. Céloron threatened to fire on them if they did not cease. The French climbed the steep bank, and encamped on the plateau above, betwixt the forest and the village, which consisted of some fifty cabins and wigwams, grouped in picturesque squalor, and tenanted by a mixed population, chiefly of Delawares, Shawanoes, and Mingoes. Here, too, were gathered many fugitives from the deserted towns above. Céloron feared a night attack. The camp was encircled by a ring of sentries; the officers walked the rounds till morning; a part of the men were kept under arms, and

---

[1] There was another Chiningué, the Shenango of the English, on the Alleghany.

the rest ordered to sleep in their clothes. Joncaire discovered through some women of his acquaintance that an attack was intended. Whatever the danger may have been, the precautions of the French averted it; and instead of a battle, there was a council. Céloron delivered to the assembled chiefs a message from the governor more conciliatory than the former: "Through the love I bear you, my children, I send you Monsieur de Céloron to open your eyes to the designs of the English against your lands. The establishments they mean to make, and of which you are certainly ignorant, tend to your complete ruin. They hide from you their plans, which are to settle here and drive you away, if I let them. As a good father who tenderly loves his children, and though far away from them bears them always in his heart, I must warn you of the danger that threatens you. The English intend to rob you of your country; and that they may succeed, they begin by corrupting your minds. As they mean to seize the Ohio, which belongs to me, I send to warn them to retire."

The reply of the chiefs, though sufficiently humble, was not all that could be wished. They begged that the intruders might stay a little longer, since the goods they brought were necessary to them. It was, in fact, these goods, cheap, excellent, and abundant as they were, which formed the only true bond between the English and the western tribes. Logstown was one of the chief resorts of the English traders; and at this moment there were ten of them in the place. Céloron warned them off. "They agreed," says the chaplain, "to all that was demanded, well resolved, no doubt, to do the contrary as soon as our backs were turned."

Having distributed gifts among the Indians, the French proceeded on their way, and at or near the mouth of Wheeling Creek buried another plate of lead. They repeated the same ceremony at the mouth of the Muskingum. Here, half a century later, when this region belonged to the United States, a party of boys, bathing in the river, saw the plate protruding from the bank where the freshets had laid it bare, knocked it down with a long stick, melted half of it into bullets, and gave what remained to a neighbor from Marietta, who, hearing of this mysterious relic, inscribed in an unknown tongue, came to rescue it from their hands.[1] It is now in the cabinet of the American Antiquarian Society.[2] On the eighteenth of August, Céloron buried yet another plate, at the mouth of the Great Kanawha. This, too, in the course of a century, was unearthed by the floods, and was found in 1846 by a boy at play, by the edge of the water.[3] The inscriptions on all these plates were much alike, with variations of date and place.

[1] O. H. Marshall, in *Magazine of American History, March,* 1878.

[2] For papers relating to it, see *Trans. Amer. Antiq. Soc.,* ii.

[3] For a facsimile of the inscription on this plate, see *Olden Time,* i. 288. Céloron calls the Kanawha, *Chinodahichetha.* The inscriptions as given in his Journal correspond with those on the plates discovered.

The weather was by turns rainy and hot; and the men, tired and famished, were fast falling ill. On the twenty-second they approached Scioto, called by the French St. Yotoc, or Sinioto, a large Shawanoe town at the mouth of the river which bears the same name. Greatly doubting what welcome awaited them, they filled their powder-horns and prepared for the worst. Joncaire was sent forward to propitiate the inhabitants; but they shot bullets through the flag that he carried, and surrounded him, yelling and brandishing their knives. Some were for killing him at once; others for burning him alive. The interposition of a friendly Iroquois saved him; and at length they let him go. Céloron was very uneasy at the reception of his messenger. "I knew," he writes, "the weakness of my party, two-thirds of which were young men who had never left home before, and would all have run at the sight of ten Indians. Still, there was nothing for me but to keep on; for I was short of provisions, my canoes were badly damaged, and I had no pitch or bark to mend them. So I embarked again, ready for whatever might happen. I had good officers, and about fifty men who could be trusted."

As they neared the town, the Indians swarmed to the shore, and began the usual salute of musketry. "They fired," says Céloron, "full a thousand shots; for the English give them powder for nothing." He prudently pitched his camp on the farther side of the river, posted guards, and kept close watch. Each party distrusted and feared the other. At length, after much ado, many debates, and some threatening movements on the part of the alarmed and excited Indians, a council took place at the tent of the French commander; the chiefs apologized for the rough treatment of Joncaire, and Céloron replied with a rebuke, which would doubtless have been less mild, had he felt himself stronger. He gave them also a message from the governor, modified, apparently, to suit the circumstances; for while warning them of the wiles of the English, it gave no hint that the King of France claimed mastery of their lands. Their answer was vague and unsatisfactory. It was plain that they were bound to the enemy by interest, if not by sympathy. A party of English traders were living in the place; and Céloron summoned them to withdraw, on pain of what might ensue. "My instructions," he says, "enjoined me to do this, and even to pillage the English; but I was not strong enough; and as these traders were established in the village and well supported by the Indians, the attempt would have failed, and put the French to shame." The assembled chiefs having been regaled with a cup of brandy each, — the only part of the proceeding which seemed to please them, — Céloron re-embarked, and continued his voyage.

On the thirtieth they reached the Great Miami, called by the French, Rivière à la Roche; and here Céloron buried the last of his leaden plates. They

now bade farewell to the Ohio, or, in the words of
the chaplain, to "La Belle Rivière, — that river so
little known to the French, and unfortunately too
well known to the English." He speaks of the multitude of Indian villages on its shores, and still more
on its northern branches. "Each, great or small,
has one or more English traders, and each of these
has hired men to carry his furs. Behold, then, the
English well advanced upon our lands, and, what is
worse, under the protection of a crowd of savages
whom they have drawn over to them, and whose
number increases daily."

The course of the party lay up the Miami; and
they toiled thirteen days against the shallow current
before they reached a village of the Miami Indians,
lately built at the mouth of the rivulet now called
Loramie Creek. Over it ruled a chief to whom the
French had given the singular name of La Demoiselle,
but whom the English, whose fast friend he was,
called Old Britain. The English traders who lived
here had prudently withdrawn, leaving only two
hired men in the place. The object of Céloron was
to induce the Demoiselle and his band to leave this
new abode and return to their old villages near the
French fort on the Maumee, where they would be
safe from English seduction. To this end, he called
them to a council, gave them ample gifts, and made
them an harangue in the name of the governor. The
Demoiselle took the gifts, thanked his French father
for his good advice, and promised to follow it at a

more convenient time.[1] In vain Céloron insisted
that he and his tribesmen should remove at once.
Neither blandishments nor threats would prevail,
and the French commander felt that his negotiation
had failed.

He was not deceived. Far from leaving his
village, the Demoiselle, who was Great Chief of the
Miami Confederacy, gathered his followers to the
spot, till, less than two years after the visit of
Céloron, its population had increased eightfold.
Pique Town, or Pickawillany, as the English called
it, became one of the greatest Indian towns of the
West, the centre of English trade and influence,
and a capital object of French jealousy.

Céloron burned his shattered canoes, and led his
party across the long and difficult portage to the
French post on the Maumee, where he found Raymond, the commander, and all his men, shivering
with fever and ague. They supplied him with
wooden canoes for his voyage down the river; and,
early in October, he reached Lake Erie, where he
was detained for a time by a drunken debauch of his
Indians, who are called by the chaplain "a species
of men made to exercise the patience of those who
have the misfortune to travel with them." In a
month more he was at Fort Frontenac; and as he
descended thence to Montreal, he stopped at the

---

[1] Céloron, *Journal.* Compare *A Message from the Twightwees
Miamis*) in *Colonial Records of Pa.*, v. 437, where they say that
they refused the gifts.

Oswegatchie, in obedience to the governor, who had
directed him to report the progress made by the
Sulpitian, Abbé Piquet, at his new mission. Piquet's
new fort had been burned by Indians, prompted, as
he thought, by the English of Oswego; but the
priest, buoyant and undaunted, was still resolute for
the glory of God and the confusion of the heretics.

At length Céloron reached Montreal; and, closing
his Journal, wrote thus: "Father Bonnecamp, who
is a Jesuit and a great mathematician, reckons that
we have travelled twelve hundred leagues; I and my
officers think we have travelled more. All I can say
is, that the nations of these countries are very ill-
disposed towards the French, and devoted entirely to
the English." [1] If his expedition had done no more,
it had at least revealed clearly the deplorable condition of French interests in the West.

While Céloron was warning English traders from
the Ohio, a plan was on foot in Virginia for a new
invasion of the French domain. An association was
formed to settle the Ohio country; and a grant of
five hundred thousand acres was procured from the
King, on condition that a hundred families should be
established upon it within seven years, a fort built,
and a garrison maintained. The Ohio Company

[1] *Journal de la Campagne que moy Céloron, Chevalier de l'Ordre
Royal et Militaire de St. Louis, Capitaine Commandant un détache-
ment envoyé dans la Belle Rivière par les ordres de M. le Marquis de
La Galissonière, etc.*

*Relation d'un voyage dans la Belle Rivière sous les ordres de M. de
Céloron, par le Père Bonnecamp, en 1749.*

numbered among its members some of the chief men
of Virginia, including two brothers of Washington;
and it had also a London partner, one Hanbury, a
person of influence, who acted as its agent in England. In the year after the expedition of Céloron,
its governing committee sent the trader Christopher
Gist to explore the country and select land. It
must be "good level land," wrote the committee;
"we had rather go quite down to the Mississippi
than take mean, broken land."[1] In November Gist
reached Logstown, the Chiningué of Céloron, where
he found what he calls a "parcel of reprobate Indian
traders." Those whom he so stigmatizes were
Pennsylvanians, chiefly Scotch-Irish, between whom
and the traders from Virginia there was great
jealousy. Gist was told that he "should never go
home safe." He declared himself the bearer of a
message from the King. This imposed respect, and
he was allowed to proceed. At the Wyandot village
of Muskingum he found the trader George Croghan,
sent to the Indians by the governor of Pennsylvania,
to renew the chain of friendship.[2] "Croghan," he
says, "is a mere idol among his countrymen, the
Irish traders;" yet they met amicably, and the Pennsylvanian had with him a companion, Andrew
Montour, the interpreter, who proved of great service

---

[1] Instructions to Gist, in appendix to Pownall, *Topographical
Description of North America.*

[2] *Mr. Croghan's Transactions with the Indians,* in *N. Y. Col. Docs.*
vii. 267; *Croghan to Hamilton,* 16 *December,* 1750.

to Gist. As Montour was a conspicuous person in his time, and a type of his class, he merits a passing notice. He was the reputed grandson of a French governor and an Indian squaw. His half-breed mother, Catharine Montour, was a native of Canada, whence she was carried off by the Iroquois, and adopted by them. She lived in a village at the head of Seneca Lake, and still held the belief, inculcated by the guides of her youth, that Christ was a Frenchman crucified by the English.[1] Her son Andrew is thus described by the Moravian Zinzendorf, who knew him: "His face is like that of a European, but marked with a broad Indian ring of bear's-grease and paint drawn completely round it. He wears a coat of fine cloth of cinnamon color, a black necktie with silver spangles, a red satin waistcoat, trousers over which hangs his shirt, shoes and stockings, a hat, and brass ornaments, something like the handle of a basket, suspended from his ears."[2] He was an excellent interpreter, and held in high account by his Indian kinsmen.

After leaving Muskingum, Gist, Croghan, and Montour went together to a village on White Woman's Creek, — so called from one Mary Harris,

[1] This is stated by Count Zinzendorf, who visited her among the Senecas. Compare "Frontenac and New France under Louis XIV.," 395. In a plan of the "Route of the Western Army," made in 1779, and of which a tracing is before me, the village where she lived is still called "French Catharine's Town."

[2] Journal of Zinzendorf, quoted in Schweinitz, *Life of David Zeisberger*, 112, *note*.

who lived here. She was born in New England, was made prisoner when a child forty years before, and had since dwelt among her captors, finding such comfort as she might in an Indian husband and a family of young half-breeds. "She still remembers," says Gist, "that they used to be very religious in New England, and wonders how white men can be so wicked as she has seen them in these woods." He and his companions now journeyed southwestward to the Shawanoe town at the mouth of the Scioto, where they found a reception very different from that which had awaited Céloron. Thence they rode northwestward along the forest path that led to Pickawillany, the Indian town on the upper waters of the Great Miami. Gist was delighted with the country, and reported to his employers that "it is fine, rich, level land, well timbered with large walnut, ash, sugar trees and cherry trees; well watered with a great number of little streams and rivulets; full of beautiful natural meadows, with wild rye, blue-grass, and clover, and abounding with turkeys, deer, elks, and most sorts of game, particularly buffaloes, thirty or forty of which are frequently seen in one meadow." A little farther west, on the plains of the Wabash and the Illinois, he would have found them by thousands.

They crossed the Miami on a raft, their horses swimming after them; and were met on landing by a crowd of warriors, who, after smoking with them, escorted them to the neighboring town, where they were greeted by a fusillade of welcome. "We entered with English colors before us, and were kindly received by their king, who invited us into his own house and set our colors upon the top of it; then all the white men and traders that were there came and welcomed us." This "king" was Old Britain, or La Demoiselle. Great were the changes here since Céloron, a year and a half before, had vainly enticed him to change his abode, and dwell in the shadow of the fleur-de-lis. The town had grown to four hundred families, or about two thousand souls; and the English traders had built for themselves and their hosts a fort of pickets, strengthened with logs.

There was a series of councils in the long house, or town-hall. Croghan made the Indians a present from the governor of Pennsylvania; and he and Gist delivered speeches of friendship and good advice, which the auditors received with the usual monosyllabic plaudits, ejected from the depths of their throats. A treaty of peace was solemnly made between the English and the confederate tribes, and all was serenity and joy; till four Ottawas, probably from Detroit, arrived with a French flag, a gift of brandy and tobacco, and a message from the French commandant inviting the Miamis to visit him. Whereupon the great war-chief rose, and, with "a fierce tone and very warlike air," said to the envoys: "Brothers the Ottawas, we let you know, by these four strings of wampum, that we will not hear anything the French say, nor do anything they bid us."

of the other.   This was not the only evil that sprang
from uncertain ownership.   "Till the line is run
between the two provinces," says Dinwiddie, governor of Virginia, "I cannot appoint magistrates to
keep the traders in good order." [1]   Hence they did
what they pleased, and often gave umbrage to the
Indians.   Clinton, of New York, appealed to his
Assembly for means to assist Pennsylvania in "securing the fidelity of the Indians on the Ohio," and the
Assembly refused. [2]   "We will take care of our
Indians, and they may take care of theirs:" such was
the spirit of their answer.   He wrote to the various
provinces, inviting them to send commissioners to
meet the tribes at Albany, "in order to defeat the
designs and intrigues of the French."   All turned
a deaf ear except Massachusetts, Connecticut, and
South Carolina, who sent the commissioners, but
supplied them very meagrely with the indispensable
presents. [3]   Clinton says further: "The Assembly of
this province have not given one farthing for Indian
affairs, nor for a year past have they provided for
the subsistence of the garrison at Oswego, which
is the key for the commerce between the colonies
and the inland nations of Indians." [4]

In the heterogeneous structure of the British

[1] *Dinwiddie to the Lords of Trade,* 6 *October,* 1752.

[2] *Journals of New York Assembly,* ii. 283, 284.   *Colonial Records
of Pa.,* v. 466.

[3] *Clinton to Hamilton,* 18 *December,* 1750.   *Clinton to Lords of
Trade,* 13 *June,* 1751; *Ibid.,* 17 *July,* 1751.

[4] *Clinton to Bedford,* 30 *July,* 1750.

colonies, their clashing interests, their internal disputes, and the misplaced economy of penny-wise and
short-sighted assembly-men, lay the hope of France.
The rulers of Canada knew the vast numerical preponderance of their rivals; but with their centralized
organization they felt themselves more than a match
for any one English colony alone.   They hoped to·
wage war under the guise of peace, and to deal with
the enemy in detail; and they at length perceived
that the fork of the Ohio, so strangely neglected by
the English, formed, together with Niagara, the key
of the Great West.   Could France hold firmly these
two controlling passes, she might almost boast herself
mistress of the continent.

NOTE. — The Journal of Céloron (Archives de la Marine) is very
long and circumstantial, including the *procès verbaux*, and reports
of councils with Indians.   The Journal of the chaplain, Bonnecamp (Dépôt de la Marine), is shorter, but is the work of an intelligent and observing man.   The author, a Jesuit, was skilled in
mathematics, made daily observations, and constructed a map of
the route, still preserved at the Dépôt de la Marine.   Concurrently
with these French narratives, one may consult the English letters
and documents bearing on the same subjects, in the Colonial
Records of Pennsylvania, the Archives of Pennsylvania, and the
Colonial Documents of New York.

Three of Céloron's leaden plates have been found, — the two
mentioned in the text, and another which was never buried, and
which the Indians, who regarded these mysterious tablets as "bad
medicine," procured by a trick from Joncaire, or, according to
Governor Clinton, stole from him.   A Cayuga chief brought it to
Colonel Johnson on the Mohawk, who interpreted the "Devilish
writing" in such a manner as best to inspire horror of French
designs.

CHAPTER III.

1749–1753.

CONFLICT FOR THE WEST.

The Five Nations. — Caughnawaga. — Abbé Piquet: his Schemes; his Journey. — Fort Frontenac. — Toronto. — Niagara. — Oswego. — Success of Piquet. — Detroit. — La Jonquière: his Intrigues; his Trials; his Death. — English Intrigues. — Critical State of the West. — Pickawillany destroyed. — Duquesne: his Grand Enterprise.

The Iroquois, or Five Nations, sometimes called Six Nations after the Tuscaroras joined them, had been a power of high importance in American international politics. In a certain sense they may be said to have held the balance between their French and English neighbors; but their relative influence had of late declined. So many of them had emigrated and joined the tribes of the Ohio, that the centre of Indian population had passed to that region. Nevertheless, the Five Nations were still strong enough in their ancient abodes to make their alliance an object of the utmost consequence to both the European rivals. At the western end of their "Long House," or belt of confederated villages, Joncaire intrigued to gain them for France; while in the east he was counteracted by the young colonel of militia,

William Johnson, who lived on the Mohawk, and
was already well skilled in managing Indians.
Johnson sometimes lost his temper; and once wrote
to Governor Clinton to complain of the "confounded
wicked things the French had infused into the Indians'
heads; among the rest that the English were determined, the first opportunity, to destroy them all. I
assure your Excellency I had hard work to beat these
and several other cursed villanous things, told them
by the French, out of their heads."[1]

In former times the French had hoped to win over
the Five Nations in a body, by wholesale conversion
to the Faith; but the attempt had failed. They had,
however, made within their own limits an asylum for
such converts as they could gain, whom they collected
together at Caughnawaga, near Montreal, to the
number of about three hundred warriors.[2] These
could not be trusted to fight their kinsmen, but
willingly made forays against the English borders.
Caughnawaga, like various other Canadian missions,
was divided between the Church, the army, and the
fur-trade. It had a chapel, fortifications, and storehouses; two Jesuits, an officer, and three chief
traders. Of these last, two were maiden ladies, the
Demoiselles Desauniers; and one of the Jesuits, their
friend Father Tournois, was their partner in business. They carried on by means of the Mission

---

[1] *Johnson to Clinton*, 28 *April*, 1749.
[2] The estimate of a French official report, 1736, and of Sir
William Johnson, 1763.

Indians, and in collusion with influential persons in
the colony, a trade with the Dutch at Albany, illegal,
but very profitable.[1]

Besides this Iroquois mission, which was chiefly
composed of Mohawks and Oneidas, another was
now begun farther westward, to win over the Onondagas, Cayugas, and Senecas. This was the establishment of Father Piquet, which Céloron had visited
in its infancy when on his way to the Ohio, and
again on his return. Piquet was a man in the prime
of life, of an alert, vivacious countenance, by no
means unprepossessing;[2] an enthusiastic schemer,
with great executive talents; ardent, energetic, vain,
self-confident, and boastful. The enterprise seems
to have been of his own devising; but it found warm
approval from the government.[3] La Présentation,
as he called the new mission, stood on the bank of
the river Oswegatchie where it enters the St.
Lawrence. Here the rapids ceased, and navigation
was free to Lake Ontario. The place commanded
the main river, and could bar the way to hostile war-
parties or contraband traders. Rich meadows, forests,
and abundance of fish and game, made it attractive

---

[1] *La Jonquière au Ministre*, 27 *Février*, 1750. *Ibid.*, 29 *Octobre*,
1751. *Ordres du Roy et Dépêches des Ministres*, 1751. *Notice biographique de La Jonquière.* La Jonquière, governor of Canada, at
last broke up their contraband trade, and ordered Tournois to
Quebec.

[2] I once saw a contemporary portrait of him at the mission of
Two Mountains, where he had been stationed.

[3] *Rouillé à La Jonquière*, 1749. The intendant Bigot gave him
money and provisions. *N. Y. Col. Docs.*, x. 204.

to Indians, and the Oswegatchie gave access to the
Iroquois towns. Piquet had chosen his site with
great skill. His activity was admirable. His first
stockade was burned by Indian incendiaries; but it
rose quickly from its ashes, and within a year or two
the mission of La Présentation had a fort of palisades
flanked with blockhouses, a chapel, a storehouse, a
barn, a stable, ovens, a saw-mill, broad fields of corn
and beans, and three villages of Iroquois, containing,
in all, forty-nine bark lodges, each holding three or
four families, more or less converted to the Faith;
and, as time went on, this number increased. The
governor had sent a squad of soldiers to man the
fort, and five small cannon to mount upon it. The
place was as safe for the new proselytes as it was
convenient and agreeable. The Pennsylvanian interpreter, Conrad Weiser, was told at Onondaga, the
Iroquois capital, that Piquet had made a hundred
converts from that place alone; and that, "having
clothed them all in very fine clothes, laced with
silver and gold, he took them down and presented
them to the French governor at Montreal, who received them very kindly, and made them large
presents." [1]

Such were some of the temporal attractions of La
Présentation. The nature of the spiritual instruction bestowed by Piquet and his fellow-priests may
be partly inferred from the words of a proselyte
warrior, who declared with enthusiasm that he had

[1] *Journal of Conrad Weiser,* 1750.

learned from the Sulpitian missionary that the King
of France was the eldest son of the wife of Jesus
Christ.[1] This he of course took in a literal sense,
the mystic idea of the Church as the spouse of Christ
being beyond his savage comprehension. The effect
was to stimulate his devotion to the Great Onontio
beyond the sea, and to the lesser Onontio who represented him as governor of Canada.

Piquet was elated by his success; and early in
1752 he wrote to the governor and intendant: "It is
a great miracle that, in spite of envy, contradiction,
and opposition from nearly all the Indian villages, I
have formed in less than three years one of the most
flourishing missions in Canada. I find myself in a
position to extend the empire of my good masters,
Jesus Christ and the King, even to the extremities
of this new world; and, with some little help from
you, to do more than France and England have been
able to do with millions of money and all their
troops."[2]

The letter from which this is taken was written to
urge upon the government a scheme in which the
zealous priest could see nothing impracticable. He
proposed to raise a war-party of thirty-eight hundred

[1] Lalande, *Notice de l'Abbé Piquet*, in *Lettres Édifiantes*. See
also Tassé in *Revue Canadienne*, 1870, p. 9.

[2] *Piquet à La Jonquière et Bigot*, 8 *Février*, 1752. See Appendix
A. In spite of Piquet's self-laudation, and in spite also of the
detraction of the author of the *Mémoires sur le Canada*, 1749-1760,
there can be no doubt of his practical capacity and his fertility of
resource. Duquesne, when governor of the colony, highly praises
" ses talents et son activité pour le service de Sa Majesté."

Indians, eighteen hundred of whom were to be drawn from the Canadian missions, the Five Nations, and the tribes of the Ohio, while the remaining two thousand were to be furnished by the Flatheads, or Choctaws, who were at the same time to be supplied with missionaries. The united force was first to drive the English from the Ohio, and next attack the Dog Tribe, or Cherokees, who lived near the borders of Virginia, with the people of which they were on friendly terms. "If," says Piquet, "the English of Virginia give any help to this last-named tribe, — which will not fail to happen, — they [*the war-party*] will do their utmost against them, through a grudge they bear them by reason of some old quarrels." In other words, the missionary hopes to set a host of savages to butchering English settlers in time of peace![1] His wild project never took effect, though the governor, he says, at first approved it.

In the preceding year the "Apostle of the Iroquois," as he was called, made a journey to muster recruits for his mission, and kept a copious diary on the way. By accompanying him, one gets a clear view of an important part of the region in dispute between the rival nations. Six Canadians paddled him up the St. Lawrence, and five Indian converts followed in another canoe. Emerging from among the Thousand Islands, they stopped at Fort Frontenac, where Kingston now stands. Once the place was a great

[1] Appendix A.

resort of Indians; now none were here, for the English post of Oswego, on the other side of the lake,
had greater attractions. Piquet and his company
found the pork and bacon very bad, and he complains that "there was not brandy enough in the fort
to wash a wound." They crossed to a neighboring
island, where they were soon visited by the chaplain
of the fort, the storekeeper, his wife, and three
young ladies, glad of an excursion to relieve the
monotony of the garrison. "My hunters," says
Piquet, "had supplied me with means of giving
them a pretty good entertainment. We drank, with
all our hearts, the health of the authorities, temporal
and ecclesiastical, to the sound of our musketry,
which was very well fired, and delighted the islanders."
These islanders were a band of Indians who lived
here. Piquet gave them a feast, then discoursed of
religion, and at last persuaded them to remove to
the new mission.

During eight days he and his party coasted the
northern shore of Lake Ontario, with various inci-
dents, such as an encounter between his dog Cerberus
and a wolf, to the disadvantage of the latter, and the
meeting with "a very fine negro of twenty-two years,
a fugitive from Virginia." On the twenty-sixth of
June they reached the new fort of Toronto, which
offered a striking contrast to their last stopping-
place. "The wine here is of the best; there is nothing wanting in this fort; everything is abundant,
fine, and good." There was reason for this. The

northern Indians were flocking with their beaver-skins to the English of Oswego; and in April, 1749, an officer named Portneuf had been sent with soldiers and workmen to build a stockaded trading-house at Toronto, in order to intercept them, — not by force, which would have been ruinous to French interests, but by a tempting supply of goods and brandy.[1] Thus the fort was kept well stocked, and with excellent effect. Piquet found here a band of Mississagas, who would otherwise, no doubt, have carried their furs to the English. He was strongly impelled to persuade them to migrate to La Présentation; but the governor had told him to confine his efforts to other tribes; and lest, he says, the ardor of his zeal should betray him to disobedience, he re-embarked, and encamped six leagues from temptation.

Two days more brought him to Niagara, where he was warmly received by the commandant, the chaplain, and the storekeeper, — the triumvirate who ruled these forest outposts, and stood respectively for their three vital principles, war, religion, and trade. Here Piquet said mass; and after resting a day, set out for the trading-house at the portage of the cataract, recently built, like Toronto, to stop the Indians on their way to Oswego.[2] Here he found Joncaire, and here also was encamped a large band of Senecas;

[1] On Toronto, *La Jonquière et Bigot au Ministre,* 1749. *La Jonquière au Ministre,* 30 *Août,* 1750. *N. Y. Col. Docs.,* x. 201, 246.

[2] *La Jonquière au Ministre,* 23 *Février,* 1750. *Ibid.,* 6 *Octobre,* 1751. Compare *Colonial Records of Pa.,* v. 508.

though, being all drunk, men, women, and children, they were in no condition to receive the Faith, or appreciate the temporal advantages that attended it. On the next morning, finding them partially sober, he invited them to remove to La Présentation; "but as they had still something left in their bottles, I could get no answer till the following day." "I pass in silence," pursues the missionary, "an infinity of talks on this occasion. Monsieur de Joncaire forgot nothing that could help me, and behaved like a great servant of God and the King. My recruits increased every moment. I went to say my breviary while my Indians and the Senecas, without loss of time, assembled to hold a council with Monsieur de Joncaire." The result of the council was an entreaty to the missionary not to stop at Oswego, lest evil should befall him at the hands of the English. He promised to do as they wished, and presently set out on his return to Fort Niagara, attended by Joncaire and a troop of his new followers. The journey was a triumphal progress. "Whenever we passed a camp or a wigwam, the Indians saluted me by firing their guns, which happened so often that I thought all the trees along the way were charged with gunpowder; and when we reached the fort, Monsieur de Becancour received us with great ceremony and the firing of cannon, by which my savages were infinitely flattered."

His neophytes were gathered into the chapel for the first time in their lives, and there rewarded with

a few presents.   He now prepared to turn homeward,
his flock at the mission being left in his absence
without a shepherd; and on the sixth of July he
embarked, followed by a swarm of canoes.   On the
twelfth they stopped at the Genesee, and went to
visit the Falls, where the city of Rochester now
stands.   On the way, the Indians found a populous
resort of rattlesnakes, and attacked the gregarious
reptiles with great animation, to the alarm of the
missionary, who trembled for his bare-legged retainers.
His fears proved needless.   Forty-two dead snakes,
as he avers, requited the efforts of the sportsmen,
and not one of them was bitten.   When he returned
to camp in the afternoon he found there a canoe
loaded with kegs of brandy.   "The English," he
says, "had sent it to meet us, well knowing that this
was the best way to cause disorder among my new
recruits and make them desert me.   The Indian in
charge of the canoe, who had the look of a great
rascal, offered some to me first, and then to my
Canadians and Indians.   I gave out that it was very
probably poisoned, and immediately embarked again."

He encamped on the fourteenth at Sodus Bay, and
strongly advises the planting of a French fort there.
"Nevertheless," he adds, "it would be still better to
destroy Oswego, and on no account let the English
build it again."   On the sixteenth he came in sight
of this dreaded post.   Several times on the way he
had met fleets of canoes going thither or returning,
in spite of the rival attractions of Toronto and

Niagara. No English establishment on the continent was of such ill omen to the French. It not only
robbed them of the fur-trade, by which they lived,
but threatened them with military and political, no
less than commercial, ruin. They were in constant
dread lest ships of war should be built here, strong
enough to command Lake Ontario, thus separating
Canada from Louisiana, and cutting New France
asunder. To meet this danger, they soon after built
at Fort Frontenac a large three-masted vessel,
mounted with heavy cannon; thus, as usual, fore-
stalling their rivals by promptness of action.[1] The
ground on which Oswego stood was claimed by the
Province of New York, which alone had control of it;
but through the purblind apathy of the Assembly,
and their incessant quarrels with the governor, it
was commonly left to take care of itself. For some
time they would vote no money to pay the feeble
little garrison; and Clinton, who saw the necessity
of maintaining it, was forced to do so on his own
personal credit.[2] "Why can't your governor and
your great men [the Assembly] agree?" asked a
Mohawk chief of the interpreter, Conrad Weiser.[3]

Piquet kept his promise not to land at the English
fort; but he approached in his canoe, and closely
observed it. The shores, now covered by the city of
Oswego, were then a desolation of bare hills and

1 *Lieutenant Lindesay to Johnson, July,* 1751.
2 *Clinton to Lords of Trade,* 30 *July,* 1750.
3 *Journal of Conrad Weiser,* 1750.

fields, studded with the stumps of felled trees, and
hedged about with a grim border of forests. Near
the strand, by the mouth of the Onondaga, were the
houses of some of the traders; and on the higher
ground behind them stood a huge blockhouse with
a projecting upper story. This building was surrounded by a rough wall of stone, with flankers
at the angles, forming what was called the fort.[1]
Piquet reconnoitred it from his canoe with the eye
of a soldier. "It is commanded," he says, "on
almost every side; two batteries, of three twelve-
pounders each, would be more than enough to reduce
it to ashes." And he enlarges on the evils that arise
from it. "It not only spoils our trade, but puts the
English into communication with a vast number of
our Indians, far and near. It is true that they like
our brandy better than English rum; but they prefer
English goods to ours, and can buy for two beaver-
skins at Oswego a better silver bracelet than we sell
at Niagara for ten."

The burden of these reflections was lightened
when he approached Fort Frontenac. "Never was
reception more solemn. The Nipissings and Algonquins, who were going on a war-party with Monsieur
Belêtre, formed a line of their own accord, and
saluted us with three volleys of musketry, and cries
of joy without end. All our little bark vessels
replied in the same way. Monsieur de Verchères
and Monsieur de Valtry ordered the cannon of the

[1] Compare *Doc. Hist. N. Y.*, i. 463.

fort to be fired; and my Indians, transported with joy at the honor done them, shot off their guns incessantly, with cries and acclamations that delighted everybody." A goodly band of recruits joined him, and he pursued his voyage to La Présentation, while the canoes of his proselytes followed in a swarm to their new home; "that establishment"—thus in a burst of enthusiasm he closes his Journal—"that establishment which I began two years ago, in the midst of opposition; that establishment which may be regarded as a key of the colony; that establishment which officers, interpreters, and traders thought a chimera,—that establishment, I say, forms already a mission of Iroquois savages whom I assembled at first to the number of only six, increased last year to eighty-seven, and this year to three hundred and ninety-six, without counting more than a hundred and fifty whom Monsieur Chabert de Joncaire is to bring me this autumn. And I certify that thus far I have received from His Majesty—for all favor, grace, and assistance—no more than a half pound of bacon and two pounds of bread for daily rations; and that he has not yet given a pin to the chapel, which I have maintained out of my own pocket, for the greater glory of my masters, God and the King."[1]

[1] *Journal qui peut servir de Mémoire et de Relation du Voyage que j'ay fait sur le Lac Ontario pour attirer au nouvel Établissement de La Présentation les Sauvages Iroquois des Cinq Nations*, 1751. The last passage given above is condensed in the rendering, as the original is extremely involved and ungrammatical.

In his late journey he had made the entire circuit
of Lake Ontario. Beyond lay four other inland
oceans, to which Fort Niagara was the key. As that
all-essential post controlled the passage from Ontario
to Erie, so did Fort Detroit control that from Erie to
Huron, and Fort Michilimackinac that from Huron
to Michigan; while Fort Ste. Marie, at the outlet of
Lake Superior, had lately received a garrison, and
changed from a mission and trading-station to a post
of war.[1] This immense extent of inland navigation
was safe in the hands of France so long as she held
Niagara. Niagara lost, not only the lakes, but also
the Valley of the Ohio was lost with it. Next in
importance was Detroit. This was not a military
post alone, but also a settlement; and, except the
hamlets about Fort Chartres, the only settlement
that France owned in all the West. There were, it
is true, but a few families; yet the hope of growth
seemed good; for to such as liked a wilderness home,
no spot in America had more attraction. Father
Bonnecamp stopped here for a day on his way back
from the expedition of Céloron. "The situation,"
he says, "is charming. A fine river flows at the foot
of the fortifications; vast meadows, asking only to
be tilled, extend beyond the sight. Nothing can be
more agreeable than the climate. Winter lasts hardly
two months. European grains and fruits grow here
far better than in many parts of France. It is the
Touraine and Beauce of Canada."[2] The white flag

[1] *La Jonquière au Ministre,* 24 *Août,* 1750.
[2] *Relation du Voiage de la Belle Rivière,* 1749.

of the Bourbons floated over the compact little pali-
saded town, with its population of soldiers and fur-
traders; and from the blockhouses which served as
bastions, one saw on either hand the small solid
dwellings of the *habitants*, ranged at intervals along
the margin of the water; while at a little distance
three Indian villages — Ottawa, Pottawattamie, and
Wyandot — curled their wigwam smoke into the pure
summer air.[1]

When Céloron de Bienville returned from the
Ohio, he went, with a royal commission, sent him a
year before, to command at Detroit.[2] His late chaplain, the very intelligent Father Bonnecamp, speaks
of him as fearless, energetic, and full of resource;
but the governor calls him haughty and insubordinate.
Great efforts were made, at the same time, to build
up Detroit as a centre of French power in the West.
The methods employed were of the debilitating,
paternal character long familiar to Canada. All
emigrants with families were to be carried thither at
the King's expense; and every settler was to receive
in free gift a gun, a hoe, an axe, a ploughshare, a
scythe, a sickle, two augers, large and small, a sow,
six hens, a cock, six pounds of powder, and twelve
pounds of lead; while to these favors were added
many others. The result was that twelve families

---

[1] A plan of Detroit is before me, made about this time by the
engineer Lery.

[2] *Le Ministre à La Jonquière et Bigot*, 14 *Mai*, 1749. *Le Ministre à
Céloron*, 23 *Mai*, 1749.

VOL. I. — 6

were persuaded to go, or about a twentieth part of the number wanted.[1] Detroit was expected to furnish supplies to the other posts for five hundred miles around, control the neighboring Indians, thwart English machinations, and drive off English interlopers.

La Galissonière no longer governed Canada. He had been honorably recalled, and the Marquis de la Jonquière sent in his stead.[2] La Jonquière, like his predecessor, was a naval officer of high repute; he was tall and imposing in person, and of undoubted capacity and courage; but old and, according to his enemies, very avaricious.[3] The colonial minister gave him special instructions regarding that thorn in the side of Canada, Oswego. To attack it openly would be indiscreet, as the two nations were at peace; but there was a way of dealing with it less hazardous, if not more lawful. This was to attack it vicariously by means of the Iroquois. "If Abbé Piquet succeeds in his mission," wrote the minister to the new governor, "we can easily persuade these

[1] *Ordonnance du 2 Janvier*, 1750. *La Jonquière et Bigot au Ministre*, 1750. Forty-six persons of all ages and both sexes had been induced by La Galissonière to go the year before. *Lettres communes de La Jonquière et Bigot*, 1749. The total fixed population of Detroit and its neighborhood in 1750 is stated at four hundred and eighty-three souls. In the following two years, a considerable number of young men came of their own accord, and Céloron wrote to Montreal to ask for girls to marry them.

[2] *Le Ministre à La Galissonière*, 14 *Mai*, 1749.

[3] *Mémoires sur le Canada*, 1749–1760. The charges made here and elsewhere are denied, somewhat faintly, by a descendant of La Jonquière in his elaborate *Notice biographique* of his ancestor.

savages to destroy Oswego. This is of the utmost importance; but act with great caution."[1] In the next year the minister wrote again: "The only means that can be used for such an operation in time of peace are those of the Iroquois. If by making these savages regard such an establishment [*Oswego*] as opposed to their liberty, and, so to speak, a usurpation by which the English mean to get possession of their lands, they could be induced to undertake its destruction, an operation of the sort is not to be neglected; but M. le Marquis de la Jonquière should feel with what circumspection such an affair should be conducted, and he should labor to accomplish it in a manner not to commit himself."[2] To this La Jonquière replies that it will need time; but that he will gradually bring the Iroquois to attack and destroy the English post. He received stringent orders to use every means to prevent the English from encroaching, but to act towards them at the same time "with the greatest politeness."[3] This last injunction was scarcely fulfilled in a correspondence which he had with Clinton, governor of New York, who had written to complain of the new post at the Niagara portage as an invasion of English territory, and also of the arrest of four English

[1] *Le Ministre à La Jonquière, Mai,* 1749. The instructions given to La Jonquière before leaving France also urge the necessity of destroying Oswego.

[2] *Ordres du Roy et Dépêches des Ministres ; à MM. de La Jonquièr et Bigot,* 15 *Avril,* 1750. See Appendix A for original.

[3] *Ordres du Roy et Dépêches des Ministres,* 1750.

traders in the country of the Miamis. Niagara, like
Oswego, was in the country of the Five Nations,
whom the treaty of Utrecht declared "subject to the
dominion of Great Britain."[1] This declaration, preposterous in itself, was binding on France, whose
plenipotentiaries had signed the treaty. The treaty
also provided that the subjects of the two Crowns
"shall enjoy full liberty of going and coming on
account of trade," and Clinton therefore demanded
that La Jonquière should disavow the arrest of the
four traders and punish its authors. The French
governor replied with great asperity, spurned the
claim that the Five Nations were British subjects,
and justified the arrest.[2] He presently went further.
Rewards were offered by his officers for the scalps
of Croghan and of another trader named Lowry.[3]
When this reached the ears of William Johnson, on
the Mohawk, he wrote to Clinton in evident anxiety
for his own scalp: "If the French go on so, there is
no man can be safe in his own house; for I can at
any time get an Indian to kill any man for a small
matter. Their going on in that manner is worse
than open war."

The French on their side made counter-accusa-
tions. The captive traders were examined on oath
before La Jonquière, and one of them, John Patton,

[1] Chalmers, *Collection of Treaties*, i. 382.

[2] *La Jonquière à Clinton*, 10 *Août*, 1751.

[3] Deposition of Morris Turner and Ralph Kilgore, in *Colonial
Records of Pa.*, v. 482. The deponents had been prisoners at
Detroit.

is reported to have said that Croghan had instigated Indians to kill Frenchmen.[1] French officials declared that other English traders were guilty of the same practices; and there is very little doubt that the charge was true.

The dispute with the English was not the only source of trouble to the governor. His superiors at Versailles would not adopt his views, and looked on him with distrust. He advised the building of forts near Lake Erie, and his advice was rejected. "Niagara and Detroit," he was told, "will secure forever our communications with Louisiana."[2]   "His Majesty," again wrote the colonial minister, "thought that expenses would diminish after the peace; but, on the contrary, they have increased. There must be great abuses. You and the intendant must look to it."[3]   Great abuses there were; and of the money sent to Canada for the service of the King the larger part found its way into the pockets of peculators. The colony was eaten to the heart with official corruption; and the centre of it was François Bigot, the intendant. The minister directed La Jonquière's attention to certain malpractices which had been reported to him; and the old man, deeply touched, replied: "I have reached the age of sixty-six years, and there is not a drop of blood in my veins that does not thrill for the service of my King. I will not

[1] *Précis des Faits, avec leurs Pièces justificatives,* 100.
[2] *Ordres du Roy et Dépêches des Ministres,* 1750.
[3] *Ibid.,* 6 *Juin,* 1751.

conceal from you that the slightest suspicion on your part against me would cut the thread of my days." [1]

Perplexities increased; affairs in the West grew worse and worse. La Jonquière ordered Céloron to attack the English at Pickawillany; and Céloron could not or would not obey. "I cannot express," writes the governor, "how much this business troubles me; it robs me of sleep; it makes me ill." Another letter of rebuke presently came from Versailles. "Last year you wrote that you would soon drive the English from the Ohio; but private letters say that you have done nothing. This is deplorable. If not expelled, they will seem to acquire a right against us. Send force enough at once to drive them off, and cure them of all wish to return." [2] La Jonquière answered with bitter complaints against Céloron, and then begged to be recalled. His health, already shattered, was ruined by fatigue and vexation; and he took to his bed. Before spring he was near his end. [3] It is said that, though very rich, his habits of thrift so possessed his last hours that, seeing wax candles burning in his chamber, he ordered others of tallow to be brought instead, as being good enough to die by. Thus frugally lighted on its way, his spirit fled; and the Baron de Longueuil took his place till a new governor should arrive.

[1] La Jonquière au Ministre, 19 Octobre, 1751.

[2] Ordres du Roy et Dépêches des Ministres, 1751.

[3] He died on the sixth of March, 1752 (Bigot au Ministre, 6 Mai); not on the seventeenth of May, as stated in the Mémoires sur le Canada, 1749-1760.

Sinister tidings came thick from the West. Raymond, commandant at the French fort on the Maumee, close to the centre of intrigue, wrote: "My people are leaving me for Detroit. Nobody wants to stay here and have his throat cut. All the tribes who go to the English at Pickawillany come back loaded with gifts. I am too weak to meet the danger. Instead of twenty men, I need five hundred. . . . We have made peace with the English, yet they try continually to make war on us by means of the Indians; they intend to be masters of all this upper country. The tribes here are leaguing together to kill all the French, that they may have nobody on their lands but their English brothers. This I am told by Coldfoot, a great Miami chief, whom I think an honest man, if there is any such thing among Indians. . . . If the English stay in this country we are lost. We must attack, and drive them out." And he tells of war-belts sent from tribe to tribe, and rumors of plots and conspiracies far and near.

Without doubt, the English traders spared no pains to gain over the Indians by fair means or foul; sold them goods at low rates, made ample gifts, and gave gunpowder for the asking. Saint-Ange, who commanded at Vincennes, wrote that a storm would soon burst on the heads of the French. Joncaire reported that all the Ohio Indians sided with the English. Longueuil informed the minister that the Miamis had scalped two soldiers; that the Piankishaws had killed seven Frenchmen; and that a squaw who had lived with one of the slain declared that the tribes of the Wabash and Illinois were leaguing with the Osages for a combined insurrection. Every letter brought news of murder. Small-pox had broken out at Detroit. "It is to be wished," says Longueuil, "that it would spread among our rebels; it would be fully as good as an army. . . . We are menaced with a general outbreak, and even Toronto is in danger. . . . Before long the English on the Miami will gain over all the surrounding tribes, get possession of Fort Chartres, and cut our communications with Louisiana." [1]

The moving spirit of disaffection was the chief called Old Britain, or the Demoiselle, and its focus was his town of Pickawillany, on the Miami. At this place it is said that English traders sometimes mustered to the number of fifty or more. "It is they," wrote Longueuil, "who are the instigators of revolt and the source of all our woes." [2] Whereupon the colonial minister reiterated his instructions to drive them off and plunder them, which he thought would "effectually disgust them," and bring all trouble to an end. [3]

La Jonquière's remedy had been more heroic, for he had ordered Céloron to attack the English and their red allies alike; and he charged that officer

[1] *Dépêches de Longueuil; Lettres de Raymond; Benoît de Saint-Clerc à La Jonquière, Octobre,* 1751.

[2] *Longueuil au Ministre,* 21 *Avril,* 1752.

[3] *Le Ministre à La Jonquière,* 1752. *Le Ministre à Duquesne,* 9 *Juillet,* 1752.

with arrogance and disobedience because he had not
done so. It is not certain that obedience was easy;
for though, besides the garrison of regulars, a strong
body of militia was sent up to Detroit to aid the
stroke,[1] the Indians of that post, whose co-operation
was thought necessary, proved half-hearted, intractable and even touched with disaffection. Thus the
enterprise languished till, in June, aid came from
another quarter. Charles Langlade, a young French
trader married to a squaw at Green Bay, and strong
in influence with the tribes of that region, came down
the lakes from Michilimackinac with a fleet of canoes
manned by two hundred and fifty Ottawa and Ojibwa
warriors; stopped a while at Detroit; then embarked
again, paddled up the Maumee to Raymond's fort at
the portage, and led his greased and painted rabble
through the forest to attack the Demoiselle and his
English friends. They approached Pickawillany at
about nine o'clock on the morning of the twenty-
first. The scared squaws fled from the cornfields into
the town, where the wigwams of the Indians clustered
about the fortified warehouse of the traders. Of
these there were at the time only eight in the place.
Most of the Indians also were gone on their summer
hunt, though the Demoiselle remained with a band of
his tribesmen. Great was the screeching of war-whoops
and clatter of guns. Three of the traders were
caught outside the fort. The remaining five closed
the gate, and stood on their defence. The fight was

---

[1] *La Jonquière à Céloron*, 1 *Octobre*, 1751.

soon over. Fourteen Miamis were shot down, the Demoiselle among the rest. The five white men held out till the afternoon, when three of them surrendered, and two, Thomas Burney and Andrew McBryer, made their escape. One of the English prisoners being wounded, the victors stabbed him to death. Seventy years of missionaries had not weaned them from cannibalism, and they boiled and ate the Demoiselle.[1]

The captive traders, plundered to the skin, were carried by Langlade to Duquesne, the new governor, who highly praised the bold leader of the enterprise, and recommended him to the minister for such reward as befitted one of his station. "As he is not in the King's service, and has married a squaw, I will ask for him only a pension of two hundred francs, which will flatter him infinitely."

The Marquis Duquesne, sprung from the race of the great naval commander of that name, had arrived towards midsummer; and he began his rule by a general review of troops and militia. His lofty bearing offended the Canadians; but he compelled their respect, and, according to a writer of the time, showed from the first that he was born to command. He presently took in hand an enterprise which his predecessor would probably have accomplished, had the home government encouraged him. Duquesne, profiting by the infatuated neglect of the British

[1] On the attack of Pickawillany, *Longueuil au Ministre*, 18 *Août*, 1752; *Duquesne au Ministre*, 25 *Octobre*, 1752; *Colonial Records of Pa.*, v. 599; *Journal of William Trent*, 1752. Trent was on the spot a few days after the affair.

provincial assemblies, prepared to occupy the upper
waters of the Ohio, and secure the passes with forts
and garrisons. Thus the Virginian and Pennsylvanian traders would be debarred all access to the
West, and the tribes of that region, bereft henceforth
of English guns, knives, hatchets, and blankets, English gifts and English cajoleries, would be thrown
back to complete dependence on the French. The
moral influence, too, of such a movement would be incalculable; for the Indian respects nothing so much
as a display of vigor and daring, backed by force.
In short, the intended enterprise was a master-stroke,
and laid the axe to the very root of disaffection. It
is true that, under the treaty, commissioners had
been long in session at Paris to settle the question of
American boundaries; but there was no likelihood
that they would come to agreement; and if France
would make good her western claims, it behooved
her, while there was yet time, to prevent her rival
from fastening a firm grasp on the countries in
dispute.

Yet the colonial minister regarded the plan with
distrust. "Be on your guard," he wrote to Duquesne,
"against new undertakings; private interests are
generally at the bottom of them. It is through these
that new posts are established. Keep only such as
are indispensable, and suppress the others. The
expenses of the colony are enormous; and they have
doubled since the peace." Again, a little later
"Build on the Ohio such forts as are absolutely

necessary, but no more.   Remember that His Majesty
suspects your advisers of interested views." [1]

No doubt there was justice in the suspicion.
Every military movement, and above all the establishment of every new post, was an opportunity to the
official thieves with whom the colony swarmed.
Some bands of favored knaves grew rich; while a
much greater number, excluded from sharing the
illicit profits, clamored against the undertaking, and
wrote charges of corruption to Versailles.   Thus the
minister was kept tolerably well informed, but was
scarcely the less helpless, for with the Atlantic
between, the disorders of Canada defied his control.
Duquesne was exasperated by the opposition that
met him on all hands, and wrote to the minister:
"There are so many rascals in this country that one
is forever the butt of their attacks." [2]

It seems that unlawful gain was not the only secret
spring of the movement.   An officer of repute says
that the intendant, Bigot, enterprising in his pleasures
as in his greed, was engaged in an intrigue with the
wife of Chevalier Péan; and wishing at once to console the husband and to get rid of him, sought for
him a high command at a distance from the colony.
Therefore while Marin, an able officer, was made
first in rank, Péan was made second.   The same
writer hints that Duquesne himself was influenced by
similar motives in his appointment of leaders. [3]

[1] *Ordres du Roy et Dépêches des Ministres,* 1753.

[2] *Duquesne au Ministre,* 29 *Septembre,* 1754.

[3] Pouchot, *Mémoire sur la dernière Guerre de l'Amérique septentrionale* (ed. 1781), i. 8.

He mustered the colony troops, and ordered out the Canadians. With the former he was but half satisfied; with the latter he was delighted; and he praises highly their obedience and alacrity. "I had not the least trouble in getting them to march. They came on the minute, bringing their own guns, though many people tried to excite them to revolt; for the whole colony opposes my operations." The expedition set out early in the spring of 1753. The whole force was not much above a thousand men, increased by subsequent detachments to fifteen hundred; but to the Indians it seemed a mighty host; and one of their orators declared that the lakes and rivers were covered with boats and soldiers from Montreal to Presqu'isle.[1] Some Mohawk hunters by the St. Lawrence saw them as they passed, and hastened home to tell the news to Johnson, whom they wakened at midnight, "whooping and hollowing in a frightful manner."[2] Lieutenant Holland at Oswego saw a fleet of canoes upon the lake, and was told by a roving Frenchman that they belonged to an army of six thousand men going to the Ohio, "to cause all the English to quit those parts."[3]

The main body of the expedition landed at Presqu'isle, on the southeastern shore of Lake Erie, where the town of Erie now stands; and here for a while we leave them.

---

[1] *Duquesne au Ministre,* 27 *Octobre,* 1753.

[2] *Johnson to Clinton,* 20 *April,* 1753, in *N. Y. Col. Docs.,* **vi.** 778.

[3] *Holland to Clinton,* 15 *May,* 1753, in *N. Y. Col. Docs.,* **vi.** 780.

CHAPTER IV.

1710–1754.

CONFLICT FOR ACADIA.

ACADIA CEDED TO ENGLAND. — ACADIANS SWEAR FIDELITY. —
HALIFAX FOUNDED. — FRENCH INTRIGUE. — ACADIAN PRIESTS. —
MILDNESS OF ENGLISH RULE. — COVERT HOSTILITY OF ACA-
DIANS. — THE NEW OATH. — TREACHERY OF VERSAILLES. —
INDIANS INCITED TO WAR. — CLERICAL AGENTS OF REVOLT.
— ABBÉ LE LOUTRE. — ACADIANS IMPELLED TO EMIGRATE. —
MISERY OF THE EMIGRANTS. — HUMANITY OF CORNWALLIS AND
HOPSON. — FANATICISM AND VIOLENCE OF LE LOUTRE. — CAP-
TURE OF THE "ST. FRANÇOIS." — THE ENGLISH AT BEAU-
BASSIN. — LE LOUTRE DRIVES OUT THE INHABITANTS. — MURDER
OF HOWE. — BEAUSÉJOUR. — INSOLENCE OF LE LOUTRE : HIS
HARSHNESS TO THE ACADIANS. — THE BOUNDARY COMMISSION :
ITS FAILURE. — APPROACHING WAR.

WHILE in the West all the signs of the sky fore-
boded storm, another tempest was gathering in the
East, less in extent, but not less in peril. The conflict in Acadia has a melancholy interest, since it
ended in a catastrophe which prose and verse have
joined to commemorate, but of which the causes
have not been understood.

Acadia — that is to say, the peninsula of Nova
Scotia, with the addition, as the English claimed, of
the present New Brunswick and some adjacent
country — was conquered by General Nicholson in

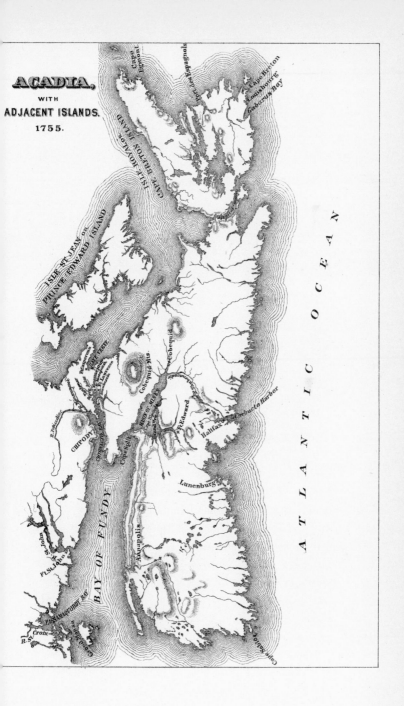

ACADIA,
WITH
ADJACENT ISLANDS.
1755.

1710, and formally transferred by France to the British Crown, three years later, by the treaty of Utrecht. By that treaty it was "expressly provided" that such of the French inhabitants as "are willing to remain there and to be subject to the Kingdom of Great Britain, are to enjoy the free exercise of their religion according to the usage of the Church of Rome, as far as the laws of Great Britain do allow the same;" but that any who choose may remove, with their effects, if they do so within a year. Very few availed themselves of this right; and after the end of the year those who remained were required to take an oath of allegiance to King George. There is no doubt that in a little time they would have complied, had they been let alone; but the French authorities of Canada and Cape Breton did their utmost to prevent them, and employed agents to keep them hostile to England. Of these the most efficient were the French priests, who, in spite of the treaty, persuaded their flocks that they were still subjects of King Louis. Hence rose endless perplexity to the English commanders at Annapolis, who more than suspected that the Indian attacks with which they were harassed were due mainly to French instigation.[1] It was not till seventeen years after the treaty that the Acadians could be brought to take the oath without qualifications which made it almost useless.

[1] See the numerous papers in *Selections from the Public Documents of the Province of Nova Scotia* (Halifax, 1869), pp. 1-165; a government publication of great value.

The English authorities seem to have shown through-out an unusual patience and forbearance. At length, about 1730, nearly all the inhabitants signed by crosses, since few of them could write, an oath recog-nizing George II. as sovereign of Acadia, and promis-ing fidelity and obedience to him.[1] This restored comparative quiet till the war of 1745, when some of the Acadians remained neutral, while some took arms against the English, and many others aided the enemy with information and supplies.

English power in Acadia, hitherto limited to a feeble garrison at Annapolis and a feebler one at Canseau, received at this time a great accession. The fortress of Louisbourg, taken by the English during the war, had been restored by the treaty; and the French at once prepared to make it a mili-tary and naval station more formidable than ever. Upon this the British ministry resolved to establish another station as a counterpoise; and the harbor of Chebucto, on the south coast of Acadia, was chosen as the site of it. Thither in June, 1749, came a fleet of transports loaded with emigrants, tempted by offers of land and a home in the New World. Some were mechanics, tradesmen, farmers, and laborers; others were sailors, soldiers, and subaltern officers thrown out of employment by the peace. Including

[1] The oath was *literatim* as follows : " Je Promets et Jure Sincere-ment en Foi de Chrétien que Je serai entierement Fidele, et Obeierai Vraiment Sa Majesté Le Roy George Second, qui [sic] Je reconnoi pour Le Souvrain Seigneur de l'Accadie ou Nouvelle Ecosse. Ainsi Dieu me Soit en Aide."

women and children, they counted in all about twenty-five hundred. Alone of all the British colonies on the continent, this new settlement was the offspring, not of private enterprise, but of royal authority. Yet it was free like the rest, with the same popular representation and local self-government. Edward Cornwallis, uncle of Lord Cornwallis of the Revolutionary War, was made governor and commander-in-chief. Wolfe calls him "a man of approved courage and fidelity;" and even the caustic Horace Walpole speaks of him as "a brave, sensible young man, of great temper and good nature."

Before summer was over, the streets were laid out, and the building-lot of each settler was assigned to him; before winter closed, the whole were under shelter, the village was fenced with palisades and defended by redoubts of timber, and the battalions lately in garrison at Louisbourg manned the wooden ramparts. Succeeding years brought more emigrants, till in 1752 the population was above four thousand. Thus was born into the world the city of Halifax. Along with the crumbling old fort and miserably disciplined garrison at Annapolis, besides six or seven small detached posts to watch the Indians and Acadians, it comprised the whole British force on the peninsula; for Canseau had been destroyed by the French.

The French had never reconciled themselves to the loss of Acadia, and were resolved, by diplomacy or force, to win it back again; but the building of

Halifax showed that this was to be no easy task, and
filled them at the same time with alarm for the safety
of Louisbourg. On one point, at least, they saw
their policy clear. The Acadians, though those of
them who were not above thirty-five had been born
under the British flag, must be kept French at
heart, and taught that they were still French subjects. In 1748 they numbered eighty-eight hundred
and fifty communicants, or from twelve to thirteen
thousand souls; but an emigration, of which the
causes will soon appear, had reduced them in 1752
to but little more than nine thousand.[1] These were
divided into six principal parishes, one of the largest
being that of Annapolis. Other centres of population were Grand Pré, on the Basin of Mines; Beaubassin, at the head of Chignecto Bay; Pisiquid, now
Windsor; and Cobequid, now Truro. Their priests,
who were missionaries controlled by the diocese of
Quebec, acted also as their magistrates, ruling them
for this world and the next. Being subject to a
French superior, and being, moreover, wholly French
at heart, they formed in this British province a wheel
within a wheel, the inner movement always opposing
the outer.

Although, by the twelfth article of the treaty of
Utrecht, France had solemnly declared the Acadians

[1] *Description de l'Acadie, avec le Nom des Paroisses et le Nombre
des Habitants*, 1748. *Mémoire à présenter à la Cour sur la Necessité
de fixer les Limites de l'Acadie*, par l'Abbé de l'Isle-Dieu, 1753
(1754?). Compare the estimates in *Censuses of Canada* (Ottawa,
1876).

of the said month [*August*], to the effect that if the
inhabitants will remain faithful subjects of the King
of Great Britain, he will allow them priests and
public exercise of their religion, with the understanding that no priest shall officiate without his
permission or before taking an oath of fidelity to the
King of Great Britain. Secondly, that the inhabitants shall not be exempted from defending their
houses, their lands, and the Government. Thirdly,
that they shall take an oath of fidelity to the King
of Great Britain, on the twenty-sixth of this month,
before officers sent them for that purpose."

La Jonquière proceeds to say that on hearing these
conditions the Acadians were filled with perplexity
and alarm, and that he, the governor, had directed
Boishébert, his chief officer on the Acadian frontier,
to encourage them to leave their homes and seek
asylum on French soil. He thus recounts the steps
he has taken to harass the English of Halifax by
means of their Indian neighbors. As peace had been
declared, the operation was delicate; and when three
of these Indians came to him from their missionary,
Le Loutre, with letters on the subject, La Jonquière
was discreetly reticent. "I did not care to give
them any advice upon the matter, and confined myself to a promise that I would on no account abandon
them; and I have provided for supplying them with
everything, whether arms, ammunition, food, or
other necessaries. It is to be desired that these
savages should succeed in thwarting the designs of

the English, and even their settlement at Halifax.
They are bent on doing so; and if they can carry
out their plans, it is certain that they will give the
English great trouble, and so harass them that they
will be a great obstacle in their path.　These savages
are to act alone; neither soldier nor French inhabit-
ant is to join them; everything will be done of their
own motion, and without showing that I had any
knowledge of the matter.　This is very essential;
therefore I have written to the Sieur de Boishébert to
observe great prudence in his measures, and to act
very secretly, in order that the English may not
perceive that we are providing for the needs of the
said savages.

"It will be the missionaries who will manage all
the negotiation, and direct the movements of the
savages, who are in excellent hands, as the Reverend
Father Germain and Monsieur l'Abbé Le Loutre are
very capable of making the most of them, and using
them to the greatest advantage for our interests.
They will manage their intrigue in such a way as
not to appear in it."

La Jonquière then recounts the good results which
he expects from these measures: first, the English
will be prevented from making any new settlements;
secondly, we shall gradually get the Acadians out
of their hands; and lastly, they will be so discouraged by constant Indian attacks that they will
renounce their pretensions to the parts of the
country belonging to the King of France.　"I feel,

Monseigneur," — thus the governor concludes his
despatch, — "all the delicacy of this negotiation; be
assured that I will conduct it with such precaution
that the English will not be able to say that my
orders had any part in it." [1]

He kept his word, and so did the missionaries.
The Indians gave great trouble on the outskirts of
Halifax, and murdered many harmless settlers; yet
the English authorities did not at first suspect that
they were hounded on by their priests, under the
direction of the governor of Canada, and with the
privity of the minister at Versailles. More than
this; for, looking across the sea, we find royalty
itself lending its august countenance to the machina-
tion. Among the letters read before the King in his
cabinet in May, 1750, was one from Desherbiers, then
commanding at Louisbourg, saying that he was advising the Acadians not to take the oath of allegiance
to the King of England; another from Le Loutre,
declaring that he and Father Germain were consulting together how to disgust the English with their
enterprise of Halifax; and a third from the intendant,
Bigot, announcing that Le Loutre was using the
Indians to harass the new settlement, and that he
himself was sending them powder, lead, and merchandise, "to confirm them in their good designs." [2]

To this the minister replies in a letter to Desherbiers: "His Majesty is well satisfied with all you

---

[1] *La Jonquière au Ministre,* 9 *Octobre,* 1749. See Appendix B.
[2] *Résumé des Lettres lues au Travail du Roy, Mai,* 1750.

have done to thwart the English in their new establishment. If the dispositions of the savages are such as they seem, there is reason to hope that in the course of the winter they will succeed in so harassing the settlers that some of them will become disheartened." Desherbiers is then told that His Majesty desires him to aid English deserters in escaping from Halifax.[1] Supplies for the Indians are also promised; and he is informed that twelve medals are sent him by the frigate "La Mutine," to be given to the chiefs who shall most distinguish themselves. In another letter Desherbiers is enjoined to treat the English authorities with great politeness.[2]

When Count Raymond took command at Louisbourg, he was instructed, under the royal hand, to give particular attention to the affairs of Acadia, especially in two points, — the management of the Indians, and the encouraging of Acadian emigration to countries under French rule. "His Majesty," says the document, "has already remarked that the savages have been most favorably disposed. It is of the utmost importance that no means be neglected to keep them so. The missionaries among them are in a better position than anybody to contribute to this end, and His Majesty has reason to be satisfied with the pains they take therein. The Sieur de

---

[1] In 1750 nine captured deserters from Phillips's regiment declared on their trial that the French had aided them and supplied them all with money. *Public Documents of Nova Scotia*, 193.

[2] *Le Ministre à Desherbiers*, 23 *Mai*, 1750; *Ibid.*, 31 *Mai*, 1750.

Raymond will excite these missionaries not to slacken
their efforts; but he will warn them at the same time
so to contain their zeal as not to compromise themselves with the English, and give just occasion of
complaint." [1] That is, the King orders his representative to encourage the missionaries in instigating their
flocks to butcher English settlers, but to see that
they take care not to be found out. The injunction
was hardly needed. "Monsieur Desherbiers," says a
letter of earlier date, "has engaged Abbé Le Loutre
to distribute the usual presents among the savages,
and Monsieur Bigot has placed in his hands an additional gift of cloth, blankets, powder, and ball, to be
given them in case they harass the English at
Halifax. This missionary is to induce them to do
so." [2] In spite of these efforts, the Indians began to
relent in their hostilities; and when Longueuil
became provisional governor of Canada, he complained to the minister that it was very difficult to
prevent them from making peace with the English,
though Father Germain was doing his best to keep
them on the war-path.[3] La Jonquière, too, had done
his best, even to the point of departing from his
original policy of allowing no soldier or Acadian to
take part with them. He had sent a body of troops
under La Corne, an able partisan officer, to watch

[1] *Mémoire du Roy pour servir d'Instruction au Comte de Raymond,*
24 *Avril,* 1751.

[2] *Lettre commune de Desherbiers et Bigot au Ministre 15 Août,*
1749.

[3] *Longueuil au Ministre,* 26 *Avril,* 1752.

the English frontier; and in the same vessel was sent
a supply of "merchandise, guns, and munitions for
the savages and the Acadians who may take up arms
with them; and the whole is sent under pretext of
trading in furs with the savages." [1]   On another occasion La Jonquière wrote: "In order that the savages
may do their part courageously, a few Acadians,
dressed and painted in their way, could join them to
strike the English. I cannot help consenting to
what these savages do, because we have our hands
tied [*by the peace*], and so can do nothing ourselves.
Besides, I do not think that any inconvenience will
come of letting the Acadians mingle among them,
because if they [*the Acadians*] are captured, we shall
say that they acted of their own accord." [2]   In other
words, he will encourage them to break the peace;
and then, by means of a falsehood, have them pun-
ished as felons. Many disguised Acadians did in
fact join the Indian war-parties; and their doing so
was no secret to the English. "What we call here
an Indian war," wrote Hopson, successor of Cornwallis, "is no other than a pretence for the French
to commit hostilities on His Majesty's subjects."

At length the Indians made peace, or pretended
to do so. The chief of Le Loutre's mission, who
called himself Major Jean-Baptiste Cope, came to
Halifax with a deputation of his tribe, and they all
affixed their totems to a solemn treaty. In the next

---

[1] *Bigot au Ministre*, 1749.
[2] *Dépêches de La Jonquière*, 1 *Mai*, 1751.   See Appendix B.

summer they returned with ninety or a hundred
warriors, were well entertained, presented with gifts,
and sent homeward in a schooner. On the way they
seized the vessel and murdered the crew. This is
told by Prévost, intendant at Louisbourg, who does
not say that French instigation had any part in the
treachery.[1] It is nevertheless certain that the Indians
were paid for this or some contemporary murder;
for Prévost, writing just four weeks later, says:
"Last month the savages took eighteen English
scalps, and Monsieur Le Loutre was obliged to pay
them eighteen hundred livres, Acadian money,
which I have reimbursed him."[2]

From the first, the services of this zealous missionary had been beyond price. Prévost testifies
that, though Cornwallis does his best to induce the
Acadians to swear fidelity to King George, Le Loutre
keeps them in allegiance to King Louis, and
threatens to set his Indians upon them unless they
declare against the English. "I have already," adds
Prévost, "paid him 11,183 livres for his daily
expenses; and I never cease advising him to be as
economical as possible, and always to take care not
to compromise himself with the English Government."[3] In consequence of "good service to religion
and the state," Le Loutre received a pension of eight

[1] *Prévost au Ministre,* 12 *Mars,* 1753; *Ibid.,* 17 *Juillet,* 1753. Prévost was *ordonnateur,* or intendant, at Louisbourg. The treaty will
be found in full in *Public Documents of Nova Scotia,* 683.

[2] *Prévost au Ministre,* 16 *Août,* 1753.

[3] *Ibid.,* 22 *Juillet,* 1750.

hundred livres, as did also Maillard, his brother missionary on Cape Breton. "The fear is," writes the colonial minister to the governor of Louisbourg, "that their zeal may carry them too far. Excite them to keep the Indians in our interest, but do not let them compromise us. Act always so as to make the English appear as aggressors."[1]

All the Acadian clergy, in one degree or another, seem to have used their influence to prevent the inhabitants from taking the oath, and to persuade them that they were still French subjects. Some were noisy, turbulent, and defiant; others were too tranquil to please the officers of the Crown. A missionary at Annapolis is mentioned as old, and therefore inefficient; while the curé at Grand Pré, also an elderly man, was too much inclined to confine himself to his spiritual functions. It is everywhere apparent that those who chose these priests, and sent them as missionaries into a British province, expected them to act as enemies of the British Crown. The maxim is often repeated that duty to religion is inseparable

---

[1] *Le Ministre au Comte de Raymond*, 21 *Juillet*, 1752. It is curious to compare these secret instructions, given by the minister to the colonial officials, with a letter which the same minister, Rouillé, wrote ostensibly to La Jonquière, but which was really meant for the eye of the British minister at Versailles, Lord Albemarle, to whom it was shown in proof of French good faith. It was afterwards printed, along with other papers, in a small volume called *Précis des Faits, avec leurs Pièces justificatives*, which was sent by the French government to all the courts of Europe to show that the English alone were answerable for the war. The letter, it is needless to say, breathes the highest sentiments of international honor.

from duty to the King of France. The Bishop of
Quebec desired the Abbé de l'Isle-Dieu to represent
to the Court the need of more missionaries to keep
the Acadians Catholic and French; but, he adds,
there is danger that they (the missionaries) will be
required to take an oath to do nothing contrary to
the interests of the King of Great Britain.[1] It is a
wonder that such a pledge was not always demanded.
It was exacted in a few cases, notably in that of
Girard, priest at Cobequid, who, on charges of instigating his flock to disaffection, had been sent prisoner
to Halifax, but released on taking an oath in the
above terms. Thereupon he wrote to Longueuil at
Quebec that his parishioners wanted to submit to the
English, and that he, having sworn to be true to the
British King, could not prevent them. "Though I
don't pretend to be a casuist," writes Longueuil, "I
could not help answering him that he is not obliged
to keep such an oath, and that he ought to labor in
all zeal to preserve and increase the number of the
faithful." Girard, to his credit, preferred to leave
the colony, and retired to Isle St. Jean.[2]

Cornwallis soon discovered to what extent the
clergy stirred their flocks to revolt; and he wrote
angrily to the Bishop of Quebec: "Was it you who
sent Le Loutre as a missionary to the Micmacs? and
is it for their good that he excites these wretches to

[1] L'Isle-Dieu, *Mémoire sur l'État actuel des Missions*, 1753
(1754?).

[2] *Longueuil au Ministre*, 27 *Avril*, 1752.

practise their cruelties against those who have shown them every kindness? The conduct of the priests of Acadia has been such that by command of His Majesty I have published an Order declaring that if any one of them presumes to exercise his functions without my express permission he shall be dealt with according to the laws of England."[1]

The English, bound by treaty to allow the Acadians the exercise of their religion, at length conceived the idea of replacing the French priests by others to be named by the Pope at the request of the British government. This, becoming known to the French, greatly alarmed them, and the intendant at Louisbourg wrote to the minister that the matter required serious attention.[2] It threatened, in fact, to rob them of their chief agents of intrigue; but their alarm proved needless, as the plan was not carried into execution.

The French officials would have been better pleased had the conduct of Cornwallis been such as to aid their efforts to alienate the Acadians; and one writer, while confessing the "favorable treatment" of the English towards the inhabitants, denounces it as a snare.[3] If so, it was a snare intended simply to reconcile them to English rule. Nor was it without effect. "We must give up altogether the idea of an

---

[1] *Cornwallis to the Bishop of Quebec*, 1 *December*, 1749.

[2] *Daudin, prêtre, à Prévost*, 23 *Octobre*, 1753. *Prévost au Ministre*, 24 *Novembre*, 1753.

[3] *Mémoire à présenter à la Cour*, 1753.

insurrection in Acadia," writes an officer of Cape
Breton. " The Acadians cannot be trusted; they are
controlled by fear of the Indians, which leads them
to breathe French sentiments, even when their inclinations are English. They will yield to their interests;
and the English will make it impossible that they should
either hurt them or serve us, unless we take measures
different from those we have hitherto pursued." [1]

During all this time, constant efforts were made to
stimulate Acadian emigration to French territory,
and thus to strengthen the French frontier. In
this work the chief agent was Le Loutre. " This
priest," says a French writer of the time, "urged the
people of Les Mines, Port Royal [*Annapolis*], and
other places, to come and join the French, and
promised to all, in the name of the governor, to settle
and support them for three years, and even indemnify
them for any losses they might incur; threatening if
they did not do as he advised, to abandon them,
deprive them of their priests, have their wives and
children carried off, and their property laid waste by
the Indians." [2] Some passed over the isthmus to the
shores of the gulf, and others made their way to the
Strait of Canseau. Vessels were provided to convey
them, in the one case to Isle St. Jean, now Prince
Edward Island, and in the other to Isle Royale,
called by the English, Cape Breton. Some were
eager to go; some went with reluctance; some would

---

[1] *Roma au Ministre*, 11 *Mars*, 1750.
[2] *Mémoires sur le Canada*, 1749-1760.

scarcely be persuaded to go at all. "They leave
their homes with great regret," reports the governor
of Isle St. Jean, speaking of the people of Cobequid,
"and they began to move their luggage only when
the savages compelled them."[1] These savages were
the flock of Abbé Le Loutre, who was on the spot to
direct the emigration. Two thousand Acadians are
reported to have left the peninsula before the end of
1751, and many more followed within the next two
years. Nothing could exceed the misery of a great
part of these emigrants, who had left perforce most
of their effects behind. They became disheartened
and apathetic. The intendant at Louisbourg says
that they will not take the trouble to clear the land,
and that some of them live, like Indians, under huts
of spruce-branches.[2] The governor of Isle St. Jean
declares that they are dying of hunger.[3] Girard, the
priest who had withdrawn to this island rather than
break his oath to the English, writes: "Many of
them cannot protect themselves day or night from
the severity of the cold. Most of the children are
entirely naked; and when I go into a house they are
all crouched in the ashes, close to the fire. They
run off and hide themselves, without shoes, stockings, or shirts. They are not all reduced to this
extremity, but nearly all are in want."[4] Mortality

[1] *Bonaventure à Desherbiers, 26 Juin,* 1751.
[2] *Prévost au Ministre,* 25 *Novembre,* 1750.
[3] *Bonaventure, ut supra.*
[4] *Girard à (Bonaventure?), 27 Octobre,* 1753.

among them was great, and would have been greater but for rations supplied by the French government.

During these proceedings, the English governor, Cornwallis, seems to have justified the character of good temper given him by Horace Walpole. His attitude towards the Acadians remained on the whole patient and conciliatory. "My friends," he replied to a deputation of them asking a general permission to leave the province, "I am not ignorant of the fact that every means has been used to alienate the hearts of the French subjects of His Britannic Majesty. Great advantages have been promised you elsewhere, and you have been made to imagine that your religion was in danger. Threats even have been resorted to in order to induce you to remove to French territory. The savages are made use of to molest you; they are to cut the throats of all who remain in their native country, attached to their own interests and faithful to the Government. You know that certain officers and missionaries, who came from Canada last autumn, have been the cause of all our trouble during the winter. Their conduct has been horrible, without honor, probity, or conscience. Their aim is to embroil you with the Government. I will not believe that they are authorized to do so by the Court of France, that being contrary to good faith and the friendship established between the two Crowns."

What foundation there was for this amiable confidence in the Court of Versailles has been seen already.

"When you declared your desire to submit yourselves to another Government," pursues Cornwallis,
"our determination was to hinder nobody from following what he imagined to be his interest. We
know that a forced service is worth nothing, and that
a subject compelled to be so against his will is not
far from being an enemy. We confess, however,
that your determination to go gives us pain. We
are aware of your industry and temperance, and that
you are not addicted to any vice or debauchery.
This province is your country. You and your
fathers have cultivated it; naturally you ought yourselves to enjoy the fruits of your labor. Such was
the design of the King, our master. You know that
we have followed his orders. You know that we
have done everything to secure to you not only the
occupation of your lands, but the ownership of them
forever. We have given you also every possible
assurance of the free and public exercise of the
Roman Catholic religion. But I declare to you
frankly that, according to our laws, nobody can possess lands or houses in the province who shall refuse
to take the oath of allegiance to his King when
required to do so. You know very well that there
are ill-disposed and mischievous persons among you
who corrupt the others. Your inexperience, your
ignorance of the affairs of government, and your habit
of following the counsels of those who have not your
real interests at heart, make it an easy matter to
seduce you. In your petitions you ask for a general

leave to quit the province. The only manner in which
you can do so is to follow the regulations already
established, and provide yourselves with our pass-
port. And we declare that nothing shall prevent us
from giving such passports to all who ask for them,
the moment peace and tranquillity are re-established." [1] He declares as his reason for not giving
them at once, that on crossing the frontier "you will
have to pass the French detachments and savages
assembled there, and that they compel all the inhabitants who go there to take up arms" against the
English. How well this reason was founded will
soon appear.

Hopson, the next governor, described by the
French themselves as a "mild and peaceable officer,"
was no less considerate in his treatment of the
Acadians; and at the end of 1752 he issued the following order to his military subordinates: "You are
to look on the French inhabitants in the same light
as the rest of His Majesty's subjects, as to the protection of the laws and government; for which reason
nothing is to be taken from them by force, or any
price set upon their goods but what they themselves
agree to. And if at any time the inhabitants should
obstinately refuse to comply with what His Majesty's
service may require of them, you are not to redress

---

[1] The above passages are from two addresses of Cornwallis,
read to the Acadian deputies in April and May, 1750. The combined extracts here given convey the spirit of the whole. See
Public Documents of Nova Scotia, 185-190.

yourself by military force or in any unlawful manner, but to lay the case before the Governor and wait his orders thereon."[1]   Unfortunately, the mild rule of Cornwallis and Hopson was not always maintained under their successor, Lawrence.

Louis Joseph Le Loutre, vicar-general of Acadia and missionary to the Micmacs, was the most conspicuous person in the province, and more than any other man was answerable for the miseries that overwhelmed it.   The sheep of which he was the shepherd dwelt, at a day's journey from Halifax, by the banks of the river Shubenacadie, in small cabins of logs, mixed with wigwams of birch-bark.   They were not a docile flock; and to manage them needed address, energy, and money, — with all of which the missionary was provided.   He fed their traditional dislike of the English, and fanned their fanaticism, born of the villanous counterfeit of Christianity which he and his predecessors had imposed on them.   Thus he contrived to use them on the one hand to murder the English, and on the other to terrify the Acadians; yet not without cost to the French government; for they had learned the value of money, and, except when their blood was up, were slow to take scalps without pay.   Le Loutre was a man of boundless egotism, a violent spirit of domination, an intense hatred of the English, and a fanaticism that stopped at nothing.   Towards the Acadians he was a despot; and this simple and superstitious people, extremely

[1] *Public Documents of Nova Scotia,* 197.

susceptible to the influence of their priests, trembled before him. He was scarcely less masterful in his dealings with the Acadian clergy; and, aided by his quality of the bishop's vicar-general, he dragooned even the unwilling into aiding his schemes. Three successive governors of New France thought him invaluable, yet feared the impetuosity of his zeal, and vainly tried to restrain it within safe bounds. The bishop, while approving his objects, thought his medicines too violent, and asked in a tone of reproof: "Is it right for you to refuse the Acadians the sacraments, to threaten that they shall be deprived of the services of a priest, and that the savages shall treat them as enemies?"[1] "Nobody," says a French Catholic contemporary, "was more fit than he to carry discord and desolation into a country."[2] Cornwallis called him "a good-for-nothing scoundrel," and offered a hundred pounds for his head.[3]

The authorities at Halifax, while exasperated by the perfidy practised on them, were themselves not always models of international virtue. They seized a French vessel in the Gulf of St. Lawrence, on the charge — probably true — that she was carrying arms and ammunition to the Acadians and Indians. A less defensible act was the capture of the armed brig

[1] *L'Évêque de Québec à Le Loutre;* translation in *Public Documents of Nova Scotia,* 240.

[2] *Mémoires sur le Canada,* 1749-1760.

[3] On Le Loutre, compare *Public Documents of Nova Scotia,* 178-180, *note,* with authorities there cited; *N. Y. Col. Docs.,* x. 11; *Mémoires sur le Canada,* 1749-1760 (Quebec, 1838).

"St. François," laden with supplies for a fort lately re-established by the French, at the mouth of the river St. John, on ground claimed by both nations. Captain Rous, a New England officer commanding a frigate in the royal navy, opened fire on the "St. François," took her after a short cannonade, and carried her into Halifax, where she was condemned by the court. Several captures of small craft, accused of illegal acts, were also made by the English. These proceedings, being all of an overt nature, gave the officers of Louis XV. precisely what they wanted, — an occasion for uttering loud complaints, and denouncing the English as breakers of the peace.

But the movement most alarming to the French was the English occupation of Beaubassin, — an act perfectly lawful in itself, since, without reasonable doubt, the place was within the limits of Acadia, and therefore on English ground.[1] Beaubassin was a considerable settlement on the isthmus that joins the Acadian peninsula to the mainland. Northwest of the settlement lay a wide marsh, through which ran a stream called the Missaguash, some two miles beyond which rose a hill called Beauséjour. On and near this hill were stationed the troops and Canadians sent under Boishébert and La Corne to watch the English frontier. This French force excited disaffection among the Acadians through all the

[1] La Jonquière himself admits that he thought so. " Cette partie là étant, à ce que je crois, dépendante de l'Acadie." — *La Jonquière au Ministre, 3 Octobre,* 1750.

neighboring districts, and constantly helped them to
emigrate. Cornwallis therefore resolved to send an
English force to the spot; and accordingly, towards
the end of April, 1750, Major Lawrence landed at
Beaubassin with four hundred men. News of their
approach had come before them, and Le Loutre was
here with his Micmacs, mixed with some Acadians
whom he had persuaded or bullied to join him.
Resolved that the people of Beaubassin should not
live under English influence, he now with his own
hand set fire to the parish church, while his white
and red adherents burned the houses of the inhabitants, and thus compelled them to cross to the French
side of the river.[1] This was the first forcible removal
of the Acadians. It was as premature as it was
violent; since Lawrence, being threatened by La
Corne, whose force was several times greater than
his own, presently re-embarked. In the following
September he returned with seventeen small vessels
and about seven hundred men, and again attempted
to land on the strand of Beaubassin. La Jonquière
says that he could only be resisted indirectly, because
he was on the English side of the river. This

---

[1] It has been erroneously stated that Beaubassin was burned
by its own inhabitants. "Laloutre, ayant vu que les Acadiens ne
paroissoient pas fort pressés d'abandonner leurs biens, avoit lui-
même mis le feu à l'Église, et l'avoit fait mettre aux maisons des
habitants par quelques-uns de ceux qu'il avoit gagnés," etc.
Mémoires sur le Canada, 1749-1760. "Les sauvages y mirent le
feu." *Précis des Faits*, 85. "Les sauvages mirent le feu aux
maisons." *Prévost au Ministre*, 22 *Juillet*, 1750.

and accompanied by a few officers and men, went towards the river to hear what he had to say. As they drew near, his looks and language excited their suspicion. But it was too late; for a number of Indians, who had hidden behind the dike during the night, fired upon Howe across the stream, and mortally wounded him. They continued their fire on his companions, but could not prevent them from carrying the dying man to the fort. The French officers, indignant at this villany, did not hesitate to charge it upon Le Loutre; "for," says one of them, "what is not a wicked priest capable of doing?" But Le Loutre's brother missionary, Maillard, declares that it was purely an effect of religious zeal on the part of the Micmacs, who, according to him, bore a deadly grudge against Howe because, fourteen years before, he had spoken words disrespectful to the Holy Virgin.[1] Maillard adds that the Indians were much pleased with what they had done. Finding, however, that they could effect little against the English troops, they changed their field of action, repaired to the outskirts of Halifax, murdered about thirty settlers, and carried off eight or ten prisoners.

Strong reinforcements came from Canada. The

---

[1] Maillard, *Les Missions Micmaques.* On the murder of Howe, *Public Documents of Nova Scotia,* 194, 195, 210; *Mémoires sur le Canada,* 1749–1760, where it is said that Le Loutre was present at the deed; La Vallière, *Journal,* who says that some Acadians took part in it; *Dépêches de La Jonquière,* who says "les sauvages de l'Abbé le Loutre l'ont tué par trahison;" and *Prévost au Ministre* 27 *Octobre,* 1750.

French began a fort on the hill of Beauséjour, and the Acadians were required to work at it with no compensation but rations. They were thinly clad, some had neither shoes nor stockings, and winter was begun. They became so dejected that it was found absolutely necessary to give them wages enough to supply their most pressing needs. In the following season Fort Beauséjour was in a state to receive a garrison. It stood on the crown of the hill, and a vast panorama stretched below and around it. In front lay the Bay of Chignecto, winding along the fertile shores of Chipody and Memeramcook. Far on the right spread the great Tantemar marsh; on the left lay the marsh of the Missaguash; and on a knoll beyond it, not three miles distant, the red flag of England waved over the palisades of Fort Lawrence, while hills wrapped in dark forests bounded the horizon.

How the homeless Acadians from Beaubassin lived through the winter is not very clear. They probably found shelter at Chipody and its neighborhood, where there were thriving settlements of their countrymen. Le Loutre, fearing that they would return to their lands and submit to the English, sent some of them to Isle St. Jean. "They refused to go," says a French writer; "but he compelled them at last, by threatening to make the Indians pillage them, carry off their wives and children, and even kill them before their eyes. Nevertheless he kept about him such as were most submissive to his

to settle the question of boundaries between France
and England in America had been in session at Paris,
waging interminable war on paper; La Galissonière
and Silhouette for France, Shirley and Mildmay for
England. By the treaty of Utrecht, Acadia belonged
to England; but what was Acadia? According to
the English commissioners, it comprised not only the
peninsula now called Nova Scotia, but all the immense tract of land between the river St. Lawrence
on the north, the gulf of the same name on the east,
the Atlantic on the south, and New England on the
west.[1] The French commissioners, on their part,
maintained that the name Acadia belonged of right
only to about a twentieth part of this territory, and
that it did not even cover the whole of the Acadian
peninsula, but only its southern coast, with an
adjoining belt of barren wilderness. When the
French owned Acadia, they gave it boundaries as
comprehensive as those claimed for it by the English
commissioners; now that it belonged to a rival, they
cut it down to a paring of its former self. The
denial that Acadia included the whole peninsula was
dictated by the need of a winter communication
between Quebec and Cape Breton, which was possible only with the eastern portions in French hands.
So new was this denial that even La Galissonière

[1] The commission of De Monts, in 1603, defines Acadia as extending from the fortieth to the forty-sixth degrees of latitude, —
that is, from central New Brunswick to southern Pennsylvania.
Neither party cared to produce the document.

himself, the foremost in making it, had declared
without reservation two years before that Acadia was
the entire peninsula.[1] "If," says a writer on the
question, "we had to do with a nation more tractable,
less grasping, and more conciliatory, it would be
well to insist also that Halifax should be given up to
us." He thinks that, on the whole, it would be well
to make the demand in any case, in order to gain
some other point by yielding this one.[2] It is curious
that while denying that the country was Acadia, the
French invariably called the inhabitants Acadians.
Innumerable public documents, commissions, grants,
treaties, edicts, signed by French kings and ministers, had recognized Acadia as extending over New
Brunswick and a part of Maine. Four censuses of
Acadia while it belonged to the French had recognized the mainland as included in it; and so do also
the early French maps. Its prodigious shrinkage
was simply the consequence of its possession by an
alien.

Other questions of limits, more important and
equally perilous, called loudly for solution. What
line should separate Canada and her western dependencies from the British colonies? Various principles
of demarcation were suggested, of which the most
prominent on the French side was a geographical

---

[1] "L'Acadie suivant ses anciennes limites est la presquisle
bornée par son isthme." *La Galissonnière au Ministre, 25 Juillet,*
1749. The English commissioners were, of course, ignorant of
this admission.

[2] *Mémoire de l'Abbé de l'Isle-Dieu,* 1753 (1754 ?).

one. All countries watered by streams falling into the St. Lawrence, the Great Lakes, and the Mississippi were to belong to her. This would have planted her in the heart of New York and along the crests of the Alleghanies, giving her all the interior of the continent, and leaving nothing to England but a strip of sea-coast. Yet in view of what France had achieved; of the patient gallantry of her explorers, the zeal of her missionaries, the adventurous hardihood of her bushrangers, revealing to civilized mankind the existence of this wilderness world, while her rivals plodded at their workshops, their farms, or their fisheries, — in view of all this, her pretensions were moderate and reasonable compared with those of England. The treaty of Utrecht had declared the Iroquois, or Five Nations, to be British subjects; therefore it was insisted that all countries conquered by them belonged to the British Crown. But what was an Iroquois conquest? The Iroquois rarely occupied the countries they overran. Their military expeditions were mere raids, great or small. Sometimes, as in the case of the Hurons, they made a solitude and called it peace; again, as in the case of the Illinois, they drove off the occupants of the soil, who returned after the invaders were gone. But the range of their war-parties was prodigious; and the English laid claim to every mountain, forest, or prairie where an Iroquois had taken a scalp. This would give them not only the country between the Alleghanies and the Mississippi, but also that

between Lake Huron and the Ottawa, thus reducing
Canada to the patch on the American map now
represented by the province of Quebec, — or rather,
by a part of it, since the extension of Acadia to the
St. Lawrence would cut off the present counties of
Gaspé, Rimouski, and Bonaventure.   Indeed, among
the advocates of British claims there were those who
denied that France had any rights whatever on the
south side of the St. Lawrence.[1] Such being the
attitude of the two contestants, it was plain that
there was no resort but the last argument of kings.
Peace must be won with the sword.

The commissioners at Paris broke up their sessions, leaving as the monument of their toils four
quarto volumes of allegations, arguments, and docu-
mentary proofs.[2] Out of the discussion rose also a
swarm of fugitive publications in French, English,
and Spanish; for the question of American bounda-

[1] The extent of British claims is best shown on two maps of
the time, Mitchell's *Map of the British and French Dominions in
North America* and Huske's *New and Accurate Map of North
America*; both are in the British Museum. Dr. John Mitchell, in
his *Contest in America* (London, 1757), pushes the English claim to
its utmost extreme, and denies that the French were rightful
owners of anything in North America except the town of Quebec
and the trading-post of Tadoussac. Besides the claim founded
on the subjection of the Iroquois to the British Crown, the English somewhat inconsistently advanced others founded on titles
obtained by treaty from these same tribes, and others still, founded
on the original grants of some of the colonies, which ran indefi-
nitely westward across the continent.

[2] *Mémoires des Commissaires de Sa Majesté Très Chrétienne et de
ceux de Sa Majesté Brittanique.* Paris, 1755. Several editions
appeared.

ries had become European. There was one among
them worth notice from its amusing absurdity. It is
an elaborate disquisition, under the title of *Roman
politique*, by an author faithful to the traditions of
European diplomacy, and inspired at the same time
by the new philosophy of the school of Rousseau.
He insists that the balance of power must be preserved in America as well as in Europe, because
"Nature," "the aggrandizement of the human soul,"
and the "felicity of man" are unanimous in demanding it. The English colonies are more populous and
wealthy than the French; therefore the French
should have more land, to keep the balance. Nature,
the human soul, and the felicity of man require that
France should own all the country beyond the Alleghanies and all Acadia but a strip of the south coast,
according to the "sublime negotiations" of the
French commissioners, of which the writer declares
himself a "religious admirer." [1]

We know already that France had used means
sharper than negotiation to vindicate her claim to the
interior of the continent; had marched to the sources
of the Ohio to intrench herself there, and hold the
passes of the West against all comers. It remains to
see how she fared in her bold enterprise.

[1] *Roman politique sur l'État présent des Affaires de l'Amérique*
(Amsterdam, 1756). For extracts from French Documents, see
Appendix B.

Washington could prevent his red allies from staying at the fort, conquered by French blandishments.

After leaving Venango on his return, he found the horses so weak that, to arrive the sooner, he left them and their drivers in charge of Vanbraam and pushed forward on foot, accompanied by Gist alone. Each was wrapped to the throat in an Indian "match-coat," with a gun in his hand and a pack at his back. Passing an old Indian hamlet called Murdering Town, they had an adventure which threatened to make good the name. A French Indian, whom they met in the forest, fired at them, pretending that his gun had gone off by chance. They caught him, and Gist would have killed him; but Washington interposed, and they let him go.[1] Then, to escape pursuit from his tribesmen, they walked all night and all the next day. This brought them to the banks of the Alleghany. They hoped to have found it dead frozen; but it was all alive and turbulent, filled with ice sweeping down the current. They made a raft, shoved out into the stream, and were soon caught helplessly in the drifting ice. Washington, pushing hard with his setting-pole, was jerked into the freezing river, but caught a log of the raft, and dragged himself out. By no efforts could they reach the farther bank, or regain that which they had left; but they were driven against an island, where they landed, and left the raft to its fate. The night was

[1] *Journal of Mr. Christopher Gist*, in *Mass. Hist. Coll.* 3rd Series, v.

excessively cold, and Gist's feet and hands were badly frost-bitten. In the morning, the ice had set, and the river was a solid floor. They crossed it, and succeeded in reaching the house of the trader Fraser, on the Monongahela. It was the middle of January when Washington arrived at Williamsburg and made his report to Dinwiddie.

Robert Dinwiddie was lieutenant-governor of Virginia, in place of the titular governor, Lord Albemarle, whose post was a sinecure. He had been clerk in a government office in the West Indies; then surveyor of customs in the "Old Dominion," — a position in which he made himself cordially disliked; and when he rose to the governorship he carried his unpopularity with him. Yet Virginia and all the British colonies owed him much; for, though past sixty, he was the most watchful sentinel against French aggression and its most strenuous opponent. Scarcely had Marin's vanguard appeared at Presqu'isle, when Dinwiddie warned the home government of the danger, and urged, what he had before urged in vain on the Virginian Assembly, the immediate building of forts on the Ohio. There came in reply a letter, signed by the King, authorizing him to build the forts at the cost of the colony, and to repel force by force in case he was molested or obstructed. Moreover, the King wrote: "If you shall find that any number of persons shall presume to erect any fort or forts within the limits of our province of Virginia, you are first to require of them

peaceably to depart; and if, notwithstanding your
admonitions, they do still endeavor to carry out any
such unlawful and unjustifiable designs, we do hereby
strictly charge and command you to drive them off
by force of arms." [1]

The order was easily given; but to obey it needed
men and money, and for these Dinwiddie was
dependent on his Assembly, or House of Burgesses.
He convoked them for the first of November, sending
Washington at the same time with the summons to
Saint-Pierre. The burgesses met. Dinwiddie exposed the danger, and asked for means to meet it. [2]
They seemed more than willing to comply; but
debates presently arose concerning the fee of a pistole,
which the governor had demanded on each patent of
land issued by him. The amount was trifling, but
the principle was doubtful. The aristocratic republic
of Virginia was intensely jealous of the slightest
encroachment on its rights by the Crown or its representative. The governor defended the fee. The
burgesses replied that "subjects cannot be deprived
of the least part of their property without their consent," declared the fee unlawful, and called on Dinwiddie to confess it to be so. He still defended it.
They saw in his demand for supplies a means of
bringing him to terms, and refused to grant money
unless he would recede from his position. Dinwiddie

[1] *Instructions to Our Trusty and Well-beloved Robert Dinwiddie, Esq.,*
28 *August,* 1753.

[2] *Address of Lieutenant-Governor Dinwiddie to the Council and Bur-*
gesses, 1 *November,* 1753.

rebuked them for "disregarding the designs of the French, and disputing the rights of the Crown;" and he "prorogued them in some anger." [1]

Thus he was unable to obey the instructions of the King. As a temporary resource, he ventured to order a draft of two hundred men from the militia. Washington was to have command, with the trader, William Trent, as his lieutenant. His orders were to push with all speed to the forks of the Ohio, and there build a fort; "but in case any attempts are made to obstruct the works by any persons whatsoever, to restrain all such offenders, and, in case of resistance, to make prisoners of, or kill and destroy them." [2] The governor next sent messengers to the Catawbas, Cherokees, Chickasaws, and Iroquois of the Ohio, inviting them to take up the hatchet against the French, "who, under pretence of embracing you, mean to squeeze you to death." Then he wrote urgent letters to the governors of Pennsylvania, the Carolinas, Maryland, and New Jersey, begging for contingents of men, to be at Will's Creek in March at the latest. But nothing could be done without money; and trusting for a change of heart on the part of the burgesses, he summoned them to meet again on the fourteenth of February. "If they come in good temper," he wrote to Lord Fairfax, a nobleman settled in the colony, "I hope they will lay a fund to qualify me to send four or five hundred men

---

[1] *Dinwiddie Papers.*
[2] *Ibid. Instructions to Major George Washington, January,* 1754.

more to the Ohio, which, with the assistance of our
neighboring colonies, may make some figure."

The session began. Again, somewhat oddly, yet
forcibly, the governor set before the Assembly the
peril of the situation, and begged them to postpone
less pressing questions to the exigency of the hour.[1]
This time they listened, and voted ten thousand
pounds in Virginia currency to defend the frontier.
The grant was frugal, and they jealously placed its
expenditure in the hands of a committee of their
own.[2] Dinwiddie, writing to the Lords of Trade,
pleads necessity as his excuse for submitting to their
terms. "I am sorry," he says, "to find them too
much in a republican way of thinking." What
vexed him still more was their sending an agent to
England to complain against him on the irrepressible
question of the pistole fee; and he writes to his
London friend, the merchant Hanbury: "I have had
a great deal of trouble from the factious disputes and
violent heats of a most impudent, troublesome party
here in regard to that silly fee of a pistole. Surely
every thinking man will make a distinction between
a fee and a tax. Poor people! I pity their ignorance and narrow, ill-natured spirits. But, my
friend, consider that I could by no means give up
this fee without affronting the Board of Trade and
the Council here who established it." His thoughts

---

[1] Speech of Lieutenant-Governor Dinwiddie to the Council and Burgesses, 14 February, 1754.

[2] See the bill in Hening, Statutes of Virginia, vi. 417.

were not all of this harassing nature, and he ends his
letter with the following petition: "Now, sir, as His
Majesty is pleased to make me a military officer,
please send for Scott, my tailor, to make me a proper
suit of regimentals, to be here by His Majesty's
birthday. I do not much like gayety in dress, but I
conceive this necessary. I do not much care for lace
on the coat, but a neat embroidered button-hole;
though you do not deal that way, I know you have a
good taste, that I may show my friend's fancy in that
suit of clothes; a good laced hat and two pair stockings, one silk, the other fine thread." [1]

If the governor and his English sometimes provoke
a smile, he deserves admiration for the energy with
which he opposed the public enemy, under circumstances the most discouraging. He invited the
Indians to meet him in council at Winchester, and,
as bait to attract them, coupled the message with a
promise of gifts. He sent circulars from the King
to the neighboring governors, calling for supplies,
and wrote letter upon letter to rouse them to effort.
He wrote also to the more distant governors, Delancey
of New York, and Shirley of Massachusetts, begging
them to make what he called a "faint" against
Canada, to prevent the French from sending so large
a force to the Ohio. It was to the nearer colonies,
from New Jersey to South Carolina, that he looked
for direct aid; and their several governors were all
more or less active to procure it; but as most of them

[1] *Dinwiddie to Hanbury,* 12 *March,* 1754; *Ibid.,* 10 *May,* 1754.

had some standing dispute with their assemblies, they could get nothing except on terms with which they would not, and sometimes could not, comply. As the lands invaded by the French belonged to one of the two rival claimants, Virginia and Pennsylvania, the other colonies had no mind to vote money to defend them. Pennsylvania herself refused to move. Hamilton, her governor, could do nothing against the placid obstinacy of the Quaker non-combatants and the stolid obstinacy of the German farmers who chiefly made up his Assembly. North Carolina alone answered the appeal, and gave money enough to raise three or four hundred men. Two independent companies maintained by the King in New York, and one in South Carolina, had received orders from England to march to the scene of action; and in these, with the scanty levies of his own and the adjacent province, lay Dinwiddie's only hope. With men abundant and willing, there were no means to put them into the field, and no commander whom they would all obey.

From the brick house at Williamsburg pompously called the Governor's Palace, Dinwiddie despatched letters, orders, couriers, to hasten the tardy reinforcements of North Carolina and New York, and push on the raw soldiers of the Old Dominion, who now numbered three hundred men. They were called the Virginia regiment; and Joshua Fry, an English gentleman, bred at Oxford, was made their colonel, with Washington as next in command.

Fry was at Alexandria with half the so-called regiment, trying to get it into marching order; Washington, with the other half, had pushed forward to the Ohio Company's storehouse at Will's Creek, which was to form a base of operations. His men were poor whites, brave, but hard to discipline; without tents, ill armed, and ragged as Falstaff's recruits. Besides these, a band of backwoodsmen under Captain Trent had crossed the mountains in February to build a fort at the forks of the Ohio, where Pittsburg now stands, — a spot which Washington had examined when on his way to Fort Le Bœuf, and which he had reported as the best for the purpose. The hope was that Trent would fortify himself before the arrival of the French, and that Washington and Fry would join him in time to secure the position. Trent had begun the fort, but for some unexplained reason had gone back to Will's Creek, leaving Ensign Ward with forty men at work upon it. Their labors were suddenly interrupted. On the seventeenth of April a swarm of bateaux and canoes came down the Alleghany, bringing, according to Ward, more than a thousand Frenchmen, though in reality not much above five hundred, who landed, planted cannon against the incipient stockade, and summoned the ensign to surrender, on pain of what might ensue.[1] He complied, and was allowed to depart with his men. Retracing his steps over the mountains, he reported his mishap to Washington; while the French

---

[1] See the summons in *Précis des Faits*, 101.

demolished his unfinished fort, began a much larger and better one, and named it Fort Duquesne.

They had acted with their usual promptness. Their governor, a practised soldier, knew the value of celerity, and had set his troops in motion with the first opening of spring. He had no refractory assembly to hamper him; no lack of money, for the King supplied it; and all Canada must march at his bidding. Thus, while Dinwiddie was still toiling to muster his raw recruits, Duquesne's lieutenant, Contrecœur, successor of Saint-Pierre, had landed at Presqu'isle with a much greater force, in part regulars, and in part Canadians.

Dinwiddie was deeply vexed when a message from Washington told him how his plans were blighted; and he spoke his mind to his friend Hanbury: "If our Assembly had voted the money in November which they did in February, it's more than probable the fort would have been built and garrisoned before the French had approached; but these things cannot be done without money. As there was none in our treasury, I have advanced my own to forward the expedition; and if the independent companies from New York come soon, I am in hopes the eyes of the other colonies will be opened; and if they grant a proper supply of men, I hope we shall be able to dislodge the French or build a fort on that river. I congratulate you on the increase of your family. My wife and two girls join in our most sincere respects to good Mrs. Hanbury." [1]

[1] *Dinwiddie to Hanbury,* 10 *May,* 1754.

The seizure of a king's fort by planting cannon against it and threatening it with destruction was in his eyes a beginning of hostilities on the part of the French; and henceforth both he and Washington acted much as if war had been declared. From their station at Will's Creek, the distance by the traders' path to Fort Duquesne was about a hundred and forty miles. Midway was a branch of the Monongahela called Redstone Creek, at the mouth of which the Ohio Company had built another storehouse. Dinwiddie ordered all the forces to cross the mountains and assemble at this point, until they should be strong enough to advance against the French. The movement was critical in presence of an enemy as superior in discipline as he was in numbers, while the natural obstacles were great. A road for cannon and wagons must be cut through a dense forest and over two ranges of high mountains, besides countless hills and streams. Washington set all his force to the work, and they spent a fortnight in making twenty miles. Towards the end of May, however, Dinwiddie learned that he had crossed the main ridge of the Alleghanies, and was encamped with a hundred and fifty men near the parallel ridge of Laurel Hill, at a place called the Great Meadows. Trent's backwoodsmen had gone off in disgust; Fry, with the rest of the regiment, was still far behind; and Washington was daily expecting an attack. Close upon this, a piece of good news, or what seemed such, came over the mountains and gladdened the heart of the governor. He heard that a French detachment had tried to surprise Washington, and that he had killed or captured the whole. The facts were as follows.

Washington was on the Youghiogany, a branch of the Monongahela, exploring it in hopes that it might prove navigable, when a messenger came to him from his old comrade, the Half-King, who was on the way to join him. The message was to the effect that the French had marched from their fort, and meant to attack the first English they should meet. A report came soon after that they were already at the ford of the Youghiogany, eighteen miles distant. Washington at once repaired to the Great Meadows, a level tract of grass and bushes, bordered by wooded hills, and traversed in one part by a gully, which with a little labor the men turned into an intrenchment, at the same time cutting away the bushes and clearing what the young commander called "a charming field for an encounter." Parties were sent out to scour the woods, but they found no enemy. Two days passed; when, on the morning of the twenty-seventh, Christopher Gist, who had lately made a settlement on the farther side of Laurel Hill, twelve or thirteen miles distant, came to the camp with news that fifty Frenchmen had been at his house towards noon of the day before, and would have destroyed everything but for the intervention of two Indians whom he had left in charge during his absence. Washington sent seventy-five men to look for the party; but the search was vain, the French having hidden themselves so well as to escape any eye but that of an Indian. In the evening a runner came from the Half-King, who was encamped with a few warriors some miles distant. He had sent to tell Washington that he had found the tracks of two men, and traced them towards a dark glen in the forest, where in his belief all the French were lurking.

Washington seems not to have hesitated a moment. Fearing a stratagem to surprise his camp, he left his main force to guard it, and at ten o'clock set out for the Half-King's wigwams at the head of forty men. The night was rainy, and the forest, to use his own words, "as black as pitch." "The path," he continues, "was hardly wide enough for one man; we often lost it, and could not find it again for fifteen or twenty minutes, and we often tumbled over each other in the dark."[1] Seven of his men were lost in the woods and left behind. The rest groped their way all night, and reached the Indian camp at sunrise. A council was held with the Half-King, and he and his warriors agreed to join in striking the French. Two of them led the way. The tracks of the two French scouts seen the day before were again found, and, marching in single file, the party pushed through the forest into the rocky hollow where the

[1] *Journal of Washington* in *Précis des Faits*, 109. This Journal, which is entirely distinct from that before cited, was found by the French among the baggage left on the field after the defeat of Braddock in 1755, and a translation of it was printed by them as above. The original has disappeared.

French were supposed to be concealed. They were there in fact; and they snatched their guns the moment they saw the English. Washington gave the word to fire. A short fight ensued. Coulon de Jumonville, an ensign in command, was killed, with nine others; twenty-two were captured, and none escaped but a Canadian who had fled at the beginning of the fray. After it was over, the prisoners told Washington that the party had been sent to bring him a summons from Contrecœur, the commandant at Fort Duquesne.

Five days before, Contrecœur had sent Jumonville to scour the country as far as the dividing ridge of the Alleghanies. Under him were another officer, three cadets, a volunteer, an interpreter, and twenty-eight men. He was provided with a written summons, to be delivered to any English he might find. It required them to withdraw from the domain of the King of France, and threatened compulsion by force of arms in case of refusal. But before delivering the summons Jumonville was ordered to send two couriers back with all speed to Fort Duquesne to inform the commandant that he had found the English, and to acquaint him when he intended to communicate with them.[1] It is difficult to imagine any object for such an order except that of enabling Contrecœur to send to the spot whatever force might be needed to attack the English on their refusal to

[1] The summons and the instructions to Jumonville are in *Préci des Faits.*

withdraw. Jumonville had sent the two couriers, and had hidden himself, apparently to wait the result. He lurked nearly two days within five miles of Washington's camp, sent out scouts to reconnoitre it, but gave no notice of his presence; played to perfection the part of a skulking enemy, and brought destruction on himself by conduct which can only be ascribed to a sinister motive on the one hand, or to extreme folly on the other. French deserters told Washington that the party came as spies, and were to show the summons only if threatened by a superior force. This last assertion is confirmed by the French officer Pouchot, who says that Jumonville, seeing himself the weaker party, tried to show the letter he had brought.[1]

French writers say that, on first seeing the English, Jumonville's interpreter called out that he had something to say to them; but Washington, who was at the head of his men, affirms this to be absolutely false. The French say further that Jumonville was killed in the act of reading the summons. This is also denied by Washington, and rests only on the assertion of the Canadian who ran off at the outset, and on the alleged assertion of Indians who, if present at all, which is unlikely, escaped like the Canadian before the fray began. Druillon, an officer with Jumonville, wrote two letters to Dinwiddie after his capture, to claim the privileges of the bearer of a summons; but while bringing forward

[1] Pouchot, *Mémoire sur la dernière Guerre.*

every other circumstance in favor of the claim, he does not pretend that the summons was read or shown either before or during the action. The French account of the conduct of Washington's Indians is no less erroneous. "This murder," says a chronicler of the time, "produced on the minds of the savages an effect very different from that which the cruel Washington had promised himself. They have a horror of crime; and they were so indignant at that which had just been perpetrated before their eyes, that they abandoned him, and offered themselves to us in order to take vengeance." [1] Instead of doing this, they boasted of their part in the fight, scalped all the dead Frenchmen, sent one scalp to the Delawares as an invitation to take up the hatchet for the English, and distributed the rest among the various Ohio tribes to the same end.

Coolness of judgment, a profound sense of public duty, and a strong self-control, were even then the characteristics of Washington; but he was scarcely twenty-two, was full of military ardor, and was vehement and fiery by nature. Yet it is far from certain that, even when age and experience had ripened him, he would have forborne to act as he did, for there was every reason for believing that the designs of the French were hostile; and though by passively waiting the event he would have thrown upon them the responsibility of striking the first blow, he would have exposed his small party to

[1] Poulin de Lumina, *Histoire de la Guerre contre les Anglois*, 15.

capture or destruction by giving them time to gain reinforcements from Fort Duquesne. It was inevitable that the killing of Jumonville should be greeted in France by an outcry of real or assumed horror; but the Chevalier de Lévis, second in command to Montcalm, probably expresses the true opinion of Frenchmen best fitted to judge when he calls it "a pretended assassination."[1] Judge it as we may, this obscure skirmish began the war that set the world on fire.[2]

Washington returned to the camp at the Great Meadows; and, expecting soon to be attacked, sent for reinforcements to Colonel Fry, who was lying dangerously ill at Will's Creek. Then he set his men to work at an intrenchment, which he named Fort Necessity, and which must have been of the slightest, as they finished it within three days.[3] The

[1] Lévis, *Mémoire sur la Guerre du Canada.*

[2] On this affair Sparks, *Writings of Washington,* ii. 25–48, 447. *Dinwiddie Papers. Letter of Contrecœur* in *Précis des Faits. Journal of Washington, Ibid. Washington to Dinwiddie,* 3 *June,* 1754. Dussieux, *Le Canada sous la Domination Française,* 118. Gaspé, *Anciens Canadiens,* Appendix, 396. The assertion of Abbé de l'Isle-Dieu, that Jumonville showed a flag of truce, is unsupported. Adam Stephen, who was in the fight, says that the guns of the English were so wet that they had to trust mainly to the bayonet. The Half King boasted that he killed Jumonville with his tomahawk. Dinwiddie highly approved Washington's conduct.

In 1755 the widow of Jumonville received a pension of one hundred and fifty francs. In 1775, his daughter, Charlotte Aimable, wishing to become a nun, was given by the King six hundred francs for her "trousseau" on entering the convent. *Dossier de Jumonville et de sa Veuve,* 22 *Mars,* 1755. *Mémoire pour Mlle. de Jumonville,* 10 *Juillet,* 1775. *Réponse du Garde des Sceaux,* 25 *Juillet,* 1775.

[3] *Journal of Washington* in *Précis des Faits.*

Half-King now joined him, along with the female potentate known as Queen Alequippa, and some thirty Indian families. A few days after, Gist came from Will's Creek with news that Fry was dead. Washington succeeded to the command of the regiment, the remaining three companies of which presently appeared and joined their comrades, raising the whole number to three hundred. Next arrived the independent company from South Carolina; and the Great Meadows became an animated scene, with the wigwams of the Indians, the camp-sheds of the rough Virginians, the cattle grazing on the tall grass or drinking at the lazy brook that traversed it; the surrounding heights and forests; and over all, four miles away, the lofty green ridge of Laurel Hill.

The presence of the company of regulars was a doubtful advantage. Captain Mackay, its commander, holding his commission from the King, thought himself above any officer commissioned by the governor. There was great courtesy between him and Washington; but Mackay would take no orders, nor even the countersign, from the colonel of volunteers. Nor would his men work, except for an additional shilling a day. To give this was impossible, both from want of money, and from the discontent it would have bred in the Virginians, who worked for nothing besides their daily pay of eightpence. Washington, already a leader of men, possessed himself in a patience extremely difficult to his passionate temper; but the position was untenable, and the presence of the military drones demoralized his soldiers. Therefore, leaving Mackay at the Meadows, he advanced towards Gist's settlement, cutting a wagon road as he went.

On reaching the settlement the camp was formed and an intrenchment thrown up. Deserters had brought news that strong reinforcements were expected at Fort Duquesne, and friendly Indians repeatedly warned Washington that he would soon be attacked by overwhelming numbers. Forty Indians from the Ohio came to the camp, and several days were spent in councils with them; but they proved for the most part to be spies of the French. The Half-King stood fast by the English, and sent out three of his young warriors as scouts. Reports of attack thickened. Mackay and his men were sent for, and they arrived on the twenty-eighth of June. A council of war was held at Gist's house; and as the camp was commanded by neighboring heights, it was resolved to fall back. The horses were so few that the Virginians had to carry much of the baggage on their backs, and drag nine swivels over the broken and rocky road. The regulars, though they also were raised in the provinces, refused to give the slightest help. Toiling on for two days, they reached the Great Meadows on the first of July. The position, though perhaps the best in the neighborhood, was very unfavorable, and Washington would have retreated farther, but for the condition of his men.

They were spent with fatigue, and there was no choice but to stay and fight.

Strong reinforcements had been sent to Fort Duquesne in the spring, and the garrison now consisted of about fourteen hundred men. When news of the death of Jumonville reached Montreal, Coulon de Villiers, brother of the slain officer, was sent to the spot with a body of Indians from all the tribes in the colony. He made such speed that at eight o'clock on the morning of the twenty-sixth of June he reached the fort with his motley following. Here he found that five hundred Frenchmen and a few Ohio Indians were on the point of marching against the English, under Chevalier Le Mercier; but in view of his seniority in rank and his relationship to Jumonville, the command was now transferred to Villiers. Hereupon, the march was postponed; the newly-arrived warriors were called to council, and Contrecœur thus harangued them: "The English have murdered my children; my heart is sick; to-morrow I shall send my French soldiers to take revenge. And now, men of the Saut St. Louis, men of the Lake of Two Mountains, Hurons, Abenakis, Iroquois of La Présentation, Nipissings, Algonquins, and Ottawas, — I invite you all by this belt of wampum to join your French father and help him to crush the assassins. Take this hatchet, and with it two barrels of wine for a feast." Both hatchet and wine were cheerfully accepted. Then Contrecœur turned to the Delawares, who were also present:

"By these four strings of wampum I invite you, if you are true children of Onontio, to follow the example of your brethren;" and with some hesitation they also took up the hatchet.

The next day was spent by the Indians in making moccasons for the march, and by the French in preparing for an expedition on a larger scale than had been at first intended. Contrecœur, Villiers, Le Mercier, and Longueuil, after deliberating together, drew up a paper to the effect that "it was fitting (*convenable*) to march against the English with the greatest possible number of French and savages, in order to avenge ourselves and chastise them for having violated the most sacred laws of civilized nations;" that, though their conduct justified the French in disregarding the existing treaty of peace, yet, after thoroughly punishing them, and compelling them to withdraw from the domain of the King, they should be told that, in pursuance of his royal orders, the French looked on them as friends. But it was further agreed that should the English have withdrawn to their own side of the mountains, "they should be followed to their settlements to destroy them and treat them as enemies, till that nation should give ample satisfaction and completely change its conduct." [1]

---

[1] *Journal de Campagne de M. de Villiers depuis son Arrivée au Fort Duquesne jusqu'à son Retour au dit Fort.* These and other passages are omitted in the Journal as printed in *Précis des Faits.* Before me is a copy from the original in the Archives de la Marine.

The party set out on the next morning, paddled
their canoes up the Monongahela, encamped, heard
mass; and on the thirtieth reached the deserted storehouse of the Ohio Company at the mouth of Redstone
Creek. It was a building of solid logs, well loopholed for musketry. To please the Indians by
asking their advice, Villiers called all the chiefs to
council; which being concluded to their satisfaction,
he left a sergeant's guard at the storehouse to watch
the canoes, and began his march through the forest.
The path was so rough that at the first halt the chaplain declared he could go no farther, and turned
back for the storehouse, though not till he had
absolved the whole company in a body. Thus lightened of their sins, they journeyed on, constantly
sending out scouts. On the second of July they
reached the abandoned camp of Washington at Gist's
settlement; and here they bivouacked, tired, and
drenched all night by rain. At daybreak they
marched again, and passed through the gorge of
Laurel Hill. It rained without ceasing; but Villiers
pushed his way through the dripping forest to see
the place, half a mile from the road, where his
brother had been killed, and where several bodies
still lay unburied. They had learned from a deserter
the position of the enemy, and Villiers filled the
woods in front with a swarm of Indian scouts. The
crisis was near. He formed his men in column, and
ordered every officer to his place.

Washington's men had had a full day at Fort

Necessity; but they spent it less in resting from their
fatigue than in strengthening their rampart with
logs.   The fort was a simple square enclosure, with
a trench said by a French writer to be only knee
deep.   On the south, and partly on the west, there
was an exterior embankment, which seems to have
been made, like a rifle-pit, with the ditch inside.
The Virginians had but little ammunition, and no
bread whatever, living chiefly on fresh beef.   They
knew the approach of the French, who were reported
to Washington as nine hundred strong, besides
Indians.   Towards eleven o'clock a wounded sentinel
came in with news that they were close at hand; and
they presently appeared at the edge of the woods,
yelling, and firing from such a distance that their
shot fell harmless.   Washington drew up his men
on the meadow before the fort, thinking, he says,
that the enemy, being greatly superior in force, would
attack at once; and choosing for some reason to meet
them on the open plain.   But Villiers had other
views.   "We approached the English," he writes, "as
near as possible, without uselessly exposing the lives
of the King's subjects;" and he and his followers
made their way through the forest till they came
opposite the fort, where they stationed themselves on
two densely wooded hills, adjacent, though separated by a small brook.   One of these was about a
hundred paces from the English, and the other about
sixty.   Their position was such that the French and
Indians, well sheltered by trees and bushes, and with

the advantage of higher ground, could cross their
fire upon the fort and enfilade a part of it. Washington had meanwhile drawn his followers within the
intrenchment; and the firing now began on both
sides. Rain fell all day. The raw earth of the
embankment was turned to soft mud, and the men in
the ditch of the outwork stood to the knee in water.
The swivels brought back from the camp at Gist's
farm were mounted on the rampart; but the gunners
were so ill protected that the pieces were almost
silenced by the French musketry. The fight lasted
nine hours. At times the fire on both sides was
nearly quenched by the showers, and the bedrenched
combatants could do little but gaze at each other
through a gray veil of mist and rain. Towards
night, however, the fusillade revived, and became
sharp again until dark. At eight o'clock the French
called out to propose a parley.

Villiers thus gives his reasons for these overtures.
"As we had been wet all day by the rain, as the
soldiers were very tired, as the savages said that they
would leave us the next morning, and as there was
a report that drums and the firing of cannon had
been heard in the distance, I proposed to M. Le
Mercier to offer the English a conference." He says
further that ammunition was falling short, and that
he thought the enemy might sally in a body and
attack him.[1] The English, on their side, were in a

---

[1] *Journal de Villiers,* original. Omitted in the Journal as printed
by the French government. A short and very incorrect abstract
of this Journal will be found in *N. Y. Col. Docs.,* x.

worse plight. They were half starved, their powder
was nearly spent, their guns were foul, and among
them all they had but two screw-rods to clean them.
In spite of his desperate position, Washington
declined the parley, thinking it a pretext to introduce
a spy; but when the French repeated their proposal
and requested that he would send an officer to them,
he could hesitate no longer. There were but two
men with him who knew French, Ensign Peyroney,
who was disabled by a wound, and the Dutchman,
Captain Vanbraam. To him the unpalatable errand
was assigned. After a long absence he returned with
articles of capitulation offered by Villiers; and while
the officers gathered about him in the rain, he read
and interpreted the paper by the glimmer of a sput-
tering candle kept alight with difficulty. Objection
was made to some of the terms, and they were
changed. Vanbraam, however, apparently anxious
to get the capitulation signed and the affair ended,
mistranslated several passages, and rendered the
words *l'assassinat du Sieur de Jumonville* as *the death
of the Sieur de Jumonville.*[1] As thus understood, the
articles were signed about midnight. They provided
that the English should march out with drums beating and the honors of war, carrying with them one
of their swivels and all their other property; that

[1] See Appendix C. On the fight at Great Meadows, compare
Sparks, *Writings of Washington*, ii. 456–468; also a letter of Colonel
Innes to Governor Hamilton, written a week after the event, in
Colonial Records of Pa., vi. 50, and a letter of Adam Stephen, in
Pennsylvania Gazette, 1754.

they should be protected against insult from French or Indians; that the prisoners taken in the affair of Jumonville should be set free; and that two officers should remain as hostages for their safe return to Fort Duquesne. The hostages chosen were Van-braam and a brave but eccentric Scotchman, Robert Stobo, an acquaintance of the novelist Smollett, said to be the original of his Lismahago.

Washington reports that twelve of the Virginians were killed on the spot, and forty-three wounded, while of the casualties in Mackay's company no returns appear. Villiers reports his own loss at only twenty in all.[1] The numbers engaged are uncertain. The six companies of the Virginia regiment counted three hundred and five men and officers, and Mackay's company one hundred; but many were on the sick list, and some had deserted. About three hundred and fifty may have taken part in the fight. On the side of the French, Villiers says that the detachment as originally formed consisted of five hundred white men. These were increased after his arrival at Fort Duquesne, and one of the party reports that seven hundred marched on the expedition.[2] The number

[1] Dinwiddie writes to the Lords of Trade that thirty in all were killed, and seventy wounded, on the English side; and the commissary Varin writes to Bigot that the French lost seventy-two killed and wounded.

[2] *A Journal had from Thomas Forbes, lately a Private Soldier in the King of France's Service.* (Public Record Office.) Forbes was one of Villiers's soldiers. The commissary Varin puts the number of French at six hundred, besides Indians.

of Indians joining them is not given; but as nine tribes and communities contributed to it, and as two barrels of wine were required to give the warriors a parting feast, it must have been considerable. White men and red, it seems clear that the French force was more than twice that of the English, while they were better posted and better sheltered, keeping all day under cover, and never showing themselves on the open meadow. There were no Indians with Washington. Even the Half-King held aloof; though, being of a caustic turn, he did not spare his comments on the fight, telling Conrad Weiser, the provincial interpreter, that the French behaved like cowards, and the English like fools.[1]

In the early morning the fort was abandoned and the retreat began. The Indians had killed all the horses and cattle, and Washington's men were so burdened with the sick and wounded, whom they were obliged to carry on their backs, that most of the baggage was perforce left behind. Even then they could march but a few miles, and then encamped to wait for wagons. The Indians increased the confusion by plundering, and threatening an attack. They knocked to pieces the medicine-chest, thus

[1] *Journal of Conrad Weiser*, in *Colonial Records of Pa.*, vi. 150. The Half-King also remarked that Washington " was a good-natured man, but had no experience, and would by no means take advice from the Indians, but was always driving them on to fight by his directions; that he lay at one place from one full moon to the other, and made no fortifications at all, except that little thing upon the meadow, where he thought the French would come up to him in open field."

causing great distress to the wounded, two of whom
they murdered and scalped.   For a time there was
danger of panic; but order was restored, and the
wretched march began along the forest road that led
over the Alleghanies, fifty-two miles to the station
at Will's Creek.   Whatever may have been the feel-
ings of Washington, he has left no record of them.
His immense fortitude was doomed to severer trials
in the future; yet perhaps this miserable morning
was the darkest of his life.   He was deeply moved
by sights of suffering; and all around him were
wounded men borne along in torture, and weary men
staggering under the living load.   His pride was
humbled, and his young ambition seemed blasted in
the bud.   It was the fourth of July.   He could not
foresee that he was to make that day forever glorious
to a new-born nation hailing him as its father.

The defeat at Fort Necessity was doubly disastrous
to the English, since it was a new step and a long
one towards the ruin of their interest with the
Indians; and when, in the next year, the smouldering war broke into flame, nearly all the western tribes
drew their scalping-knives for France.

Villiers went back exultant to Fort Duquesne,
burning on his way the buildings of Gist's settlement
and the storehouse at Redstone Creek.   Not an
English flag now waved beyond the Alleghanies.[1]

[1] See Appendix C.

CHAPTER VI.

1754, 1755.

THE SIGNAL OF BATTLE.

Troubles of Dinwiddie. — Gathering of the Burgesses. — Virginian Society. — Refractory Legislators. — The Quaker Assembly: it refuses to resist the French. — Apathy of New York. — Shirley and the General Court of Massachusetts. — Short-sighted Policy. — Attitude of Royal Governors. — Indian Allies waver. — Convention at Albany. — Scheme of Union: it fails. — Dinwiddie and Glen. — Dinwiddie calls on England for Help. — The Duke of Newcastle. — Weakness of the British Cabinet. — Attitude of France. — Mutual Dissimulation. — Both Powers send Troops to America. — Collision. — Capture of the "Alcide" and the "Lis."

THE defeat of Washington was a heavy blow to the governor, and he angrily ascribed it to the delay of the expected reinforcements. The King's companies from New York had reached Alexandria, and crawled towards the scene of action with thin ranks, bad discipline, thirty women and children, no tents, no blankets, no knapsacks, and for munitions one barrel of spoiled gunpowder.[1] The case was still worse with the regiment from North Carolina. It was commanded by Colonel Innes, a countryman and

[1] *Dinwiddie to the Lords of Trade*, 24 *July*, 1754. *Ibid. to Delancey* 20 *June*, 1754.

friend of Dinwiddie, who wrote to him: "Dear James, I now wish that we had none from your colony but yourself, for I foresee nothing but confusion among them." The men were, in fact, utterly unmanageable. They had been promised three shillings a day, while the Virginians had only eightpence; and when they heard on the march that their pay was to be reduced, they mutinied, disbanded, and went home.

"You may easily guess," says Dinwiddie to a London correspondent, "the great fatigue and trouble I have had, which is more than I ever went through in my life." He rested his hopes on the session of his Assembly, which was to take place in August; for he thought that the late disaster would move them to give him money for defending the colony. These meetings of the burgesses were the great social as well as political event of the Old Dominion, and gave a gathering signal to the Virginian gentry scattered far and wide on their lonely plantations. The capital of the province was Williamsburg, a village of about a thousand inhabitants, traversed by a straight and very wide street, and adorned with various public buildings, conspicuous among which was William and Mary College, a respectable structure, unjustly likened by Jefferson to a brick kiln with a roof. The capitol, at the other end of the town, had been burned some years before, and had just risen from its ashes. Not far distant was the so-called Governor's Palace, where Dinwiddie with

his wife and two daughters exercised such official
hospitality as his moderate salary and Scottish thrift
would permit.[1]

In these seasons of festivity the dull and quiet
village was transfigured. The broad, sandy street,
scorching under a southern sun, was thronged with
coaches and chariots brought over from London at
heavy cost in tobacco, though soon to be bedimmed
by Virginia roads and negro care; racing and hard-
drinking planters; clergymen of the Establishment,
not much more ascetic than their boon companions
of the laity; ladies, with manners a little rusted by
long seclusion; black coachmen and footmen, proud
of their masters and their liveries; young cavaliers,
booted and spurred, sitting their thoroughbreds with
the careless grace of men whose home was the saddle.
It was a proud little provincial society, which might
seem absurd in its lofty self-appreciation, had it not
soon approved itself so prolific in ability and worth.[2]

The burgesses met, and Dinwiddie made them an
opening speech, inveighing against the aggressions
of the French, their "contempt of treaties," and
"ambitious views for universal monarchy;" and he
concluded: "I could expatiate very largely on these

[1] For a contemporary account of Williamsburg, Burnaby,
Travels in North America, 6. Smyth, *Tour in America*, i. 17, describes it some years later.

[2] The English traveller Smyth, in his *Tour*, gives a curious and
vivid picture of Virginian life. For the social condition of this
and other colonies before the Revolution, one cannot do better
than to consult Lodge's *Short History of the English Colonies.*

affairs, but my heart burns with resentment at their insolence.   I think there is no room for many arguments to induce you to raise a considerable supply to enable me to defeat the designs of these troublesome people and enemies of mankind."   The burgesses in their turn expressed the "highest and most becoming resentment," and promptly voted twenty thousand pounds; but on the third reading of the bill they added to it a rider which touched the old question of the pistole fee, and which, in the view of the governor, was both unconstitutional and offensive.   He remonstrated in vain; the stubborn republicans would not yield, nor would he; and again he prorogued them.   This unexpected defeat depressed him greatly. " A governor," he wrote, "is really to be pitied in the discharge of his duty to his king and country, in having to do with such obstinate, self-conceited people. . . . I cannot satisfy the burgesses unless I prostitute the rules of government.   I have gone through monstrous fatigues.   Such wrong-headed people, I thank God, I never had to do with before." [1] A few weeks later he was comforted; for, having again called the burgesses, they gave him the money, without trying this time to humiliate him.[2]

In straining at a gnat and swallowing a camel, aristocratic Virginia was far outdone by democratic Pennsylvania.   Hamilton, her governor, had laid

---

[1] *Dinwiddie to Hamilton*, 6 *September*, 1754.   *Ibid. to J. Abercrombie*, 1 *September*, 1754.

[2] Hening, vi. 435.

before the Assembly a circular letter from the Earl
of Holdernesse, directing him, in common with other
governors, to call on his province for means to repel
any invasion which might be made "within the
undoubted limits of His Majesty's dominion."[1]   The
Assembly of Pennsylvania was curiously unlike that
of Virginia, as half and often more than half of its
members were Quaker tradesmen in sober raiment
and broad-brimmed hats; while of the rest, the
greater part were Germans who cared little whether
they lived under English rule or French, provided
that they were left in peace upon their farms.   The
House replied to the governor's call: "It would be
highly presumptuous in us to pretend to judge of the
undoubted limits of His Majesty's dominions;" and
they added: "the Assemblies of this province are
generally composed of a majority who are constitu-
tionally principled against war, and represent a well-
meaning, peaceable people."[2]   They then adjourned,
telling the governor that, "As those our limits have
not been clearly ascertained to our satisfaction, we
fear the precipitate call upon us as the province
invaded cannot answer any good purpose at this
time."

In the next month they met again, and again
Hamilton asked for means to defend the country.
The question was put, Should the Assembly give

[1] *The Earl of Holdernesse to the Governors in America*, 28 *August,*
1753.
[2] *Colonial Records of Pa.*, v. 748.

money for the King's use? and the vote was feebly
affirmative. Should the sum be twenty thousand
pounds? The vote was overwhelming in the nega-
tive. Fifteen thousand, ten thousand, and five
thousand were successively proposed, and the answer
was always, No. The House would give nothing but
five hundred pounds for a present to the Indians;
after which they adjourned "to the sixth of the
month called May."[1] At their next meeting they
voted to give the governor ten thousand pounds; but
under conditions which made them for some time
independent of his veto, and which, in other respects,
were contrary to his instructions from the King, as
well as from the proprietaries of the province, to
whom he had given bonds to secure his obedience.
He therefore rejected the bill, and they adjourned.
In August they passed a similar vote, with the same
result. At their October meeting they evaded his
call for supplies. In December they voted twenty
thousand pounds, hampered with conditions which
were sure to be refused, since Morris, the new governor, who had lately succeeded Hamilton, was under
the same restrictions as his predecessor. They told
him, however, that in the present case they felt
themselves bound by no Act of Parliament, and
added: "We hope the Governor, notwithstanding
any penal bond he may have entered into, will on
reflection think himself at liberty and find it con-

[1] *Pennsylvania Archives*, ii. 235. *Colonial Records of Pa.*, vi. 22-
26. *Works of Franklin*, iii. 265.

sistent with his safety and honor to give his assent
to this bill." Morris, who had taken the highest
legal advice on the subject in England, declined to
compromise himself, saying: "Consider, gentlemen,
in what light you will appear to His Majesty while,
instead of contributing towards your own defence,
you are entering into an ill-timed controversy concerning the validity of royal instructions which may
be delayed to a more convenient time without the
least injury to the rights of the people."[1] They
would not yield, and told him "that they had rather
the French should conquer them than give up their
privileges."[2] "Truly," remarks Dinwiddie, "I think
they have given their senses a long holiday."

New York was not much behind her sisters in con-
tentious stubbornness. In answer to the governor's
appeal, the Assembly replied: "It appears that the
French have built a fort at a place called French
Creek, at a considerable distance from the River
Ohio, which may, but does not by any evidence or
information appear to us to be an invasion of any of
His Majesty's colonies."[3] So blind were they as yet
to "manifest destiny!" Afterwards, however, on
learning the defeat of Washington, they gave five
thousand pounds to aid Virginia.[4] Maryland, after
long delay, gave six thousand. New Jersey felt

[1] *Colonial Records of Pa.*, vi. 215.

[2] *Morris to Penn*, 1 *January*, 1755.

[3] *Address of the Assembly to Lieutenant-Governor Delancey*, 23
April, 1754. *Lords of Trade to Delancey*, 5 *July*, 1754.

[4] *Delancey to Lords of Trade*, 8 *October*, 1754.

herself safe behind the other colonies, and would give nothing.   New England, on the other hand, and especially Massachusetts, had suffered so much from French war-parties that they were always ready to fight.   Shirley, the governor of Massachusetts, had returned from his bootless errand to settle the boundary question at Paris.   His leanings were strongly monarchical; yet he believed in the New Englanders, and was more or less in sympathy with them.   Both he and they were strenuous against the French, and they had mutually helped each other to reap laurels in the last war.   Shirley was cautious of giving umbrage to his Assembly, and rarely quarrelled with it, except when the amount of his salary was in question.   He was not averse to a war with France; for though bred a lawyer, and now past middle life, he flattered himself with hopes of a high military command.   On the present occasion, making use of a rumor that the French were seizing the carrying-place between the Chaudière and the Kennebec, he drew from the Assembly a large grant of money, and induced them to call upon him to march in person to the scene of danger.   He accordingly repaired to Falmouth (now Portland); and, though the rumor proved false, sent eight hundred men under Captain John Winslow to build two forts on the Kennebec as a measure of precaution.[1]

1 *Massachusetts Archives*, 1754.   Hutchinson, iii. 26.   *Conduct of Major-General Shirley briefly stated*.   *Journals of the Board of Trade*, 1754.

While to these northern provinces Canada was an old and pestilent enemy, those towards the south scarcely knew her by name; and the idea of French aggression on their borders was so novel and strange that they admitted it with difficulty. Mind and heart were engrossed in strife with their governors: the universal struggle for virtual self-rule. But the war was often waged with a passionate stupidity. The colonist was not then an American; he was simply a provincial, and a narrow one. The time was yet distant when these dissevered and jealous communities should weld themselves into one broad nationality, capable, at need, of the mightiest efforts to purge itself of disaffection and vindicate its commanding unity.

In the interest of that practical independence which they had so much at heart, two conditions were essential to the colonists. The one was a field for expansion, and the other was mutual help. Their first necessity was to rid themselves of the French, who, by shutting them between the Alleghanies and the sea, would cramp them into perpetual littleness. With France on their backs, growing while they had no room to grow, they must remain in helpless wardship, dependent on England, whose aid they would always need; but with the West open before them, their future was their own. King and Parliament would respect perforce the will of a people spread from the ocean to the Mississippi, and united in action as in aims. But in the middle of the last

century the vision of the ordinary colonist rarely
reached so far. The immediate victory over a governor, however slight the point at issue, was more
precious in his eyes than the remote though decisive
advantage which he saw but dimly.

The governors, representing the central power,
saw the situation from the national point of view.
Several of them, notably Dinwiddie and Shirley, were
filled with wrath at the proceedings of the French;
and the former was exasperated beyond measure at
the supineness of the provinces. He had spared no
effort to rouse them, and had failed. His instincts
were on the side of authority; but, under the circumstances, it is hardly to be imputed to him as a
very deep offence against human liberty that he
advised the compelling of the colonies to raise men
and money for their own defence, and proposed,
in view of their "intolerable obstinacy and disobedience to his Majesty's commands," that Parliament
should tax them half-a-crown a head. The approaching war offered to the party of authority tempta-
tions from which the colonies might have saved it
by opening their purse-strings without waiting to be
told.

The home government, on its part, was but half-
hearted in the wish that they should unite in opposition to the common enemy. It was very willing
that the several provinces should give money and
men, but not that they should acquire military habits
and a dangerous capacity of acting together. There

was one kind of union, however, so obviously necessary, and at the same time so little to be dreaded,
that the British Cabinet, instructed by the governors,
not only assented to it, but urged it.   This was joint
action in making treaties with the Indians.   The
practice of separate treaties, made by each province in
its own interest, had bred endless disorders.   The
adhesion of all the tribes had been so shaken, and the
efforts of the French to alienate them were so vigorous and effective, that not a moment was to be lost.
Joncaire had gained over most of the Senecas, Piquet
was drawing the Onondagas more and more to his
mission, and the Dutch of Albany were alienating
their best friends, the Mohawks, by encroaching on
their lands.   Their chief, Hendrick, came to New
York with a deputation of the tribe to complain of
their wrongs; and finding no redress, went off in
anger, declaring that the covenant chain was broken.[1]
The authorities in alarm called William Johnson to
their aid.   He succeeded in soothing the exasperated
chief, and then proceeded to the confederate council
at Onondaga, where he found the assembled sachems
full of anxieties and doubts.   " We don't know what
you Christians, English and French, intend," said
one of their orators.   "We are so hemmed in by you
both that we have hardly a hunting-place left.   In a
little while, if we find a bear in a tree, there will
immediately appear an owner of the land to claim the
property and hinder us from killing it, by which

[1] *N. Y. Col. Docs.*, vi. 788.   *Colonial Records of Pa.*, v. 625.

we live. We are so perplexed between you that we
hardly know what to say or think."[1] No man had
such power over the Five Nations as Johnson. His
dealings with them were at once honest, downright,
and sympathetic. They loved and trusted him as
much as they detested the Indian commissioners at
Albany, whom the province of New York had charged
with their affairs, and who, being traders, grossly
abused their office.

It was to remedy this perilous state of things that
the Lords of Trade and Plantations directed the
several governors to urge on their assemblies the
sending of commissioners to make a joint treaty with
the wavering tribes.[2] Seven of the provinces, New
York, Pennsylvania, Maryland, and the four New
England colonies, acceded to the plan, and sent to
Albany, the appointed place of meeting, a body of
men who for character and ability had never had an
equal on the continent, but whose powers from their
respective assemblies were so cautiously limited as
to preclude decisive action. They met in the court-
house of the little frontier city. A large "chain-
belt" of wampum was provided, on which the King
was symbolically represented, holding in his embrace
the colonies, the Five Nations, and all their allied
tribes. This was presented to the assembled war-

---

[1] *N. Y. Col. Docs.*, vi. 813.
[2] *Circular Letter of Lords of Trade to Governors in America*, 18
September, 1753. *Lords of Trade to Sir Danvers Osborne*, in *N. Y.
Col. Docs.*, vi. 800.

riors, with a speech in which the misdeeds of the
French were not forgotten. The chief, Hendrick,
made a much better speech in reply. "We do now
solemnly renew and brighten the covenant chain.
We shall take the chain-belt to Onondaga, where
our council-fire always burns, and keep it so safe
that neither thunder nor lightning shall break it."
The commissioners had blamed them for allowing so
many of their people to be drawn away to Piquet's
mission. "It is true," said the orator, "that we live
disunited. We have tried to bring back our brethren,
but in vain; for the Governor of Canada is like a
wicked, deluding spirit. You ask why we are so
dispersed. The reason is that you have neglected us
for these three years past." Here he took a stick
and threw it behind him. "You have thus thrown
us behind your back; whereas the French are a
subtle and vigilant people, always using their utmost
endeavors to seduce and bring us over to them."
He then told them that it was not the French alone
who invaded the country of the Indians. "The
Governor of Virginia and the Governor of Canada
are quarrelling about lands which belong to us, and
their quarrel may end in our destruction." And he
closed with a burst of sarcasm. "We would have
taken Crown Point [*in the last war*], but you prevented us. Instead, you burned your own fort at
Saratoga and ran away from it, — which was a shame
and a scandal to you. Look about your country and
see: you have no fortifications; no, not even in this

city. It is but a step from Canada hither, and the
French may come and turn you out of doors. You
desire us to speak from the bottom of our hearts, and
we shall do it. Look at the French: they are men;
they are fortifying everywhere. But you are all like
women, bare and open, without fortifications." [1]

Hendrick's brother Abraham now took up the
word, and begged that Johnson might be restored to
the management of Indian affairs, which he had
formerly held; "for," said the chief, "we love him
and he us, and he has always been our good and
trusty friend." The commissioners had not power
to grant the request, but the Indians were assured
that it should not be forgotten; and they returned to
their villages soothed, but far from satisfied. Nor
were the commissioners empowered to take any
effective steps for fortifying the frontier.

The congress now occupied itself with another
matter. Its members were agreed that great danger
was impending; that without wise and just treatment of the tribes, the French would gain them all,
build forts along the back of the British colonies,
and, by means of ships and troops from France,
master them one by one, unless they would combine
for mutual defence. The necessity of some form of
union had at length begun to force itself upon the
colonial mind. A rough woodcut had lately appeared

---

[1] *Proceedings of the Congress at Albany, N. Y. Col. Docs.,* vi. 853.
A few verbal changes, for the sake of brevity, are made in the
above extracts.

in the "Pennsylvania Gazette," figuring the provinces under the not very flattering image of a snake cut to pieces, with the motto, "Join, or die." A writer of the day held up the Five Nations for emulation, observing that if ignorant savages could confederate, British colonists might do as much.[1] Franklin, the leading spirit of the congress, now laid before it his famous project of union, which has been too often described to need much notice here. Its fate is well known. The Crown rejected it because it gave too much power to the colonies; the colonies, because it gave too much power to the Crown, and because it required each of them to transfer some of its functions of self-government to a central council. Another plan was afterwards devised by the friends of prerogative, perfectly agreeable to the King, since it placed all power in the hands of a council of governors, and since it involved compulsory taxation of the colonists, who, for the same reasons, would have doggedly resisted it, had an attempt been made to carry it into effect.[2]

Even if some plan of union had been agreed upon, long delay must have followed before its machinery could be set in motion; and meantime there was

[1] Kennedy, *Importance of gaining and preserving the Friendship of the Indians.*

[2] On the Albany plan of union, *Franklin's Works,* i. 177. Shirley thought it " a great strain upon the prerogative of the Crown," and was for requiring the colonies to raise money and men "without farther consulting them upon any points whatever." *Shirley to Robinson,* 24 *December,* 1754.

need of immediate action. War-parties of Indians
from Canada, set on, it was thought, by the governor,
were already burning and murdering among the
border settlements of New York and New Hampshire.
In the south Dinwiddie grew more and more alarmed,
"for the French are like so many locusts; they are
collected in bodies in a most surprising manner;
their number now on the Ohio is from twelve hundred to fifteen hundred." He writes to Lord Gran
ville that, in his opinion, they aim to conquer the
continent, and that "the obstinacy of this stubborn
generation" exposes the country "to the merciless
rage of a rapacious enemy." What vexed him even
more than the apathy of the assemblies was the conduct of his brother-governor, Glen of South Carolina,
who, apparently piqued at the conspicuous part
Dinwiddie was acting, wrote to him in a "very dic-
tatorial style," found fault with his measures, jested
at his activity in writing letters, and even questioned
the right of England to lands on the Ohio; till he
was moved at last to retort: "I cannot help observing that your letters and arguments would have been
more proper from a French officer than from one of
His Majesty's governors. My conduct has met with
His Majesty's gracious approbation; and I am sorry
it has not received yours." Thus discouraged, even
in quarters where he had least reason to expect it,
he turned all his hopes to the home government;
again recommended a tax by Act of Parliament, and
begged, in repeated letters, for arms, munitions, and

two regiments of infantry.[1] His petition was not made in vain.

England at this time presented the phenomenon of a prime minister who could not command the respect of his own servants. A more preposterous figure than the Duke of Newcastle never stood at the head of a great nation. He had a feverish craving for place and power, joined to a total unfitness for both. He was an adept in personal politics, and was so busied with the arts of winning and keeping office that he had no leisure, even if he had had ability, for the higher work of government. He was restless, quick in movement, rapid and confused in speech, lavish of worthless promises, always in a hurry, and at once headlong, timid, and rash. "A borrowed importance and real insignificance," says Walpole, who knew him well, "gave him the perpetual air of a solicitor. . . . He had no pride, though infinite self-love. He loved business immoderately; yet was only always doing it, never did it. When left to himself, he always plunged into difficulties, and then shuddered for the consequences." Walpole gives an anecdote showing the state of his ideas on colonial matters. General Ligonier suggested to him that Annapolis ought to be defended. "To which he replied with his lisping, evasive hurry: 'Annapolis, Annapolis! Oh, yes, Annapolis must be defended; to be sure, Annapolis should be defended, — where

[1] *Dinwiddie Papers;* letters to Granville, Albemarle, Halifax, Fox, Holdernesse, Horace Walpole, and Lords of Trade.

is Annapolis?'"[1] Another contemporary, Smollett,
ridicules him in his novel of "Humphrey Clinker,"
and tells a similar story, which, founded in fact or
not, shows in what estimation the minister was held:
"Captain C. treated the Duke's character without
any ceremony. ' This wiseacre,' said he, ' is still
abed; and I think the best thing he can do is to
sleep on till Christmas; for when he gets up he does
nothing but expose his own folly. In the beginning
of the war he told me in a great fright that thirty
thousand French had marched from Acadia to Cape
Breton. Where did they find transports? said I. —
Transports! cried he, I tell you they marched by
land. — By land to the island of Cape Breton! — What,
is Cape Breton an island? — Certainly. — Ha! are you
sure of that? — When I pointed it out on the map,
he examined it earnestly with his spectacles; then,
taking me in his arms, — My dear C., cried he, you
always bring us good news. Egad! I'll go directly
and tell the King that Cape Breton is an island.'"

His wealth, county influence, flagitious use of
patronage, and long-practised skill in keeping majori-
ties in the House of Commons by means that would
not bear the light, made his support necessary to
Pitt himself, and placed a fantastic political jobber
at the helm of England in a time when she needed a
patriot and a statesman. Newcastle was the growth
of the decrepitude and decay of a great party, which
had fulfilled its mission and done its work. But if

[1] Walpole, *George II.*, i. 344.

the Whig soil had become poor for a wholesome crop, it was never so rich for toadstools.

Sir Thomas Robinson held the Southern Department, charged with the colonies; and Lord Mahon remarks of him that the duke had achieved the feat of finding a secretary of state more incapable than himself. He had the lead of the House of Commons. "Sir Thomas Robinson lead us!" said Pitt to Henry Fox; "the Duke might as well send his jackboot to lead us." The active and aspiring Halifax was at the head of the Board of Trade and Plantations. The Duke of Cumberland commanded the army, — an indifferent soldier, though a brave one; harsh, violent, and headlong. Anson, the celebrated navigator, was First Lord of the Admiralty, — a position in which he disappointed everybody.

In France the true ruler was Madame Pompadour, once the King's mistress, now his procuress, and a sort of feminine prime minister. Machault d'Arnouville was at the head of the Marine and Colonial Department. The diplomatic representatives of the two Crowns were more conspicuous for social than for political talents. Of Mirepoix, French ambassador at London, Marshal Saxe had once observed: "It is a good appointment; he can teach the English to dance." Walpole says concerning him: "He could not even learn to pronounce the names of our games of cards, — which, however, engaged most of the hours of his negotiation. We were to be bullied out of our colonies by an apprentice at whist!" Lord

Albemarle, English ambassador at Versailles, is held up by Chesterfield as an example to encourage his son in the pursuit of the graces: "What do you think made our friend Lord Albemarle colonel of a regiment of Guards, Governor of Virginia, Groom of the Stole, and ambassador to Paris, — amounting in all to sixteen or seventeen thousand pounds a year? Was it his birth? No; a Dutch gentleman only. Was it his estate? No; he had none. Was it his learning, his parts, his political abilities and application? You can answer these questions as easily and as soon as I can ask them. What was it then? Many people wondered; but I do not, for I know, and will tell you, — it was his air, his address, his manners, and his graces."

The rival nations differed widely in military and naval strength. England had afloat more than two hundred ships-of-war, some of them of great force, while the navy of France counted little more than half the number. On the other hand, England had reduced her army to eighteen thousand men, and France had nearly ten times as many under arms. Both alike were weak in leadership. That rare son of the tempest, a great commander, was to be found in neither of them since the death of Saxe.

In respect to the approaching crisis, the interests of the two Powers pointed to opposite courses of action. What France needed was time. It was her policy to put off a rupture, wreathe her face in diplomatic smiles, and pose in an attitude of peace and good faith, while increasing her navy, reinforcing her garrisons in America, and strengthening her positions there. It was the policy of England to attack at once, and tear up the young encroachments while they were yet in the sap, before they could strike root and harden into stiff resistance.

When, on the fourteenth of November, the King made his opening speech to the Houses of Parliament, he congratulated them on the prevailing peace, and assured them that he should improve it to promote the trade of his subjects, "and protect those possessions which constitute one great source of their wealth." America was not mentioned; but his hearers understood him, and made a liberal grant for the service of the year.[1] Two regiments, each of five hundred men, had already been ordered to sail for Virginia, where their numbers were to be raised by enlistment to seven hundred.[2] Major-General Braddock, a man after the Duke of Cumberland's own heart, was appointed to the chief command. The two regiments — the forty-fourth and the forty-eighth — embarked at Cork in the middle of January. The soldiers detested the service, and many had deserted. More would have done so had they foreseen what awaited them.

This movement was no sooner known at Versailles

[1] Entick, *Late War*, i. 118.

[2] *Robinson to Lords of the Admiralty*, 30 *September*, 1754. *Ibid. to Board of Ordnance*, 10 *October*, 1754. *Ibid., Circular Letter to American Governors*, 26 *October*, 1754. *Instructions to our Trusty and Well-beloved Edward Braddock*, 25 *November*, 1754.

than a counter expedition was prepared on a larger scale. Eighteen ships-of-war were fitted for sea at Brest and Rochefort, and the six battalions of La Reine, Bourgogne, Languedoc, Guienne, Artois, and Béarn, three thousand men in all, were ordered on board for Canada. Baron Dieskau, a German veteran who had served under Saxe, was made their general; and with him went the new governor of French America, the Marquis de Vaudreuil, destined to succeed Duquesne, whose health was failing under the fatigues of his office. Admiral Dubois de la Motte commanded the fleet; and lest the English should try to intercept it, another squadron of nine ships, under Admiral Macnamara, was ordered to accompany it to a certain distance from the coast. There was long and tedious delay. Doreil, commissary of war, who had embarked with Vaudreuil and Dieskau in the same ship, wrote from the harbor of Brest on the twenty-ninth of April: "At last I think we are off. We should have been outside by four o'clock this morning, if M. de Macnamara had not been obliged to ask Count Dubois de la Motte to wait till noon to mend some important part of the rigging (I don't know the name of it) which was broken. It is precious time lost, and gives the English the advantage over us of two tides. I talk of these things as a blind man does of colors. What is certain is that Count Dubois de la Motte is very impatient to get away, and that the King's fleet destined for Canada is in very able and zealous hands.

who got to sea before La Motte, stationed himself
near the southern coast of Newfoundland to cut him
off; but most of the French squadron eluded him,
and safely made their way, some to Louisbourg, and
the others to Quebec. Thus the English expedition
was, in the main, a failure. Three of the French
ships, however, lost in fog and rain, had become
separated from the rest, and lay rolling and tossing
on an angry sea not far from Cape Race. One of
them was the "Alcide," commanded by Captain
Hocquart; the others were the "Lis" and the
"Dauphin." The wind fell; but the fogs continued
at intervals; till, on the afternoon of the seventh of
June, the weather having cleared, the watchman on
the maintop saw the distant ocean studded with
ships. It was the fleet of Boscawen. Hocquart,
who gives the account, says that in the morning they
were within three leagues of him, crowding all sail
in pursuit. Towards eleven o'clock one of them, the
"Dunkirk," was abreast of him to windward, within
short speaking distance; and the ship of the admiral,
displaying a red flag as a signal to engage, was not
far off. Hocquart called out: "Are we at peace, or
war?" He declares that Howe, captain of the
"Dunkirk," replied in French: "La paix, la paix."
Hocquart then asked the name of the British admiral;
and on hearing it said: "I know him; he is a friend

cawen, *Esq., Vice-Admiral of the Blue*, 16 *April*, 1755. *Most secret
Instructions for Francis Holbourne, Esq., Rear-Admiral of the Blue*, 9
May, 1755. *Robinson to Lords of the Admiralty*, 8 *May*, 1755.

of mine." Being asked his own name in return, he
had scarcely uttered it when the batteries of the
"Dunkirk" belched flame and smoke, and volleyed a
tempest of iron upon the crowded decks of the
"Alcide." She returned the fire, but was forced at
length to strike her colors. Rostaing, second in
command of the troops, was killed; and six other
officers, with about eighty men, were killed or
wounded.[1] At the same time the "Lis" was attacked
and overpowered. She had on board eight companies
of the battalions of La Reine and Languedoc. The
third French ship, the "Dauphin," escaped under
cover of a rising fog.[2]

Here at last was an end to negotiation. The sword
was drawn and brandished in the eyes of Europe.

[1] *Liste des Officiers tués et blessés dans le Combat de l'Alcide et du
Lis.*

[2] Hocquart's account is given in full by Pichon, *Lettres et
Mémoires pour servir à l'Histoire du Cap-Breton.* The short account
in *Précis des Faits,* 272, seems, too, to be drawn from Hocquart.
Also *Boscawen to Robinson,* 22 *June,* 1755. *Vaudreuil au Ministre,*
24 *Juillet,* 1755. Entick, i. 137.

Some English accounts say that Captain Howe, in answer to the
question, "Are we at peace, or war ? " returned, "I don't know;
but you had better prepare for war." Boscawen places the action
on the tenth, instead of the eighth, and puts the English loss at
seven killed and twenty-seven wounded.

CHAPTER VII.

1755.

BRADDOCK.

ARRIVAL OF BRADDOCK: HIS CHARACTER. — COUNCIL AT ALEX-
ANDRIA. — PLAN OF THE CAMPAIGN. — APATHY OF THE COLO-
NISTS. — RAGE OF BRADDOCK. — FRANKLIN. — FORT CUMBERLAND.
— COMPOSITION OF THE ARMY. — OFFENDED FRIENDS. — THE
MARCH. — THE FRENCH FORT. — SAVAGE ALLIES. — THE CAP-
TIVE. — BEAUJEU: HE GOES TO MEET THE ENGLISH. — PAS-
SAGE OF THE MONONGAHELA. — THE SURPRISE. — THE BATTLE.
— ROUT OF BRADDOCK: HIS DEATH. — INDIAN FEROCITY. —
RECEPTION OF THE ILL NEWS. — WEAKNESS OF DUNBAR. —
THE FRONTIER ABANDONED.

"I HAVE the pleasure to acquaint you that General
Braddock came to my house last Sunday night," writes
Dinwiddie, at the end of February, to Governor
Dobbs of North Carolina. Braddock had landed
at Hampton from the ship "Centurion," along with
young Commodore Keppel, who commanded the
American squadron. "I am mighty glad," again
writes Dinwiddie, "that the General is arrived,
which I hope will give me some ease; for these
twelve months past I have been a perfect slave."
He conceived golden opinions of his guest. "He
is, I think, a very fine officer, and a sensible, considerate gentleman. He and I live in great harmony."

Had he known him better, he might have praised
him less. William Shirley, son of the governor of
Massachusetts, was Braddock's secretary; and after
an acquaintance of some months wrote to his friend
Governor Morris: "We have a general most judi-
ciously chosen for being disqualified for the service
he is employed in in almost every respect. He may
be brave for aught I know, and he is honest in pecu-
niary matters."[1] The astute Franklin, who also had
good opportunity of knowing him, says: "This
general was, I think, a brave man, and might probably have made a good figure in some European war.
But he had too much self-confidence; too high an
opinion of the validity of regular troops; too mean a
one of both Americans and Indians."[2] Horace
Walpole, in his function of gathering and immortaliz-
ing the gossip of his time, has left a sharply drawn
sketch of Braddock in two letters to Sir Horace
Mann, written in the summer of this year: "I love
to give you an idea of our characters as they rise
upon the stage of history. Braddock is a very Iroquois in disposition. He had a sister who, having
gamed away all her little fortune at Bath, hanged
herself with a truly English deliberation, leaving
only a note upon the table with those lines: ' To die
is landing on some silent shore,' etc. When Braddock was told of it, he only said: ' Poor Fanny! I
always thought she would play till she would be

---

[1] *Shirley the younger to Morris,* 23 *May,* 1755.
[2] Franklin, *Autobiography.*

forced to *tuck herself up.*'" Under the name of Miss
Sylvia S——, Goldsmith, in his life of Nash, tells
the story of this unhappy woman. She was a rash
but warm-hearted creature, reduced to penury and
dependence, not so much by a passion for cards as
by her lavish generosity to a lover ruined by his own
follies, and with whom her relations are said to have
been entirely innocent. Walpole continues: "But a
more ridiculous story of Braddock, and which is
recorded in heroics by Fielding in his ' Covent
Garden Tragedy,' was an amorous discussion he
had formerly with a Mrs. Upton, who kept him. He
had gone the greatest lengths with her pin-money,
and was still craving. One day, that he was very
pressing, she pulled out her purse and showed him
that she had but twelve or fourteen shillings left.
He twitched it from her: ' Let me see that.' Tied
up at the other end, he found five guineas. He took
them, tossed the empty purse in her face, saying,
' Did you mean to cheat me?' and never went near
her more. Now you are acquainted with General
Braddock."

"He once had a duel with Colonel Gumley, Lady
Bath's brother, who had been his great friend. As
they were going to engage, Gumley, who had good-
humor and wit (Braddock had the latter), said,
' Braddock, you are a poor dog! Here, take my
purse; if you kill me, you will be forced to run
away, and then you will not have a shilling to support you.' Braddock refused the purse, insisted on

the duel, was disarmed, and would not even ask his life. However, with all his brutality, he has lately been governor of Gibraltar, where he made himself adored, and where scarce any governor was endured before." [1]

Another story is told of him by an accomplished actress of the time, George Anne Bellamy, whom Braddock had known from girlhood, and with whom his present relations seem to have been those of an elderly adviser and friend. "As we were walking in the Park one day, we heard a poor fellow was to be chastised; when I requested the General to beg off the offender. Upon his application to the general officer, whose name was Dury, he asked Braddock how long since he had divested himself of the brutality and insolence of his manners? To which the other replied: 'You never knew me insolent to my inferiors. It is only to such rude men as yourself that I behave with the spirit which I think they deserve.'"

Braddock made a visit to the actress on the evening before he left London for America. "Before we parted," she says, "the General told me that he should never see me more; for he was going with a handful of men to conquer whole nations; and to do this they must cut their way through unknown woods. He produced a map of the country, saying

---

[1] *Letters of Horace Walpole* (1866), ii. 459, 461. It is doubtful if Braddock was ever governor of Gibraltar; though, as Mr. Sargent shows, he once commanded a regiment there.

at the same time: ' Dear Pop, we are sent like sacrifices to the altar,' "[1] — a strange presentiment for a
man of his sturdy temper.

Whatever were his failings, he feared nothing, and
his fidelity and honor in the discharge of public
trusts were never questioned. "Desperate in his
fortune, brutal in his behavior, obstinate in his sentiments," again writes Walpole, "he was still intrepid
and capable."[2] He was a veteran in years and in
service, having entered the Coldstream Guards as
ensign in 1710.

The transports bringing the two regiments from
Ireland all arrived safely at Hampton, and were
ordered to proceed up the Potomac to Alexandria,
where a camp was to be formed. Thither, towards
the end of March, went Braddock himself, along
with Keppel and Dinwiddie, in the governor's coach;
while his aide-de-camp, Orme, his secretary, Shirley,
and the servants of the party followed on horseback.
Braddock had sent for the elder Shirley and other
provincial governors to meet him in council; and on
the fourteenth of April they assembled in a tent of
the newly formed encampment. Here was Dinwiddie,
who thought his troubles at an end, and saw in the
red-coated soldiery the near fruition of his hopes.
Here, too, was his friend and ally, Dobbs of North
Carolina; with Morris of Pennsylvania, fresh from

[1] *Apology for the Life of George Anne Bellamy, written by herself*, ii.
204 (London, 1786).
[2] Walpole, *George II.*, i. 390.

Assembly quarrels; Sharpe of Maryland, who, having once been a soldier, had been made a sort of
provisional commander-in-chief before the arrival
of Braddock; and the ambitious Delancey of New
York, who had lately led the opposition against the
governor of that province, and now filled the office
himself, — a position that needed all his manifold
adroitness. But, next to Braddock, the most noteworthy man present was Shirley, governor of Massachusetts. There was a fountain of youth in this old
lawyer. A few years before, when he was boundary
commissioner in Paris, he had had the indiscretion
to marry a young Catholic French girl, the daughter
of his landlord; and now, when more than sixty
years old, he thirsted for military honors, and
delighted in contriving operations of war. He was
one of a very few in the colonies who at this time
entertained the idea of expelling the French from
the continent. He held that Carthage must be
destroyed; and, in spite of his Parisian marriage,
was the foremost advocate of the root-and-branch
policy. He and Lawrence, governor of Nova Scotia,
had concerted an attack on the French fort of
Beauséjour; and, jointly with others in New England, he had planned the capture of Crown Point,
the key of Lake Champlain. By these two strokes
and by fortifying the portage between the Kennebec
and the Chaudière, he thought that the northern
colonies would be saved from invasion, and placed
in a position to become themselves invaders. Then,

by driving the enemy from Niagara, securing that important pass, and thus cutting off the communication between Canada and her interior dependencies, all the French posts in the West would die of inanition.[1] In order to commend these schemes to the home government, he had painted in gloomy colors the dangers that beset the British colonies. Our Indians, he said, will all desert us if we submit to French encroachment. Some of the provinces are full of negro slaves, ready to rise against their masters, and of Roman Catholics, Jacobites, indented servants, and other dangerous persons, who would aid the French in raising a servile insurrection. Pennsylvania is in the hands of Quakers, who will not fight, and of Germans, who are likely enough to join the enemy. The Dutch of Albany would do anything to save their trade. A strong force of French regulars might occupy that place without resistance, then descend the Hudson, and, with the help of a naval force, capture New York and cut the British colonies asunder.[2]

The plans against Crown Point and Beauséjour had already found the approval of the home government and the energetic support of all the New England colonies. Preparation for them was in full activity; and it was with great difficulty that Shirley had disengaged himself from these cares to attend the Council at Alexandria. He and Dinwiddie stood

[1] *Correspondence of Shirley*, 1754, 1755.
[2] *Shirley to Robinson*, 24 *January*, 1755.

in the front of opposition to French designs. As
they both defended the royal prerogative and were
strong advocates of taxation by Parliament, they
have found scant justice from American writers.
Yet the British colonies owed them a debt of gratitude, and the American States owe it still.

Braddock laid his instructions before the Council,
and Shirley found them entirely to his mind; while
the general, on his part, fully approved the schemes
of the governor. The plan of the campaign was
settled. The French were to be attacked at four
points at once. The two British regiments lately
arrived were to advance on Fort Duquesne; two
new regiments, known as Shirley's and Pepperrell's,
just raised in the provinces, and taken into the King's
pay, were to reduce Niagara; a body of provincials
from New England, New York, and New Jersey was
to seize Crown Point; and another body of New
England men to capture Beauséjour and bring
Acadia to complete subjection. Braddock himself
was to lead the expedition against Fort Duquesne.
He asked Shirley, who, though a soldier only in
theory, had held the rank of colonel since the last
war, to charge himself with that against Niagara; and
Shirley eagerly assented. The movement on Crown
Point was intrusted to Colonel William Johnson, by
reason of his influence over the Indians and his reputation for energy, capacity, and faithfulness. Lastly,
the Acadian enterprise was assigned to Lieutenant-
Colonel Monckton, a regular officer of merit.

To strike this fourfold blow in time of peace was
a scheme worthy of Newcastle and of Cumberland.
The pretext was that the positions to be attacked
were all on British soil; that in occupying them the
French had been guilty of invasion; and that to
expel the invaders would be an act of self-defence.
Yet in regard to two of these positions, the French,
if they had no other right, might at least claim one
of prescription. Crown Point had been twenty-four
years in their undisturbed possession, while it was
three quarters of a century since they first occupied Niagara; and, though New York claimed the
ground, no serious attempt had been made to dislodge them.

Other matters now engaged the Council. Braddock, in accordance with his instructions, asked the
governors to urge upon their several assemblies the
establishment of a general fund for the service of
the campaign; but the governors were all of opinion
that the assemblies would refuse, — each being
resolved to keep the control of its money in its own
hands; and all present, with one voice, advised that
the colonies should be compelled by Act of Parliament to contribute in due proportion to the support
of the war. Braddock next asked if, in the judgment of the Council, it would not be well to send
Colonel Johnson with full powers to treat with the
Five Nations, who had been driven to the verge of
an outbreak by the misconduct of the Dutch Indian
commissioners at Albany. The measure was cor-

dially approved, as was also another suggestion of
the general, that vessels should be built at Oswego
to command Lake Ontario. The Council then
dissolved.

Shirley hastened back to New England, burdened
with the preparation for three expeditions and the
command of one of them. Johnson, who had been in
the camp, though not in the Council, went back to
Albany, provided with a commission as sole superintendent of Indian affairs, and charged, besides, with
the enterprise against Crown Point; while an express
was despatched to Monckton at Halifax, with orders
to set at once to his work of capturing Beauséjour.[1]

In regard to Braddock's part of the campaign,
there had been a serious error. If, instead of landing
in Virginia and moving on Fort Duquesne by the
long and circuitous route of Will's Creek, the two
regiments had disembarked at Philadelphia and
marched westward, the way would have been short-
ened, and would have lain through one of the richest
and most populous districts on the continent, filled
with supplies of every kind. In Virginia, on the
other hand, and in the adjoining province of Mary-

[1] *Minutes of a Council held at the Camp at Alexandria, in Virginia,
April* 14, 1755. *Instructions to Major-General Braddock,* 25 *November,*
1754. *Secret Instructions to Major-General Braddock, same date.
Napier to Braddock, written by Order of the Duke of Cumberland,* 25
November, 1754, in *Précis des Faits, Pièces justificatives,* 168. Orme,
*Journal of Braddock's Expedition. Instructions to Governor Shirley.
Correspondence of Shirley. Correspondence of Braddock* (Public
Record Office). *Johnson Papers. Dinwiddie Papers. Pennsylvania
Archives,* ii.

land, wagons, horses, and forage were scarce. The enemies of the Administration ascribed this blunder to the influence of the Quaker merchant, John Hanbury, whom the Duke of Newcastle had consulted as a person familiar with American affairs. Hanbury, who was a prominent stockholder in the Ohio Company, and who traded largely in Virginia, saw it for his interest that the troops should pass that way, and is said to have brought the duke to this opinion.[1] A writer of the time thinks that if they had landed in Pennsylvania, forty thousand pounds would have been saved in money, and six weeks in time.[2]

Not only were supplies scarce, but the people showed such unwillingness to furnish them, and such apathy in aiding the expedition, that even Washington was provoked to declare that "they ought to be chastised."[3] Many of them thought that the alarm about French encroachment was a device of designing politicians; and they did not awake to a full consciousness of the peril till it was forced upon them by a deluge of calamities, produced by the purblind folly of their own representatives, who, instead of frankly promoting the expedition,

[1] *Shebbeare's Tracts*, Letter I. Dr. Shebbeare was a political pamphleteer, pilloried by one ministry, and rewarded by the next. He certainly speaks of Hanbury, though he does not give his name. Compare Sargent, 107, 162.

[2] *Gentleman's Magazine, August*, 1755.

[3] *Writings of Washington*, ii. 78. He speaks of the people of Pennsylvania.

displayed a perverse and exasperating narrowness which chafed Braddock to fury. He praises the New England colonies, and echoes Dinwiddie's declaration that they have shown a "fine martial spirit," and he commends Virginia as having done far better than her neighbors; but for Pennsylvania he finds no words to express his wrath.[1] He knew nothing of the intestine war between proprietaries and people, and hence could see no palliation for a conduct which threatened to ruin both the expedition and the colony. Everything depended on speed, and speed was impossible; for stores and provisions were not ready, though notice to furnish them had been given months before. The quartermaster-general, Sir John Sinclair, "stormed like a lion rampant," but with small effect.[2] Contracts broken or disavowed, want of horses, want of wagons, want of forage, want of wholesome food, or sufficient food of any kind, caused such delay that the report of it reached England, and drew from Walpole the comment that Braddock was in no hurry to be scalped. In reality he was maddened with impatience and vexation.

A powerful ally presently came to his aid in the shape of Benjamin Franklin, then postmaster-general of Pennsylvania. That sagacious personage, — the sublime of common-sense, about equal in his instincts

[1] *Braddock to Robinson*, 18 *March*, 19 *April*, 5 *June*, 1755, etc. On the attitude of Pennsylvania, *Colonial Records of Pa.*, vi., *passim*.

[2] *Colonial Records of Pa.*, vi. 368.

and motives of character to the respectable average
of the New England that produced him, but gifted
with a versatile power of brain rarely matched on
earth, — was then divided between his strong desire
to repel a danger of which he saw the imminence,
and his equally strong antagonism to the selfish
claims of the Penns, proprietaries of .Pennsylvania.
This last motive had determined his attitude towards
their representative, the governor, and led him into
an opposition as injurious to the military good name
of the province as it was favorable to its political
longings.   In the present case there was no such
conflict of inclinations; he could help Braddock
without hurting Pennsylvania. * He and his son had
visited the camp, and found the general waiting
restlessly for the report of the agents whom he had
sent to collect wagons.   "I stayed with him," says
Franklin, "several days, and dined with him daily.
When I was about to depart, the returns of wagons
to be obtained were brought in, by which it appeared
that they amounted only to twenty-five, and not all
of these were in serviceable condition."   On this the
general and his officers declared that the expedition
was at an end, and denounced the ministry for sending them into a country void of the means of transportation.   Franklin remarked that it was a pity
they had not landed in Pennsylvania, where almost
every farmer had his wagon.   Braddock caught
eagerly at his words, and begged that he would use
his influence to enable the troops to move.   Franklin

went back to Pennsylvania, issued an address to the
farmers appealing to their interest and their fears,
and in a fortnight procured a hundred and fifty
wagons, with a large number of horses.[1] Braddock,
grateful to his benefactor, and enraged at everybody
else, pronounced him "Almost the only instance of
ability and honesty I have known in these provinces."[2]
More wagons and more horses gradually arrived, and
at the eleventh hour the march began.

On the tenth of May Braddock reached Will's
Creek, where the whole force was now gathered,
having marched thither by detachments along the
banks of the Potomac. This old trading-station of
the Ohio Company had been transformed into a
military post and named Fort Cumberland. During
the past winter the independent companies which
had failed Washington in his need had been at work
here to prepare a base of operations for Braddock.
Their axes had been of more avail than their muskets.
A broad wound had been cut in the bosom of the
forest, and the murdered oaks and chestnuts turned
into ramparts, barracks, and magazines. Fort Cumberland was an enclosure of logs set upright in the
ground, pierced with loopholes, and armed with ten
small cannon. It stood on a rising ground near the
point where Will's Creek joined the Potomac, and

[1] Franklin, *Autobiography. Advertisement of B. Franklin for
Wagons, Address to the Inhabitants of the Counties of York, Lancaster, and Cumberland,* in *Pennsylvania Archives,* ii. 294.

[2] *Braddock to Robinson,* 5 *June,* 1755. The letters of Braddock
here cited are the originals in the Public Record Office.

the forest girded it like a mighty hedge, or rather
like a paling of gaunt brown stems upholding a
canopy of green. All around spread illimitable
woods, wrapping hill, valley, and mountain. The
spot was an oasis in a desert of leaves, — if the name
oasis can be given to anything so rude and harsh. In
this rugged area, or "clearing," all Braddock's force
was now assembled, amounting, regulars, provincials,
and sailors, to about twenty-two hundred men. The
two regiments, Halket's and Dunbar's, had been
completed by enlistment in Virginia to seven hundred men each. Of Virginians there were nine
companies of fifty men, who found no favor in the
eyes of Braddock or his officers. To Ensign Allen
of Halket's regiment was assigned the duty of "making them as much like soldiers as possible," [1] — that
is, of drilling them like regulars. The general had
little hope of them, and informed Sir Thomas Robinson that "their slothful and languid disposition
renders them very unfit for military service," — a
point on which he lived to change his mind. Thirty
sailors, whom Commodore Keppel had lent him, were
more to his liking, and were in fact of value in many
ways. He had now about six hundred baggage-
horses, besides those of the artillery, all weakening
daily on their diet of leaves; for no grass was to be
found. There was great show of discipline, and little
real order. Braddock's executive capacity seems to
have been moderate, and his dogged, imperious

[1] Orme, *Journal.*

temper, rasped by disappointments, was in constant irritation. "He looks upon the country, I believe," writes Washington, "as void of honor or honesty. We have frequent disputes on this head, which are maintained with warmth on both sides, especially on his, as he is incapable of arguing without it, or giving up any point he asserts, be it ever so incompatible with reason or common sense."[1] Braddock's secretary, the younger Shirley, writing to his friend Governor Morris, spoke thus irreverently of his chief: "As the King said of a neighboring governor of yours [*Sharpe*], when proposed for the command of the American forces about a twelvemonth ago, and recommended as a very honest man, though not remarkably able, ' a little more ability and a little less honesty upon the present occasion might serve our turn better.' It is a joke to suppose that secondary officers can make amends for the defects of the first; the mainspring must be the mover. As to the others, I don't think we have much to boast; some are insolent and ignorant, others capable, but rather aiming at showing their own abilities than making a proper use of them. I have a very great love for my friend Orme, and think it uncommonly fortunate for our leader that he is under the influence of so honest and capable a man; but I wish for the sake of the public he had some more experience of business, particularly in America. I am greatly disgusted at seeing an expedition (as it is called), so ill-concerted

---

[1] *Writings of Washington,* ii. 77.

originally in England, so improperly conducted since
in America."[1]

Captain Robert Orme, of whom Shirley speaks,
was aide-de-camp to Braddock, and author of a copious and excellent Journal of the expedition, now in
the British Museum.[2] His portrait, painted at full
length by Sir Joshua Reynolds, hangs in the National
Gallery at London. He stands by his horse, a gallant
young figure, with a face pale, yet rather handsome,
booted to the knee, his scarlet coat, ample waistcoat,
and small three-cornered hat all heavy with gold lace.
The general had two other aides-de-camp, Captain
Roger Morris and Colonel George Washington,
whom he had invited, in terms that do him honor,
to become one of his military family.

It has been said that Braddock despised not only
provincials, but Indians. Nevertheless, he took
some pains to secure their aid, and complained that
Indian affairs had been so ill conducted by the provinces that it was hard to gain their confidence.
This was true; the tribes had been alienated by
gross neglect. Had they been protected from
injustice and soothed by attentions and presents, the
Five Nations, Delawares, and Shawanoes would have
been retained as friends. But their complaints had
been slighted, and every gift begrudged. The trader

[1] *Shirley the younger to Morris,* 23 *May,* 1755, in *Colonial Records
of Pa.,* vi. 404.

[2] Printed by Sargent, in his excellent monograph of Braddock's
Expedition.

Croghan brought, however, about fifty warriors, with as many women and children, to the camp at Fort Cumberland. They were objects of great curiosity to the soldiers, who gazed with astonishment on their faces, painted red, yellow, and black, their ears slit and hung with pendants, and their heads close shaved, except the feathered scalp-lock at the crown. "In the day," says an officer, "they are in our camp, and in the night they go into their own, where they dance and make a most horrible noise." Braddock received them several times in his tent, ordered the guard to salute them, made them speeches, caused cannon to be fired and drums and fifes to play in their honor, regaled them with rum, and gave them a bullock for a feast; whereupon, being much pleased, they danced a war-dance, described by one spectator as "droll and odd, showing how they scalp and fight;" after which, says another, "they set up the most horrid song or cry that ever I heard."[1] These warriors, with a few others, promised the general to join him on the march; but he apparently grew tired of them, for a famous chief, called Scarroyaddy, afterwards complained: "He looked upon us as dogs, and would never hear anything that we said to him." Only eight of them remained with him to the end.[2]

Another ally appeared at the camp. This was

[1] *Journal of a Naval Officer,* in Sargent. *The Expedition of Major-General Braddock, being Extracts of Letters from an Officer* (London, 1755).

[2] *Statement of George Croghan,* in Sargent, Appendix III.

a personage long known in Western fireside story as
Captain Jack, the Black Hunter, or the Black Rifle.
It was said of him that having been a settler on the
farthest frontier, in the Valley of the Juniata, he
returned one evening to his cabin and found it burned
to the ground by Indians, and the bodies of his wife
and children lying among the ruins. He vowed
undying vengeance, raised a band of kindred spirits,
dressed and painted like Indians, and became the
scourge of the red man and the champion of the
white. But he and his wild crew, useful as they
might have been, shocked Braddock's sense of
military fitness; and he received them so coldly that
they left him.[1]

It was the tenth of June before the army was well
on its march. Three hundred axemen led the way,
to cut and clear the road; and the long train of packhorses, wagons, and cannon toiled on behind, over
the stumps, roots, and stones of the narrow track,
the regulars and provincials marching in the forest
close on either side. Squads of men were thrown
out on the flanks, and scouts ranged the woods to
guard against surprise; for, with all his scorn of
Indians and Canadians, Braddock did not neglect
reasonable precautions. Thus, foot by foot, they
advanced into the waste of lonely mountains that
divided the streams flowing to the Atlantic from
those flowing to the Gulf of Mexico, — a realm of

---

[1] See several traditional accounts and contemporary letters in
Hazard's Pennsylvania Register, iv. 389, 390, 416; v. 191.

forests ancient as the world. The road was but
twelve feet wide, and the line of march often extended
four miles. It was like a thin, long party-colored
snake, red, blue, and brown, trailing slowly through
the depth of leaves, creeping round inaccessible
heights, crawling over ridges, moving always in
dampness and shadow, by rivulets and waterfalls,
crags and chasms, gorges and shaggy steeps. In
glimpses only, through jagged boughs and flickering
leaves, did this wild primeval world reveal itself,
with its dark green mountains, flecked with the
morning mist, and its distant summits pencilled in
dreamy blue. The army passed the main Alleghany,
Meadow Mountain, and Great Savage Mountain,
and traversed the funereal pine-forest afterwards
called the Shades of Death. No attempt was made
to interrupt their march, though the commandant of
Fort Duquesne had sent out parties for that purpose.
A few French and Indians hovered about them, now
and then scalping a straggler or inscribing filthy
insults on trees; while others fell upon the border
settlements which the advance of the troops had left
defenceless. Here they were more successful, butchering about thirty persons, chiefly women and children.

It was the eighteenth of June before the army
reached a place called the Little Meadows, less than
thirty miles from Fort Cumberland. Fever and
dysentery among the men, and the weakness and
worthlessness of many of the horses, joined to the
extreme difficulty of the road, so retarded them that

they could move scarcely more than three miles a
day. Braddock consulted with Washington, who
advised him to leave the heavy baggage to follow as
it could, and push forward with a body of chosen
troops. This counsel was given in view of a report
that five hundred regulars were on the way to reinforce Fort Duquesne. It was adopted. Colonel
Dunbar was left to command the rear division, whose
powers of movement were now reduced to the lowest
point. The advance corps, consisting of about twelve
hundred soldiers, besides officers and drivers, began
its march on the nineteenth with such artillery as
was thought indispensable, thirty wagons, and a
large number of pack-horses. "The prospect," writes
Washington to his brother, "conveyed infinite delight
to my mind, though I was excessively ill at the
time. But this prospect was soon clouded, and my
hopes brought very low indeed when I found that,
instead of pushing on with vigor without regarding
a little rough road, they were halting to level every
mole-hill, and to erect bridges over every brook, by
which means we were four days in getting twelve
miles." It was not till the seventh of July that
they neared the mouth of Turtle Creek, a stream
entering the Monongahela about eight miles from
the French fort. The way was direct and short, but
would lead them through a difficult country and a
defile so perilous that Braddock resolved to ford
the Monongahela to avoid this danger, and then
ford it again to reach his destination.

Fort Duquesne stood on the point of land where the Alleghany and the Monongahela join to form the Ohio, and where now stands Pittsburg, with its swarming population, its restless industries, the clang of its forges, and its chimneys vomiting foul smoke into the face of heaven. At that early day a white flag fluttering over a cluster of palisades and embankments betokened the first intrusion of civilized men upon a scene which, a few months before, breathed the repose of a virgin wilderness, voiceless but for the lapping of waves upon the pebbles, or the note of some lonely bird. But now the sleep of ages was broken, and bugle and drum told the astonished forest that its doom was pronounced and its days numbered. The fort was a compact little work, solidly built and strong, compared with others on the continent. It was a square of four bastions, with the water close on two sides, and the other two protected by ravelins, ditch, glacis, and covered way. The ramparts on these sides were of squared logs, filled in with earth, and ten feet or more thick. The two water sides were enclosed by a massive stockade of upright logs, twelve feet high, mortised together and loopholed. The armament consisted of a number of small cannon mounted on the bastions. A gate and drawbridge on the east side gave access to the area within, which was surrounded by barracks for the soldiers, officers' quarters, the lodgings of the commandant, a guard-house and a storehouse, all built partly of logs and partly of boards. There

were no casements, and the place was commanded
by a high woody hill beyond the Monongahela. The
forest had been cleared away to the distance of more
than a musket-shot from the ramparts, and the
stumps were hacked level with the ground. Here,
just outside the ditch, bark cabins had been built for
such of the troops and Canadians as could not find
room within; and the rest of the open space was
covered with Indian corn and other crops.[1]

The garrison consisted of a few companies of the
regular troops stationed permanently in the colony,
and to these were added a considerable number of
Canadians. Contrecœur still held the command.[2]
Under him were three other captains, Beaujeu,
Dumas, and Ligneris. Besides the troops and Canadians, eight hundred Indian warriors, mustered
from far and near, had built their wigwams and
camp-sheds on the open ground, or under the edge of
the neighboring woods, — very little to the advantage
of the young corn. Some were baptized savages
settled in Canada, — Caughnawagas from Saut St.
Louis, Abenakis from St. Francis, and Hurons from
Lorette, whose chief bore the name of Anastase, in
honor of that Father of the Church. The rest were

---

[1] M'Kinney's Description of Fort Duquesne, 1756, in Hazard's
Pennsylvania Register, viii. 318. Letters of Robert Stobo, Hostage at
Fort Duquesne, 1754, in Colonial Records of Pa., vi. 141, 161. Stobo's
Plan of Fort Duquesne, 1754. Journal of Thomas Forbes, 1755. Letter
of Captain Haslet, 1758, in Olden Time, i. 184. Plan of Fort Duquesne
in Public Record Office.

[2] See Appendix D.

unmitigated heathen, — Pottawattamies and Ojibwas
from the northern lakes under Charles Langlade, the
same bold partisan who had led them, three years
before, to attack the Miamis at Pickawillany;
Shawanoes and Mingoes from the Ohio; and Ottawas
from Detroit, commanded, it is said, by that most
redoubtable of savages, Pontiac. The law of the
survival of the fittest had wrought on this heterogeneous crew through countless generations; and
with the primitive Indian, the fittest was the hardiest,
fiercest, most adroit, and most wily. Baptized and
heathen alike, they had just enjoyed a diversion
greatly to their taste. A young Pennsylvanian
named James Smith, a spirited and intelligent boy of
eighteen, had been waylaid by three Indians on the
western borders of the province and led captive to
the fort. When the party came to the edge of the
clearing, his captors, who had shot and scalped his
companion, raised the scalp-yell; whereupon a din
of responsive whoops and firing of guns rose from all
the Indian camps, and their inmates swarmed out
like bees, while the French in the fort shot off
muskets and cannon to honor the occasion. The
unfortunate boy, the object of this obstreperous
rejoicing, presently saw a multitude of savages,
naked, hideously bedaubed with red, blue, black,
and brown, and armed with sticks or clubs, ranging
themselves in two long parallel lines, between which
he was told that he must run, the faster the better,
as they would beat him all the way. He ran with

his best speed, under a shower of blows, and had
nearly reached the end of the course, when he was
knocked down. He tried to rise, but was blinded by
a handful of sand thrown into his face; and then
they beat him till he swooned. On coming to his
senses he found himself in the fort, with the surgeon
opening a vein in his arm and a crowd of French and
Indians looking on. In a few days he was able to
walk with the help of a stick; and, coming out from
his quarters one morning, he saw a memorable
scene.[1]

Three days before, an Indian had brought the
report that the English were approaching; and the
Chevalier de la Perade was sent out to reconnoitre.[2]
He returned on the next day, the seventh, with news
that they were not far distant. On the eighth the
brothers Normanville went out, and found that they
were within six leagues of the fort. The French
were in great excitement and alarm; but Contrecœur
at length took a resolution, which seems to have
been inspired by Beaujeu.[3] It was determined to
meet the enemy on the march, and ambuscade them
if possible at the crossing of the Monongahela, or
some other favorable spot. Beaujeu proposed the

---

[1] *Account of Remarkable Occurrences in the Life of Colonel James
Smith, written by himself.* Perhaps the best of all the numerous
narratives of captives among the Indians.

[2] *Relation de Godefroy*, in Shea, *Bataille du Malangueulé* (Monongahela).

[3] Dumas, however, declares that Beaujeu adopted the plan at
his suggestion. *Dumas au Ministre*, 24 *Juillet*, 1756.

plan to the Indians, and offered them the war-
hatchet; but they would not take it. "Do you want
to die, my father, and sacrifice us besides?" That
night they held a council, and in the morning again
refused to go. Beaujeu did not despair. "I am
determined," he exclaimed, "to meet the English.
What! will you let your father go alone?"[1] The
greater part caught fire at his words, promised to
follow him, and put on their war-paint. Beaujeu
received the communion, then dressed himself like a
savage, and joined the clamorous throng. Open
barrels of gunpowder and bullets were set before the
gate of the fort, and James Smith, painfully climbing
the rampart with the help of his stick, looked down
on the warrior rabble as, huddling together, wild
with excitement, they scooped up the contents to fill
their powder-horns and pouches. Then, band after
band, they filed off along the forest track that led to
the ford of the Monongahela. They numbered six
hundred and thirty-seven; and with them went
thirty-six French officers and cadets, seventy-two
regular soldiers, and a hundred and forty-six Canadians, or about nine hundred in all.[2] At eight
o'clock the tumult was over. The broad clearing
lay lonely and still, and Contrecœur, with what was

---

[1] *Relation depuis le Départ des Trouppes de Québec jusqu'au 30 du
Mois de Septembre*, 1755.

[2] *Liste des Officiers, Cadets, Soldats, Miliciens, et Sauvages qui com-
posaient le Détachement qui a été au devant d'un Corps de 2,000 Anglois
à 3 Lieues du Fort Duquesne, le 9 Juillet*, 1755; *joint à la Lettre de M.
Bigot du 6 Août*, 1755.

left of his garrison, waited in suspense for the issue.

It was near one o'clock when Braddock crossed the Monongahela for the second time. If the French made a stand anywhere, it would be, he thought, at the fording-place; but Lieutenant-Colonel Gage, whom he sent across with a strong advance-party, found no enemy, and quietly took possession of the farther shore. Then the main body followed. To impose on the imagination of the French scouts, who were doubtless on the watch, the movement was made with studied regularity and order. The sun was cloudless, and the men were inspirited by the prospect of near triumph. Washington afterwards spoke with admiration of the spectacle.[1] The music, the banners, the mounted officers, the troop of light cavalry, the naval detachment, the red-coated regulars, the blue-coated Virginians, the wagons and tumbrils, cannon, howitzers, and coe-horns, the train of packhorses, and the droves of cattle, passed in long procession through the rippling shallows, and slowly entered the bordering forest. Here, when all were over, a short halt was ordered for rest and refreshment.

Why had not Beaujeu defended the ford? This was his intention in the morning; but he had been met by obstacles, the nature of which is not wholly clear. His Indians, it seems, had proved refractory.

[1] Compare the account of another eye-witness, Dr. Walker, in *Hazard's Pennsylvania Register*, vi. 104.

TURTLE CREEK

R. MONONGAHELA

No. 1.

A Sketch of the Field of Battle of the 9th of July, upon the Monongahela, seven miles from Fort du Quesne, shewing the Disposition of the Troops when the Action began.

EXPLANATION.

▥ British Troops; the long lines express the number of Files. ○ French and Indians. ✠ Cannon and Howitzers. ☐ Waggons, Carts, and Tumbrils. I Cattle and Packhorses.

A, French and Indians when first discovered by the Guides.

B, Guides and six light Horse.

C, Vanguard of the advanced Party.

D, Advanced Party, commanded by Lt. Col. Gage.

E, Working Party, commanded by Sir Jn. St. Clair, D.Q.M.G.

F, Two Field Pieces.

G, Waggons with Powder and Tools.

H, Rear Guard of the advanced Party.

I, Light Horse leading the Convoy. *K*, Sailors and Pioneers, with a Tumbril of Tools, etc. *L*, Three Field Pieces. *M*, General's Guard. *N*, Main Body upon the Flanks of the Convoy, with the Cattle and Packhorses between them and the Flank Guards. *O*, Field Piece in ye rear of ye Convoy. *P*, Rear Guards. *Q*, Flank Guards. *R*, A Hollow Way. *S*, a Hill which the Indians did most of the Execution from. *T*, Frazer's House.

(Signed)   Pat. Mackellar, Engr.

No. 2.

A Sketch of the Field of Battle, shewing the Disposition of the Troops about 2 o'clock, when the whole of the main Body had joined the Advanced and Working Partys, then beat back from the Ground they occupied as in Plan No. I.

EXPLANATION.

A, The French and Indians skulking behind Trees, round the British.

F, The two Field Pieces of the advanced Party abandoned.

C, *D*, *E*, *H*, *K*, *M*, *N*, *Q*, The whole Body of the British joined with little or no Order, but endeavouring to make Fronts towards yᵉ Enemies Fire. *L*, The three Field Pieces of the main Body. *P*, The rear Guard divided (round the rear of the Convoy now closed up) behind Trees having been attack'd by a few Indians.

N.B. The Disposition on both Sides continued about two hours nearly as here represented, the British endeavouring to recover the Guns (*F*) and to gain the Hill (*S*) to no purpose. The British were at length beat from the Guns (*Z*). The General was wounded soon after. They were at last beat across the Hollow Way (*R*) and made no further Stand. The Retreat was full of Confusion and Hurry, but after a few Miles there was a Body got to rally.

(Signed)   Pat. Mackellar, Engr.

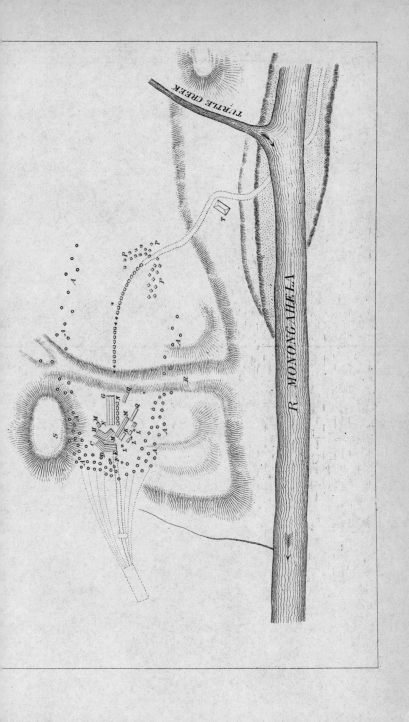

TURTLE CREEK

R. MONONGAHELA

Three hundred of them left him, went off in another
direction, and did not rejoin him till the English had
crossed the river.[1]   Hence perhaps it was that, having left Fort Duquesne at eight o'clock, he spent
half the day in marching seven miles, and was more
than a mile from the fording-place when the British
reached the eastern shore.   The delay, from whatever cause arising, cost him the opportunity of laying
an ambush either at the ford or in the gullies and
ravines that channelled the forest through which
Braddock was now on the point of marching.

Not far from the bank of the river, and close by
the British line of march, there was a clearing and
a deserted house that had once belonged to the trader
Fraser.   Washington remembered it well.   It was
here that he found rest and shelter on the winter
journey homeward from his mission to Fort Le Bœuf.
He was in no less need of rest at this moment; for
recent fever had so weakened him that he could
hardly sit his horse.   From Fraser's house to Fort
Duquesne the distance was eight miles by a rough
path, along which the troops were now beginning to
move after their halt.   It ran inland for a little,
then curved to the left, and followed a course parallel to the river along the base of a line of steep hills
that here bordered the valley.   These and all the
country were buried in dense and heavy forest,
choked with bushes and the carcasses of fallen trees.
Braddock has been charged with marching blindly

[1] *Relation de Godefroy*, in Shea, *Bataille du Malangueulé*.

that comes from despair, exciting by voice and
gesture the few soldiers that remained. The fire of
my platoon was so sharp that the enemy seemed
astonished." The Indians, encouraged, began to
rally. The French officers who commanded them
showed admirable courage and address; and while
Dumas and Ligneris, with the regulars and what
was left of the Canadians, held the ground in front,
the savage warriors, screeching their war-cries,
swarmed through the forest along both flanks of the
English, hid behind trees, bushes, and fallen trunks,
or crouched in gullies and ravines, and opened a
deadly fire on the helpless soldiery, who, themselves
completely visible, could see no enemy, and wasted
volley after volley on the impassive trees. The most
destructive fire came from a hill on the English right,
where the Indians lay in multitudes, firing from
their lurking-places on the living target below. But
the invisible death was everywhere, in front, flank,
and rear. The British cheer was heard no more.
The troops broke their ranks and huddled together in
a bewildered mass, shrinking from the bullets that
cut them down by scores.

When Braddock heard the firing in the front, he
pushed forward with the main body to the support of
Gage, leaving four hundred men in the rear, under
Sir Peter Halket, to guard the baggage. At the
moment of his arrival Gage's soldiers had abandoned
their two cannon, and were falling back to escape
the concentrated fire of the Indians. Meeting the

advancing troops, they tried to find cover behind them. This threw the whole into confusion. The men of the two regiments became mixed together; and in a short time the entire force, except the Virginians and the troops left with Halket, were massed in several dense bodies within a small space of ground, facing some one way and some another, and all alike exposed without shelter to the bullets that pelted them like hail. Both men and officers were new to this blind and frightful warfare of the savage in his native woods. To charge the Indians in their hiding-places would have been useless. They would have eluded pursuit with the agility of wild-cats, and swarmed back, like angry hornets, the moment that it ceased. The Virginians alone were equal to the emergency. Fighting behind trees like the Indians themselves, they might have held the enemy in check till order could be restored, had not Braddock, furious at a proceeding that shocked all his ideas of courage and discipline, ordered them, with oaths, to form into line. A body of them under Captain Waggoner made a dash for a fallen tree lying in the woods, far out towards the lurking-places of the Indians, and, crouching behind the huge trunk, opened fire; but the regulars, seeing the smoke among the bushes, mistook their best friends for the enemy, shot at them from behind, killed many, and forced the rest to return. A few of the regulars also tried in their clumsy way to fight behind trees; but Braddock beat them with his sword, and compelled them to stand with the rest, an open mark for the Indians. The panic increased; the soldiers crowded together, and the bullets spent themselves in a mass of human bodies. Commands, entreaties, and threats were lost upon them. "We would fight," some of them answered, "if we could see anybody to fight with." Nothing was visible but puffs of smoke. Officers and men who had stood all the afternoon under fire afterwards declared that they could not be sure they had seen a single Indian. Braddock ordered Lieutenant-Colonel Burton to attack the hill where the puffs of smoke were thickest, and the bullets most deadly. With infinite difficulty that brave officer induced a hundred men to follow him; but he was soon disabled by a wound, and they all faced about. The artillerymen stood for some time by their guns, which did great damage to the trees and little to the enemy. The mob of soldiers, stupefied with terror, stood panting, their foreheads beaded with sweat, loading and firing mechanically, sometimes into the air, sometimes among their own comrades, many of whom they killed. The ground, strewn with dead and wounded men, the bounding of maddened horses, the clatter and roar of musketry and cannon, mixed with the spiteful report of rifles and the yells that rose from the indefatigable throats of six hundred unseen savages, formed a chaos of anguish and terror scarcely paralleled even in Indian war. "I cannot describe the horrors of that scene," one of Braddock's

officers wrote three weeks after; "no pen could do
it. The yell of the Indians is fresh on my ear, and
the terrific sound will haunt me till the hour of my
dissolution."[1]

Braddock showed a furious intrepidity. Mounted
on horseback, he dashed to and fro, storming like a
madman. Four horses were shot under him, and he
mounted a fifth. Washington seconded his chief
with equal courage; he too no doubt using strong
language, for he did not measure words when the
fit was on him. He escaped as by miracle. Two
horses were killed under him, and four bullets tore
his clothes. The conduct of the British officers was
above praise. Nothing could surpass their undaunted
self-devotion; and in their vain attempts to lead on
the men, the havoc among them was frightful. Sir
Peter Halket was shot dead. His son, a lieutenant
in his regiment, stooping to raise the body of his
father, was shot dead in turn. Young Shirley,
Braddock's secretary, was pierced through the brain.
Orme and Morris, his aides-de-camp, Sinclair, the
quartermaster-general, Gates and Gage, both afterwards conspicuous on opposite sides in the War of
the Revolution, and Gladwin, who, eight years later,
defended Detroit against Pontiac, were all wounded.
Of eighty-six officers, sixty-three were killed or disabled;[2] while out of thirteen hundred and seventy-

[1] *Leslie to a Merchant of Philadelphia*, 30 *July*, 1755, in *Hazard's*
Pennsylvania Register, v. 191. Leslie was a lieutenant of the Forty-
fourth.

[2] *A List of the Officers who were present, and of those killed and*

three non-commissioned officers and privates, only four hundred and fifty-nine came off unharmed.[1]

Braddock saw that all was lost. To save the wreck of his force from annihilation, he at last commanded a retreat; and as he and such of his officers as were left strove to withdraw the half-frenzied crew in some semblance of order, a bullet struck him down. The gallant bulldog fell from his horse, shot through the arm into the lungs. It is said, though on evidence of no weight, that the bullet came from one of his own men. Be this as it may, there he lay among the bushes, bleeding, gasping, unable even to curse. He demanded to be left where he was. Captain Stewart and another provincial bore him between them to the rear.

It was about this time that the mob of soldiers, having been three hours under fire, and having spent their ammunition, broke away in a blind frenzy, rushed back towards the ford, "and when," says Washington, "we endeavored to rally them, it was with as much success as if we had attempted to stop the wild bears of the mountains." They dashed across, helter-skelter, plunging through the water to the farther bank, leaving wounded comrades, cannon,

wounded, in the Action on the Banks of the Monongahela, 9 July, 1755 (Public Record Office, _America and West Indies_, lxxxii).

[1] Statement of the engineer, Mackellar. By another account, out of a total, officers and men, of 1,460, the number of all ranks who escaped was 583. Braddock's force, originally 1,200, was increased, a few days before the battle, by detachments from Dunbar.

baggage, the military chest, and the general's papers,
a prey to the Indians. About fifty of these followed
to the edge of the river. Dumas and Ligneris, who
had now only about twenty Frenchmen with them,
made no attempt to pursue, and went back to the
fort, because, says Contrecœur, so many of the
Canadians had "retired at the first fire." The field,
abandoned to the savages, was a pandemonium of
pillage and murder.[1]

James Smith, the young prisoner at Fort Duquesne,

[1] "Nous prîmes le parti de nous retirer en vue de rallier notre
petite armée." — *Dumas au Ministre*, 24 *Juillet*, 1756.

On the defeat of Braddock, besides authorities already cited, —
Shirley to Robinson, 5 *November*, 1755, accompanying the plans of
the battle reproduced in this volume (Public Record Office, *America
and West Indies*, lxxxii.). The plans were drawn at Shirley's request
by Patrick Mackellar, chief engineer of the expedition, who was
with Gage in the advance column when the fight began. They were
examined and fully approved by the chief surviving officers, and
they closely correspond with another plan made by the aide-de-
camp Orme, — which, however, shows only the beginning of the
affair.

*Report of the Court of Inquiry into the Behavior of the Troops at the
Monongahela. Letters of Dinwiddie. Letters of Gage. Burd to Morris*, 25 *July*, 1755. *Sinclair to Robinson*, 3 *September*. *Rutherford to
——, 12 July. Writings of Washington*, ii. 68–93. *Review of Military Operations in North America*. Entick, i. 145. *Gentleman's
Magazine* (1755), 378, 426. *Letter to a Friend on the Ohio Defeat*
(Boston, 1755).

Contrecœur à Vaudreuil, 14 *Juillet*, 1755. *Estat de l'Artillerie, etc.,
qui se sont trouvés sur la Champ de Bataille. Vaudreuil au Ministre*,
5 *Août*, 1755. *Bigot au Ministre*, 27 *Août*. *Relation du Combat du
9 Juillet. Relation depuis le Départ des Trouppes de Québec jusqu'au
30 du Mois de Septembre. Lotbinière à d'Argenson*, 24 *Octobre*. *Relation officielle imprimée au Louvre. Relation de Godefroy* (Shea). *Ex-
traits du Registre du Fort Duquesne (Ibid.). Relation de diverses
Mouvements (Ibid.).* Pouchot, i. 37.

had passed a day of suspense, waiting the result. "In the afternoon I again observed a great noise and commotion in the fort, and, though at that time I could not understand French, I found it was the voice of joy and triumph, and feared that they had received what I called bad news. I had observed some of the old-country soldiers speak Dutch; as I spoke Dutch, I went to one of them and asked him what was the news. He told me that a runner had just arrived who said that Braddock would certainly be defeated; that the Indians and French had surrounded him, and were concealed behind trees and in gullies, and kept a constant fire upon the English; and that they saw the English falling in heaps; and if they did not take the river, which was the only gap, and make their escape, there would not be one man left alive before sundown. Some time after this, I heard a number of scalp-halloos, and saw a company of Indians and French coming in. I observed they had a great number of bloody scalps, grenadiers' caps, British canteens, bayonets, etc., with them. They brought the news that Braddock was defeated. After that another company came in, which appeared to be about one hundred, and chiefly Indians; and it seemed to me that almost every one of this company was carrying scalps. After this came another company with a number of wagon-horses, and also a great many scalps. Those that were coming in and those that had arrived kept a constant firing of small arms, and also the great

guns in the fort, which were accompanied with the
most hideous shouts and yells from all quarters, so
that it appeared to me as though the infernal regions
had broke loose.

"About sundown I beheld a small party coming in
with about a dozen prisoners, stripped naked, with
their hands tied behind their backs and their faces
and part of their bodies blacked; these prisoners they
burned to death on the bank of Alleghany River,
opposite the fort. I stood on the fort wall until I
beheld them begin to burn one of these men; they
had him tied to a stake, and kept touching him with
firebrands, red-hot irons, etc., and he screaming in a
most doleful manner, the Indians in the meantime
yelling like infernal spirits. As this scene appeared
too shocking for me to behold, I retired to my lodging, both sore and sorry. When I came into my
lodgings I saw Russel's *Seven Sermons*, which they
had brought from the field of battle, which a Frenchman made a present of to me."

The loss of the French was slight, but fell chiefly
on the officers, three of whom were killed, and four
wounded. Of the regular soldiers, all but four
escaped untouched. The Canadians suffered still
less, in proportion to their numbers, only five of
them being hurt. The Indians, who won the victory,
bore the principal loss. Of those from Canada,
twenty-seven were killed and wounded; while the
casualties among the western tribes are not reported.[1]

[1] *Liste des Officiers, Soldats, Miliciens, et Sauvages de Canada qui
ont été tués et blessés le 9 Juillet, 1755.*

All of these last went off the next morning with their plunder and scalps, leaving Contrecœur in great anxiety lest the remnant of Braddock's troops, reinforced by the division under Dunbar, should attack him again. His doubts would have vanished had he known the condition of his defeated enemy.

In the pain and languor of a mortal wound, Braddock showed unflinching resolution. His bearers stopped with him at a favorable spot beyond the Monongahela; and here he hoped to maintain his position till the arrival of Dunbar. By the efforts of the officers about a hundred men were collected around him; but to keep them there was impossible. Within an hour they abandoned him, and fled like the rest. Gage, however, succeeded in rallying about eighty beyond the other fording-place; and Washington, on an order from Braddock, spurred his jaded horse towards the camp of Dunbar to demand wagons, provisions, and hospital stores.

Fright overcame fatigue. The fugitives toiled on all night, pursued by spectres of horror and despair; hearing still the war-whoops and the shrieks; possessed with the one thought of escape from this wilderness of death. In the morning some order was restored. Braddock was placed on a horse; then, the pain being insufferable, he was carried on a litter, Captain Orme having bribed the carriers by the promise of a guinea and a bottle of rum apiece. Early in the succeeding night, such as had not fainted on the way reached the deserted farm of Gist. Here

they met wagons and provisions, with a detachment
of soldiers sent by Dunbar, whose camp was six
miles farther on; and Braddock ordered them to go
to the relief of the stragglers left behind.

At noon of that day a number of wagoners and
pack-horse drivers had come to Dunbar's camp with
wild tidings of rout and ruin. More fugitives followed; and soon after a wounded officer was brought
in upon a sheet. The drums beat to arms. The
camp was in commotion; and many soldiers and
teamsters took to flight, in spite of the sentinels,
who tried in vain to stop them.[1] There was a still
more disgraceful scene on the next day, after Braddock, with the wreck of his force, had arrived.
Orders were given to destroy such of the wagons,
stores, and ammunition as could not be carried back
at once to Fort Cumberland. Whether Dunbar or
the dying general gave these orders is not clear; but
it is certain that they were executed with shameful
alacrity. More than a hundred wagons were burned;
cannon, coehorns, and shells were burst or buried;
barrels of gunpowder were staved, and the contents
thrown into a brook; provisions were scattered
through the woods and swamps. Then the whole
command began its retreat over the mountains to
Fort Cumberland, sixty miles distant. This proceeding, for which, in view of the condition of
Braddock, Dunbar must be held answerable, excited

[1] *Depositions of Matthew Laird, Michael Hoover, and Jacob Hoover*
Wagoners, in *Colonial Records of Pa.*, vi. 482.

the utmost indignation among the colonists. If he could not advance, they thought, he might at least have fortified himself and held his ground till the provinces could send him help; thus covering the frontier, and holding French war-parties in check.

Braddock's last moment was near. Orme, who, though himself severely wounded, was with him till his death, told Franklin that he was totally silent all the first day, and at night said only, "Who would have thought it?" that all the next day he was again silent, till at last he muttered, "We shall better know how to deal with them another time," and died a few minutes after. He had nevertheless found breath to give orders at Gist's for the succor of the men who had dropped on the road. It is said, too, that in his last hours "he could not bear the sight of a red coat," but murmured praises of "the blues," or Virginians, and said that he hoped he should live to reward them.[1] He died at about eight o'clock in the evening of Sunday, the thirteenth. Dunbar had begun his retreat that morning, and was then encamped near the Great Meadows. On Monday the dead commander was buried in the road; and men, horses, and wagons passed over his grave, effacing every sign of it, lest the Indians should find and mutilate the body.

Colonel James Innes, commanding at Fort Cumberland, where a crowd of invalids with soldiers'

[1] *Bolling to his Son*, 13 *August*, 1755. Bolling was a Virginian gentleman whose son was at school in England.

wives and other women had been left when the
expedition marched, heard of the defeat, only two
days after it happened, from a wagoner who had fled
from the field on horseback. He at once sent a note
of six lines to Lord Fairfax: "I have this moment
received the most melancholy news of the defeat of
our troops, the General killed, and numbers of our
officers; our whole artillery taken. In short, the account I have received is so very bad, that as, please
God, I intend to make a stand here, 'tis highly
necessary to raise the militia everywhere to defend
the frontiers." A boy whom he sent out on horseback met more fugitives, and came back on the fourteenth with reports as vague and disheartening as
the first. Innes sent them to Dinwiddie.[1] Some
days after, Dunbar and his train arrived in miserable
disorder, and Fort Cumberland was turned into a
hospital for the shattered fragments of a routed and
ruined army.

On the sixteenth a letter was brought in haste to
one Buchanan at Carlisle, on the Pennsylvanian
frontier: —

SIR, — I thought it proper to let you know that I was
in the battle where we were defeated. And we had about
eleven hundred and fifty private men, besides officers and
others. And we were attacked the ninth day about twelve
o'clock, and held till about three in the afternoon, and
then we were forced to retreat, when I suppose we might
bring off about three hundred whole men, besides a vast

[1] *Innes to Dinwiddie,* 14 *July,* 1755.

many wounded.   Most of our officers were either wounded
or killed; General Braddock is wounded, but I hope not
mortal ; and Sir John Sinclair and many others, but I
hope not mortal.   All the train is cut off in a manner.
Sir Peter Halket and his son, Captain Polson, Captain
Gethen, Captain Rose, Captain Tatten killed, and many
others.   Captain Ord of the train is wounded, but I hope
not mortal. We lost all our artillery entirely, and everything else.

To Mr. John Smith and Buchannon, and give it to the
next post, and let him show this to Mr. George Gibson in
Lancaster, and Mr. Bingham, at the sign of the Ship, and
you 'll oblige,

Yours to command,

JOHN CAMPBELL, *Messenger.*[1]

The evil tidings quickly reached Philadelphia,
where such confidence had prevailed that certain
over-zealous persons had begun to collect money for
fireworks to celebrate the victory.   Two of these,
brother physicians named Bond, came to Franklin
and asked him to subscribe; but the sage looked
doubtful.   " Why, the devil! " said one of them,
"you surely don't suppose the fort will not be
taken?"   He reminded them that war is always
uncertain; and the subscription was deferred.[2]   The
governor laid the news of the disaster before his
Council, telling them at the same time that his opponents in the Assembly would not believe it, and had
insulted him in the street for giving it currency.[3]

[1] *Colonial Records of Pa.,* vi. 481.
[2] *Autobiography of Franklin.*
[3] *Colonial Records of Pa.,* vi. 480.

Dinwiddie remained tranquil at Williamsburg, sure that all would go well. The brief note of Innes, forwarded by Lord Fairfax, first disturbed his dream of triumph; but on second thought he took comfort. "I am willing to think that account was from a deserter who, in a great panic, represented what his fears suggested. I wait with impatience for another express from Fort Cumberland, which I expect will greatly contradict the former." The news got abroad, and the slaves showed signs of excitement. "The villany of the negroes on any emergency is what I always feared," continues the governor. "An example of one or two at first may prevent these creatures entering into combinations and wicked designs."[1] And he wrote to Lord Halifax: "The negro slaves have been very audacious on the news of defeat on the Ohio. These poor creatures imagine the French will give them their freedom. We have too many here; but I hope we shall be able to keep them in proper subjection." Suspense grew intolerable. "It's monstrous they should be so tardy and dilatory in sending down any farther account." He sent Major Colin Campbell for news; when, a day or two later, a courier brought him two letters, one from Orme, and the other from Washington, both written at Fort Cumberland on the eighteenth. The letter of Orme began thus: "My dear Governor, I am so extremely ill in bed with the wound I have received that I am under the necessity

[1] *Dinwiddie to Colonel Charles Carter, 18 July, 1755.*

of employing my friend Captain Dobson as my
scribe." Then he told the wretched story of defeat
and humiliation. "The officers were absolutely sac-
rificed by their unparalleled good behavior; advancing
before their men sometimes in bodies, and sometimes
separately, hoping by such an example to engage the
soldiers to follow them; but to no purpose. Poor
Shirley was shot through the head, Captain Morris
very much wounded. Mr. Washington had two
horses shot under him, and his clothes shot through
in several places; behaving the whole time with the
greatest courage and resolution."

Washington wrote more briefly, saying that, as
Orme was giving a full account of the affair, it was
needless for him to repeat it. Like many others in
the fight, he greatly underrated the force of the
enemy, which he placed at three hundred, or about a
third of the actual number, — a natural error, as most
of the assailants were invisible. "Our poor Virginians
behaved like men, and died like soldiers; for I
believe that out of three companies that were there
that day, scarce thirty were left alive. Captain
Peronney and all his officers down to a corporal were
killed. Captain Polson shared almost as hard a fate,
for only one of his escaped. In short, the das-
tardly behavior of the English soldiers exposed all
those who were inclined to do their duty to almost
certain death. It is imagined (I believe with great
justice, too) that two thirds of both killed and
wounded received their shots from our own cowardly

dogs of soldiers, who gathered themselves into a body, contrary to orders, ten and twelve deep, would then level, fire, and shoot down the men before them."[1]

To Orme, Dinwiddie replied: "I read your letter with tears in my eyes; but it gave me much pleasure to see your name at the bottom, and more so when I observed by the postscript that your wound is not dangerous. But pray, dear sir, is it not possible by a second attempt to retrieve the great loss we have sustained? I presume the General's chariot is at the fort. In it you may come here, and my house is heartily at your command. Pray take care of your valuable health; keep your spirits up, and I doubt not of your recovery. My wife and girls join me in most sincere respects and joy at your being so well, and I always am, with great truth, dear friend, your affectionate humble servant."

To Washington he is less effusive, though he had known him much longer. He begins, it is true, "Dear Washington," and congratulates him on his escape; but soon grows formal, and asks: "Pray, sir, with the number of them remaining, is there no possibility of doing something on the other side of the mountains before the winter months? Surely you must mistake. Colonel Dunbar will not march to winter-quarters in the middle of summer, and leave the frontiers exposed to the invasions of the

[1] These extracts are taken from the two letters preserved in the Public Record Office, *America and West Indies*, lxxiv., lxxxii.

enemy! No; he is a better officer, and I have a different opinion of him. I sincerely wish you health and happiness, and am, with great respect, sir, your obedient, humble servant."

Washington's letter had contained the astonishing announcement that Dunbar meant to abandon the frontier and march to Philadelphia. Dinwiddie, much disturbed, at once wrote to that officer, though without betraying any knowledge of his intention. "Sir, the melancholy account of the defeat of our forces gave me a sensible and real concern " — on which he enlarges for a while; then suddenly changes style: "Dear Colonel, is there no method left to retrieve the dishonor done to the British arms? As you now command all the forces that remain, are you not able, after a proper refreshment of your men, to make a second attempt? You have four months now to come of the best weather of the year for such an expedition. What a fine field for honor will Colonel Dunbar have to confirm and establish his character as a brave officer." Then, after suggesting plans of operation, and entering into much detail, the fervid governor concludes: "It gives me great pleasure that under our great loss and misfortunes the command devolves on an officer of so great military judgment and established character. With my sincere respect and hearty wishes for success to all your proceedings, I am, worthy sir, your most obedient, humble servant."

Exhortation and flattery were lost on Dunbar. Dinwiddie received from him in reply a short, dry note, dated on the first of August, and acquainting him that he should march for Philadelphia on the second. This, in fact, he did, leaving the fort to be defended by invalids and a few Virginians. "I acknowledge," says Dinwiddie, "I was not brought up to arms; but I think common sense would have prevailed not to leave the frontiers exposed after having opened a road over the mountains to the Ohio, by which the enemy can the more easily invade us. . . . Your great colonel," he writes to Orme, "is gone to a peaceful colony, and left our frontiers open. . . . The whole conduct of Colonel Dunbar appears to me monstrous. . . . To march off all the regulars, and leave the fort and frontiers to be defended by four hundred sick and wounded, and the poor remains of our provincial forces, appears to me absurd."[1]

He found some comfort from the burgesses, who gave him forty thousand pounds, and would, he thinks, have given a hundred thousand if another attempt against Fort Duquesne had been set afoot. Shirley, too, whom the death of Braddock had made commander-in-chief, approved the governor's plan of renewing offensive operations, and instructed Dunbar to that effect; ordering him, however, should they prove impracticable, to march for Albany in aid of the Niagara expedition.[2] The order found him safe

---

[1] Dinwiddie's view of Dunbar's conduct is fully justified by the letters of Shirley, Governor Morris, and Dunbar himself.

[2] *Orders for Colonel Thomas Dunbar*, 12 *August*, 1755. These

in Philadelphia. Here he lingered for a while; then marched to join the northern army, moving at a pace which made it certain that he could not arrive in time to be of the least use.

Thus the frontier was left unguarded; and soon, as Dinwiddie had foreseen, there burst upon it a storm of blood and fire.

supersede a previous order of August 6, by which Shirley had directed Dunbar to march northward at once.

CHAPTER VIII.

1755.

REMOVAL OF THE ACADIANS.

STATE OF ACADIA. — THREATENED INVASION. — PERIL OF THE ENG-
LISH: THEIR PLANS. — FRENCH FORTS TO BE ATTACKED. —
BEAUSÉJOUR AND ITS OCCUPANTS. — FRENCH TREATMENT OF THE
ACADIANS. — JOHN WINSLOW. — SIEGE AND CAPTURE OF BEAUSÉ-
JOUR. — ATTITUDE OF ACADIANS. — INFLUENCE OF THEIR PRIESTS:
THEY REFUSE THE OATH OF ALLEGIANCE; THEIR CONDITION
AND CHARACTER. — PRETENDED NEUTRALS. — MODERATION OF
ENGLISH AUTHORITIES. — THE ACADIANS PERSIST IN THEIR
REFUSAL. — ENEMIES OR SUBJECTS ? — CHOICE OF THE ACADI-
ANS. — THE CONSEQUENCE. — THEIR REMOVAL DETERMINED. —
WINSLOW AT GRAND PRÉ. — CONFERENCE WITH MURRAY. —
SUMMONS TO THE INHABITANTS: THEIR SEIZURE; THEIR
EMBARKATION; THEIR FATE; THEIR TREATMENT IN CANADA.
MISAPPREHENSION CONCERNING THEM.

BY the plan which the Duke of Cumberland had
ordained and Braddock had announced in the Council
at Alexandria, four blows were to be struck at once
to force back the French boundaries, lop off the
dependencies of Canada, and reduce her from a vast
territory to a petty province. The first stroke had
failed, and had shattered the hand of the striker; it
remains to see what fortune awaited the others.

It was long since a project of purging Acadia of
French influence had germinated in the fertile mind
of Shirley. We have seen in a former chapter the

condition of that afflicted province. Several thousands of its inhabitants, wrought upon by intriguing
agents of the French government; taught by their
priests that fidelity to King Louis was inseparable
from fidelity to God, and that to swear allegiance to
the British Crown was eternal perdition; threatened
with plunder and death at the hands of the savages
whom the ferocious missionary, Le Loutre, held over
them in terror, — had abandoned, sometimes willingly,
but oftener under constraint, the fields which they
and their fathers had tilled, and crossing the boundary
line of the Missaguash, had placed themselves under
the French flag planted on the hill of Beauséjour.[1]
Here, or in the neighborhood, many of them had
remained, wretched and half starved; while others
had been transported to Cape Breton, Isle St.
Jean, or the coasts of the Gulf, — not so far, however, that they could not on occasion be used to aid
in an invasion of British Acadia.[2] Those of their
countrymen who still lived under the British flag
were chiefly the inhabitants of the district of Mines
and of the valley of the river Annapolis, who, with

[1] See *ante*, Chapter IV.

[2] Rameau (*La France aux Colonies*, i. 63) estimates the total
emigration from 1748 to 1755 at 8,600 souls, — which number seems
much too large. This writer, though vehemently anti-English,
gives the following passage from a letter of a high French official:
"que les Acadiens émigrés et en grande misère comptaient se retirer
à Québec et demander des terres, mais il conviendrait mieux qu'ils
restent où ils sont, afin d'avoir le voisinage de l'Acadie bien peuplé
et défriché, pour approvisionner l'Isle Royale [*Cape Breton*] et
tomber en cas de guerre sur l'Acadie." Rameau, i. 133.

other less important settlements, numbered a little
more than nine thousand souls. We have shown
already, by the evidence of the French themselves,
that neither they nor their emigrant countrymen had
been oppressed or molested in matters temporal or
spiritual, but that the English authorities, recogniz-
ing their value as an industrious population, had
labored to reconcile them to a change of rulers which
on the whole was to their advantage. It has been
shown also how, with a heartless perfidy and a reckless disregard of their welfare and safety, the French
government and its agents labored to keep them
hostile to the Crown of which it had acknowledged
them to be subjects. The result was, that though
they did not, like their emigrant countrymen, abandon
their homes, they remained in a state of restless disaffection, refused to supply English garrisons with
provisions, except at most exorbitant rates, smuggled
their produce to the French across the line, gave
them aid and intelligence, and sometimes, disguised
as Indians, robbed and murdered English settlers.
By the new-fangled construction of the treaty of
Utrecht which the French boundary commissioners
had devised,[1] more than half the Acadian peninsula,
including nearly all the cultivated land and nearly all
the population of French descent, was claimed as
belonging to France, though England had held possession of it more than forty years. Hence, according to the political ethics adopted at the time by

[1] *Supra*, p. 128.

both nations, it would be lawful for France to reclaim
it by force. England, on her part, it will be remembered, claimed vast tracts beyond the isthmus; and,
on the same pretext, held that she might rightfully
seize them and capture Beauséjour, with the other
French garrisons that guarded them.

On the part of France, an invasion of the Acadian
peninsula seemed more than likely. Honor demanded
of her that, having incited the Acadians to disaffection, and so brought on them the indignation of the
English authorities, she should intervene to save
them from the consequences. Moreover, the loss of
the Acadian peninsula had been gall and wormwood
to her; and in losing it she had lost great material
advantages. Its possession was necessary to connect
Canada with the Island of Cape Breton and the
fortress of Louisbourg. Its fertile fields and agri-
cultural people would furnish subsistence to the
troops and garrisons in the French maritime provinces, now dependent on supplies illicitly brought by
New England traders, and liable to be cut off in time
of war when they were needed most. The harbors
of Acadia, too, would be invaluable as naval stations
from which to curb and threaten the northern English colonies. Hence the intrigues so assiduously
practised to keep the Acadians French at heart, and
ready to throw off British rule at any favorable
moment. British officers believed that should a
French squadron with a sufficient force of troops on
board appear in the Bay of Fundy, the whole popu-

lation on the Basin of Mines and along the Annapolis
would rise in arms, and that the emigrants beyond
the isthmus, armed and trained by French officers,
would come to their aid. This emigrant population,
famishing in exile, looked back with regret to the
farms they had abandoned; and, prevented as they
were by Le Loutre and his colleagues from making
their peace with the English, they would, if confident
of success, have gladly joined an invading force to
regain their homes by reconquering Acadia for Louis
XV. In other parts of the continent it was the
interest of France to put off hostilities; if Acadia
alone had been in question, it would have been her
interest to precipitate them.

Her chances of success were good. The French
could at any time send troops from Louisbourg or
Quebec to join those maintained upon the isthmus;
and they had on their side of the lines a force of
militia and Indians amounting to about two thousand, while the Acadians within the peninsula had
about an equal number of fighting men who, while
calling themselves neutrals, might be counted on to
join the invaders. The English were in no condition
to withstand such an attack. Their regular troops
were scattered far and wide through the province,
and were nowhere more than equal to the local
requirement; while of militia, except those of Halifax,
they had few or none whom they dared to trust.
Their fort at Annapolis was weak and dilapidated,
and their other posts were mere stockades. The

strongest place in Acadia was the French fort of
Beauséjour, in which the English saw a continual
menace.

Their apprehensions were well grounded. Duquesne, governor of Canada, wrote to Le Loutre,
who virtually shared the control of Beauséjour with
Vergor, its commandant: "I invite both yourself
and M. Vergor to devise a plausible pretext for
attacking them [*the English*] vigorously." [1] Three
weeks after this letter was written, Lawrence, governor of Nova Scotia, wrote to Shirley from Halifax:
"Being well informed that the French have designs
of encroaching still farther upon His Majesty's rights
in this province, and that they propose, the moment
they have repaired the fortifications of Louisbourg,
to attack our fort at Chignecto [*Fort Lawrence*], I
think it high time to make some effort to drive them
from the north side of the Bay of Fundy." [2] This
letter was brought to Boston by Lieutenant-Colonel
Monckton, who was charged by Lawrence to propose
to Shirley the raising of two thousand men in New
England for the attack of Beauséjour and its dependent forts. Almost at the moment when Lawrence
was writing these proposals to Shirley, Shirley was
writing with the same object to Lawrence, enclosing
a letter from Sir Thomas Robinson, concerning which
he said: "I construe the contents to be orders to us

[1] *Duquesne à Le Loutre,* 15 *Octobre,* 1754; extract in *Public Documents of Nova Scotia,* 239.

[2] *Lawrence to Shirley,* 5 *November,* 1754. *Instructions of Lawrence
to Monckton,* 7 *November,* 1754.

to act in concert for taking *any* advantages to drive
the French of Canada out of Nova Scotia. If that is
your sense of them, and your honor will be pleased
to let me know whether you want any and what
assistance to enable you to execute the orders, I will
endeavor to send you such assistance from this
province as you shall want." [1]

The letter of Sir Thomas Robinson, of which a
duplicate had already been sent to Lawrence, was
written in answer to one of Shirley informing the
minister that the Indians of Nova Scotia, prompted
by the French, were about to make an attack on all
the English settlements east of the Kennebec;
whereupon Robinson wrote: "You will without
doubt have given immediate intelligence thereof to
Colonel Lawrence, and will have concerted the proper-
est measures with him for taking all possible advantage in Nova Scotia itself from the absence of those
Indians, in case Mr. Lawrence shall have force
enough to attack the forts erected by the French in
those parts, without exposing the English settlements; and I am particularly to acquaint you that
if you have not already entered into such a concert
with Colonel Lawrence, it is His Majesty's pleasure
that you should immediately proceed thereupon." [2]

The Indian raid did not take place; but not the
less did Shirley and Lawrence find in the minister's
letter their authorization for the attack of Beauséjour.

[1] *Shirley to Lawrence, 7 November, 1754.*
[2] *Robinson to Shirley, 5 July, 1754.*

by force of energy, capacity, and passionate vehemence, held him in some awe, and divided his authority. The priest could count on the support of
Duquesne, who had found, says a contemporary,
that "he promised more than he could perform, and
that he was a knave," but who nevertheless felt
compelled to rely upon him for keeping the Acadians
on the side of France. There was another person in
the fort worthy of notice. This was Thomas Pichon,
commissary of stores, a man of education and intelligence, born in France of an English mother. He
was now acting the part of a traitor, carrying on a
secret correspondence with the commandant of Fort
Lawrence, and acquainting him with all that passed
at Beauséjour. It was partly from this source that
the hostile designs of the French became known to
the authorities of Halifax, and more especially the
proceedings of "Moses," by which name Pichon
always designated Le Loutre, because he pretended
to have led the Acadians from the land of bondage.[1]

These exiles, who cannot be called self-exiled, in
view of the outrageous means used to force most of
them from their homes, were in a deplorable condition. They lived in constant dread of Le Loutre,
backed by Vergor and his soldiers. The savage missionary, bad as he was, had in him an ingredient of

[1] Pichon, called also Tyrrell from the name of his mother, was
author of *Genuine Letters and Memoirs relating to Cape Breton*, — a
book of some value. His papers are preserved at Halifax, and
some of them are printed in the *Public Documents of Nova Scotia*.

honest fanaticism, both national and religious; though hatred of the English held a large share in it. He would gladly, if he could, have formed the Acadians into a permanent settlement on the French side of the line, not out of love for them, but in the interest of the cause with which he had identified his own ambition. His efforts had failed. There was not land enough for their subsistence and that of the older settlers; and the suffering emigrants pined more and more for their deserted farms. Thither he was resolved that they should not return. "If you go," he told them, "you will have neither priests nor sacraments, but will die like miserable wretches."[1] The assertion was false. Priests and sacraments had never been denied them. It is true that Daudin, priest of Pisiquid, had lately been sent to Halifax for using insolent language to the commandant, threatening him with an insurrection of the inhabitants, and exciting them to sedition; but on his promise to change conduct, he was sent back to his parishioners.[2] Vergor sustained Le Loutre, and threatened to put in irons any of the exiles who talked of going back to the English. Some of them bethought themselves of an appeal to Duquesne, and drew up a petition asking leave to return home. Le Loutre told the signers that if they did not efface their marks from the paper they should have neither

[1] *Pichon to Captain Scott,* 14 *October,* 1754, in *Public Documents of Nova Scotia,* 229.

[2] *Public Documents of Nova Scotia,* 223, 224, 226, 227, 238.

Saturday the following mandate went forth: "The men will behave very orderly on the Sabbath Day, and either stay on board their transports, or else go to church, and not stroll up and down the streets." The transports, consisting of about forty sloops and schooners, lay at Long Wharf; and here on Monday a grand review took place, — to the gratification, no doubt, of a populace whose amusements were few. All was ready except the muskets, which were expected from England, but did not come. Hence the delay of a month, threatening to ruin the enterprise. When Shirley returned from Alexandria he found, to his disgust, that the transports still lay at the wharf where he had left them on his departure.[1] The muskets arrived at length, and the fleet sailed on the twenty-second of May. Three small frigates, the "Success," the "Mermaid," and the "Siren," commanded by the ex-privateersman, Captain Rous, acted as convoy; and on the twenty-sixth the whole force safely reached Annapolis. Thence after some delay they sailed up the Bay of Fundy, and at sunset on the first of June anchored within five miles of the hill of Beauséjour.

At two o'clock on the next morning a party of Acadians from Chipody roused Vergor with the news. In great alarm, he sent a messenger to Louisbourg to beg for help, and ordered all the fighting men of the neighborhood to repair to the fort. They counted in

[1] *Shirley to Robinson*, 20 *June*, 1755.

all between twelve and fifteen hundred;[1] but they
had no appetite for war. The force of the invaders
daunted them; and the hundred and sixty regulars
who formed the garrison of Beauséjour were too few
to revive their confidence. Those of them who had
crossed from the English side dreaded what might
ensue should they be caught in arms; and, to prepare
an excuse beforehand, they begged Vergor to threaten
them with punishment if they disobeyed his order.
He willingly complied, promised to have them killed
if they did not fight, and assured them at the same
time that the English could never take the fort.[2]
Three hundred of them thereupon joined the garrison, and the rest, hiding their families in the woods,
prepared to wage guerilla war against the invaders.

Monckton, with all his force, landed unopposed,
and encamped at night on the fields around Fort
Lawrence, whence he could contemplate Fort Beauséjour at his ease. The regulars of the English garrison joined the New England men; and then, on
the morning of the fourth, they marched to the
attack. Their course lay along the south bank of
the Missaguash to where it was crossed by a bridge
called Pont-à-Buot. This bridge had been destroyed;
and on the farther bank there was a large blockhouse and a breastwork of timber defended by four

[1] *Mémoires sur le Canada,* 1749–1760. An English document,
State of the English and French Forts in Nova Scotia, says 1,200 to
1,400.

[2] *Mémoires sur le Canada,* 1749–1760.

hundred regulars, Acadians, and Indians. They
lay silent and unseen till the head of the column
reached the opposite bank; then raised a yell and
opened fire, causing some loss. Three field-pieces
were brought up, the defenders were driven out, and
a bridge was laid under a spattering fusillade from
behind bushes, which continued till the English had
crossed the stream. Without further opposition,
they marched along the road to Beauséjour, and,
turning to the right, encamped among the woody
hills half a league from the fort. That night there
was a grand illumination, for Vergor set fire to the
church and all the houses outside the ramparts.[1]

The English spent some days in preparing their
camp and reconnoitring the ground. Then Scott,
with five hundred provincials, seized upon a ridge
within easy range of the works. An officer named
Vannes came out to oppose him with a hundred and
eighty men, boasting that he would do great things;
but on seeing the enemy, quietly returned, to become
the laughing-stock of the garrison. The fort fired
furiously, but with little effect. In the night of the
thirteenth, Winslow, with a part of his own battalion,
relieved Scott, and planted in the trenches two small
mortars, brought to the camp on carts. On the next
day they opened fire. One of them was disabled by
the French cannon, but Captain Hazen brought up

[1] Winslow, *Journal and Letter Book*. *Mémoires sur le Canada*,
1749–1760. Letters from officers on the spot in *Boston Evening Post*
and *Boston News Letter*. *Journal of Surgeon John Thomas*.

two more, of larger size, on ox-wagons; and, in spite of heavy rain, the fire was brisk on both sides.

Captain Rous, on board his ship in the harbor, watched the bombardment with great interest. Having occasion to write to Winslow, he closed his letter in a facetious strain. "I often hear of your success in plunder, particularly a coach.[1] I hope you have some fine horses for it, at least four, to draw it, that it may be said a New England colonel [*rode in*] his coach and four in Nova Scotia. If you have any good saddle-horses in your stable, I should be obliged to you for one to ride round the ship's deck on for exercise, for I am not likely to have any other."

Within the fort there was little promise of a strong defence. Le Loutre, it is true, was to be seen in his shirt-sleeves, with a pipe in his mouth, directing the Acadians in their work of strengthening the fortifications.[2] They, on their part, thought more of escape than of fighting. Some of them vainly begged to be allowed to go home; others went off without leave, — which was not difficult, as only one side of the place was attacked. Even among the officers there were some in whom interest was stronger than honor, and who would rather rob the King than die for him. The general discouragement was redoubled when, on the fourteenth, a letter came from the commandant

[1] "11 June. Capt. Adams went with a Cómpany of Raingers, and Returned at 11 Clock with a Coach and Sum other Plunder." — *Journal of John Thomas.*

[2] *Journal of Pichon,* cited by Beamish Murdoch.

of Louisbourg to say that he could send no help, as British ships blocked the way. On the morning of the sixteenth, a mischance befell, recorded in these words in the Diary of Surgeon John Thomas: "One of our large shells fell through what they called their bomb-proof, where a number of their officers were sitting, killed six of them dead, and one Ensign Hay, which the Indians had took prisoner a few days agone and carried to the fort." The party was at breakfast when the unwelcome visitor burst in. Just opposite was a second bomb-proof, where was Vergor himself, with Le Loutre, another priest, and several officers, who felt that they might at any time share the same fate. The effect was immediate. The English, who had not yet got a single cannon into position, saw to their surprise a white flag raised on the rampart. Some officers of the garrison protested against surrender; and Le Loutre, who thought that he had everything to fear at the hands of the victors, exclaimed that it was better to be buried under the ruins of the fort than to give it up; but all was in vain, and the valiant Vannes was sent out to propose terms of capitulation. They were rejected, and others offered, to the following effect: the garrison to march out with the honors of war and to be sent to Louisbourg at the charge of the King of England, but not to bear arms in America for the space of six months; the Acadians to be pardoned the part they had just borne in the defence, "seeing that they had been compelled to take arms on pain of death."

Confusion reigned all day at Beauséjour. The
Acadians went home loaded with plunder. The
French officers were so busy in drinking and pillag-
ing that they could hardly be got away to sign the
capitulation. At the appointed hour, seven in the
evening, Scott marched in with a body of provincials,
raised the British flag on the ramparts, and saluted
it by a general discharge of the French cannon, while
Vergor as a last act of hospitality gave a supper to
the officers.[1]

Le Loutre was not to be found; he had escaped in
disguise with his box of papers, and fled to Baye
Verte to join his brother missionary, Manach.
Thence he made his way to Quebec, where the
bishop received him with reproaches. He soon
embarked for France; but the English captured him
on the way, and kept him eight years in Elizabeth
Castle, on the Island of Jersey. Here on one occasion a soldier on guard made a dash at the father,
tried to stab him with his bayonet, and was prevented
with great difficulty. He declared that, when he was
with his regiment in Acadia, he had fallen into the
hands of Le Loutre, and narrowly escaped being
scalped alive, the missionary having doomed him to
this fate, and with his own hand drawn a knife round
his head as a beginning of the operation. The man
swore so fiercely that he would have his revenge

[1] On the capture of Beauséjour, *Mémoires sur le Canada*, 1749–
1760; Pichon, *Cape Breton*, 318; *Journal of Pichon,* cited by Murdoch; and the English accounts already mentioned.

that the officer in command transferred him to another post.[1]

Throughout the siege, the Acadians outside the fort, aided by Indians, had constantly attacked the English, but were always beaten off with loss. There was an affair of this kind on the morning of the surrender, during which a noted Micmac chief was shot, and being brought into the camp, recounted the losses of his tribe; "after which, and taking a dram or two, he quickly died," writes Winslow in his Journal.

Fort Gaspereau, at Baye Verte, twelve miles distant, was summoned by letter to surrender. Villeray, its commandant, at once complied; and Winslow went with a detachment to take possession.[2] Nothing remained but to occupy the French post at the mouth of the St. John. Captain Rous, relieved at last from inactivity, was charged with the task; and on the thirtieth he appeared off the harbor, manned his boats, and rowed for shore. The French burned their fort, and withdrew beyond his reach.[3] A hundred and fifty Indians, suddenly converted from enemies to pretended friends, stood on the strand, firing their guns into the air as a salute, and declaring themselves brothers of the English. All Acadia was now in British hands. Fort Beauséjour

---

[1] Knox, *Campaigns in North America,* i. 114, *note.* Knox, who was stationed in Nova Scotia, says that Le Loutre left behind him "a most remarkable character for inhumanity."

[2] Winslow, *Journal. Villeray au Ministre,* 20 *Septembre,* 1755.

[3] *Drucour au Ministre,* 1 *Décembre,* 1755.

became Fort Cumberland, — the second fort in America that bore the name of the royal duke.

The defence had been of the feeblest. Two years later, on pressing demands from Versailles, Vergor was brought to trial, as was also Villeray. The governor, Vaudreuil, and the intendant, Bigot, who had returned to Canada, were in the interest of the chief defendant. The court-martial was packed; adverse evidence was shuffled out of sight; and Vergor, acquitted and restored to his rank, lived to inflict on New France another and a greater injury.[1]

Now began the first act of a deplorable drama. Monckton, with his small body of regulars, had pitched their tents under the walls of Beauséjour. Winslow and Scott, with the New England troops, lay not far off. There was little intercourse between the two camps. The British officers bore themselves towards those of the provincials with a supercilious coldness common enough on their part throughout the war. July had passed in what Winslow calls "an indolent manner," with prayers every day in the Puritan camp, when, early in August, Monckton sent for him, and made an ominous declaration. "The said Monckton was so free as to acquaint me that it was determined to remove all the French inhabitants out of the province, and that he should send for all the adult males from Tantemar, Chipody, Aulac, Beauséjour, and Baye Verte to read the Governor's

---

[1] *Mémoire sur les Fraudes commises dans la Colonie,* 1779. *Mémoires sur le Canada,* 1749–1760.

orders; and when that was done, was determined to
retain them all prisoners in the fort. And this is
the first conference of a public nature I have had
with the colonel since the reduction of Beauséjour;
and I apprehend that no officer of either corps has
been made more free with."

Monckton sent accordingly to all the neighboring
settlements, commanding the male inhabitants to
meet him at Beauséjour. Scarcely a third part of
their number obeyed. These arrived on the tenth,
and were told to stay all night under the guns of the
fort. What then befell them will appear from an
entry in the diary of Winslow under date of August
eleventh: "This day was one extraordinary to the
inhabitants of Tantemar, Oueskak, Aulac, Baye
Verte, Beauséjour, and places adjacent; the male
inhabitants, or the principal of them, being collected
together in Fort Cumberland to hear the sentence,
which determined their property, from the Governor
and Council of Halifax; which was that they were
declared rebels, their lands, goods, and chattels forfeited to the Crown, and their bodies to be imprisoned.
Upon which the gates of the fort were shut, and they
all confined, to the amount of four hundred men and
upwards." Parties were sent to gather more, but
caught very few, the rest escaping to the woods.

Some of the prisoners were no doubt among those
who had joined the garrison at Beauséjour, and had
been pardoned for doing so by the terms of the
capitulation. It was held, however, that, though

forgiven this special offence, they were not exempted
from the doom that had gone forth against the great
body of their countrymen. We must look closely at
the motives and execution of this stern sentence.

At any time up to the spring of 1755 the emigrant
Acadians were free to return to their homes on taking the ordinary oath of allegiance required of British
subjects. The English authorities of Halifax used
every means to persuade them to do so; yet the
greater part refused. This was due not only to Le
Loutre and his brother priests, backed by the military power, but also to the bishop of Quebec, who
enjoined the Acadians to demand of the English certain concessions, the chief of which were that the
priests should exercise their functions without being
required to ask leave of the governor, and that the
inhabitants should not be called upon for military
service of any kind. The bishop added that the
provisions of the treaty of Utrecht were insufficient,
and that others ought to be exacted.[1] The oral
declaration of the English authorities, that for the
present the Acadians should not be required to bear
arms, was not thought enough. They, or rather
their prompters, demanded a written pledge.

The refusal to take the oath without reservation
was not confined to the emigrants. Those who
remained in the peninsula equally refused it, though
most of them were born and had always lived under

[1] *L'Évêque de Québec à Le Loutre, Novembre,* 1754, in *Public Docu
ments of Nova Scotia,* 240.

the British flag. Far from pledging themselves to complete allegiance, they showed continual signs of hostility. In May three pretended French deserters were detected among them inciting them to take arms against the English.[1]

On the capture of Beauséjour the British authorities found themselves in a position of great difficulty. The New England troops were enlisted for the year only, and could not be kept in Acadia. It was likely that the French would make a strong effort to recover the province, sure as they were of support from the great body of its people. The presence of this disaffected population was for the French commanders a continual inducement to invasion; and Lawrence was not strong enough to cope at once with attack from without and insurrection from within.

Shirley had held for some time that there was no safety for Acadia but in ridding it of the Acadians. He had lately proposed that the lands of the district of Chignecto, abandoned by their emigrant owners, should be given to English settlers, who would act as a check and a counterpoise to the neighboring French population. This advice had not been acted upon. Nevertheless Shirley and his brother governor of Nova Scotia were kindred spirits, and inclined to similar measures. Colonel Charles Lawrence had not the good-nature and conciliatory temper which marked his predecessors, Cornwallis and Hopson. His energetic will was not apt to relent under the

[1] *L'Évêque de Québec à Le Loutre, Novembre*, 1754, in *Public Doc uments of Nova Scotia*, 242.

softer sentiments, and the behavior of the Acadians was fast exhausting his patience. More than a year before, the Lords of Trade had instructed him that they had no right to their lands if they persisted in refusing the oath.[1] Lawrence replied, enlarging on their obstinacy, treachery, and "ingratitude for the favor, indulgence, and protection they have at all times so undeservedly received from His Majesty's Government;" declaring at the same time that, "while they remain without taking the oaths, and have incendiary French priests among them, there are no hopes of their amendment;" and that "it would be much better, if they refuse the oaths, that they were away."[2] "We were in hopes," again wrote the Lords of Trade, "that the lenity which had been shown to those people by indulging them in the free exercise of their religion and the quiet possession of their lands, would by degrees have gained their friendship and assistance, and weaned their affections from the French; but we are sorry to find that this lenity has had so little effect, and that they still hold the same conduct, furnishing them with labor, provisions, and intelligence, and concealing their designs from us." In fact, the Acadians, while calling themselves neutrals, were an enemy encamped in the heart of the province. These are the reasons which explain and palliate a measure too harsh and indiscriminate to be wholly justified.

Abbé Raynal, who never saw the Acadians, has

---

[1] Lords of Trade to Lawrence, 4 March, 1754.
[2] Lawrence to Lords of Trade, 1 August, 1754.

made an ideal picture of them,[1] since copied and
improved in prose and verse, till Acadia has become
Arcadia. The plain realities of their condition and
fate are touching enough to need no exaggeration.
They were a simple and very ignorant peasantry,
industrious and frugal till evil days came to discourage them; living aloof from the world, with little of
that spirit of adventure which an easy access to the
vast fur-bearing interior had developed in their
Canadian kindred; having few wants, and those of
the rudest; fishing a little and hunting in the winter,
but chiefly employed in cultivating the meadows
along the river Annapolis, or rich marshes reclaimed
by dikes from the tides of the Bay of Fundy. The
British government left them entirely free of taxation. They made clothing of flax and wool of their
own raising, hats of similar materials, and shoes or
moccasons of moose and seal skin. They bred cattle,
sheep, hogs, and horses in abundance; and the valley
of the Annapolis, then as now, was known for the
profusion and excellence of its apples. For drink,
they made cider or brewed spruce-beer. French
officials describe their dwellings as wretched wooden
boxes, without ornaments or conveniences, and
scarcely supplied with the most necessary furniture.[2]
Two or more families often occupied the same house;
and their way of life, though simple and virtuous,

---

[1] *Histoire philosophique et politique*, vi. 242 (ed. 1772).
[2] *Beauharnois et Hocquart au Comte de Maurepas*, 12 *Septembre*,
1745.

was by no means remarkable for cleanliness. Such as it was, contentment reigned among them, undisturbed by what modern America calls progress. Marriages were early, and population grew apace. This humble society had its disturbing elements; for the Acadians, like the Canadians, were a litigious race, and neighbors often quarrelled about their boundaries. Nor were they without a bountiful share of jealousy, gossip, and backbiting, to relieve the monotony of their lives; and every village had its turbulent spirits, sometimes by fits, though rarely long, contumacious even toward the curé, the guide, counsellor, and ruler of his flock. Enfeebled by hereditary mental subjection, and too long kept in leading-strings to walk alone, they needed him, not for the next world only, but for this; and their submission, compounded of love and fear, was commonly without bounds. He was their true government; to him they gave a frank and full allegiance, and dared not disobey him if they would. Of knowledge he gave them nothing; but he taught them to be true to their wives and constant at confession and mass, to stand fast for the Church and King Louis, and to resist heresy and King George; for, in one degree or another, the Acadian priest was always the agent of a double-headed foreign power, — the bishop of Quebec allied with the governor of Canada.[1]

When Monckton and the Massachusetts men laid

[1] Franquet, *Journal*, 1751, says of the Acadians: " Ils aiment l'argent, n'ont dans toute leur conduite que leur intérêt pour objet,

siege to Beauséjour, Governor Lawrence thought the moment favorable for exacting an unqualified oath of allegiance from the Acadians. The presence of a superior and victorious force would help, he thought, to bring them to reason; and there were some indications that this would be the result. A number of Acadian families, who at the promptings of Le Loutre had emigrated to Cape Breton, had lately returned to Halifax, promising to be true subjects of King George if they could be allowed to repossess their lands. They cheerfully took the oath; on which they were reinstated in their old homes, and supplied with food for the winter.[1] Their example unfortunately found few imitators.

Early in June the principal inhabitants of Grand Pré and other settlements about the Basin of Mines brought a memorial, signed with their crosses, to Captain Murray, the military commandant in their district, and desired him to send it to Governor Lawrence, to whom it was addressed. Murray reported that when they brought it to him they behaved with the greatest insolence, though just before they had been unusually submissive. He thought that this change of demeanor was caused by a report which had lately got among them of a French fleet in the Bay of Fundy; for it had been observed

sont, indifféremment des deux sexes, d'une inconsidération dans leurs discours qui dénote de la méchanceté." Another observer, Dieréville, gives a more favorable picture.

[1] *Public Documents of Nova Scotia*, 228.

that any rumor of an approaching French force
always had a similar effect. The deputies who
brought the memorial were sent with it to Halifax,
where they laid it before the governor and Council.
It declared that the signers had kept the qualified
oath they had taken, "in spite of the solicitations
and dreadful threats of another power," and that they
would continue to prove "an unshaken fidelity to
His Majesty, provided that His Majesty shall allow
us the same liberty that he has [*hitherto*] granted
us." Their memorial then demanded, in terms
highly offensive to the Council, that the guns,
pistols, and other weapons, which they had lately
been required to give up, should be returned to
them. They were told in reply that they had
been protected for many years in the enjoyment of
their lands, though they had not complied with
the terms on which the lands were granted; "that
they had always been treated by the Government
with the greatest lenity and tenderness, had enjoyed more privileges than other English subjects,
and had been indulged in the free exercise of their
religion;" all which they acknowledged to be true.
The governor then told them that their conduct had
been undutiful and ungrateful; "that they had discovered a constant disposition to assist His Majesty's
enemies and to distress his subjects; that they had
not only furnished the enemy with provisions and
ammunition, but had refused to supply the [*English*]
inhabitants or Government, and when they did supply

them, had exacted three times the price for which they were sold at other markets." The hope was then expressed that they would no longer obstruct the settlement of the province by aiding the Indians to molest and kill English settlers; and they were rebuked for saying in their memorial that they would be faithful to the King only on certain conditions. The governor added that they had some secret reason for demanding their weapons, and flattered themselves that French troops were at hand to support their insolence. In conclusion, they were told that now was a good opportunity to prove their sincerity by taking the oath of allegiance, in the usual form, before the Council. They replied that they had not made up their minds on that point, and could do nothing till they had consulted their constituents. Being reminded that the oath was personal to themselves, and that six years had already been given them to think about it, they asked leave to retire and confer together. This was granted, and at the end of an hour they came back with the same answer as before; whereupon they were allowed till ten o'clock on the next morning for a final decision.[1]

At the appointed time the Council again met, and the deputies were brought in. They persisted stubbornly in the same refusal. "They were then informed," says the record, "that the Council could no longer look on them as subjects to His Britannic

[1] *Minutes of Council at Halifax,* 3 *July,* 1755, in *Public Documents of Nova Scotia,* 247–255.

Majesty, but as subjects to the King of France, and as such they must hereafter be treated; and they were ordered to withdraw." A discussion followed in the Council. It was determined that the Acadians should be ordered to send new deputies to Halifax, who should answer for them, once for all, whether they would accept the oath or not; that such as refused it should not thereafter be permitted to take it; and "that effectual measures ought to be taken to remove all such recusants out of the province."

The deputies, being then called in and told this decision, became alarmed, and offered to swear allegiance in the terms required. The answer was that it was too late; that as they had refused the oath under persuasion, they could not be trusted when they took it under compulsion. It remained to see whether the people at large would profit by their example.

"I am determined," wrote Lawrence to the Lords of Trade, "to bring the inhabitants to a compliance, or rid the province of such perfidious subjects."[1] First, in answer to the summons of the Council, the deputies from Annapolis appeared, declaring that they had always been faithful to the British Crown, but flatly refusing the oath. They were told that, far from having been faithful subjects, they had always secretly aided the Indians, and that many of them had been in arms against the English; that the French were threatening the province; and that its

[1] *Lawrence to Lords of Trade,* 18 *July,* 1755.

affairs had reached a crisis when its inhabitants must either pledge themselves without equivocation to be true to the British Crown, or else must leave the country. They all declared that they would lose their lands rather than take the oath. The Council urged them to consider the matter seriously, warning them that, if they now persisted in refusal, no farther choice would be allowed them; and they were given till ten o'clock on the following Monday to make their final answer.

When that day came, another body of deputies had arrived from Grand Pré and the other settlements of the Basin of Mines; and being called before the Council, both they and the former deputation absolutely refused to take the oath of aliegiance. These two bodies represented nine-tenths of the Acadian population within the peninsula. "Nothing," pursues the record of the Council, "now remained to be considered but what measures should be taken to send the inhabitants away, and where they should be sent to." If they were sent to Canada, Cape Breton, or the neighboring islands, they would strengthen the enemy, and still threaten the province. It was therefore resolved to distribute them among the various English colonies, and to hire vessels for the purpose with all despatch.[1]

---

[1] *Minutes of Council, 4 July–28 July,* in *Public Documents of Nova Scotia,* 255–267. Copies of these and other parts of the record were sent at the time to England, and are now in the Public Record Office along with the letters of Lawrence.

The oath, the refusal of which had brought such consequences, was a simple pledge of fidelity and allegiance to King George II. and his successors. Many of the Acadians had already taken an oath of fidelity, though with the omission of the word "allegiance," and, as they insisted, with a saving clause exempting them from bearing arms. The effect of this was that they did not regard themselves as British subjects, and claimed, falsely as regards most of them, the character of neutrals. It was to put an end to this anomalous state of things that the oath without reserve had been demanded of them. Their rejection of it, reiterated in full view of the consequences, is to be ascribed partly to a fixed belief that the English would not execute their threats, partly to ties of race and kin, but mainly to superstition. They feared to take part with heretics against the King of France, whose cause, as already stated, they had been taught to regard as one with the cause of God; they were constrained by the dread of perdition. "If the Acadians are miserable, remember that the priests are the cause of it," writes the French officer Boishébert to the missionary Manach.[1]

---

[1] On the oath and its history, compare a long note by Mr. Akin in *Public Documents of Nova Scotia*, 263–267. Winslow in his Journal gives an abstract of a memorial sent him by the Acadians, in which they say that they had refused the oath, and so forfeited their lands, from motives of religion. I have shown in a former chapter that the priests had been the chief instruments in preventing them from accepting the English government. Add the following : —

"Les malheurs des Accadiens sont beaucoup moins leur ouvrage

The Council having come to a decision, Lawrence acquainted Monckton with the result, and ordered him to seize all the adult males in the neighborhood of Beauséjour; and this, as we have seen, he promptly did. It remains to observe how the rest of the sentence was carried into effect.

Instructions were sent to Winslow to secure the inhabitants on or near the Basin of Mines and place them on board transports, which, he was told, would soon arrive from Boston. His orders were stringent: "If you find that fair means will not do with them, you must proceed by the most vigorous measures possible, not only in compelling them to embark, but in depriving those who shall escape of all means of shelter or support, by burning their houses and by destroying everything that may afford them the means of subsistence in the country." Similar orders were given to Major Handfield, the regular officer in command at Annapolis.

que le fruit des sollicitations et des démarches des missionnaires." — *Vaudreuil au Ministre, 6 Mai,* 1760.

"Si nous avons la guerre, et si les Accadiens sont misérables, souvenez-vous que ce sont les prêtres qui en sont la cause." — *Boishébert à Manach,* 21 *Février,* 1760. Both these writers had encouraged the priests in their intrigues so long as these were likely to profit the French government, and only blamed them after they failed to accomplish what was expected of them.

"Nous avons six missionnaires dont l'occupation perpetuelle est de porter les esprits au fanatisme et à la vengeance. . . . Je ne puis supporter dans nos prêtres ces odieuses déclamations qu'ils font tous les jours aux sauvages : 'Les Anglois sont les ennemis de Dieu, les compagnons du Diable.'" — Pichon, *Lettres et Mémoires pour servir à l'Histoire du Cap-Breton,* 160, 161. **(La Haye, 1760.)**

On the fourteenth of August Winslow set out from
his camp at Fort Beauséjour, or Cumberland, on his
unenviable errand. He had with him but two hundred and ninety-seven men. His mood of mind was
not serene. He was chafed because the regulars had
charged his men with stealing sheep; and he was
doubly vexed by an untoward incident that happened
on the morning of his departure. He had sent forward his detachment under Adams, the senior captain, and they were marching by the fort with drums
beating and colors flying, when Monckton sent out
his aide-de-camp with a curt demand that the colors
should be given up, on the ground that they ought
to remain with the regiment. Whatever the sound-
ness of the reason, there was no courtesy in the
manner of enforcing it. "This transaction raised my
temper some," writes Winslow in his Diary; and he
proceeds to record his opinion that "it is the most
ungenteel, ill-natured thing that ever I saw." He
sent Monckton a quaintly indignant note, in which
he observed that the affair "looks odd, and will
appear so in future history;" but his commander,
reckless of the judgments of posterity, gave him little
satisfaction.

Thus ruffled in spirit, he embarked with his men
and sailed down Chignecto Channel to the Bay of
Fundy. Here, while they waited the turn of the
tide to enter the Basin of Mines, the shores of Cumberland lay before them dim in the hot and hazy air,
and the promontory of Cape Split, like some mis-

shapen monster of primeval chaos, stretched its portentous length along the glimmering sea, with head of yawning rock, and ridgy back bristled with forests. Borne on the rushing flood, they soon drifted through the inlet, glided under the rival promontory of Cape Blomedon, passed the red sandstone cliffs of Lyon's Cove, and descried the mouths of the rivers Canard and Des Habitants, where fertile marshes, diked against the tide, sustained a numerous and thriving population. Before them spread the boundless meadows of Grand Pré, waving with harvests or alive with grazing cattle; the green slopes behind were dotted with the simple dwellings of the Acadian farmers, and the spire of the village church rose against a background of woody hills. It was a peaceful, rural scene, soon to become one of the most wretched spots on earth. Winslow did not land for the present, but held his course to the estuary of the river Pisiquid, since called the Avon. Here, where the town of Windsor now stands, there was a stockade called Fort Edward, where a garrison of regulars under Captain Alexander Murray kept watch over the surrounding settlements. The New England men pitched their tents on shore, while the sloops that had brought them slept on the soft bed of tawny mud left by the fallen tide.

Winslow found a warm reception, for Murray and his officers had been reduced too long to their own society not to welcome the coming of strangers. The two commanders conferred together. Both had been ordered by Lawrence to "clear the whole country of such bad subjects;" and the methods of doing so had been outlined for their guidance. Having come to some understanding with his brother officer concerning the duties imposed on both, and begun an acquaintance which soon grew cordial on both sides, Winslow embarked again and retraced his course to Grand Pré, the station which the governor had assigned him. "Am pleased," he wrote to Lawrence, "with the place proposed by your Excellency for our reception [*the village church*]. I have sent for the elders to remove all sacred things, to prevent their being defiled by heretics." The church was used as a storehouse and place of arms; the men pitched their tents between it and the graveyard; while Winslow took up his quarters in the house of the priest, where he could look from his window on a tranquil scene. Beyond the vast tract of grassland to which Grand Pré owed its name, spread the blue glistening breast of the Basin of Mines; beyond this again, the distant mountains of Cobequid basked in the summer sun; and nearer, on the left, Cape Blomedon reared its bluff head of rock and forest above the sleeping waves.

As the men of the settlement greatly outnumbered his own, Winslow set his followers to surrounding the camp with a stockade. Card-playing was forbidden, because it encouraged idleness, and pitching quoits in camp, because it spoiled the grass. Presently there came a letter from Lawrence expressing a

fear that the fortifying of the camp might alarm the
inhabitants. To which Winslow replied that the
making of the stockade had not alarmed them in the
least, since they took it as a proof that the detachment was to spend the winter with them; and he
added, that as the harvest was not yet got in, he and
Murray had agreed not to publish the governor's
commands till the next Friday. He concludes:
"Although it is a disagreeable part of duty we are put
upon, I am sensible it is a necessary one, and shall
endeavor strictly to obey your Excellency's orders."

On the thirtieth, Murray, whose post was not many
miles distant, made him a visit. They agreed that
Winslow should summon all the male inhabitants
about Grand Pré to meet him at the church and hear
the King's orders, and that Murray should do the
same for those around Fort Edward. Winslow then
called in his three captains, — Adams, Hobbs, and
Osgood, — made them swear secrecy, and laid before
them his instructions and plans; which latter they
approved. Murray then returned to his post, and on
the next day sent Winslow a note containing the
following: "I think the sooner we strike the stroke
the better, therefore will be glad to see you here as
soon as conveniently you can. I shall have the
orders for assembling ready written for your approbation, only the day blank, and am hopeful everything
will succeed according to our wishes. The gentlemen join me in our best compliments to you and the
Doctor."

On the next day, Sunday, Winslow and the Doctor, whose name was Whitworth, made the tour of the neighborhood, with an escort of fifty men, and found a great quantity of wheat still on the fields. On Tuesday Winslow "set out in a whale-boat with Dr. Whitworth and Adjutant Kennedy, to consult with Captain Murray in this critical conjuncture." They agreed that three in the afternoon of Friday should be the time of assembling; then between them they drew up a summons to the inhabitants, and got one Beauchamp, a merchant, to "put it into French." It ran as follows: —

By John Winslow, Esquire, Lieutenant-Colonel and Commander of His Majesty's troops at Grand Pré, Mines, River Canard, and places adjacent.

To the inhabitants of the districts above named, as well ancients as young men and lads.

Whereas His Excellency the Governor has instructed us of his last resolution respecting the matters proposed lately to the inhabitants, and has ordered us to communicate the same to the inhabitants in general in person, His Excellency being desirous that each of them should be fully satisfied of His Majesty's intentions, which he has also ordered us to communicate to you, such as they have been given him.

We therefore order and strictly enjoin by these presents to all the inhabitants, as well of the above-named districts as of all the other districts, both old men and young men, as well as all the lads of ten years of age, to attend at the church in Grand Pré on Friday, the fifth instant, at three of the clock in the afternoon, that we may impart what we are ordered to communicate to them; declaring that no excuse will be admitted on any pretence whatsoever, on pain of forfeiting goods and chattels in default.

Given at Grand Pré, the second of September, in the twenty-ninth year of His Majesty's reign, A.D. 1755.

A similar summons was drawn up in the name of Murray for the inhabitants of the district of Fort Edward.

Captain Adams made a reconnoissance of the rivers Canard and Des Habitants, and reported "a fine country and full of inhabitants, a beautiful church, and abundance of the goods of the world." Another reconnoissance by Captains Hobbs and Osgood among the settlements behind Grand Pré brought reports equally favorable. On the fourth, another letter came from Murray: "All the people quiet, and very busy at their harvest; if this day keeps fair, all will be in here in their barns. I hope to-morrow will crown all our wishes." The Acadians, like the bees, were to gather a harvest for others to enjoy. The summons was sent out that afternoon. Powder and ball were served to the men, and all were ordered to keep within the lines.

On the next day the inhabitants appeared at the hour appointed, to the number of four hundred and eighteen men. Winslow ordered a table to be set in the middle of the church, and placed on it his instructions and the address he had prepared. Here he took his stand in his laced uniform, with one or two subalterns from the regulars at Fort Edward, and such of the Massachusetts officers as were not on

guard duty; strong, sinewy figures, bearing, no
doubt, more or less distinctly, the peculiar stamp
with which toil, trade, and Puritanism had imprinted
the features of New England. Their commander
was not of the prevailing type. He was fifty-three
years of age, with double chin, smooth forehead,
arched eyebrows, close powdered wig, and round,
rubicund face, from which the weight of an odious
duty had probably banished the smirk of self-satis-
faction that dwelt there at other times.[1] Nevertheless, he had manly and estimable qualities. The
congregation of peasants, clad in rough homespun,
turned their sunburned faces upon him, anxious and
intent; and Winslow "delivered them by interpreters the King's orders in the following words," which,
retouched in orthography and syntax, ran thus: —

GENTLEMEN, — I have received from His Excellency,
Governor Lawrence, the King's instructions, which I have
in my hand. By his orders you are called together to
hear His Majesty's final resolution concerning the French
inhabitants of this his province of Nova Scotia, who for
almost half a century have had more indulgence granted
them than any of his subjects in any part of his dominions.
What use you have made of it you yourselves best know.

The duty I am now upon, though necessary, is very disagreeable to my natural make and temper, as I know it must
be grievous to you, who are of the same species. But it
is not my business to animadvert on the orders I have
received, but to obey them; and therefore without hesita-

---

[1] See his portrait, at the rooms of the Massachusetts Historical
Society.

tion I shall deliver to you His Majesty's instructions and commands, which are that your lands and tenements and cattle and live-stock of all kinds are forfeited to the Crown, with all your other effects, except money and household goods, and that you yourselves are to be removed from this his province.

The peremptory orders of His Majesty are that all the French inhabitants of these districts be removed; and through His Majesty's goodness I am directed to allow you the liberty of carrying with you your money and as many of your household goods as you can take without overloading the vessels you go in. I shall do everything in my power that all these goods be secured to you, and that you be not molested in carrying them away, and also that whole families shall go in the same vessel; so that this removal, which I am sensible must give you a great deal of trouble, may be made as easy as His Majesty's service will admit; and I hope that in whatever part of the world your lot may fall, you may be faithful subjects, and a peaceable and happy people.

I must also inform you that it is His Majesty's pleasure that you remain in security under the inspection and direction of the troops that I have the honor to command.

He then declared them prisoners of the King. "They were greatly struck," he says, "at this determination, though I believe they did not imagine that they were actually to be removed." After delivering the address, he returned to his quarters at the priest's house, whither he was followed by some of the elder prisoners, who begged leave to tell their families what had happened, "since they were fearful that the surprise of their detention would quite overcome them." Winslow consulted with his officers, and it was arranged that the Acadians should choose twenty of their number each day to revisit their homes, the rest being held answerable for their return.

A letter, dated some days before, now came from Major Handfield at Annapolis, saying that he had tried to secure the men of that neighborhood, but that many of them had escaped to the woods. Murray's report from Fort Edward came soon after, and was more favorable: "I have succeeded finely, and have got a hundred and eighty-three men into my possession." To which Winslow replies: "I have the favor of yours of this day, and rejoice at your success, and also for the smiles that have attended the party here." But he adds mournfully: "Things are now very heavy on my heart and hands." The prisoners were lodged in the church, and notice was sent to their families to bring them food. "Thus," says the Diary of the commander, "ended the memorable fifth of September, a day of great fatigue and trouble."

There was one quarter where fortune did not always smile. Major Jedediah Preble, of Winslow's battalion, wrote to him that Major Frye had just returned from Chipody, whither he had gone with a party of men to destroy the settlements and bring off the women and children. After burning two hundred and fifty-three buildings he had re-embarked, leaving fifty men on shore at a place called Peticodiac to give a finishing stroke to the work by burning the

"Mass House," or church. While thus engaged, they were set upon by three hundred Indians and Acadians, led by the partisan officer Boishébert. More than half their number were killed, wounded, or taken. The rest ensconced themselves behind the neighboring dikes, and Frye, hastily landing with the rest of his men, engaged the assailants for three hours, but was forced at last to re-embark.[1] Captain Speakman, who took part in the affair, also sent Winslow an account of it, and added: "The people here are much concerned for fear your party should meet with the same fate (being in the heart of a numerous devilish crew), which I pray God avert."

Winslow had indeed some cause for anxiety. He had captured more Acadians since the fifth; and had now in charge nearly five hundred able-bodied men, with scarcely three hundred to guard them. As they were allowed daily exercise in the open air, they might by a sudden rush get possession of arms and make serious trouble. On the Wednesday after the scene in the church some unusual movements were observed among them, and Winslow and his officers became convinced that they could not safely be kept in one body. Five vessels, lately arrived from Boston, were lying within the mouth of the neighboring river. It was resolved to place fifty of the prisoners on board each of these, and keep them

---

[1] Also *Boishébert à Drucour*, 10 *Octobre*, 1755, an exaggerated account. *Vaudreuil au Ministre*, 18 *Octobre*, 1755, sets Boishébert's force at one hundred and twenty-five men.

anchored in the Basin.   The soldiers were all ordered
under arms, and posted on an open space beside the
church and behind the priest's house.   The prisoners
were then drawn up before them, ranked six deep, —
the young unmarried men, as the most dangerous,
being told off and placed on the left, to the number
of a hundred and forty-one.   Captain Adams, with
eighty men, was then ordered to guard them to the
vessels.   Though the object of the movement had
been explained to them, they were possessed with the
idea that they were to be torn from their families and
sent away at once; and they all, in great excitement,
refused to go.   Winslow told them that there must
be no parley or delay; and as they still refused, a
squad of soldiers advanced towards them with fixed
bayonets; while he himself, laying hold of the foremost young man, commanded him to move forward.
" He obeyed; and the rest followed, though slowly,
and went off praying, singing, and crying, being met
by the women and children all the way (which is a
mile and a half) with great lamentation, upon their
knees, praying."   When the escort returned, about a
hundred of the married men were ordered to follow
the first party; and, " the ice being broken," they
readily complied.   The vessels were anchored at a
little distance from shore, and six soldiers were placed
on board each of them as a guard.   The prisoners
were offered the King's rations, but preferred to be
supplied by their families, who, it was arranged,
should go in boats to visit them every day; " and

thus," says Winslow, "ended this troublesome job." He was not given to effusions of feeling, but he wrote to Major Handfield: "This affair is more grievous to me than any service I was ever employed in." [1]

Murray sent him a note of congratulation: "I am extremely pleased that things are so clever at Grand Pré, and that the poor devils are so resigned. Here they are more patient than I could have expected for people in their circumstances; and what surprises me still more is the indifference of the women, who really are, or seem, quite unconcerned. I long much to see the poor wretches embarked and our affair a little settled; and then I will do myself the pleasure of meeting you and drinking their good voyage."

This agreeable consummation was still distant. There was a long and painful delay. The provisions for the vessels which were to carry the prisoners did not come; nor did the vessels themselves, excepting the five already at Grand Pré. In vain Winslow wrote urgent letters to George Saul, the commissary, to bring the supplies at once. Murray, at Fort Edward, though with less feeling than his brother officer, was quite as impatient of the burden of suffering humanity on his hands. "I am amazed what can keep the transports and Saul. Surely our

---

[1] Haliburton, who knew Winslow's Journal only by imperfect extracts, erroneously states that the men put on board the vessels were sent away immediately. They remained at Grand Pré several weeks, and were then sent off at intervals with their families.

friend at Chignecto is willing to give us as much of our neighbors' company as he well can." [1]　Saul came at last with a shipload of provisions; but the lagging transports did not appear.　Winslow grew heartsick at the daily sight of miseries which he himself had occasioned, and wrote to a friend at Halifax: "I know they deserve all and more than they feel; yet it hurts me to hear their weeping and wailing and gnashing of teeth.　I am in hopes our affairs will soon put on another face, and we get transports, and I rid of the worst piece of service that ever I was in."

After weeks of delay, seven transports came from Annapolis; and Winslow sent three of them to Murray, who joyfully responded: "Thank God, the transports are come at last.　So soon as I have shipped off my rascals, I will come down and settle matters with you, and enjoy ourselves a little."

Winslow prepared for the embarkation.　The Acadian prisoners and their families were divided into groups answering to their several villages, in order that those of the same village might, as far as possible, go in the same vessel.　It was also provided that the members of each family should remain together; and notice was given them to hold themselves in readiness.　"But even now," he writes, "I could not persuade the people I was in earnest." Their doubts were soon ended.　The first embarkation took place on the eighth of October, under which date the Diary contains this entry: "Began to embark

[1] *Murray to Winslow,* 26 *September,* 1755.

the inhabitants, who went off very solentarily [*sic*] and unwillingly, the women in great distress, carrying off their children in their arms; others carrying their decrepit parents in their carts, with all their goods; moving in great confusion, and appeared a scene of woe and distress."[1]

Though a large number were embarked on this occasion, still more remained; and as the transports slowly arrived, the dismal scene was repeated at intervals, with more order than at first, as the Acadians had learned to accept their fate as a certainty. So far as Winslow was concerned, their treatment seems to have been as humane as was possible under the circumstances; but they complained of the men, who disliked and despised them. One soldier received thirty lashes for stealing fowls from them; and an order was issued forbidding soldiers or sailors, on pain of summary punishment, to leave their quarters without permission, "that an end may be put to distressing this distressed people." Two of the prisoners, however, while trying to escape, were shot by a reconnoitring party.

At the beginning of November Winslow reported that he had sent off fifteen hundred and ten persons, in nine vessels, and that more than six hundred still remained in his district.[2] The last of these were not embarked till late in December. Murray finished

---

[1] In spite of Winslow's care, some cases of separation of families occurred; but they were not numerous.

[2] *Winslow to Monckton, 3 November,* 1755.

his part of the work at the end of October, having sent from the district of Fort Edward eleven hundred persons in four frightfully crowded transports.[1] At the close of that month sixteen hundred and sixty-four had been sent from the district of Annapolis, where many others escaped to the woods.[2] A detachment which was ordered to seize the inhabitants of the district of Cobequid failed entirely, finding the settlements abandoned. In the country about Fort Cumberland, Monckton, who directed the operation in person, had very indifferent success, catching in all but little more than a thousand.[3] Le Guerne, missionary priest in this neighborhood, gives a characteristic and affecting incident of the embarkation. "Many unhappy women, carried away by excessive attachment to their husbands, whom they had been allowed to see too often, and closing their ears to the voice of religion and their missionary, threw themselves blindly and despairingly into the English vessels. And now was seen the saddest of spectacles; for some of these women, solely from a religious motive, refused to take with them their grown-up sons and daughters."[4] They would expose their own souls to perdition among heretics, but not those of their children.

When all, or nearly all, had been sent off from the

---

[1] *Winslow to Monckton, 3 November,* 1755.

[2] *Captain Adams to Winslow, 29 November,* 1755; see also **Knox,** i. 85, who exactly confirms Adams's figures.

[3] *Monckton to Winslow, 7 October,* 1755.

[4] *Le Guerne à Prévost,* 10 *Mars,* 1756.

various points of departure, such of the houses and barns as remained standing were burned, in obedience to the orders of Lawrence, that those who had escaped might be forced to come in and surrender themselves. The whole number removed from the province, men, women, and children, was a little above six thousand. Many remained behind; and while some of these withdrew to Canada, Isle St. Jean, and other distant retreats, the rest lurked in the woods or returned to their old haunts, whence they waged, for several years, a guerilla warfare against the English. Yet their strength was broken, and they were no longer a danger to the province.

Of their exiled countrymen, one party overpowered the crew of the vessel that carried them, ran her ashore at the mouth of the St. John, and escaped.[1] The rest were distributed among the colonies from Massachusetts to Georgia, the master of each transport having been provided with a letter from Lawrence addressed to the governor of the province to which he was bound, and desiring him to receive the unwelcome strangers. The provincials were vexed at the burden imposed upon them; and though the Acadians were not in general ill-treated, their lot was a hard one. Still more so was that of those among them who escaped to Canada. The chronicle of the Ursulines of Quebec, speaking of these last, says that their misery was indescribable, and at-

[1] *Lettre commune de Drucour et Prévost au Ministre, 6 Avril,* 1756. *Vaudreuil au Ministre,* 1 *Juin,* 1756.

tributes it to the poverty of the colony. But there
were other causes. The exiles found less pity from
kindred and fellow-Catholics than from the heretics
of the English colonies. Some of them who had
made their way to Canada from Boston, whither
they had been transported, sent word to a gentleman
of that place who had befriended them that they
wished to return.[1] Bougainville, the celebrated
navigator, then aide-de-camp to Montcalm, says
concerning them: "They are dying by wholesale.
Their past and present misery, joined to the rapacity
of the Canadians, who seek only to squeeze out of
them all the money they can, and then refuse them
the help so dearly bought, are the cause of this
mortality." "A citizen of Quebec," he says farther
on, "was in debt to one of the partners of the Great
Company [*Government officials leagued for plunder*].
He had no means of paying. They gave him a great
number of Acadians to board and lodge. He starved
them with hunger and cold, got out of them what
money they had, and paid the extortioner. *Quel
pays! Quels mœurs!*"[2]

Many of the exiles eventually reached Louisiana,
where their descendants now form a numerous and
distinct population. Some, after incredible hardship,
made their way back to Acadia, where, after the
peace, they remained unmolested, and, with those

[1] Hutchinson, *Hist. Mass.*, iii. 42, *note*.
[2] Bougainville, *Journal*, 1756–1758. His statements are sustained
by *Mémoires sur le Canada*, 1749–1760.

who had escaped seizure, became the progenitors of the present Acadians, now settled in various parts of the British maritime provinces, notably at Madawaska, on the upper St. John, and at Clare, in Nova Scotia. Others were sent from Virginia to England; and others again, after the complete conquest of the country, found refuge in France.

In one particular the authors of the deportation were disappointed in its results. They had hoped to substitute a loyal population for a disaffected one; but they failed for some time to find settlers for the vacated lands. The Massachusetts soldiers, to whom they were offered, would not stay in the province; and it was not till five years later that families of British stock began to occupy the waste fields of the Acadians. This goes far to show that a longing to become their heirs had not, as has been alleged, any considerable part in the motives for their removal.

New England humanitarianism, melting into sentimentality at a tale of woe, has been unjust to its own. Whatever judgment may be passed on the cruel measure of wholesale expatriation, it was not put in execution till every resource of patience and persuasion had been tried in vain. The agents of the French court, civil, military, and ecclesiastical, had made some act of force a necessity. We have seen by what vile practices they produced in Acadia a state of things intolerable, and impossible of continuance. They conjured up the tempest; and when it burst on the heads of the unhappy people, they

gave no help.   The government of Louis XV. began
with making the Acadians its tools, and ended with
making them its victims.[1]

---

[1] It may not be remembered that the predecessor of Louis XV.,
without the slightest provocation or the pretence of any, gave
orders that the whole Protestant population of the colony of New
York, amounting to about eighteen thousand, should be seized,
despoiled of their property, placed on board his ships, and dispersed among the other British colonies in such a way that they
could not reunite.   Want of power alone prevented the execution
of the order.   See "Frontenac and New France under Louis XIV.,"
198, 199.

CHAPTER IX.

1755.

DIESKAU.

EXPEDITION AGAINST CROWN POINT. — WILLIAM JOHNSON. — VAU-
DREUIL. — DIESKAU. — JOHNSON AND THE INDIANS. — THE PRO-
VINCIAL ARMY. — DOUBTS AND DELAYS. — MARCH TO LAKE
GEORGE. — SUNDAY IN CAMP. — ADVANCE OF DIESKAU: HE
CHANGES PLAN. — MARCHES AGAINST JOHNSON. — AMBUSH. —
ROUT OF PROVINCIALS. — BATTLE OF LAKE GEORGE. — ROUT
OF THE FRENCH. — RAGE OF THE MOHAWKS. — PERIL OF DIES-
KAU. — INACTION OF JOHNSON. — THE HOMEWARD MARCH. —
LAURELS OF VICTORY.

THE next stroke of the campaign was to be the
capture of Crown Point, that dangerous neighbor
which, for a quarter of a century, had threatened the
northern colonies. Shirley, in January, had proposed
an attack on it to the ministry; and in February,
without waiting their reply, he laid the plan before
his Assembly. They accepted it, and voted money
for the pay and maintenance of twelve hundred men,
provided the adjacent colonies would contribute in
due proportion.[1] Massachusetts showed a military

[1] *Governor Shirley's Message to his Assembly*, 13 *February*, 1755.
Resolutions of the Assembly of Massachusetts, 18 *February*, 1755. Shirley's original idea was to build a fort on a rising ground near
Crown Point, in order to command it. This was soon abandoned
for the more honest and more practical plan of direct attack.

THE REGION OF

LAKE GEORGE

from surveys made in

1762

Miles.

Crown Point

FART OF LAKE CHAMPLAIN

Ticonderoga

Trout Brook

Rogers Rock

Sabbath Day Pt.

LAKE GEORGE

Two Rocks

Drowned Lands

NORTH WEST BAY

Tongue Mt.

SOUTH BAY

Path of Dieskau

Creek

Wood

William Henry

French Mt.

BATTLE FIELD

Road to Fort Edward

Old Fort Anne

activity worthy of the reputation she had won. Forty-five hundred of her men, or one in eight of her adult males, volunteered to fight the French, and enlisted for the various expeditions, some in the pay of the province, and some in that of the King.[1] It remained to name a commander for the Crown Point enterprise. Nobody had power to do so, for Braddock was not yet come; but that time might not be lost, Shirley, at the request of his Assembly, took the responsibility on himself. If he had named a Massachusetts officer, it would have roused the jealousy of the other New England colonies; and he therefore appointed William Johnson of New York, thus gratifying that important province and pleasing the Five Nations, who at this time looked on Johnson with even more than usual favor. Hereupon, in reply to his request, Connecticut voted twelve hundred men, New Hampshire five hundred, and Rhode Island four hundred, all at their own charge; while New York, a little later, promised eight hundred more. When, in April, Braddock and the Council at Alexandria approved the plan and the commander, Shirley gave Johnson the commission of major-general of the levies of Massachusetts; and the governors of the other provinces contributing to the expedition gave him similar commissions for their respective contingents. Never did general take the field with authority so heterogeneous.

[1] *Correspondence of Shirley, February,* 1755. The number was much increased later in the season.

He had never seen service, and knew nothing of war. By birth he was Irish, of good family, being nephew of Admiral Sir Peter Warren, who, owning extensive wild lands on the Mohawk, had placed the young man in charge of them nearly twenty years before. Johnson was born to prosper. He had ambition, energy, an active mind, a tall, strong person, a rough, jovial temper, and a quick adaptation to his surroundings. He could drink flip with Dutch boors, or Madeira with royal governors. He liked the society of the great, would intrigue and flatter when he had an end to gain, and foil a rival without looking too closely at the means; but compared with the Indian traders who infested the border, he was a model of uprightness. He lived by the Mohawk in a fortified house which was a stronghold against foes and a scene of hospitality to friends, both white and red. Here — for his tastes were not fastidious — presided for many years a Dutch or German wench whom he finally married; and after her death a young Mohawk squaw took her place. Over his neighbors, the Indians of the Five Nations, and all others of their race with whom he had to deal, he acquired a remarkable influence. He liked them, adopted their ways, and treated them kindly or sternly as the case required, but always with a justice and honesty in strong contrast with the rascalities of the commission of Albany traders who had lately managed their affairs, and whom they so detested that one of their chiefs called them "not

men, but devils." Hence, when Johnson was made
Indian superintendent there was joy through all the
Iroquois confederacy. When, in addition, he was
made a general, he assembled the warriors in council
to engage them to aid the expedition.

This meeting took place at his own house, known
as Fort Johnson; and as more than eleven hundred
Indians appeared at his call, his larder was sorely
taxed to entertain them. The speeches were interminable. Johnson, a master of Indian rhetoric, knew
his audience too well not to contest with them the
palm of insufferable prolixity. The climax was
reached on the fourth day, and he threw down the
war-belt. An Oneida chief took it up; Stevens, the
interpreter, began the war-dance, and the assembled
warriors howled in chorus. Then a tub of punch
was brought in, and they all drank the King's
health.[1] They showed less alacrity, however, to
fight his battles, and scarcely three hundred of them
would take the war-path. Too many of their friends
and relatives were enlisted for the French.

While the British colonists were preparing to
attack Crown Point, the French of Canada were
preparing to defend it. Duquesne, recalled from his
post, had resigned the government to the Marquis de
Vaudreuil, who had at his disposal the battalions of
regulars that had sailed in the spring from Brest
under Baron Dieskau. His first thought was to use

[1] *Report of Conference between Major-General Johnson and the
Indians, June,* 1755.

them for the capture of Oswego; but the letters of
Braddock, found on the battle-field, warned him of
the design against Crown Point; while a reconnoitring
party which had gone as far as the Hudson brought
back news that Johnson's forces were already in the
field. Therefore the plan was changed, and Dieskau
was ordered to lead the main body of his troops, not
to Lake Ontario, but to Lake Champlain. He passed
up the Richelieu, and embarked in boats and canoes
for Crown Point. The veteran knew that the foes
with whom he had to deal were but a mob of countrymen. He doubted not of putting them to rout, and
meant never to hold his hand till he had chased them
back to Albany.[1] "Make all haste," Vaudreuil
wrote to him; "for when you return we shall send
you to Oswego to execute our first design."[2]

Johnson on his part was preparing to advance.
In July about three thousand provincials were encamped near Albany, some on the "Flats" above the
town, and some on the meadows below. Hither,
too, came a swarm of Johnson's Mohawks, — warriors,
squaws, and children. They adorned the general's
face with war-paint, and he danced the war-dance;
then with his sword he cut the first slice from the ox
that had been roasted whole for their entertainment.
"I shall be glad," wrote the surgeon of a New England regiment, "if they fight as eagerly as they ate
their ox and drank their wine."

[1] *Bigot au Ministre,* 27 *Août,* 1755. *Ibid.,* 5 *Septembre,* 1755.

[2] *Mémoire pour servir d'Instruction à M. le Baron de Dieskau,
Maréchal des Camps et Armées du Roy,* 15 *Août,* 1755.

Above all things the expedition needed promptness; yet everything moved slowly. Five popular legislatures controlled the troops and the supplies. Connecticut had refused to send her men till Shirley promised that her commanding officer should rank next to Johnson. The whole movement was for some time at a deadlock because the five governments could not agree about their contributions of artillery and stores.[1] The New Hampshire regiment had taken a short cut for Crown Point across the wilderness of Vermont, but had been recalled in time to save them from probable destruction. They were now with the rest in the camp at Albany, in such distress for provisions that a private subscription was proposed for their relief.[2]

Johnson's army, crude as it was, had in it good material. Here was Phineas Lyman, of Connecticut, second in command, once a tutor at Yale College, and more recently a lawyer, — a raw soldier, but a vigorous and brave one; Colonel Moses Titcomb, of Massachusetts, who had fought with credit at Louisbourg; and Ephraim Williams, also colonel of a Massachusetts regiment, a tall and portly man, who had been a captain in the last war, member of the General Court, and deputy sheriff. He made his will in the camp at Albany, and left a legacy to

---

[1] *The Conduct of Major-General Shirley briefly stated* (London, 1758).

[2] *Blanchard to Wentworth, 28 August, 1755,* in *Provincial Papers of New Hampshire,* vi. 429.

found the school which has since become Williams College. His relative, Stephen Williams, was chaplain of his regiment, and his brother Thomas was its surgeon. Seth Pomeroy, gunsmith at Northampton, who, like Titcomb, had seen service at Louisbourg, was its lieutenant-colonel. He had left a wife at home, an excellent matron, to whom he was continually writing affectionate letters, mingling household cares with news of the camp, and charging her to see that their eldest boy, Seth, then in college at New Haven, did not run off to the army. Pomeroy had with him his brother Daniel; and this he thought was enough. Here, too, was a man whose name is still a household word in New England, — the sturdy Israel Putnam, private in a Connecticut regiment and another as bold as he, John Stark, lieutenant in the New Hampshire levies, and the future victor of Bennington.

The soldiers were no soldiers, but farmers and farmers' sons who had volunteered for the summer campaign. One of the corps had a blue uniform faced with red. The rest wore their daily clothing. Blankets had been served out to them by the several provinces, but the greater part brought their own guns; some under the penalty of a fine if they came without them, and some under the inducement of a reward.[1] They had no bayonets, but carried hatchets in their belts as a sort of substitute.[2] At their sides

[1] *Proclamation of Governor Shirley*, 1755.
[2] *Second Letter to a Friend on the Battle of Lake George.*

were slung powder-horns, on which, in the leisure
of the camp, they carved quaint devices with the
points of their jack-knives. They came chiefly from
plain New England homesteads, — rustic abodes,
unpainted and dingy, with long well-sweeps, capacious
barns, rough fields of pumpkins and corn, and vast
kitchen chimneys, above which in winter hung
squashes to keep them from frost, and guns to keep
them from rust.

As to the manners and morals of the army there is
conflict of evidence. In some respects nothing could
be more exemplary. "Not a chicken has been
stolen," says William Smith, of New York; while,
on the other hand, Colonel Ephraim Williams writes
to Colonel Israel Williams, then commanding on the
Massachusetts frontier: "We are a wicked, profane
army, especially the New York and Rhode Island
troops. Nothing to be heard among a great part of
them but the language of Hell. If Crown Point is
taken, it will not be for our sakes, but for those good
people left behind." [1] There was edifying regularity
in respect to form. Sermons twice a week, daily
prayers, and frequent psalm-singing alternated with
the much-needed military drill.[2] "Prayers among
us night and morning," writes Private Jonathan
Caswell, of Massachusetts, to his father. "Here we
lie, knowing not when we shall march for Crown
Point; but I hope not long to tarry. Desiring your

---

[1] *Papers of Colonel Israel Williams.*
[2] *Massachusetts Archives.*

prayers to God for me as I am agoing to war, I am
Your Ever Dutiful Son."[1]

To Pomeroy and some of his brothers in arms it
seemed that they were engaged in a kind of crusade
against the myrmidons of Rome.   "As you have at
heart the Protestant cause," he wrote to his friend
Israel Williams, "so I ask an interest in your prayers
that the Lord of Hosts would go forth with us and
give us victory over our unreasonable, encroaching,
barbarous, murdering enemies."

Both Williams the surgeon and Williams the
colonel chafed at the incessant delays.   "The expedition goes on very much as a snail runs," writes the
former to his wife; "it seems we may possibly see
Crown Point this time twelve months."   The colonel
was vexed because everything was out of joint in the
department of transportation: wagoners mutinous for
want of pay; ordnance stores, camp-kettles, and
provisions left behind.   "As to rum," he complains,
"it won't hold out nine weeks.   Things appear
most melancholy to me."   Even as he was writing, a
report came of the defeat of Braddock; and, shocked
at the blow, his pen traced the words: "The Lord
have mercy on poor New England!"

Johnson had sent four Mohawk scouts to Canada.
They returned on the twenty-first of August with
the report that the French were all astir with preparation, and that eight thousand men were coming to
defend Crown Point.   On this a council of war was

[1] *Jonathan Caswell to John Caswell, 6 July,* 1755.

called; and it was resolved to send to the several colonies for reinforcements.[1] Meanwhile the main body had moved up the river to the spot called the Great Carrying Place, where Lyman had begun a fortified storehouse, which his men called Fort Lyman, but which was afterwards named Fort Edward. Two Indian trails led from this point to the waters of Lake Champlain, one by way of Lake George, and the other by way of Wood Creek. There was doubt which course the army should take. A road was begun to Wood Creek; then it was countermanded, and a party was sent to explore the path to Lake George. "With submission to the general officers," Surgeon Williams again writes, "I think it a very grand mistake that the business of reconnoitring was not done months agone." It was resolved at last to march for Lake George; gangs of axemen were sent to hew out the way; and on the twenty-sixth two thousand men were ordered to the lake, while Colonel Blanchard, of New Hampshire, remained with five hundred to finish and defend Fort Lyman.

The train of Dutch wagons, guarded by the homely soldiery, jolted slowly over the stumps and roots of the newly made road, and the regiments followed at their leisure. The hardships of the way were not without their consolations. The jovial Irishman who held the chief command made himself very agreeable

---

[1] *Minutes of Council of War, 22 August, 1755. Ephraim Williams to Benjamin Dwight, 22 August, 1755.*

to the New England officers. "We went on about four or five miles," says Pomeroy in his Journal, "then stopped, ate pieces of broken bread and cheese, and drank some fresh lemon-punch and the best of wine with General Johnson and some of the field-officers." It was the same on the next day. "Stopped about noon and dined with General Johnson by a small brook under a tree; ate a good dinner of cold boiled and roast venison; drank good fresh lemon-punch and wine."

That afternoon they reached their destination, fourteen miles from Fort Lyman. The most beautiful lake in America lay before them; then more beautiful than now, in the wild charm of untrodden mountains and virgin forests. "I have given it the name of Lake George," wrote Johnson to the Lords of Trade, "not only in honor of His Majesty, but to ascertain his undoubted dominion here." His men made their camp on a piece of rough ground by the edge of the water, pitching their tents among the stumps of the newly felled trees. In their front was a forest of pitch-pine; on their right, a marsh, choked with alders and swamp-maples; on their left, the low hill where Fort George was afterwards built; and at their rear, the lake. Little was done to clear the forest in front, though it would give excellent cover to an enemy. Nor did Johnson take much pains to learn the movements of the French in the direction of Crown Point, though he sent scouts towards South Bay and Wood Creek. Every day stores and bateaux,

or flat boats, came on wagons from Fort Lyman; and
preparation moved on with the leisure that had
marked it from the first. About three hundred
Mohawks came to the camp, and were regarded by
the New England men as nuisances. On Sunday
the gray-haired Stephen Williams preached to these
savage allies a long Calvinistic sermon, which must
have sorely perplexed the interpreter whose business
it was to turn it into Mohawk; and in the afternoon
young Chaplain Newell, of Rhode Island, expounded
to the New England men the somewhat untimely
text, "Love your enemies." On the next Sunday,
September seventh, Williams preached again, this
time to the whites from a text in Isaiah. It was a
peaceful day, fair and warm, with a few light
showers; yet not wholly a day of rest, for two hundred wagons came up from Fort Lyman, loaded with
bateaux. After the sermon there was an alarm.
An Indian scout came in about sunset, and reported
that he had found the trail of a body of men moving
from South Bay towards Fort Lyman. Johnson
called for a volunteer to carry a letter of warning
to Colonel Blanchard, the commander. A wagoner
named Adams offered himself for the perilous service,
mounted, and galloped along the road with the letter.
Sentries were posted, and the camp fell asleep.

While Johnson lay at Lake George, Dieskau prepared a surprise for him. The German baron had
reached Crown Point at the head of three thousand
five hundred and seventy-three men, regulars, Cana-

dians, and Indians.[1] He had no thought of waiting
there to be attacked. The troops were told to hold
themselves ready to move at a moment's notice.
Officers — so ran the order — will take nothing with
them but one spare shirt, one spare pair of shoes, a
blanket, a bearskin, and provisions for twelve days;
Indians are not to amuse themselves by taking scalps
till the enemy is entirely defeated, since they can kill
ten men in the time required to scalp one.[2] Then
Dieskau moved on, with nearly all his force, to
Carillon, or Ticonderoga, a promontory commanding
both the routes by which alone Johnson could
advance, that of Wood Creek and that of Lake
George.

The Indian allies were commanded by Legardeur
de Saint-Pierre, the officer who had received Washington on his embassy to Fort Le Bœuf. These
unmanageable warriors were a constant annoyance to
Dieskau, being a species of humanity quite new to
him. "They drive us crazy," he says, "from morning till night. There is no end to their demands.
They have already eaten five oxen and as many hogs,
without counting the kegs of brandy they have
drunk. In short, one needs the patience of an angel
to get on with these devils; and yet one must always
force himself to seem pleased with them."[3]

They would scarcely even go out as scouts. At

[1] *Vaudreuil au Ministre*, 25 *Septembre*, 1755.

[2] *Livre d'Ordres, Août, Septembre*, 1755.

[3] *Dieskau à Vaudreuil*, 1 *Septembre*, 1755.

last, however, on the fourth of September, a reconnoitring party came in with a scalp and an English
prisoner caught near Fort Lyman. He was questioned under the threat of being given to the Indians
for torture if he did not tell the truth; but, nothing daunted, he invented a patriotic falsehood; and
thinking to lure his captors into a trap, told them
that the English army had fallen back to Albany,
leaving five hundred men at Fort Lyman, which he
represented as indefensible. Dieskau resolved on a
rapid movement to seize the place. At noon of the
same day, leaving a part of his force at Ticonderoga,
he embarked the rest in canoes and advanced along
the narrow prolongation of Lake Champlain that
stretched southward through the wilderness to where
the town of Whitehall now stands. He soon came
to a point where the lake dwindled to a mere canal,
while two mighty rocks, capped with stunted forests,
faced each other from the opposing banks. Here he
left an officer named Roquemaure with a detachment
of troops, and again advanced along a belt of quiet
water traced through the midst of a deep marsh,
green at that season with sedge and water-weeds, and
known to the English as the Drowned Lands.
Beyond, on either hand, crags feathered with birch
and fir, or hills mantled with woods, looked down on
the long procession of canoes.[1] As they neared the
site of Whitehall, a passage opened on the right, the

[1] I passed this way three weeks ago. There are some points
where the scene is not much changed since Dieskau saw it.

entrance to a sheet of lonely water slumbering in the shadow of woody mountains, and forming the lake then, as now, called South Bay. They advanced to its head, landed where a small stream enters it, left the canoes under a guard, and began their march through the forest. They counted in all two hundred and sixteen regulars of the battalions of Languedoc and La Reine, six hundred and eighty-four Canadians, and about six hundred Indians.[1] Every officer and man carried provisions for eight days in his knapsack. They encamped at night by a brook, and in the morning, after hearing mass, marched again. The evening of the next day brought them near the road that led to Lake George. Fort Lyman was but three miles distant. A man on horseback galloped by; it was Adams, Johnson's unfortunate messenger. The Indians shot him, and found the letter in his pocket. Soon after, ten or twelve wagons appeared in charge of mutinous drivers, who had left the English camp without orders. Several of them were shot, two were taken, and the rest ran off. The two captives declared that, contrary to the assertion of the prisoner at Ticonderoga, a large force lay encamped at the lake. The Indians now held a council, and presently gave out that they would not attack the fort, which they thought well supplied with cannon, but that they were willing to attack the camp at Lake George. Remonstrance was lost upon them. Dieskau was not young, but he was

[1] *Mémoire sur l'Affaire du 8 Septembre.*

daring to rashness, and inflamed to emulation by the victory over Braddock.   The enemy were reported greatly to outnumber him; but his Canadian advisers had assured him that the English colony militia were the worst troops on the face of the earth.   "The more there are," he said to the Canadians and Indians, "the more we shall kill;" and in the morning the order was given to march for the lake.

They moved rapidly on through the waste of pines, and soon entered the rugged valley that led to Johnson's camp.   On their right was a gorge where, shadowed in bushes, gurgled a gloomy brook; and beyond rose the cliffs that buttressed the rocky heights of French Mountain, seen by glimpses between the boughs.   On their left rose gradually the lower slopes of West Mountain.   All was rock, thicket, and forest; there was no open space but the road along which the regulars marched, while the Canadians and Indians pushed their way through the woods in such order as the broken ground would permit.

They were three miles from the lake, when their scouts brought in a prisoner who told them that a column of English troops was approaching.   Dieskau's preparations were quickly made.   While the regulars halted on the road, the Canadians and Indians moved to the front, where most of them hid in the forest along the slopes of West Mountain, and the rest lay close among the thickets on the other side.   Thus, when the English advanced to attack the regulars in front, they would find themselves caught in a double ambush. No sight or sound betrayed the snare; but behind every bush crouched a Canadian or a savage, with gun cocked and ears intent, listening for the tramp of the approaching column.

The wagoners who escaped the evening before had reached the camp about midnight, and reported that there was a war-party on the road near Fort Lyman. Johnson had at this time twenty-two hundred effective men, besides his three hundred Indians.[1] He called a council of war in the morning, and a resolution was taken which can only be explained by a complete misconception as to the force of the French. It was determined to send out two detachments of five hundred men each, one towards Fort Lyman, and the other towards South Bay, the object being, according to Johnson, "to catch the enemy in their retreat."[2] Hendrick, chief of the Mohawks, a brave and sagacious warrior, expressed his dissent after a fashion of his own. He picked up a stick and broke it; then he picked up several sticks, and showed that together they could not be broken. The hint was taken, and the two detachments were joined in one. Still the old savage shook his head. "If they are to be killed," he said, "they are too many; if

[1] *Wraxall to Lieutenant-Governor Delancey*, 10 *September*, 1755. Wraxall was Johnson's aide-de-camp and secretary. The *Second Letter to a Friend* says twenty-one hundred whites and two hundred or three hundred Indians. Blodget, who was also on the spot, sets the whites at two thousand.

[2] *Letter to the Governors of the Several Colonies*, 9 *September*, 1755.

they are to fight, they are too few." Nevertheless, he resolved to share their fortunes; and mounting on a gun-carriage, he harangued his warriors with a voice so animated and gestures so expressive that the New England officers listened in admiration, though they understood not a word. One difficulty remained. He was too old and fat to go afoot; but Johnson lent him a horse, which he bestrode, and trotted to the head of the column, followed by two hundred of his warriors as fast as they could grease, paint, and befeather themselves.

Captain Elisha Hawley was in his tent, finishing a letter which he had just written to his brother Joseph; and these were the last words: "I am this minute agoing out in company with five hundred men to see if we can intercept 'em in their retreat, or find their canoes in the Drowned Lands; and therefore must conclude this letter." He closed and directed it; and in an hour received his death-wound.

It was soon after eight o'clock when Ephraim Williams left the camp with his regiment, marched a little distance, and then waited for the rest of the detachment under Lieutenant-Colonel Whiting. Thus Dieskau had full time to lay his ambush. When Whiting came up, the whole moved on together, so little conscious of danger that no scouts were thrown out in front or flank; and, in full security, they entered the fatal snare. Before they were completely involved in it, the sharp eye of old Hendrick detected some sign of an enemy. At that instant, whether by accident or design, a gun was fired from the bushes. It is said that Dieskau's Iroquois, seeing Mohawks, their relatives, in the van, wished to warn them of danger. If so, the warning came too late. The thickets on the left blazed out a deadly fire, and the men fell by scores. In the words of Dieskau, the head of the column "was doubled up like a pack of cards." Hendrick's horse was shot down, and the chief was killed with a bayonet as he tried to rise. Williams, seeing a rising ground on his right, made for it, calling on his men to follow; but as he climbed the slope, guns flashed from the bushes, and a shot through the brain laid him dead. The men in the rear pressed forward to support their comrades, when a hot fire was suddenly opened on them from the forest along their right flank. Then there was a panic; some fled outright, and the whole column recoiled. The van now became the rear, and all the force of the enemy rushed upon it, shouting and screeching. There was a moment of total confusion; but a part of Williams's regiment rallied under command of Whiting, and covered the retreat, fighting behind trees like Indians, and firing and falling back by turns, bravely aided by some of the Mohawks and by a detachment which Johnson sent to their aid. "And a very handsome retreat they made," writes Pomeroy; "and so continued till they came within about three quarters of a mile of our camp. This was the last fire our men gave our enemies, which killed great numbers of them; they were seen to drop as pigeons." So ended the fray long known in New England fireside story as the "bloody morning scout." Dieskau now ordered a halt, and sounded his trumpets to collect his scattered men. His Indians, however, were sullen and unmanageable, and the Canadians also showed signs of wavering. The veteran who commanded them all, Legardeur de Saint-Pierre, had been killed. At length they were persuaded to move again, the regulars leading the way.

About an hour after Williams and his men had begun their march, a distant rattle of musketry was heard at the camp; and as it grew nearer and louder, the listeners knew that their comrades were on the retreat. Then, at the eleventh hour, preparations were begun for defence. A sort of barricade was made along the front of the camp, partly of wagons, and partly of inverted bateaux, but chiefly of the trunks of trees hastily hewn down in the neighboring forest and laid end to end in a single row. The line extended from the southern slopes of the hill on the left across a tract of rough ground to the marshes on the right. The forest, choked with bushes and clumps of rank ferns, was within a few yards of the barricade, and there was scarcely time to hack away the intervening thickets. Three cannon were planted to sweep the road that descended through the pines, and another was dragged up to the ridge of the hill. The defeated party began to come in; first, scared fugitives both white and red; then, gangs of men bringing the wounded; and at last, an hour and a half after the first fire was heard, the main detachment was seen marching in compact bodies down the road.

Five hundred men were detailed to guard the flanks of the camp. The rest stood behind the wagons or lay flat behind the logs and inverted bateaux, the Massachusetts men on the right, and the Connecticut men on the left. Besides Indians, this actual fighting force was between sixteen and seventeen hundred rustics, very few of whom had been under fire before that morning. They were hardly at their posts when they saw ranks of white-coated soldiers moving down the road, and bayonets that to them seemed innumerable glittering between the boughs. At the same time a terrific burst of war-whoops rose along the front; and, in the words of Pomeroy, "the Canadians and Indians, helter-skelter, the woods full of them, came running with undaunted courage right down the hill upon us, expecting to make us flee."[1] Some of the men grew uneasy; while the chief officers, sword in hand, threatened instant death to any who should stir from their posts.[2] If Dieskau had made an assault at that instant, there could be little doubt of the result.

This he well knew; but he was powerless. He had his small force of regulars well in hand; but the rest, red and white, were beyond control, scattering

[1] *Seth Pomeroy to his Wife*, 10 *September*, 1755.
[2] *Dr. Perez Marsh to William Williams*, 25 *September*, 1755.

through the woods and swamps, shouting, yelling, and firing from behind trees. The regulars advanced with intrepidity towards the camp where the trees were thin, deployed, and fired by platoons, till Captain Eyre, who commanded the artillery, opened on them with grape, broke their ranks, and compelled them to take to cover. The fusillade was now general on both sides, and soon grew furious. "Perhaps," Seth Pomeroy wrote to his wife, two days after, "the hailstones from heaven were never much thicker than their bullets came; but, blessed be God! that did not in the least daunt or disturb us." Johnson received a flesh-wound in the thigh, and spent the rest of the day in his tent. Lyman took command; and it is a marvel that he escaped alive, for he was four hours in the heat of the fire, directing and animating the men. "It was the most awful day my eyes ever beheld," wrote Surgeon Williams to his wife; "there seemed to be nothing but thunder and lightning and perpetual pillars of smoke." To him, his colleague Doctor Pynchon, one assistant, and a young student called "Billy," fell the charge of the wounded of his regiment. "The bullets flew about our ears all the time of dressing them; so we thought best to leave our tent and retire a few rods behind the shelter of a log-house." On the adjacent hill stood one Blodget, who seems to have been a sutler, watching, as well as bushes, trees, and smoke would let him, the progress of the fight, of which he soon after made and published a curious bird's-eye

Canadians and Indians had left the field and returned to the scene of the morning fight, to plunder and scalp the dead. They were resting themselves near a pool in the forest, close beside the road, when their repose was interrupted by a volley of bullets. It was fired by a scouting party from Fort Lyman, chiefly backwoodsmen, under Captains Folsom and McGinnis. The assailants were greatly outnumbered; but after a hard fight the Canadians and Indians broke and fled. McGinnis was mortally wounded. He continued to give orders till the firing was over; then fainted, and was carried, dying, to the camp. The bodies of the slain, according to tradition, were thrown into the pool, which bears to this day the name of Bloody Pond.

The various bands of fugitives rejoined each other towards night, and encamped in the forest, then made their way round the southern shoulder of French Mountain, till, in the next evening, they reached their canoes. Their plight was deplorable; for they had left their knapsacks behind, and were spent with fatigue and famine.

Meanwhile their captive general was not yet out of danger. The Mohawks were furious at their losses in the ambush of the morning, and above all at the death of Hendrick. Scarcely were Dieskau's wounds dressed, when several of them came into the tent. There was a long and angry dispute in their own language between them and Johnson, after which they went out very sullenly. Dieskau asked

what they wanted. "What do they want?" returned
Johnson. "To burn you, by God, eat you, and
smoke you in their pipes, in revenge for three or four
of their chiefs that were killed. But never fear;
you shall be safe with me, or else they shall kill us
both." [1] The Mohawks soon came back, and another
talk ensued, excited at first, and then more calm;
till at length the visitors, seemingly appeased, smiled,
gave Dieskau their hands in sign of friendship, and
quietly went out again. Johnson warned him that
he was not yet safe; and when the prisoner, fearing
that his presence might incommode his host, asked
to be removed to another tent, a captain and fifty
men were ordered to guard him. In the morning
an Indian, alone and apparently unarmed, loitered
about the entrance, and the stupid sentinel let him
pass in. He immediately drew a sword from under
a sort of cloak which he wore, and tried to stab
Dieskau, but was prevented by the colonel to whom
the tent belonged, who seized upon him, took away
his sword, and pushed him out. As soon as his
wounds would permit, Dieskau was carried on a
litter, strongly escorted, to Fort Lyman, whence he
was sent to Albany, and afterwards to New York.
He is profuse in expressions of gratitude for the
kindness shown him by the colonial officers, and
especially by Johnson. Of the provincial soldiers he

---

[1] See the story as told by Dieskau to the celebrated Diderot, at
Paris, in 1760. *Mémoires de Diderot*, i. 402 (1830). Compare *N. Y.
Col. Docs.*, x. 343.

remarked soon after the battle that in the morning
they fought like good boys, about noon like men, and
in the afternoon like devils.[1] In the spring of 1757
he sailed for England, and was for a time at Falmouth; whence Colonel Matthew Sewell, fearing
that he might see and learn too much, wrote to the
Earl of Holdernesse: "The Baron has great penetra-
tion and quickness of apprehension. His long service under Marshal Saxe renders him a man of real
consequence, to be cautiously observed. His circumstances deserve compassion, for indeed they are
very melancholy, and I much doubt of his being ever
perfectly cured." He was afterwards a long time at
Bath, for the benefit of the waters. In 1760 the
famous Diderot met him at Paris, cheerful and full
of anecdote, though wretchedly shattered by his
wounds. He died a few years later.

On the night after the battle the yeomen warriors
felt the truth of the saying that, next to defeat, the
saddest thing is victory. Comrades and friends by
scores lay scattered through the forest. As soon as
he could snatch a moment's leisure, the overworked
surgeon sent the dismal tidings to his wife: "My
dear brother Ephraim was killed by a ball through
his head; poor brother Josiah's wound I fear will
prove mortal; poor Captain Hawley is yet alive,
though I did not think he would live two hours after
bringing him in." Daniel Pomeroy was shot dead;
and his brother Seth wrote the news to his wife

---

[1] *Dr. Perez Marsh to William Williams,* 25 *September,* 1755.

Rachel, who was just delivered of a child: "Dear Sister, this brings heavy tidings; but let not your heart sink at the news, though it be your loss of a dear husband. Monday the eighth instant was a memorable day; and truly you may say, had not the Lord been on our side, we must all have been swallowed up. My brother, being one that went out in the first engagement, received a fatal shot through the middle of the head." Seth Pomeroy found a moment to write also to his own wife, whom he tells that another attack is expected; adding, in quaintly pious phrase: "But as God hath begun to show mercy, I hope he will go on to be gracious." Pomeroy was employed during the next few days with four hundred men in what he calls "the melancholy piece of business" of burying the dead. A letter-writer of the time does not approve what was done on this occasion. "Our people," he says, "not only buried the French dead, but buried as many of them as might be without the knowledge of our Indians, to prevent their being scalped. This I call an excess of civility;" his reason being that Braddock's dead soldiers had been left to the wolves.

The English loss in killed, wounded, and missing was two hundred and sixty-two;[1] and that of the French by their own account, two hundred and twenty-eight,[2] — a somewhat modest result of five

[1] *Return of Killed, Wounded, and Missing at the Battle of Lake George.*

[2] *Doreil au Ministre,* 20 *Octobre,* 1755. Surgeon Williams gives

hours' fighting. The English loss was chiefly in the ambush of the morning, where the killed greatly outnumbered the wounded, because those who fell and could not be carried away were tomahawked by Dieskau's Indians. In the fight at the camp, both Indians and Canadians kept themselves so well under cover that it was very difficult for the New England men to pick them off, while they on their part lay close behind their row of logs. On the French side, the regular officers and troops bore the brunt of the battle and suffered the chief loss, nearly all of the former and nearly half of the latter being killed or wounded.

Johnson did not follow up his success. He says that his men were tired. Yet five hundred of them had stood still all day, and boats enough for their transportation were lying on the beach. Ten miles down the lake, a path led over a gorge of the mountains to South Bay, where Dieskau had left his canoes and provisions. It needed but a few hours to reach and destroy them; but no such attempt was made. Nor, till a week after, did Johnson send out scouts to learn the strength of the enemy at Ticonderoga. Lyman strongly urged him to make an effort to seize that important pass; but Johnson thought only of holding his own position. "I think," he wrote, "we may expect very shortly a more

---

the English loss as two hundred and sixteen killed, and ninety-six wounded. Pomeroy thinks that the French lost four or five hundred. Johnson places their loss at four hundred.

formidable attack." He made a solid breastwork to defend his camp; and as reinforcements arrived, set them at building a fort on a rising ground by the lake. It is true that just after the battle he was deficient in stores, and had not bateaux enough to move his whole force. It is true, also, that he was wounded, and that he was too jealous of Lyman to delegate the command to him; and so the days passed till, within a fortnight, his nimble enemy were intrenched at Ticonderoga in force enough to defy him.

The Crown Point expedition was a failure disguised under an incidental success. The northern provinces, especially Massachusetts and Connecticut, did what they could to forward it, and after the battle sent a herd of raw recruits to the scene of action. Shirley wrote to Johnson from Oswego; declared that his reasons for not advancing were insufficient, and urged him to push for Ticonderoga at once. Johnson replied that he had not wagons enough, and that his troops were ill-clothed, ill-fed, discontented, insubordinate, and sickly. He complained that discipline was out of the question, because the officers were chosen by popular election; that many of them were no better than the men, unfit for command, and like so many "heads of a mob." [1] The reinforcements began to come in, till, in October, there were thirty-six hundred men in the camp; and as most of them wore summer clothing

[1] *Shirley to Johnson, 19 September, 1755. Ibid., 24 September, 1755. Johnson to Shirley, 22 September, 1755. Johnson to Phipps, 10 October, 1755* (Massachusetts Archives).

and had but one thin domestic blanket, they were half frozen in the chill autumn nights.

Johnson called a council of war; and as he was suffering from inflamed eyes, and was still kept in his tent by his wound, he asked Lyman to preside, — not unwilling, perhaps, to shift the responsibility upon him. After several sessions and much debate, the assembled officers decided that it was inexpedient to proceed.[1] Yet the army lay more than a month longer at the lake, while the disgust of the men increased daily under the rains, frosts, and snows of a dreary November. On the twenty-second, Chandler, chaplain of one of the Massachusetts regiments, wrote in the interleaved almanac that served him as a diary: "The men just ready to mutiny. Some clubbed their firelocks and marched, but returned back. Very rainy night. Miry water standing in the tents. Very distressing time among the sick." The men grew more and more unruly, and went off in squads without asking leave. A difficult question arose: Who should stay for the winter to garrison the new forts, and who should command them? It was settled at last that a certain number of soldiers from each province should be assigned to this ungrateful service, and that Massachusetts should have the first officer, Connecticut the second, and New York the third. Then the camp broke up. "Thursday the 27th," wrote the chaplain in his almanac, "we set out about ten of the clock, marched in a

[1] *Reports of Council of War*, 11–21 *October*, 1755.

body, about three thousand, the wagons and baggage in the centre, our colonel much insulted by the way." The soldiers dispersed to their villages and farms, where in blustering winter nights, by the blazing logs of New England hearthstones, they told their friends and neighbors the story of the campaign.

The profit of it fell to Johnson. If he did not gather the fruits of victory, at least he reaped its laurels. He was a courtier in his rough way. He had changed the name of Lac St. Sacrement to Lake George, in compliment to the King. He now changed that of Fort Lyman to Fort Edward, in compliment to one of the King's grandsons; and, in compliment to another, called his new fort at the lake, William Henry. Of General Lyman he made no mention in his report of the battle, and his partisans wrote letters traducing that brave officer; though Johnson is said to have confessed in private that he owed him the victory. He himself found no lack of eulogists; and, to quote the words of an able but somewhat caustic and prejudiced opponent, "to the panegyrical pen of his secretary, Mr. Wraxall, and the *sic volo sic jubeo* of Lieutenant-Governor Delancey, is to be ascribed that mighty renown which echoed through the colonies, reverberated to Europe, and elevated a raw, inexperienced youth into a kind of second Marlborough."[1] Parliament gave him five

[1] *Review of Military Operations in North America, in a Letter to a Nobleman* (ascribed to William Livingston).

On the Battle of Lake George a mass of papers will be found in

thousand pounds, and the King made him a
baronet.

the *N. Y. Col. Docs.*, vols. vi. and x. Those in Vol. VI., taken
chiefly from the archives of New York, consist of official and private letters, reports, etc., on the English side. Those in Vol. X.
are drawn chiefly from the archives of the French War Department, and include the correspondence of Dieskau and his adjutant
Montreuil. I have examined most of them in the original. Besides
these I have obtained from the Archives de la Marine and other
sources a number of important additional papers, which have never
been printed, including Vaudreuil's reports to the Minister of War,
and his strictures on Dieskau, whom he accuses of disobeying
orders by dividing his force ; also the translation of an English
journal of the campaign found in the pocket of a captured officer,
and a long account of the battle sent by Bigot to the minister of
marine, 4 October, 1755.

I owe to the kindness of Theodore Pomeroy, Esq., a copy of the
Journal of Lieutenant-Colonel Seth Pomeroy, whose letters also are
full of interest ; as are those of Surgeon Williams, from the collection of William L. Stone, Esq. The papers of Colonel Israel Williams, in the Library of the Massachusetts Historical Society, contain many other curious letters relating to the campaign, extracts
from some of which are given in the text. One of the most curious
records of the battle is *A Prospective-Plan of the Battle near Lake
George, with an Explanation thereof, containing a full, though short, History of that important Affair, by Samuel Blodget, occasionally at the
Camp when the Battle was fought.* It is an engraving, printed at
Boston soon after the fight, of which it gives a clear idea. Four
years after, Blodget opened a shop in Boston, where, as appears by
his advertisements in the newspapers, he sold "English Goods, also
English Hatts, etc." The Engraving is reproduced in the *Docu-
mentary History of New York,* iv., and elsewhere. The *Explanation
thereof* is only to be found complete in the original. This, as well
as the anonymous *Second Letter to a Friend,* also printed at Boston
in 1755, is excellent for the information it gives as to the condition
of the ground where the conflict took place, and the position of the
combatants. The unpublished Archives of Massachusetts ; the
correspondence of Sir William Johnson ; the *Review of Military
Operations in North America ;* Dwight, *Travels in New England and
New York,* iii. ; and Hoyt, *Antiquarian Researches on Indian Wars,*

— should also be mentioned.   Dwight and Hoyt drew their information from aged survivors of the battle.   I have repeatedly examined the localities.

In the odd effusion of the colonial muse called *Tilden's Poems, chiefly to Animate and Rouse the Soldiers, printed* 1756, is a piece styled *The Christian Hero, or New England's Triumph,* beginning with the invocation, —

> " O Heaven, indulge my feeble Muse,
> Teach her what numbers for to choose!"

and containing the following stanza, —

> " Their Dieskau we from them detain,
>   While Canada aloud complains
> And counts the numbers of their slain
>   And makes a dire complaint;
>   The Indians to their demon gods;
> And with the French there's little odds,
> While images receive their nods,
>   Invoking rotten saints."

CHAPTER X.

1755, 1756.

SHIRLEY. — BORDER WAR.

THE capture of Niagara was to finish the work of
the summer. This alone would have gained for
England the control of the valley of the Ohio, and
made Braddock's expedition superfluous. One
marvels at the short-sightedness, the dissensions, the
apathy which had left this key of the interior so long
in the hands of France without an effort to wrest it
from her. To master Niagara would be to cut the
communications of Canada with the whole system of
French forts and settlements in the West, and leave
them to perish like limbs of a girdled tree.

Major-General Shirley, in the flush of his new
martial honors, was to try his prentice hand at the
work. The lawyer-soldier could plan a campaign

boldly and well. It remained to see how he would
do his part towards executing it. In July he arrived
at Albany, the starting-point of his own expedition
as well as that of Johnson. This little Dutch city
was an outpost of civilization. The Hudson, descend-
ing from the northern wilderness, connected it with
the lakes and streams that formed the thoroughfare
to Canada; while the Mohawk, flowing from the
west, was a liquid pathway to the forest homes of
the Five Nations. Before the war was over, a little
girl, Anne MacVicar, daughter of a Highland officer,
was left at Albany by her father, and spent several
years there in the house of Mrs. Schuyler, aunt of
General Schuyler of the Revolution. Long after,
married and middle-aged, she wrote down her recol-
lections of the place, — the fort on the hill behind;
the great street, grassy and broad, that descended
thence to the river, with market, guard-house, town-
hall, and two churches in the middle, and rows of
quaint Dutch-built houses on both sides, each detached from its neighbors, each with its well, garden,
and green, and its great overshadowing tree. Before
every house was a capacious porch, with seats where
the people gathered in the summer twilight; old men
at one door, matrons at another, young men and girls
mingling at a third; while the cows with their tinkling
bells came from the common at the end of the town,
each stopping to be milked at the door of its owner;
and children, porringer in hand, sat on the steps, watching the process and waiting their evening meal.

Such was the quiet picture painted on the memory of Anne MacVicar, and reproduced by the pen of Mrs. Anne Grant.[1] The patriarchal, semi-rural town had other aspects, not so pleasing. The men were mainly engaged in the fur-trade, sometimes legally with the Five Nations, and sometimes illegally with the Indians of Canada, — an occupation which by no means tends to soften the character. The Albany Dutch traders were a rude, hard race, loving money, and not always scrupulous as to the means of getting it. Coming events, too, were soon to have their effect on this secluded community. Regiments, red and blue, trumpets, drums, banners, artillery trains, and all the din of war transformed its peaceful streets, and brought some attaint to domestic morals hitherto commendable; for during the next five years Albany was to be the principal base of military operations on the continent.

Shirley had left the place, and was now on his way up the Mohawk. His force, much smaller than at first intended, consisted of the New Jersey regiment, which mustered five hundred men, known as the "Jersey Blues," and of the fiftieth and fifty-first regiments, called respectively Shirley's and Pepperrell's. These, though paid by the King and counted as regulars, were in fact raw provincials, just raised in the colonies, and wearing their gay uniforms with an

[1] *Memoirs of an American Lady* (Mrs. Schuyler), chap. vi. A genuine picture of colonial life, and a charming book, though far from being historically trustworthy. Compare the account of Albany in Kalm, ii. 102.

awkward, unaccustomed air.   How they gloried in them may be gathered from a letter of Sergeant James Gray, of Pepperrell's, to his brother John: "I have two Holland shirts, found me by the King, and two pair of shoes and two pair of worsted stockings; a good silver-laced hat (the lace I could sell for four dollars); and my clothes is as fine scarlet broadcloth as ever you did see.   A sergeant here in the King's regiment is counted as good as an ensign with you; and one day in every week we must have our hair or wigs powdered." [1]   Most of these gorgeous warriors were already on their way to Oswego, their first destination.

Shirley followed, embarking at the Dutch village of Schenectady, and ascending the Mohawk with about two hundred of the so-called regulars in bateaux.   They passed Fort Johnson, the two villages of the Mohawks, and the Palatine settlement of German Flats; left behind the last trace of civilized man, rowed sixty miles through a wilderness, and reached the Great Carrying Place, which divided the waters that flow to the Hudson from those that flow to Lake Ontario.   Here now stands the city which the classic zeal of its founders has adorned with the name of Rome.   Then all was swamp and forest, traversed by a track that led to Wood Creek, — which is not to be confounded with the Wood Creek of Lake Champlain.   Thither the bateaux were dragged on sledges and launched on the dark and tortuous

[1] *James Gray to John Gray,* 11 *July,* 1755.

stream, which, fed by a decoction of forest leaves that oozed from the marshy shores, crept in shadow through depths of foliage, with only a belt of illumined sky gleaming between the jagged tree-tops. Tall and lean with straining towards the light, their rough, gaunt stems trickling with perpetual damps, stood on either hand the silent hosts of the forest. The skeletons of their dead, barkless, blanched, and shattered, strewed the mudbanks and shallows; others lay submerged, like bones of drowned mammoths, thrusting lank, white limbs above the sullen water; and great trees, entire as yet, were flung by age or storms athwart the current, — a bristling barricade of matted boughs. There was work for the axe as well as for the oar; till at length Lake Oneida opened before them, and they rowed all day over its sunny breast, reached the outlet, and drifted down the shallow eddies of the Onondaga, between walls of verdure, silent as death, yet haunted everywhere with ambushed danger. It was twenty days after leaving Schenectady when they neared the mouth of the river; and Lake Ontario greeted them, stretched like a sea to the pale brink of the northern sky, while on the bare hill at their left stood the miserable little fort of Oswego.

Shirley's whole force soon arrived; but not the needful provisions and stores. The machinery of transportation and the commissariat was in the bewildered state inevitable among a peaceful people at the beginning of a war; while the news of Braddock's

defeat produced such an effect on the boatmen and
the draymen at the carrying-places that the greater
part deserted.   Along with these disheartening tidings, Shirley learned the death of his eldest son,
killed at the side of Braddock.   He had with him a
second son, Captain John Shirley, a vivacious young
man, whom his father and his father's friends in
their familiar correspondence always called "Jack."
John Shirley's letters give a lively view of the
situation.

"I have sat down to write to you," — thus he
addresses Governor Morris, of Pennsylvania, who
seems to have had a great liking for him, — "because
there is an opportunity of sending you a few lines;
and if you will promise to excuse blots, interlinea-
tions, and grease (for this is written in the open air,
upon the head of a pork-barrel, and twenty people
about me), I will begin another half-sheet.   We are
not more than about fifteen hundred men fit for
duty; but that, I am pretty sure, if we can go in
time in our sloop, schooner, row-galleys, and whaleboats, will be sufficient to take Frontenac; after
which we may venture to go upon the attack of
Niagara, but not before.   I have not the least doubt
with myself of knocking down both these places yet
this fall, if we can get away in a week.   If we take
or destroy their two vessels at Frontenac, and ruin
their harbor there, and destroy the two forts of that
and Niagara, I shall think we have done great things.
Nobody holds it out better than my father and

myself. We shall all of us relish a good house over
our heads, being all encamped, except the General
and some few field-officers, who have what are called
at Oswego houses; but they would in other countries
be called only sheds, except the fort, where my
father is. Adieu, dear sir; I hope my next will be
directed from Frontenac. Yours most affectionately,
John Shirley." [1]

Fort Frontenac lay to the northward, fifty miles or
more across the lake. Niagara lay to the westward,
at the distance of four or five days by boat or canoe
along the south shore. At Frontenac there was a
French force of fourteen hundred regulars and
Canadians. [2] They had vessels and canoes to cross
the lake and fall upon Oswego as soon as Shirley
should leave it to attack Niagara; for Braddock's
captured papers had revealed to them the English
plan. If they should take it, Shirley would be cut

---

[1] The young author of this letter was, like his brother, a victim
of the war.

"Permit me, good sir, to offer you my hearty condolence upon
the death of my friend Jack, whose worth I admired, and feel for
him more than I can express. . . . Few men of his age had so many
friends." — *Governor Morris to Shirley,* 27 *November,* 1755.

"My heart bleeds for Mr. Shirley. He must be overwhelmed
with Grief when he hears of Capt. John Shirley's Death, of which
I have an Account by the last Post from New York, where he died
of a Flux and Fever that he had contracted at Oswego. The loss
of Two Sons in one Campaign scarcely admits of Consolation. I
feel the Anguish of the unhappy Father, and mix my Tears very
heartily with his. I have had an intimate Acquaintance with Both
of Them for many Years, and know well their inestimable Value."
— *Morris to Dinwiddie,* 29 *November,* 1755.

[2] *Bigot au Ministre,* 27 *Août,* 1755.

off from his supplies and placed in desperate jeopardy, with the enemy in his rear. Hence it is that John Shirley insists on taking Frontenac before attempting Niagara. But the task was not easy; for the French force at the former place was about equal in effective strength to that of the English at Oswego. At Niagara, too, the French had, at the end of August, nearly twelve hundred Canadians and Indians from Fort Duquesne and the upper lakes.[1] Shirley was but imperfectly informed by his scouts of the unexpected strength of the opposition that awaited him; but he knew enough to see that his position was a difficult one. His movement on Niagara was stopped, first by want of provisions, and secondly because he was checkmated by the troops at Frontenac. He did not despair. Want of courage was not among his failings, and he was but too ready to take risks. He called a council of officers, told them that the total number of men fit for duty was thirteen hundred and seventy-six, and that as soon as provisions enough should arrive he would embark for Niagara with six hundred soldiers and as many Indians as possible, leaving the rest to defend Oswego against the expected attack from Fort Frontenac.[2]

"All I am uneasy about is our provisions," writes John Shirley to his friend Morris; "our men have been upon half allowance of bread these three weeks past, and no rum given to 'em. My father yesterday

---

[1] *Bigot au Ministre*, 5 *Septembre*, 1755.
[2] *Minutes of a Council of War at Oswego*, 18 *September*, 1755.

called all the Indians together and made 'em a speech
on the subject of General Johnson's engagement,
which he calculated to inspire them with a spirit of
revenge." After the speech he gave them a bullock
for a feast, which they roasted and ate, pretending
that they were eating the governor of Canada! Some
provisions arriving, orders were given to embark on
the next day; but the officers murmured their dissent. The weather was persistently bad, their vessels
would not hold half the party, and the bateaux,
made only for river navigation, would infallibly
founder on the treacherous and stormy lake. "All
the field-officers," says John Shirley, "think it too
rash an attempt; and I have heard so much of it that
I think it my duty to let my father know what I
hear." Another council was called; and the general,
reluctantly convinced of the danger, put the question
whether to go or not. The situation admitted but
one reply. The council was of opinion that for
the present the enterprise was impracticable; that
Oswego should be strengthened, more vessels built,
and preparation made to renew the attempt as soon
as spring opened.[1] All thoughts of active operations were now suspended, and during what was
left of the season the troops exchanged the musket
for the spade, saw, and axe. At the end of October, leaving seven hundred men at Oswego, Shirley
returned to Albany, and narrowly escaped drowning
on the way, while passing a rapid in a whale-boat,

[1] *Minutes of a Council of War at Oswego,* 27 *September,* 1755.

to try the fitness of that species of craft for river navigation.[1]

Unfortunately for him, he had fallen out with Johnson, whom he had made what he was, but who now turned against him, — a seeming ingratitude not wholly unprovoked. Shirley had diverted the New Jersey regiment, destined originally for Crown Point, to his own expedition against Niagara. Naturally inclined to keep all the reins in his own hands, he had encroached on Johnson's new office of Indian superintendent, held conferences with the Five Nations, and employed agents of his own to deal with them. These agents were persons obnoxious to Johnson, being allied with the clique of Dutch traders at Albany, who hated him because he had supplanted them in the direction of Indian affairs; and in a violent letter to the Lords of Trade, he inveighs against their "licentious and abandoned proceedings," "villanous conduct," "scurrilous false-hoods," and "base and insolent behavior."[2] "I am considerable enough," he says, "to have enemies and to be envied;"[3] and he declares he has proof that Shirley told the Mohawks that he, Johnson, was an

[1] On the Niagara expedition, *Braddock's Instructions to Major-General Shirley*. *Correspondence of Shirley*, 1755. *Conduct of Major-General Shirley* (London, 1758). Letters of John Shirley in *Pennsylvania Archives*, ii. *Bradstreet to Shirley*, 17 *August*, 1755. MSS. in Massachusetts Archives. *Review of Military Operations in North America*. *Gentleman's Magazine*, 1757, p. 73. *London Magazine*, 1759, p. 594. Trumbull, *Hist. Connecticut*, ii. 370.

[2] *Johnson to the Lords of Trade*, 3 *September*, 1755.

[3] *Ibid.*, 17 *January*, 1756.

upstart of his creating, whom he had set up and
could pull down. Again, he charges Shirley's agents
with trying to "debauch the Indians from joining
him;" while Shirley, on his side, retorts the same
complaint against his accuser.[1] When, by the death
of Braddock, Shirley became commander-in-chief,
Johnson grew so restive at being subject to his
instructions that he declined to hold the management
of Indian affairs unless it was made independent of
his rival. The dispute became mingled with the
teapot-tempest of New York provincial politics.
The lieutenant-governor, Delancey, a politician of
restless ambition and consummate dexterity, had
taken umbrage at Shirley, of whose rising honors,
not borne with remarkable humility, he appears to
have been jealous. Delancey had hitherto favored
the Dutch faction in the Assembly, hostile to Johnson; but he now changed attitude, and joined hands
with him against the object of their common dislike.
The one was strong in the prestige of a loudly
trumpeted victory, and the other had means of influence over the ministry. Their coalition boded ill to
Shirley, and he soon felt its effects.[2]

The campaign was now closed, — a sufficiently
active one, seeing that the two nations were nomi-

[1] *John Shirley to Governor Morris*, 12 *August*, 1755.
[2] On this affair, see various papers in *N. Y. Col. Docs.*, vi., vii.
Smith, *Hist. New York*, Part II., Chaps. IV. V. *Review of Military
Operations in North America*. Both Smith and Livingston, the
author of the *Review*, were personally cognizant of the course of
the dispute.

nally at peace.   A disastrous rout on the Monongahela, failure at Niagara, a barren victory at Lake
George, and three forts captured in Acadia, were
the disappointing results on the part of England.
Nor had her enemies cause to boast. The Indians,
it is true, had won a battle for them: but they had
suffered mortifying defeat from a raw militia; their
general was a prisoner; and they had lost Acadia
past hope.

The campaign was over; but not its effects. It
remains to see what befell from the rout of Braddock
and the unpardonable retreat of Dunbar from the
frontier which it was his duty to defend. Dumas
had replaced Contrecœur in the command of Fort
Duquesne; and his first care was to set on the
western tribes to attack the border settlements. His
success was triumphant. The Delawares and Shawanoes, old friends of the English, but for years past
tending to alienation through neglect and ill-usage,
now took the lead against them. Many of the
Mingoes, or Five Nation Indians on the Ohio, also
took up the hatchet, as did various remoter tribes.
The West rose like a nest of hornets, and swarmed
in fury against the English frontier. Such was the
consequence of the defeat of Braddock aided by the
skilful devices of the French commander. "It is by
means such as I have mentioned," says Dumas, "varied
in every form to suit the occasion, that I have succeeded in ruining the three adjacent provinces, Pennsylvania, Maryland, and Virginia, driving off the

inhabitants, and totally destroying the settlements
over a tract of country thirty leagues wide, reckoning
from the line of Fort Cumberland. M. de Contrecœur
had not been gone a week before I had six or seven
different war-parties in the field at once, always
accompanied by Frenchmen. Thus far, we have
lost only two officers and a few soldiers; but the
Indian villages are full of prisoners of every age and
sex. The enemy has lost far more since the battle
than on the day of his defeat." [1]

Dumas, required by the orders of his superiors to
wage a detestable warfare against helpless settlers
and their families, did what he could to temper its
horrors, and enjoined the officers who went with the
Indians to spare no effort to prevent them from tor-
turing prisoners. [2] The attempt should be set down
to his honor; but it did not avail much. In the
record of cruelties committed this year on the
borders, we find repeated instances of children scalped
alive. "They kill all they meet," writes a French
priest; "and after having abused the women and
maidens, they slaughter or burn them." [3]

Washington was now in command of the Virginia

---

[1] *Dumas au Ministre*, 24 *Juillet*, 1756.

[2] *Mémoires de Famille de l'Abbé Casgrain*, cited in *Le Foyer Can-
adien*, iii. 26, where an extract is given from an order of Dumas to
Baby, a Canadian officer. Orders of Contrecœur and Ligneris to
the same effect are also given. A similar order, signed by Dumas,
was found in the pocket of Douville, an officer killed by the English on the frontier. *Writings of Washington*, ii. 137, *note*.

[3] *Rev. Claude Godefroy Cocquard, S. J., à son Frère, Mars* (?),
1757.

regiment, consisting of a thousand men, raised afterwards to fifteen hundred. With these he was to protect a frontier of three hundred and fifty miles
against more numerous enemies, who could choose
their time and place of attack. His headquarters
were at Winchester. His men were an ungovernable
crew, enlisted chiefly on the turbulent border, and
resenting every kind of discipline as levelling them
with negroes; while the sympathizing House of
Burgesses hesitated for months to pass any law for
enforcing obedience, lest it should trench on the
liberties of free white men. The service was to the
last degree unpopular. "If we talk of obliging men
to serve their country," wrote Landon Carter, "we
are sure to hear a fellow mumble over the words
'liberty' and 'property' a thousand times."[1] The
people, too, were in mortal fear of a slave insurrection, and therefore dared not go far from home.[2]
Meanwhile a panic reigned along the border. Captain Waggoner, passing a gap in the Blue Ridge,
could hardly make his way for the crowd of fugitives.
"Every day," writes Washington, "we have accounts
of such cruelties and barbarities as are shocking to
human nature. It is not possible to conceive the
situation and danger of this miserable country. Such
numbers of French and Indians are all around that
no road is safe."

These frontiers had always been at peace. No

[1] Extract in *Writings of Washington*, ii. 145, *note*.
[2] *Letters of Dinwiddie*, 1755.

forts of refuge had thus far been built, and the
scattered settlers had no choice but flight.   Their first
impulse was to put wife and children beyond reach
of the tomahawk.   As autumn advanced, the invading bands grew more and more audacious.   Braddock
had opened a road for them by which they could
cross the mountains at their ease; and scouts from
Fort Cumberland reported that this road was beaten
by as many feet as when the English army passed
last summer.   Washington was beset with difficulties.
Men and officers alike were unruly and mutinous.
He was at once blamed for their disorders and refused
the means of repressing them.   Envious detractors
published slanders against him.   A petty Maryland
captain, who had once had a commission from the
King, refused to obey his orders, and stirred up
factions among his officers.   Dinwiddie gave him
cold support.   The temper of the old Scotchman,
crabbed at the best, had been soured by disappoint-
ment, vexation, weariness, and ill-health.   He had,
besides, a friend and countryman, Colonel Innes,
whom, had he dared, he would gladly have put in
Washington's place.   He was full of zeal in the
common cause, and wanted to direct the defence of
the borders from his house at Williamsburg, two
hundred miles distant.   Washington never hesitated
to obey; but he accompanied his obedience by a
statement of his own convictions and his reasons for
them, which, though couched in terms the most
respectful, galled his irascible chief.   The governor

acknowledged his merit, but bore him no love, and
sometimes wrote to him in terms which must have
tried his high temper to the utmost. Sometimes,
though rarely, he gave words to his emotion.

"Your Honor," he wrote in April, "may see to
what unhappy straits the distressed inhabitants and
myself are reduced. I see inevitable destruction in
so clear a light that unless vigorous measures are
taken by the Assembly, and speedy assistance sent
from below, the poor inhabitants that are now in
forts must unavoidably fall, while the remainder are
flying before the barbarous foe. In fine, the melancholy situation of the people; the little prospect of
assistance; the gross and scandalous abuse cast upon
the officers in general, which is reflecting upon me in
particular for suffering misconduct of such extraordinary kinds; and the distant prospect, if any, of
gaining honor and reputation in the service, — cause
me to lament the hour that gave me a commission,
and would induce me at any other time than this of
imminent danger to resign, without one hesitating
moment, a command from which I never expect to
reap either honor or benefit, but, on the contrary,
have almost an absolute certainty of incurring dis-
pleasure below, while the murder of helpless families
may be laid to my account here.

"The supplicating tears of the women and moving
petitions of the men melt me into such deadly sorrow that I solemnly declare, if I know my own
mind, I could offer myself a willing sacrifice to the

butchering enemy, provided that would contribute to the people's ease." [1]

In the turmoil around him, patriotism and public duty seemed all to be centred in the breast of one heroic youth. He was respected and generally beloved, but he did not kindle enthusiasm. His were the qualities of an unflagging courage, an all-enduring fortitude, and a deep trust. He showed an astonishing maturity of character, and the kind of mastery over others which begins with mastery over self. At twenty-four he was the foremost man, and acknowledged as such, along the whole long line of the western border.

To feel the situation, the nature of these frontiers must be kept in mind. Along the skirts of the southern and middle colonies ran for six or seven hundred miles a loose, thin, dishevelled fringe of population, the half-barbarous pioneers of advancing civilization. Their rude dwellings were often miles apart. Buried in woods, the settler lived in an appalling loneliness. A low-browed cabin of logs, with moss stuffed in the chinks to keep out the wind, roof covered with sheets of bark, chimney of sticks and clay, and square holes closed by a shutter in place of windows; an unkempt matron, lean with hard work, and a brood of children with bare heads and tattered garments eked out by deerskin, — such was the home of the pioneer in the remoter and wilder districts. The scene around bore witness to his

[1] *Writings of Washington*, ii. 143.

labors. It was the repulsive transition from savagery
to civilization, from the forest to the farm. The
victims of his axe lay strewn about the dismal "clearing" in a chaos of prostrate trunks, tangled boughs,
and withered leaves, waiting for the fire that was to
be the next agent in the process of improvement;
while around, voiceless and grim, stood the living
forest, gazing on the desolation, and biding its own
day of doom. The owner of the cabin was miles
away, hunting in the woods for the wild turkey and
venison which were the chief food of himself and his
family till the soil could be tamed into the bearing
of crops.

Towards night he returned; and as he issued from
the forest shadows he saw a column of blue smoke
rising quietly in the still evening air. He ran to the
spot; and there, among the smouldering logs of his
dwelling, lay, scalped and mangled, the dead bodies
of wife and children. A war-party had passed that
way. Breathless, palpitating, his brain on fire, he
rushed through the thickening night to carry the
alarm to his nearest neighbor, three miles distant.

Such was the character and the fate of many incipient settlements of the utmost border. Farther east,
they had a different aspect. Here, small farms with
well-built log-houses, cattle, crops of wheat, and
Indian corn, were strung at intervals along some
woody valley of the lower Alleghanies: yesterday a
scene of hardy toil; to-day swept with destruction
from end to end. There was no warning; no time

for concert, perhaps none for flight. Sudden as the leaping panther, a pack of human wolves burst out of the forest, did their work, and vanished.

If the country had been an open one, like the plains beyond the Mississippi, the situation would have been less frightful; but the forest was everywhere, rolled over hill and valley in billows of interminable green, — a leafy maze, a mystery of shade, a universal hiding-place, where murder might lurk unseen at its victim's side, and Nature seemed formed to nurse the mind with wild and dark imaginings. The detail of blood is set down in the untutored words of those who saw and felt it. But there was a suffering that had no record, — the mortal fear of women and children in the solitude of their wilderness homes, haunted, waking and sleeping, with nightmares of horror that were but the forecast of an imminent reality. The country had in past years been so peaceful, and the Indians so friendly, that many of the settlers, especially on the Pennsylvanian border, had no arms, and were doubly in need of help from the government. In Virginia they had it, such as it was. In Pennsylvania they had for months none whatever; and the Assembly turned a deaf ear to their cries.

Far to the east, sheltered from danger, lay staid and prosperous Philadelphia, the home of order and thrift. It took its stamp from the Quakers, its original and dominant population, set apart from the other colonists not only in character and creed, but

in the outward symbols of a peculiar dress and a daily
sacrifice of grammar on the altar of religion. The
even tenor of their lives counteracted the effects of
climate, and they are said to have been perceptibly
more rotund in feature and person than their neighbors. Yet, broad and humanizing as was their faith,
they were capable of extreme bitterness towards opponents, clung tenaciously to power, and were jealous
for the ascendency of their sect, which had begun to
show signs of wavering. On other sects they looked
askance, and regarded the Presbyterians in particular
with a dislike which in moments of crisis rose to
detestation.[1] They held it sin to fight, and above all
to fight against Indians.

Here was one cause of military paralysis. It was
reinforced by another. The old standing quarrel
between governor and assembly had grown more
violent than ever; and this as a direct consequence
of the public distress, which above all things demanded harmony. The dispute turned this time on
a single issue, — that of the taxation of the proprietary estates. The estates in question consisted
of vast tracts of wild land, yielding no income, and
at present to a great extent worthless, being overrun
by the enemy.[2] The Quaker Assembly had refused
to protect them; and on one occasion had rejected an

[1] See a crowd of party pamphlets, Quaker against Presbyterian,
which appeared at Philadelphia in 1764, abusively acrimonious on
both sides.

[2] The productive estates of the proprietaries were taxed through
the tenants.

offer of the proprietaries to join them in paying the cost of their defence.[1] But though they would not defend the land, they insisted on taxing it; and farther insisted that the taxes upon it should be laid by the provincial assessors. By a law of the province, these assessors were chosen by popular vote; and in consenting to this law, the proprietaries had expressly provided that their estates should be exempted from all taxes to be laid by officials in whose appointment they had no voice.[2] Thomas and Richard Penn, the present proprietaries, had debarred their deputy, the governor, both by the terms of his commission and by special instruction, from consenting to such taxation, and had laid him under heavy bonds to secure his obedience. Thus there was another side to the question than that of the Assembly; though our American writers have been slow to acknowledge it.

Benjamin Franklin was leader in the Assembly and shared its views. The feudal proprietorship of the Penn family was odious to his democratic nature. It was, in truth, a pestilent anomaly, repugnant to the genius of the people; and the disposition and character of the present proprietaries did not tend to render it less vexatious. Yet there were considera-

[1] The proprietaries offered to contribute to the cost of building and maintaining a fort on the spot where the French soon after built Fort Duquesne. This plan, vigorously executed, would have saved the province from a deluge of miseries. One of the reasons assigned by the Assembly for rejecting it was that it would irritate the enemy. See *supra*, 64.

[2] *A Brief View of the Conduct of Pennsylvania for the year* 1755.

tions which might have tempered the impatient hatred
with which the colonists regarded it. The first
proprietary, William Penn, had used his feudal rights
in the interest of a broad liberalism; and through
them had established the popular institutions and
universal tolerance which made Pennsylvania the
most democratic province in America, and nursed the
spirit of liberty which now revolted against his heirs.
The one absorbing passion of Pennsylvania was
resistance to their deputy, the governor. The badge
of feudalism, though light, was insufferably irritat-
ing; and the sons of William Penn were moreover
detested by the Quakers as renegades from the faith
of their father. Thus the immediate political conflict engrossed mind and heart; and in the rancor of
their quarrel with the proprietaries, the Assembly
forgot the French and Indians.

In Philadelphia and the eastern districts the
Quakers could ply their trades, tend their shops, till
their farms, and discourse at their ease on the wickedness of war. The midland counties, too, were for
the most part tolerably safe. They were occupied
mainly by crude German peasants, who nearly
equalled in number all the rest of the population,
and who, gathered at the centre of the province,
formed a mass politically indigestible. Translated
from servitude to the most ample liberty, they hated
the thought of military service, which reminded them
of former oppression, cared little whether they lived
under France or England, and, thinking themselves

out of danger, had no mind to be taxed for the
defence of others. But while the great body of the
Germans were sheltered from harm, those of them
who lived farther westward were not so fortunate.
Here, mixed with Scotch Irish Presbyterians and
Celtic Irish Catholics, they formed a rough border
population, the discordant elements of which could
rarely unite for common action; yet, though confused
and disjointed, they were a living rampart to the rest
of the colony. Against them raged the furies of
Indian war; and, maddened with distress and terror,
they cried aloud for help.

Petition after petition came from the borders for
arms and ammunition, and for a militia law to enable
the people to organize and defend themselves. The
Quakers resisted. "They have taken uncommon
pains," writes Governor Morris to Shirley, "to prevent the people from taking up arms." [1] Braddock's
defeat, they declared, was a just judgment on him
and his soldiers for molesting the French in their
settlements on the Ohio. [2] A bill was passed by the
Assembly for raising fifty thousand pounds for the
King's use by a tax which included the proprietary
lands. The governor, constrained by his instructions
and his bonds, rejected it. "I can only say," he told
them, "that I will readily pass a bill for striking
any sum in paper money the present exigency may
require, provided funds are established for sinking

[1] *Morris to Shirley,* 16 *August,* 1755.
[2] *Morris to Sir Thomas Robinson.* 28 *August,* 1755.

the same in five years." Messages long and acrimonious were exchanged between the parties. The
Assembly, had they chosen, could easily have raised
money enough by methods not involving the point in
dispute; but they thought they saw in the crisis a
means of forcing the governor to yield. The Quakers
had an alternative motive: if the governor gave way,
it was a political victory; if he stood fast, their non-
resistance principles would triumph, and in this
triumph their ascendency as a sect would be confirmed. The debate grew every day more bitter and
unmannerly. The governor could not yield; the
Assembly would not. There was a complete deadlock. The Assembly requested the governor "not to
make himself the hateful instrument of reducing a
free people to the abject state of vassalage." [1] As
the raising of money and the control of its expenditure was in their hands; as he could not prorogue or
dissolve them, and as they could adjourn on their
own motion to such time as pleased them; as they
paid his support, and could withhold it if he offended
them, — which they did in the present case, — it
seemed no easy task for him to reduce them to vassalage. "What must we do," pursued the Assembly,
"to please this kind governor, who takes so much
pains to render us obnoxious to our sovereign and
odious to our fellow-subjects? If we only tell him
that the difficulties he meets with are not owing to
the causes he names, — which indeed have no exist-

[1] *Colonial Records of Pa.*, vi. 584.

ence, — but to his own want of skill and abilities for his station, he takes it extremely amiss, and says 'we forget all decency to those in authority.' We are apt to think there is likewise some decency due to the Assembly as a part of the government; and though we have not, like the governor, had a courtly education, but are plain men, and must be very imperfect in our politeness, yet we think we have no chance of improving by his example." [1] Again, in another Message, the Assembly, with a thrust at Morris himself, tell him that colonial governors have often been "transient persons, of broken fortunes, greedy of money, destitute of all concern for those they govern, often their enemies, and endeavoring not only to oppress, but to defame them." [2] In such unseemly fashion was the battle waged. Morris, who was himself a provincial, showed more temper and dignity; though there was not too much on either side. "The Assembly," he wrote to Shirley, "seem determined to take advantage of the country's distress to get the whole power of government into their own hands." And the Assembly proclaimed on their part that the governor was taking advantage of the country's distress to reduce the province to "Egyptian bondage."

Petitions poured in from the miserable frontiersmen. "How long will those in power, by their

[1] *Message of the Assembly to the Governor*, 29 *September*, 1755 (written by Franklin), in *Colonial Records of Pa.*, vi. 631, 632.

[2] *Writings of Franklin*, iii. 447. The Assembly at first suppressed this paper, but afterwards printed it.

quarrels, suffer us to be massacred?" demanded
William Trent, the Indian trader. "Two and forty
bodies have been buried on Patterson's Creek; and
since they have killed more, and keep on killing." [1]
Early in October news came that a hundred persons
had been murdered near Fort Cumberland. Repeated
tidings followed of murders on the Susquehanna;
then it was announced that the war-parties had
crossed that stream, and were at their work on the
eastern side. Letter after letter came from the
sufferers, bringing such complaints as this: "We are
in as bad circumstances as ever any poor Christians
were ever in; for the cries of widowers, widows,
fatherless and motherless childen, are enough to pierce
the most hardest of hearts. Likewise it's a very
sorrowful spectacle to see those that escaped with
their lives with not a mouthful to eat, or bed to lie
on, or clothes to cover their nakedness, or keep them
warm, but all they had consumed into ashes. These
deplorable circumstances cry aloud for your Honor's
most wise consideration; for it is really very shocking for the husband to see the wife of his bosom her
head cut off, and the children's blood drunk like
water, by these bloody and cruel savages." [2]

Morris was greatly troubled. "The conduct of the
Assembly," he wrote to Shirley, "is to me shocking
beyond parallel." "The inhabitants are abandoning
their plantations, and we are in a dreadful situation,"

[1] *Trent to James Burd, 4 October, 1755.*
[2] *Adam Hoops to Governor Morris, 3 November, 1755.*

wrote John Harris from the east bank of the Susquehanna. On the next day he wrote again: "The
Indians are cutting us off every day, and I had a
certain account of about fifteen hundred Indians,
besides French, being on their march against us and
Virginia, and now close on our borders, their scouts
scalping our families on our frontiers daily." The
report was soon confirmed; and accounts came that
the settlements in the valley called the Great Cove
had been completely destroyed. All this was laid
before the Assembly. They declared the accounts
exaggerated, but confessed that outrages had been
committed; hinted that the fault was with the proprietaries; and asked the governor to explain why
the Delawares and Shawanoes had become unfriendly.
"If they have suffered wrongs," said the Quakers,
"we are resolved to do all in our power to redress
them, rather than entail upon ourselves and our
posterity the calamities of a cruel Indian war." The
Indian records were searched, and several days spent
in unsuccessful efforts to prove fraud in a late land-
purchase.

Post after post still brought news of slaughter.
The upper part of Cumberland County was laid
waste. Edward Biddle wrote from Reading: "The
drum is beating and bells ringing, and all the people
under arms. This night we expect an attack. The
people exclaim against the Quakers." "We seem to
be given up into the hands of a merciless enemy,"
wrote John Elder from Paxton. And he declares

that more than forty persons have been killed in that neighborhood, besides numbers carried off. Meanwhile the governor and Assembly went on fencing with words and exchanging legal subtleties; while, with every cry of distress that rose from the west, each hoped that the other would yield.

On the eighth of November the Assembly laid before Morris for his concurrence a bill for remitting bills of credit to the amount of sixty thousand pounds, to be sunk in four years by a tax including the proprietary estates.[1] "I shall not," he replied, "enter into a dispute whether the proprietaries ought to be taxed or not. It is sufficient for me that they have given me no power in that case; and I cannot think it consistent either with my duty or safety to exceed the powers of my commission, much less to do what that commission expressly prohibits."[2] He stretched his authority, however, so far as to propose a sort of compromise by which the question should be referred to the King; but they refused it; and the quarrel and the murders went on as before. "We have taken," said the Assembly, "every step in our power, consistent with the just rights of the freemen of Pennsylvania, for the relief of the poor distressed inhabitants; and we have reason to believe that they themselves would not wish us to go farther. Those who would give up essential liberty to purchase a

[1] *Colonial Records of Pa.*, vi. 682.
[2] *Message of the Governor to the Assembly, 8 November, 1755, in Colonial Records of Pa.*, vi. 684.

little temporary safety deserve neither liberty nor
safety."[1]   Then the borderers deserved neither; for,
rather than be butchered, they would have let the
proprietary lands lie untaxed for another year.
"You have in all," said the governor, "proposed to
me five money bills, three of them rejected because
contrary to royal instructions; the other two on
account of the unjust method proposed for taxing the
proprietary estate. If you are disposed to relieve
your country, you have many other ways of granting
money to which I shall have no objection. I shall
put one proof more both of your sincerity and mine
in our professions of regard for the public, by offer-
ing to agree to any bill in the present exigency which
it is consistent with my duty to pass; lest, before our
present disputes can be brought to an issue, we
should neither have a privilege to dispute about, nor
a country to dispute in."[2]   They stood fast; and
with an obstinacy for which the Quakers were chiefly
answerable, insisted that they would give nothing,
except by a bill taxing real estate, and including that
of the proprietaries.

But now the Assembly began to feel the ground
shaking under their feet. A paper, called a "Representation," signed by some of the chief citizens,
was sent to the House, calling for measures of
defence. "You will forgive us, gentlemen," such

[1] *Message of the Assembly to the Governor*, 11 *November*, 1755, in
Colonial Records of Pa., vi. 692. The words are Franklin's.

[2] *Message of the Governor to the Assembly*, 22 *November*, 1755, *Ibid.*,
vi. 714.

was its language, "if we assume characters somewhat
higher than that of humble suitors praying for the
defence of our lives and properties as a matter of
grace or favor on your side.   You will permit us to
make a positive and immediate demand of it." [1]   This
drove the Quakers mad.   Preachers, male and female,
harangued in the streets, denouncing the iniquity of
war.   Three of the sect from England, two women
and a man, invited their brethren of the Assembly to
a private house, and fervently exhorted them to stand
firm.   Some of the principal Quakers joined in an
address to the House, in which they declared that
any action on its part "inconsistent with the peaceable testimony we profess and have borne to the
world appears to us in its consequences to be destructive of our religious liberties." [2]   And they protested
that they would rather "suffer" than pay taxes for
such ends.   Consistency, even in folly, has in it
something respectable; but the Quakers were not
consistent.   A few years after, when heated with
party passion and excited by reports of an irruption
of incensed Presbyterian borderers, some of the
pacific sectaries armed for battle; and the streets of
Philadelphia beheld the curious conjunction of
musket and broad-brimmed hat. [3]

The mayor, aldermen, and common council next
addressed the Assembly, adjuring them, "in the
most solemn manner, before God and in the name of

[1] *Pennsylvania Archives,* ii. 485.   [2] *Ibid.,* ii. 487.
[3] See "Conspiracy of Pontiac," chap. xxv.

all our fellow-citizens," to provide for defending the
lives and property of the people.[1] A deputation from
a band of Indians on the Susquehanna, still friendly
to the province, came to ask whether the English
meant to fight or not; for, said their speaker, "if
they will not stand by us, we will join the French."
News came that the settlement of Tulpehocken, only
sixty miles distant, had been destroyed; and then
that the Moravian settlement of Gnadenhütten was
burned, and nearly all its inmates massacred. Colonel
William Moore wrote to the governor that two
thousand men were coming from Chester County
to compel him and the Assembly to defend the
province; and Conrad Weiser wrote that more were
coming from Berks on the same errand. Old friends
of the Assembly began to cry out against them.
Even the Germans, hitherto their fast allies, were
roused from their attitude of passivity, and four hundred of them came in procession to demand measures
of war. A band of frontiersmen presently arrived,
bringing in a wagon the bodies of friends and relatives
lately murdered, displaying them at the doors of the
Assembly, cursing the Quakers, and threatening
vengeance.[2]

Finding some concession necessary, the House at
length passed a militia law, — probably the most
futile ever enacted. It specially exempted the
Quakers, and constrained nobody; but declared it

---

[1] *A Remonstrance*, etc., in *Colonial Records of Pa.*, vi. 734.
[2] Mante, 47; Entick, i. 377.

lawful, for such as chose, to form themselves into companies and elect officers by ballot. The company officers thus elected might, if they saw fit, elect, also by ballot, colonels, lieutenant-colonels, and majors. These last might then, in conjunction with the governor, frame articles of war; to which, however, no officer or man was to be subjected unless, after three days' consideration, he subscribed them in presence of a justice of the peace, and declared his willingness to be bound by them.[1]

This mockery could not appease the people; the Assembly must raise money for men, arms, forts, and all the detested appliances of war. Defeat absolute and ignominious seemed hanging over the House, when an incident occurred which gave them a decent pretext for retreat. The governor informed them that he had just received a letter from the proprietaries, giving to the province five thousand pounds sterling to aid in its defence, on condition that the money should be accepted as a free gift, and not as their proportion of any tax that was or might be laid by the Assembly. They had not learned the deplorable state of the country, and had sent the money in view of the defeat of Braddock and its probable consequences. The Assembly hereupon yielded, struck out from the bill before them the clause tax-

[1] This remarkable bill, drawn by Franklin, was meant for political rather than military effect. It was thought that Morris would refuse to pass it, and could therefore be accused of preventing the province from defending itself; but he avoided the snare by signing it.

ing the proprietary estates, and, thus amended, presented it to the governor, who by his signature made
it a law.[1]

The House had failed to carry its point. The
result disappointed Franklin, and doubly disappointed
the Quakers. His maxim was: Beat the governor
first, and then beat the enemy; theirs: Beat the governor, and let the enemy alone. The measures that
followed, directed in part by Franklin himself, held
the Indians in check, and mitigated the distress of
the western counties; yet there was no safety for
them throughout the two or three years when France
was cheering on her hell-hounds against this tormented frontier.

As in Pennsylvania, so in most of the other colonies
there was conflict between assemblies and governors,
to the unspeakable detriment of the public service.
In New York, though here no obnoxious proprietary
stood between the people and the Crown, the strife
was long and severe. The point at issue was an
important one, — whether the Assembly should continue their practice of granting yearly supplies to the
governor, or should establish a permanent fund for
the ordinary expenses of government, — thus placing
him beyond their control. The result was a victory
for the Assembly.

Month after month the great continent lay wrapped
in snow. Far along the edge of the western wilderness men kept watch and ward in lonely block-

[1] *Minutes of Council,* 27 *November,* 1755.

houses, or scoured the forest on the track of prowling war-parties. The provincials in garrison at Forts Edward, William Henry, and Oswego dragged out the dreary winter; while bands of New England rangers, muffled against the piercing cold, caps of fur on their heads, hatchets in their belts, and guns in their mittened hands, glided on skates along the gleaming ice-floor of Lake George, to spy out the secrets of Ticonderoga, or seize some careless sentry to tell them tidings of the foe. Thus the petty war went on; but the big war was frozen into torpor, ready, like a hibernating bear, to wake again with the birds, the bees, and the flowers.[1]

[1] On Pennsylvanian disputes, — *A Brief State of the Province of Pennsylvania* (London, 1755). *A Brief View of the Conduct of Pennsylvania* (London, 1756). These are pamphlets on the governor's side, by William Smith, D. D., Provost of the College of Pennsylvania. *An Answer to an invidious Pamphlet, intituled a Brief State,* etc. (London, 1755). Anonymous. *A True and Impartial State of the Province of Pennsylvania* (Philadelphia, 1759). Anonymous. The last two works attack the first two with great vehemence. The *True and Impartial State* is an able presentation of the case of the Assembly, omitting, however, essential facts. But the most elaborate work on the subject is the *Historical Review of the Constitution and Government of Pennsylvania,* inspired and partly written by Franklin. It is hotly partisan, and sometimes sophistical and unfair. Articles on the quarrel will also be found in the provincial newspapers, especially the *New York Mercury,* and in the *Gentleman's Magazine* for 1755 and 1756. But it is impossible to get any clear and just view of it without wading through the interminable documents concerning it in the *Colonial Records of Pennsylvania* and the *Pennsylvania Archives.*

CHAPTER XI.

1712–1756.

MONTCALM.

War declared. — State of Europe. — Pompadour and Maria Theresa. — Infatuation of the French Court. — The European War. — Montcalm to command in America: his early Life; an intractable Pupil; his Marriage; his Family; his Campaigns; Preparation for America; his Associates. — Lévis, Bourlamaque, Bougainville. — Embarkation. — The Voyage. — Arrival. — Vaudreuil. — Forces of Canada. — Troops of the Line, Colony Troops, Militia, Indians. — The Military Situation. — Capture of Fort Bull. — Montcalm at Ticonderoga.

ON the eighteenth of May, 1756, England, after a year of open hostility, at length declared war. She had attacked France by land and sea, turned loose her ships to prey on French commerce, and brought some three hundred prizes into her ports. It was the act of a weak government, supplying by spasms of violence what it lacked in considerate resolution. France, no match for her amphibious enemy in the game of marine depredation, cried out in horror; and to emphasize her complaints and signalize a pretended good faith which her acts had belied, ostentatiously released a British frigate captured by her cruisers. She in her turn declared war on the ninth of June:

and now began the most terrible conflict of the eighteenth century, — one that convulsed Europe and shook America, India, the coasts of Africa, and the islands of the sea.

In Europe the ground was trembling already with the coming earthquake. Such smothered discords, such animosities, ambitions, jealousies, possessed the rival governments; such entanglements of treaties and alliances, offensive or defensive, open or secret, — that a blow at one point shook the whole fabric. Hanover, like the heel of Achilles, was the vulnerable part for which England was always trembling. Therefore she made a defensive treaty with Prussia, by which each party bound itself to aid the other, should its territory be invaded. England thus sought a guarantee against France, and Prussia against Russia. She had need. Her King, Frederic the Great, had drawn upon himself an avalanche. Three women — two empresses and a concubine — controlled the forces of the three great nations, Austria, Russia, and France; and they all hated him: Elizabeth of Russia, by reason of a distrust fomented by secret intrigue and turned into gall by the biting tongue of Frederic himself, who had gibed at her amours, compared her to Messalina, and called her "*infâme catin du Nord;*" Maria Theresa of Austria, because she saw in him a rebellious vassal of the Holy Roman Empire, and, above all, because he had robbed her of Silesia; Madame de Pompadour, because when she sent him a message of compliment, he answered, "*Je ne la connais pas*," forbade his ambassador to visit her, and in his mocking wit spared neither her nor her royal lover. Feminine pique, revenge, or vanity had then at their service the mightiest armaments of Europe.

The recovery of Silesia and the punishment of Frederic for his audacity in seizing it, possessed the mind of Maria Theresa with the force of a ruling passion. To these ends she had joined herself in secret league with Russia; and now at the prompting of her minister Kaunitz she courted the alliance of France. It was a reversal of the hereditary policy of Austria; joining hands with an old and deadly foe, and spurning England, of late her most trusty ally. But France could give powerful aid against Frederic; and hence Maria Theresa, virtuous as she was high-born and proud, stooped to make advances to the all-powerful mistress of Louis XV., wrote her flattering letters, and addressed her, it is said, as "*Ma chère cousine.*" Pompadour was delighted, and could hardly do enough for her imperial friend. She ruled the King, and could make and unmake ministers at will. They hastened to do her pleasure, disguising their subserviency by dressing it out in specious reasons of state. A conference at her summer-house, called Babiole, "Bawble," prepared the way for a treaty which involved the nation in the anti-Prussian war, and made it the instrument of Austria in the attempt to humble Frederic, — an attempt which if successful would give the hereditary enemy of France a predominance over Germany. France engaged to aid the cause with twenty-four thousand men, but in the zeal of her rulers began with a hundred thousand. Thus the three great Powers stood leagued against Prussia. Sweden and Saxony joined them; and the Empire itself, of which Prussia was a part, took arms against its obnoxious member.

Never in Europe had power been more centralized, and never in France had the reins been held by persons so pitiful, impelled by motives so contemptible. The levity, vanity, and spite of a concubine became a mighty engine to influence the destinies of nations. Louis XV., enervated by pleasures and devoured by *ennui*, still had his emotions; he shared Pompadour's detestation of Frederic, and he was tormented at times by a lively fear of damnation. But how damn a king who had entered the lists as champion of the Church? England was Protestant, and so was Prussia; Austria was supremely Catholic. Was it not a merit in the eyes of God to join her in holy war against the powers of heresy? The King of the Parc-aux-Cerfs would propitiate Heaven by a new crusade.

Henceforth France was to turn her strength against her European foes; and the American war, the occasion of the universal outbreak, was to hold in her eyes a second place. The reasons were several: the vanity of Pompadour, infatuated by the advances of the Empress-Queen, and eager to secure her good graces; the superstition of the King; the anger of both against Frederic; the desire of D'Argenson, minister of war, that the army, and not the navy, should play the foremost part; and the passion of courtiers and nobles, ignorant of the naval service, to win laurels in a continental war, — all conspired to one end. It was the interest of France to turn her strength against her only dangerous rival; to continue as she had begun, in building up a naval power that could face England on the seas and sustain her own rising colonies in America, India, and the West Indies; for she too might have multiplied herself, planted her language and her race over all the globe, and grown with the growth of her children, had she not been at the mercy of an effeminate profligate, a mistress turned procuress, and the favorites to whom they delegated power.

Still, something must be done for the American war; at least there must be a new general to replace Dieskau. None of the court favorites wanted a command in the backwoods, and the minister of war was free to choose whom he would. His choice fell on Louis Joseph, Marquis de Montcalm-Gozon de Saint-Véran.

Montcalm was born in the south of France, at the Château of Candiac, near Nîmes, on the twenty-ninth of February, 1712. At the age of six he was placed in the charge of one Dumas, a natural son of his grandfather. This man, a conscientious pedant, with many theories of education, ruled his pupil stiffly; and, before the age of fifteen, gave him a good knowledge of Latin, Greek, and history. Young

Montcalm had a taste for books, continued his reading in such intervals of leisure as camps and garrisons afforded, and cherished to the end of his life the ambition of becoming a member of the Academy. Yet, with all his liking for study, he sometimes revolted against the sway of the pedagogue who wrote letters of complaint to his father protesting against the "judgments of the vulgar, who, contrary to the experience of ages, say that if children are well reproved they will correct their faults." Dumas, however, was not without sense, as is shown by another letter to the elder Montcalm, in which he says that the boy had better be ignorant of Latin and Greek "than know them as he does without knowing how to read, write, and speak French well." The main difficulty was to make him write a good hand, — a point in which he signally failed to the day of his death. So refractory was he at times that his master despaired. "M. de Montcalm," Dumas informs the father, "has great need of docility, industry, and willingness to take advice. What will become of him?" The pupil, aware of these aspersions, met them by writing to his father his own ideas of what his aims should be. "First, to be an honorable man, of good morals, brave, and a Christian. Secondly, to read in moderation; to know as much Greek and Latin as most men of the world; also the four rules of arithmetic, and something of history, geography, and French and Latin *belles-lettres*, as well as to have a taste for the arts and sciences. Thirdly, and above all, to be obedient, docile, and very submissive to your orders and those of my dear mother; and also to defer to the advice of M. Dumas. Fourthly, to fence and ride as well as my small abilities will permit."[1]

If Louis de Montcalm failed to satisfy his preceptor, he had a brother who made ample amends. Of this infant prodigy it is related that at six years he knew Latin, Greek, and Hebrew, and had some acquaintance with arithmetic, French history, geography, and heraldry. He was destined for the Church, but died at the age of seven; his precocious brain having been urged to fatal activity by the exertions of Dumas.

Other destinies and a more wholesome growth were the lot of young Louis. At fifteen he joined the army as ensign in the regiment of Hainaut. Two years after, his father bought him a captaincy, and he was first under fire at the siege of Philipsbourg. His father died in 1735, and left him heir to a considerable landed estate, much embarrassed by debt. The Marquis de la Fare, a friend of the family, soon after sought for him an advantageous marriage to strengthen his position and increase his prospects of promotion; and he accordingly espoused Mademoiselle Angélique Louise Talon du Boulay, — a union which brought him influential alliances and some property. Madame de Montcalm bore him ten children, of whom only two sons and four daughters

---

[1] This passage is given by Somervogel from the original letter.

were living in 1752. "May God preserve them all," he writes in his autobiography, "and make them prosper for this world and the next! Perhaps it will be thought that the number is large for so moderate a fortune, especially as four of them are girls; but does God ever abandon his children in their need?

"'Aux petits des oiseaux il donne la pâture,
    Et sa bonté s'étend sur toute la nature.'"

He was pious in his soldierly way, and ardently loyal to Church and King.

His family seat was Candiac; where, in the intervals of campaigning, he found repose with his wife, his children, and his mother, who was a woman of remarkable force of character and who held great influence over her son. He had a strong attachment to this home of his childhood; and in after years, out of the midst of the American wilderness, his thoughts turned longingly towards it. "*Quand reverrai-je mon cher Candiac !*"

In 1741 Montcalm took part in the Bohemian campaign. He was made colonel of the regiment of Auxerrois two years later, and passed unharmed through the severe campaign of 1744. In the next year he fought in Italy under Maréchal de Maillebois. In 1746, at the disastrous action under the walls of Piacenza, where he twice rallied his regiment, he received five sabre-cuts, — two of which were in the head, — and was made prisoner. Returning to France on parole, he was promoted in the year fol-

lowing to the rank of brigadier; and being soon after
exchanged, rejoined the army, and was again wounded
by a musket-shot. The peace of Aix-la-Chapelle
now gave him a period of rest.[1] At length, being on
a visit to Paris late in the autumn of 1755, the
minister, D'Argenson, hinted to him that he might
be appointed to command the troops in America.
He heard no more of the matter till, after his return
home, he received from D'Argenson a letter dated at
Versailles the twenty-fifth of January, at midnight.
"Perhaps, Monsieur," it began, "you did not expect
to hear from me again on the subject of the conversation I had with you the day you came to bid me
farewell at Paris. Nevertheless I have not forgotten
for a moment the suggestion I then made you; and
it is with the greatest pleasure that I announce to
you that my views have prevailed. The King has
chosen you to command his troops in North America,
and will honor you on your departure with the rank
of major-general."

The Chevalier de Lévis, afterwards Marshal of
France, was named as his second in command with
the rank of brigadier, and the Chevalier de Bourlamaque as his third, with the rank of colonel; but

---

[1] The account of Montcalm up to this time is chiefly from his
unpublished autobiography, preserved by his descendants, and en-
titled *Mémoires pour servir à l'Histoire de ma Vie.* Somervogel,
Comme on servait autrefois; Bonnechose, *Montcalm et le Canada;*
Martin, *Le Marquis de Montcalm; Éloge de Montcalm; Autre Éloge
de Montcalm; Mémoires sur le Canada,* 1749–1760, and other writings
in print and manuscript have also been consulted.

what especially pleased him was the appointment of
his eldest son to command a regiment in France.
He set out from Candiac for the court, and occupied
himself on the way with reading Charlevoix. "I
take great pleasure in it," he writes from Lyons to
his mother; "he gives a pleasant account of Quebec.
But be comforted; I shall always be glad to come
home." At Paris he writes again: "Don't expect
any long letter from me before the first of March;
all my business will be done by that time, and I
shall begin to breathe again. I have not yet seen
the Chevalier de Montcalm [*his son*]. Last night I
came from Versailles, and am going back to-morrow.
The King gives me twenty-five thousand francs a
year, as he did to M. Dieskau, besides twelve thousand for my equipment, which will cost me above a
thousand crowns more; but I cannot stop for that.
I embrace my dearest and all the family." A few
days later his son joined him. "He is as thin and
delicate as ever, but grows prodigiously tall."

On the second of March he informs his mother:
"My affairs begin to get on. A good part of the
baggage went off the day before yesterday in the
King's wagons; an assistant-cook and two livery-
men yesterday. I have got a good cook. Estève,
my secretary, will go on the eighth; Joseph and
Déjean will follow me. To-morrow evening I go to
Versailles till Sunday, and will write from there to
Madame de Montcalm [*his wife*]. I have three aides-
de-camp; one of them, Bougainville, a man of parts,

pleasant company. Madame Mazade was happily delivered on Wednesday; in extremity on Friday with a malignant fever; Saturday and yesterday, reports favorable. I go there twice a day, and am just going now. She has a girl. I embrace you all." Again, on the fifteenth: "In a few hours I set out for Brest. Yesterday I presented my son, with whom I am well pleased, to all the royal family. I shall have a secretary at Brest, and will write more at length." On the eighteenth he writes from Rennes to his wife: "I arrived, dearest, this morning, and stay here all day. I shall be at Brest on the twenty-first. Everything will be on board on the twenty-sixth. My son has been here since yesterday for me to coach him and get him a uniform made, in which he will give thanks for his regiment at the same time that I take leave in my embroidered coat. Perhaps I shall leave debts behind. I wait impatiently for the bills. You have my will; I wish you would get it copied, and send it to me before I sail."

Reaching Brest, the place of embarkation, he writes to his mother: "I have business on hand still. My health is good, and the passage will be a time of rest. I embrace you, and my dearest, and my daughters. Love to all the family. I shall write up to the last moment."

No translation can give an idea of the rapid, abrupt, elliptical style of this familiar correspondence, where the meaning is sometimes suggested by a single word,

unintelligible to any but those for whom it is
written.

At the end of March Montcalm, with all his following, was ready to embark; and three ships-of-the-
line, the "Léopard," the "Héros," and the "Illustre,"
fitted out as transports, were ready to receive the
troops; while the general, with Lévis and Bourlamaque, were to take passage in the frigates "Licorne,"
"Sauvage," and "Sirène." "I like the Chevalier de
Lévis," says Montcalm, "and I think he likes me."
His first aide-de-camp, Bougainville, pleased him, if
possible, still more. This young man, son of a
notary, had begun life as an advocate in the Parliament of Paris, where his abilities and learning had
already made him conspicuous, when he resigned the
gown for the sword, and became a captain of dra-
goons. He was destined in later life to win laurels
in another career, and to become one of the most
illustrious of French navigators. Montcalm, himself
a scholar, prized his varied talents and accomplish-
ments, and soon learned to feel for him a strong
personal regard.

The troops destined for Canada were only two
battalions, one belonging to the regiment of La
Sarre, and the other to that of Royal Roussillon.
Louis XV. and Pompadour sent a hundred thousand
men to fight the battles of Austria, and could spare
but twelve hundred to reinforce New France. These
troops marched into Brest at early morning, breakfasted in the town, and went at once on board the

transports, "with an incredible gayety," says Bougainville. "What a nation is ours! Happy he who
commands it, and commands it worthily!"[1] Montcalm and he embarked in the "Licorne," and sailed
on the third of April, leaving Lévis and Bourlamaque
to follow a few days after.[2]

The voyage was a rough one. "I have been fortunate," writes Montcalm to his wife, "in not being ill
nor at all incommoded by the heavy gale we had in
Holy Week. It was not so with those who were with
me, especially M. Estève, my secretary, and Joseph,
who suffered cruelly, — seventeen days without being
able to take anything but water. The season was
very early for such a hard voyage, and it was fortunate that the winter has been so mild. We had very
favorable weather till Monday the twelfth; but since
then till Saturday evening we had rough weather, with
a gale that lasted ninety hours, and put us in real
danger. The forecastle was always under water, and
the waves broke twice over the quarter-deck. From
the twenty-seventh of April to the evening of the
fourth of May we had fogs, great cold, and an amazing
quantity of icebergs. On the thirtieth, when luckily
the fog lifted for a time, we counted sixteen of them.
The day before, one drifted under the bowsprit,
grazed it, and might have crushed us if the deck-
officer had not called out quickly, *Luff*. After

---

[1] *Journal de Bougainville.* This is a fragment; his Journal proper
begins a few weeks later.

[2] *Lévis à* ——, 5 *Avril,* 1756.

speaking of our troubles and sufferings, I must tell you of our pleasures, which were fishing for cod and eating it. The taste is exquisite. The head, tongue, and liver are morsels worthy of an epicure. Still, I would not advise anybody to make the voyage for their sake. My health is as good as it has been for a long time. I found it a good plan to eat little and take no supper; a little tea now and then, and plenty of lemonade. Nevertheless I have taken very little liking for the sea, and think that when I shall be so happy as to rejoin you I shall end my voyages there. I don't know when this letter will go. I shall send it by the first ship that returns to France, and keep on writing till then. It is pleasant, I know, to hear particulars about the people one loves, and I thought that my mother and you, my dearest and most beloved, would be glad to read all these dull details. We heard mass on Easter Day. All the week before, it was impossible, because the ship rolled so that I could hardly keep my legs. If I had dared, I think I should have had myself lashed fast. I shall not soon forget that Holy Week."

This letter was written on the eleventh of May, in the St. Lawrence, where the ship lay at anchor, ten leagues below Quebec, stopped by ice from proceeding farther. Montcalm made his way to the town by land, and soon after learned with great satisfaction that the other ships were safe in the river below. "I see," he writes again, "that I shall have plenty of work. Our campaign will soon begin. Everything

is in motion. Don't expect details about our operations; generals never speak of movements till they
are over. I can only tell you that the winter has
been quiet enough, though the savages have made
great havoc in Pennsylvania and Virginia, and
carried off, according to their custom, men, women,
and children. I beg you will have High Mass said
at Montpellier or Vauvert to thank God for our safe
arrival and ask for good success in future." [1]

Vaudreuil, the governor-general, was at Montreal,
and Montcalm sent a courier to inform him of his
arrival. He soon went thither in person, and the
two men met for the first time. The new general
was not welcome to Vaudreuil, who had hoped to
command the troops himself, and had represented
to the court that it was needless and inexpedient to
send out a general officer from France. [2] The court
had not accepted his views; [3] and hence it was with
more curiosity than satisfaction that he greeted the
colleague who had been assigned him. He saw
before him a man of small stature, with a lively
countenance, a keen eye, and, in moments of animation, rapid, vehement utterance, and nervous gesticu-
lation. Montcalm, we may suppose, regarded the
governor with no less attention. Pierre François
Rigaud, Marquis de Vaudreuil, was son of Philippe
de Vaudreuil, who had governed Canada early in

[1] These extracts are translated from copies of the original letters,
in possession of the present Marquis de Montcalm.

[2] *Vaudreuil au Ministre, 30 Octobre, 1755.*

[3] *Ordres du Roy et Dépêches des Ministres, Février, 1756.*

the century; and he himself had been governor of
Louisiana. He had not the force of character which
his position demanded, lacked decision in times of
crisis; and though tenacious of authority, was more
jealous in asserting than self-reliant in exercising it.
One of his traits was a sensitive egotism, which made
him forward to proclaim his own part in every success, and to throw on others the burden of every
failure. He was facile by nature, and capable of
being led by such as had skill and temper for the
task. But the impetuous Montcalm was not of their
number; and the fact that he was born in France
would in itself have thrown obstacles in his way to
the good graces of the governor. Vaudreuil, Canadian by birth, loved the colony and its people, and
distrusted Old France and all that came out of it.
He had been bred, moreover, to the naval service;
and, like other Canadian governors, his official correspondence was with the minister of marine, while
that of Montcalm was with the minister of war.
Even had Nature made him less suspicious, his relations with the general would have been critical.
Montcalm commanded the regulars from France,
whose very presence was in the eyes of Vaudreuil
an evil, though a necessary one. Their chief was,
it is true, subordinate to him in virtue of his office
of governor;[1] yet it was clear that for the conduct of

---

[1] *Le Ministre à Vaudreuil*, 15 *Mars*, 1756. *Commission du Marquis
de Montcalm. Mémoire du Roy pour servir d'Instruction au Marquis de
Montcalm.*

the war the trust of the government was mainly in
Montcalm; and the minister of war had even suggested that he should have the immediate command,
not only of the troops from France, but of the colony
regulars and the militia. An order of the King to
this effect was sent to Vaudreuil, with instructions
to communicate it to Montcalm or withhold it, as he
should think best.[1] He lost no time in replying that
the general "ought to concern himself with nothing
but the command of the troops from France;" and
he returned the order to the minister who sent it.[2]
The governor and the general represented the two
parties which were soon to divide Canada, — those of
New France and of Old.

A like antagonism was seen in the forces commanded by the two chiefs. These were of three
kinds, — the *troupes de terre*, troops of the line, or
regulars from France; the *troupes de la marine*, or
colony regulars; and lastly the militia. The first
consisted of the four battalions that had come over
with Dieskau and the two that had come with Montcalm, comprising in all a little less than three thousand men.[3] Besides these, the battalions of Artois

[1] *Ordres du Roy et Dépêches des Ministres*, 1756. *Le Ministre à
Vaudreuil*, 15 *Mars*, 1756.

[2] *Vaudreuil au Ministre*, 16 *Juin*, 1756. "Qu'il ne se mêle que du
commandement des troupes de terre."

[3] Of about twelve hundred who came with Montcalm, nearly
three hundred were now in hospital. The four battalions that came
with Dieskau are reported at the end of May to have sixteen hundred and fifty-three effective men. *État de la Situation actuelle des
Bataillons*, appended to Montcalm's despatch of 12 June. Another

and Bourgogne, to the number of eleven hundred men, were in garrison at Louisbourg. All these troops wore a white uniform, faced with blue, red, yellow, or violet,[1] a black three-cornered hat, and gaiters, generally black, from the foot to the knee. The subaltern officers in the French service were very numerous, and were drawn chiefly from the class of lesser nobles. A well-informed French writer calls them "a generation of *petits-maîtres*, dissolute, frivolous, heedless, light-witted; but brave always, and ready to die with their soldiers, though not to suffer with them."[2] In fact, the course of the war was to show plainly that in Europe the regiments of France were no longer what they had once been. It was not so with those who fought in America. Here, for enduring gallantry, officers and men alike deserve nothing but praise.

The *troupes de la marine* had for a long time formed the permanent military establishment of Canada. Though attached to the naval department, they served on land, and were employed as a police within the limits of the colony, or as garrisons of the outlying forts, where their officers busied themselves more with fur-trading than with their military duties.

document, *Détail de ce qui s'est passé en Canada, Juin,* 1755, *jusqu'à Juin,* 1756, sets the united effective strength of the battalions in Canada at twenty-six hundred and seventy-seven, which was increased by recruits which arrived from France about midsummer.

[1] Except, perhaps, the battalion of Béarn, which formerly wore, and possibly wore still, a uniform of light blue.

[2] Susane, *Ancienne Infanterie Française.* In the atlas of this work are colored plates of the uniforms of all the regiments of foot.

Thus they had become ill-disciplined and inefficient,
till the hard hand of Duquesne restored them to
order. They originally consisted of twenty-eight
independent companies, increased in 1750 to thirty
companies, at first of fifty, and afterwards of sixty-
five men each, forming a total of nineteen hundred
and fifty rank and file. In March, 1757, ten more
companies were added. Their uniform was not
unlike that of the troops attached to the War Department, being white, with black facings. They were
enlisted for the most part in France; but when their
term of service expired, and even before, in time of
peace, they were encouraged to become settlers in
the colony, as was also the case with their officers,
of whom a great part were of European birth. Thus
the relations of the *troupes de la marine* with the
colony were close; and they formed a sort of connecting link between the troops of the line and the
native militia.[1]   Besides these colony regulars, there
was a company of colonial artillery, consisting this
year of seventy men, and replaced in 1757 by two
companies of fifty men each.

All the effective male population of Canada, from
fifteen years to sixty, was enrolled in the militia,

[1] On the *troupes de la marine*, — *Mémoire pour servir d'Instruction à
MM. Jonquière et Bigot*, 30 *Avril*, 1749. *Ordres du Roy et Dépêches
des Ministres*, 1750. *Ibid.*, 1755. *Ibid.*, 1757. *Instruction pour Vaudreuil*, 22 *Mars*, 1755. *Ordonnance pour l'Augmentation de Soldats dans
les Compagnies de Canada*, 14 *Mars*, 1755. *Duquesne au Ministre*, 26
Octobre, 1753. *Ibid.*, 30 Octobre, 1753. *Ibid.*, 29 *Février*, 1754. *Duquesne à Marin*, 27 *Août*, 1753. *Atlas de Susane.*

and called into service at the will of the governor.
They received arms, clothing, equipment, and rations
from the King, but no pay; and instead of tents they
made themselves huts of bark or branches.   The best
of them were drawn from the upper parts of the
colony, where habits of bush-ranging were still in full
activity.   Their fighting qualities were much like
those of the Indians, whom they rivalled in endur-
ance and in the arts of forest war.   As bush-fighters
they had few equals; they fought well behind earth-
works, and were good at a surprise or sudden dash;
but for regular battle on the open field they were of
small account, being disorderly, and apt to break and
take to cover at the moment of crisis.   They had no
idea of the great operations of war.   At first they
despised the regulars for their ignorance of wood-
craft, and thought themselves able to defend the
colony alone; while the regulars regarded them in
turn with a contempt no less unjust.   They were
excessively given to gasconade, and every true Canadian boasted himself a match for three Englishmen
at least.   In 1750 the militia of all ranks counted
about thirteen thousand; and eight years later the
number had increased to about fifteen thousand.[1]
Until the last two years of the war, those employed
in actual warfare were but few.   Even in the critical

---

[1] *Récapitulation des Milices du Gouvernement de Canada,* 1750.
Denombrement des Milices, 1758, 1759.   On the militia, see also Bou-
gainville in Margry, *Relations et Mémoires inédits,* 60 and *N. Y. Col
Docs.,* x. 680.

year 1758 only about eleven hundred were called to
arms, except for two or three weeks in summer;[1]
though about four thousand were employed in transporting troops and supplies, for which service they
received pay.

To the white fighting force of the colony are to be
added the red men. The most trusty of them were
the Mission Indians, living within or near the settled
limits of Canada, chiefly the Hurons of Lorette, the
Abenakis of St. Francis and Batiscan, the Iroquois
of Caughnawaga, and La Présentation, and the
Iroquois and Algonquins at the Two Mountains on
the Ottawa. Besides these, all the warriors of the
West and North, from Lake Superior to the Ohio,
and from the Alleghanies to the Mississippi, were
now at the beck of France. As to the Iroquois or
Five Nations who still remained in their ancient seats
within the present limits of New York, their power
and pride had greatly fallen; and crowded as they
were between the French and the English, they were
in a state of vacillation, some leaning to one side,
some to the other, and some to each in turn. As a
whole, the best that France could expect from them
was neutrality.

Montcalm at Montreal had more visits than he
liked from his red allies. "They are *vilains messieurs*,"
he informs his mother, "even when fresh from their
toilet, at which they pass their lives. You would
not believe it, but the men always carry to war, along

[1] *Montcalm au Ministre*, 1 *Septembre*, 1758.

with their tomahawk and gun, a mirror to daub their faces with various colors, and arrange feathers on their heads and rings in their ears and noses. They think it a great beauty to cut the rim of the ear and stretch it till it reaches the shoulder. Often they wear a laced coat, with no shirt at all. You would take them for so many masqueraders or devils. One needs the patience of an angel to get on with them. Ever since I have been here, I have had nothing but visits, harangues, and deputations of these gentry. The Iroquois ladies, who always take part in their government, came also, and did me the honor to bring me belts of wampum, which will oblige me to go to their village and sing the war-song. They are only a little way off. Yesterday we had eighty-three warriors here, who have gone out to fight. They make war with astounding cruelty, sparing neither men, women, nor children, and take off your scalp very neatly, — an operation which generally kills you.

· "Everything is horribly dear in this country; and I shall find it hard to make the two ends of the year meet, with the twenty-five thousand francs the King gives me. The Chevalier de Lévis did not join me till yesterday. His health is excellent. In a few days I shall send him to one camp, and M. de Bourlamaque to another; for we have three of them: one at Carillon, eighty leagues from here, towards the place where M. de Dieskau had his affair last year, another at Frontenac, sixty leagues; and the third

at Niagara, a hundred and forty leagues. I don't
know when or whither I shall go myself; that
depends on the movements of the enemy. It seems
to me that things move slowly in this new world;
and I shall have to moderate my activity accordingly.
Nothing but the King's service and the wish to make
a career for my son could prevent me from thinking
too much of my expatriation, my distance from you,
and the dull existence here, which would be duller
still if I did not manage to keep some little of my
natural gayety."

The military situation was somewhat perplexing.
Iroquois spies had brought reports of great preparations on the part of the English. As neither party
dared offend these wavering tribes, their warriors
could pass with impunity from one to the other, and
were paid by each for bringing information, not
always trustworthy. They declared that the English
were gathering in force to renew the attempt made
by Johnson the year before against Crown Point and
Ticonderoga, as well as that made by Shirley against
Forts Frontenac and Niagara. Vaudreuil had spared
no effort to meet the double danger. Lotbinière, a
Canadian engineer, had been busied during the
winter in fortifying Ticonderoga, while Pouchot, a
captain in the battalion of Béarn, had rebuilt
Niagara, and two French engineers were at work in
strengthening the defences of Frontenac. The governor even hoped to take the offensive, anticipate the
movements of the English, capture Oswego, and

obtain the complete command of Lake Ontario. Early in the spring a blow had been struck which materially aided these schemes.

The English had built two small forts to guard the Great Carrying Place on the route to Oswego. One of these, Fort Williams, was on the Mohawk; the other, Fort Bull, a mere collection of storehouses surrounded by a palisade, was four miles distant, on the bank of Wood Creek. Here a great quantity of stores and ammunition had imprudently been collected against the opening campaign. In February Vaudreuil sent Léry, a colony officer, with three hundred and sixty-two picked men, soldiers, Canadians, and Indians, to seize these two posts. Towards the end of March, after extreme hardship, they reached the road that connected them, and at half-past five in the morning captured twelve men going with wagons to Fort Bull. Learning from them the weakness of that place, they dashed forward to surprise it. The thirty provincials of Shirley's regiment who formed the garrison had barely time to shut the gate, while the assailants fired on them through the loopholes, of which they got possession in the tumult. Léry called on the defenders to yield; but they refused, and pelted the French for an hour with bullets and hand-grenades. The gate was at last beat down with axes, and they were summoned again; but again refused, and fired hotly through the opening. The French rushed in, shouting *Vive le roi*, and a frightful struggle followed. All the

garrison were killed, except two or three who hid
themselves till the slaughter was over; the fort was
set on fire and blown to atoms by the explosion of
the magazines; and Léry then withdrew, not ventur-
ing to attack Fort Williams. Johnson, warned by
Indians of the approach of the French, had pushed
up the Mohawk with reinforcements; but came too
late.[1]

Vaudreuil, who always exaggerates any success in
which he has had part, says that besides bombs,
bullets, cannon-balls, and other munitions, forty-five
thousand pounds of gunpowder were destroyed on
this occasion. It is certain that damage enough was
done to retard English operations in the direction of
Oswego sufficiently to give the French time for
securing all their posts on Lake Ontario. Before
the end of June this was in good measure done. The
battalion of Béarn lay encamped before the now
strong fort of Niagara, and the battalions of Guienne
and La Sarre, with a body of Canadians, guarded
Frontenac against attack. Those of La Reine and
Languedoc had been sent to Ticonderoga, while the
governor, with Montcalm and Lévis, still remained
at Montreal watching the turn of events.[2] Hither,

[1] *Bigot au Ministre, 12 Avril, 1756. Vaudreuil au Ministre, 1 Juin,
1756. Ibid., 8 Juin, 1756. Journal de ce qui s'est passé en Canada
depuis le Mois d'Octobre, 1755, jusq'au Mois de Juin, 1756. Shirley to
Fox, 7 May, 1756. Conduct of Major-General Shirley briefly stated.
Information of Captain John Vicars, of the Fiftieth (Shirley's) Regiment.
Eastburn, Faithful Narrative. Entick, i. 471.* The French accounts
place the number of English at sixty or eighty.

[2] *Correspondance de Montcalm, Vaudreuil, et Lévis.*

too, came the intendant François Bigot, the most accomplished knave in Canada, yet indispensable for his vigor and executive skill; Bougainville, who had disarmed the jealousy of Vaudreuil, and now stood high in his good graces; and the adjutant-general, Montreuil, clearly a vain and pragmatic personage, who, having come to Canada with Dieskau the year before, thought it behooved him to give the general the advantage of his experience. "I like M. de Montcalm very much," he writes to the minister, "and will do the impossible to deserve his confidence. I have spoken to him in the same terms as to M. Dieskau; thus: ' Trust only the French regulars for an expedition, but use the Canadians and Indians to harass the enemy. Don't expose yourself; send me to carry your orders to points of danger.' The colony officers do not like those from France. The Canadians are independent, spiteful, lying, boastful; very good for skirmishing, very brave behind a tree, and very timid when not under cover. I think both sides will stand on the defensive. It does not seem to me that M. de Montcalm means to attack the enemy; and I think he is right. In this country a thousand men could stop three thousand." [1]

"M. de Vaudreuil overwhelms me with civilities," Montcalm writes to the minister of war. "I think that he is pleased with my conduct towards him, and that it persuades him there are general officers in France who can act under his orders without preju-

[1] *Montreuil au Ministre*, 12 *Juin*, 1756. The original is in cipher.

dice or ill-humor."[1] "I am on good terms with
him," he says again; "but not in his confidence,
which he never gives to anybody from France. His
intentions are good, but he is slow and irresolute."[2]

Indians presently brought word that ten thousand
English were coming to attack Ticonderoga. A
reinforcement of colony regulars was at once despatched to join the two battalions already there; a
third battalion, Royal Roussillon, was sent after
them. The militia were called out and ordered to
follow with all speed, while both Montcalm and
Lévis hastened to the supposed scene of danger.[3]
They embarked in canoes on the Richelieu, coasted
the shore of Lake Champlain, passed Fort Frederic
or Crown Point, where all was activity and bustle,
and reached Ticonderoga at the end of June. They
found the fort, on which Lotbinière had been at work
all winter, advanced towards completion. It stood
on the crown of the promontory, and was a square
with four bastions, a ditch, blown in some parts out
of the solid rock, bomb-proofs, barracks of stone, and
a system of exterior defences as yet only begun.
The rampart consisted of two parallel walls ten feet
apart, built of the trunks of trees, and held together
by transverse logs dovetailed at both ends, the space

[1] *Montcalm au Ministre,* 12 *Juin,* 1756.

[2] *Ibid.,* 19 *Juin,* 1756. "Je suis bien avec luy, sans sa confiance,
qu'il ne donne jamais à personne de la France." Erroneously
rendered in *N. Y. Col. Docs.,* x. 421.

[3] *Montcalm au Ministre,* 26 *Juin,* 1756. *Détail de ce qui s'est passé
Octobre,* 1755–*Juin,* 1756.

between being filled with earth and gravel well packed.[1] Such was the first Fort Ticonderoga, or Carillon, — a structure quite distinct from the later fort of which the ruins still stand on the same spot. The forest had been hewn away for some distance around, and the tents of the regulars and huts of the Canadians had taken its place; innumerable bark canoes lay along the strand; and gangs of men toiled at the unfinished works.

Ticonderoga was now the most advanced position of the French, and Crown Point, which had before held that perilous honor, was in the second line. Lévis, to whom had been assigned the permanent command of this post of danger, set out on foot to explore the neighboring woods and mountains, and slept out several nights before he reappeared at the camp. "I do not think," says Montcalm, "that many high officers in Europe would have occasion to take such tramps as this. I cannot speak too well of him. Without being a man of brilliant parts, he has good experience, good sense, and a quick eye; and, though I had served with him before, I never should have thought that he had such promptness and efficiency. He has turned his campaigns to good account."[2] Lévis writes of his chief with equal warmth. "I do not know if the Marquis de Montcalm is pleased with me, but I am sure that I am

[1] *Lotbinière au Ministre,* 31 *Octobre,* 1756. *Montcalm au Ministre,* 20 *Juillet,* 1756.

[2] *Montcalm au Ministre,* 20 *Juillet,* 1756.

very much so with him, and shall always be charmed
to serve under his orders. It is not for me, Monseigneur, to speak to you of his merit and his talents.
You know him better than anybody else; but I may
have the honor of assuring you that he has pleased
everybody in this colony, and manages affairs with
the Indians extremely well." [1]

The danger from the English proved to be still
remote, and there was ample leisure in the camp.
Duchat, a young captain in the battalion of Languedoc,
used it in writing to his father a long account of
what he saw about him, — the forests full of game;
the ducks, geese, and partridges; the prodigious
flocks of wild pigeons that darkened the air; the
bears, the beavers; and above all the Indians, their
canoes, dress, ball-play, and dances. "We are
making here," says the military prophet, "a place
that history will not forget. The English colonies
have ten times more people than ours; but these
wretches have not the least knowledge of war; and
if they go out to fight, they must abandon wives,
children, and all that they possess. Not a week
passes but the French send them a band of *hair-
dressers*, whom they would be very glad to dispense
with. It is incredible what a quantity of scalps they
bring us. In Virginia they have committed unheard-
of cruelties, carried off families, burned a great many
houses, and killed an infinity of people. These
miserable English are in the extremity of distress,

[1] *Lévis au Ministre,* 17 *Juillet,* 1756.

and repent too late the unjust war they began against us. It is a pleasure to make war in Canada. One is troubled neither with horses nor baggage; the King provides everything. But it must be confessed that if it costs no money, one pays for it in another way, by seeing nothing but pease and bacon on the mess-table. Luckily the lakes are full of fish, and both officers and soldiers have to turn fishermen." [1]

Meanwhile, at the head of Lake George, the raw bands of ever-active New England were mustering for the fray.

[1] *Relation de M. Duchat, Capitaine au Régiment de Languedoc, écrite au Camp de Carillon,* 15 *Juillet,* 1756.

CHAPTER XII.

1756.

OSWEGO.

THE NEW CAMPAIGN. — UNTIMELY CHANGE OF COMMANDERS. — ECLIPSE OF SHIRLEY. — EARL OF LOUDON. — MUSTER OF PROVINCIALS. — NEW ENGLAND LEVIES. — WINSLOW AT LAKE GEORGE. — JOHNSON AND THE FIVE NATIONS. — BRADSTREET AND HIS BOATMEN. — FIGHT ON THE ONONDAGA. — PESTILENCE AT OSWEGO. — LOUDON AND THE PROVINCIALS. — NEW ENGLAND CAMPS. — ARMY CHAPLAINS. — A SUDDEN BLOW. — MONTCALM ATTACKS OSWEGO: ITS FALL.

WHEN, at the end of the last year, Shirley returned from his bootless Oswego campaign, he called a council of war at New York and laid before it his scheme for the next summer's operations. It was a comprehensive one: to master Lake Ontario by an overpowering naval force and seize the French forts upon it, Niagara, Frontenac, and Toronto; attack Ticonderoga and Crown Point on the one hand, and Fort Duquesne on the other, and at the same time perplex and divide the enemy by an inroad down the Chaudière upon the settlements about Quebec.[1] The

---

[1] *Minutes of Council of War held at New York, 12 and 13 December, 1755. Shirley to Robinson, 19 December, 1755. The Conduct of Major-General Shirley briefly stated. Review of Military Operations in North America.*

council approved the scheme; but to execute it the provinces must raise at least sixteen thousand men. This they refused to do. Pennsylvania and Virginia would take no active part, and were content with defending themselves. The attack on Fort Duquesne was therefore abandoned, as was also the diversion towards Quebec. The New England colonies were discouraged by Johnson's failure to take Crown Point, doubtful of the military abilities of Shirley, and embarrassed by the debts of the last campaign; but when they learned that Parliament would grant a sum of money in partial compensation for their former sacrifices,[1] they plunged into new debts without hesitation, and raised more men than the general had asked; though, with their usual jealousy, they provided that their soldiers should be employed for no other purpose than the attack on Ticonderoga and Crown Point. Shirley chose John Winslow to command them, and gave him a commission to that effect; while he, to clinch his authority, asked and obtained supplementary commissions from every government that gave men to the expedition.[2] For the movement against the forts of Lake Ontario, which Shirley meant to command in person, he had the

---

[1] *Lords of Trade to Lords of the Treasury, 12 February,* 1756. *Fox to American Governors, 13 March,* 1756. *Shirley to Phipps, 15 June,* 1756. The sum was £115,000, divided in proportion to the expense incurred by the several colonies; Massachusetts having £54,000, Connecticut £26,000, and New York £15,000, the rest being given to New Hampshire, Rhode Island, and New Jersey.

[2] *Letter and Order Books of General Winslow,* 1756.

remains of his own and Pepperrell's regiments, the
two shattered battalions brought over by Braddock,
the "Jersey Blues," four provincial companies from
North Carolina, and the four King's companies of
New York. His first care was to recruit their ranks
and raise them to their full complement; which,
when effected, would bring them up to the insufficient strength of about forty-four hundred men.

While he was struggling with contradictions and
cross purposes, a withering blow fell upon him; he
learned that he was superseded in the command.
The cabal formed against him, with Delancey at its
head, had won over Sir Charles Hardy, the new
governor of New York, and had painted Shirley's
conduct in such colors that the ministry removed
him. It was essential for the campaign that a successor should be sent at once, to form plans on the
spot and make preparations accordingly. The ministry were in no such haste. It was presently
announced that Colonel Daniel Webb would be sent
to America, followed by General James Abercrombie;
who was to be followed in turn by the Earl of
Loudon, the destined commander-in-chief. Shirley
was to resign his command to Webb, Webb to
Abercrombie, and Abercrombie to Loudon.[1] It
chanced that the two former arrived in June at about

---

[1] *Fox to Shirley*, 13 *March*, 1756. *Ibid.*, 31 *March*, 1756. *Order to
Colonel Webb*, 31 *March*, 1756. *Order to Major-General Abercrombie*, 1
April, 1756. *Halifax to Shirley*, 1 *April*, 1756. *Shirley to Fox*, 13
June, 1756.

the same time, while the earl came in July; and meanwhile it devolved on Shirley to make ready for them. Unable to divine what their plans would be, he prepared the campaign in accordance with his own.

His star, so bright a twelvemonth before, was now miserably dimmed. In both his public and private life he was the butt of adversity. He had lost two promising sons; he had made a mortifying failure as a soldier; and triumphant enemies were rejoicing in his fall. It is to the credit of his firmness and his zeal in the cause that he set himself to his task with as much vigor as if he, and not others, were to gather the fruits. His chief care was for his favorite enterprise in the direction of Lake Ontario. Making Albany his headquarters, he rebuilt the fort at the Great Carrying Place destroyed in March by the French, sent troops to guard the perilous route to Oswego, and gathered provisions and stores at the posts along the way.

Meanwhile the New England men, strengthened by the levies of New York, were mustering at Albany for the attack of Crown Point. At the end of May they moved a short distance up the Hudson, and encamped at a place called Half-Moon, where the navigation was stopped by rapids. Here and at the posts above were gathered something more than five thousand men, as raw and untrained as those led by Johnson in the summer before.[1] The four New England colonies were much alike in their way of raising

---

[1] *Letter and Order Books of Winslow,* 1756.

and equipping men, and the example of Massachusetts may serve for them all. The Assembly or
"General Court" voted the required number, and
chose a committee of war authorized to impress provisions, munitions, stores, clothing, tools, and other
necessaries, for which fair prices were to be paid
within six months. The governor issued a proclamation calling for volunteers. If the full number did
not appear within the time named, the colonels of
militia were ordered to muster their regiments, and
immediately draft out of them men enough to meet
the need. A bounty of six dollars was offered this
year to stimulate enlistment, and the pay of a private
soldier was fixed at one pound six shillings a month,
Massachusetts currency. If he brought a gun, he
had an additional bounty of two dollars. A powder-
horn, bullet-pouch, blanket, knapsack, and "wooden
bottle," or canteen, were supplied by the province;
and if he brought no gun of his own, a musket was
given him, for which, as for the other articles, he
was to account at the end of the campaign. In the
next year it was announced that the soldier should
receive, besides his pay, "a coat and soldier's hat."
The coat was of coarse blue cloth, to which breeches
of red or blue were afterwards added. Along with
his rations, he was promised a gill of rum each day,
a privilege of which he was extremely jealous, deeply
resenting every abridgment of it. He was enlisted
for the campaign, and could not be required to serve
above a year at farthest.

The complement of a regiment was five hundred, divided into companies of fifty; and as the men and officers of each were drawn from the same neighborhood, they generally knew each other. The officers, though nominally appointed by the Assembly, were for the most part the virtual choice of the soldiers themselves, from whom they were often indistinguishable in character and social standing. Hence discipline was weak. The pay — or, as it was called, the wages — of a colonel was twelve pounds sixteen shillings, Massachusetts currency, a month; that of a captain, five pounds eight shillings, — an advance on the pay of the last year; and that of a chaplain, six pounds eight shillings.[1] Penalties were enacted against "irreligion, immorality, drunkenness, debauchery, and profaneness." The ordinary punishments were the wooden horse, irons, or, in bad cases, flogging.

Much difficulty arose from the different rules adopted by the various colonies for the regulation of their soldiers. Nor was this the only source of trouble. Besides its war committee, the Assembly of each of the four New England colonies chose another committee "for clothing, arming, paying, victualling, and transporting" its troops. They were to go to the scene of operations, hire wagons, oxen, and horses, build boats and vessels, and charge themselves with the conveyance of all supplies belonging to their respective governments. They were to keep

[1] *Vote of General Court*, 26 *February*, 1756.

in correspondence with the committee of war at home, to whom they were responsible; and the officer commanding the contingent of their colony was required to furnish them with guards and escorts. Thus four independent committees were engaged in the work of transportation at the same time, over the same roads, for the same object. Each colony chose to keep the control of its property in its own hands. The inconveniences were obvious. "I wish to God," wrote Lord Loudon to Winslow, "you could persuade your people to go all one way." The committees themselves did not always find their task agreeable. One of their number, John Ashley, of Massachusetts, writes in dudgeon to Governor Phips: "Sir, I am apt to think that things have been misrepresented to your Honor, or else I am certain I should not suffer in my character, and be styled a damned rascal, and ought to be put in irons, etc., when I am certain I have exerted myself to the utmost of my ability to expedite the business assigned me by the General Court." At length, late in the autumn, Loudon persuaded the colonies to forego this troublesome sort of independence, and turn over their stores to the commissary-general, receipts being duly given.[1]

---

[1] The above particulars are gathered from the voluminous papers in the State House at Boston, *Archives, Military*, vols. lxxv., lxxvi. These contain the military acts of the General Court, proclamations, reports of committees, and other papers relating to military affairs in 1755 and 1756. The *Letter and Order Books of Winslow*, in the Library of the Massachusetts Historical Society, have supplied much concurrent matter. See also *Colonial Records of R. I.*, v., and *Provincial Papers of N. H.*, vi.

From Winslow's headquarters at Half-Moon a road led along the banks of the Hudson to Stillwater, whence there was water carriage to Saratoga. Here stores were again placed in wagons and carried several miles to Upper Falls; thence by boat to Fort Edward; and thence, fourteen miles across country, to Fort William Henry at Lake George, where the army was to embark for Ticonderoga. Each of the points of transit below Fort Edward was guarded by a stockade and two or more companies of provincials. They were much pestered by Indians, who now and then scalped a straggler, and escaped with their usual nimbleness. From time to time strong bands of Canadians and Indians approached by way of South Bay or Wood Creek, and threatened more serious mischief. It is surprising that some of the trains were not cut off, for the escorts were often reckless and disorderly to the last degree. Sometimes the invaders showed great audacity. Early in June Colonel Fitch at Albany scrawls a hasty note to Winslow: "Friday, 11 o'clock: Sir, about half an hour since, a party of near fifty French and Indians had the impudence to come down to the river opposite to this city and captivate two men;" and Winslow replies with equal quaintness: "We daily discover the Indians about us; but not yet have been so happy as to obtain any of them." [1]

[1] Vaudreuil, in his despatch of 12 August, gives particulars of these raids, with an account of the scalps taken on each occasion. He thought the results disappointing.

Colonel Jonathan Bagley commanded at Fort
William Henry, where gangs of men were busied
under his eye in building three sloops and making
several hundred whaleboats to carry the army to
Ticonderoga. The season was advancing fast, and
Winslow urged him to hasten on the work; to which
the humorous Bagley answered: "Shall leave no
stone unturned; every wheel shall go that rum and
human flesh can move."[1] A fortnight after he
reports: "I must really confess I have almost wore
the men out, poor dogs. Pray where are the committee, or what are they about?" He sent scouts to
watch the enemy, with results not quite satisfactory.
"There is a vast deal of news here; every party
brings abundance, but all different." Again, a little
later: "I constantly keep out small scouting parties
to the eastward and westward of the lake, and make
no discovery but the tracks of small parties who are
plaguing us constantly; but what vexes me most, we
can't catch one of the sons of ——. I have sent
out skulking parties some distance from the sentries
in the night, to lie still in the bushes to intercept
them; but the flies are so plenty, our people can't
bear them."[2] Colonel David Wooster, at Fort
Edward, was no more fortunate in his attempts to
take satisfaction on his midnight visitors, and reports
that he has not thus far been able "to give those
villains a dressing."[3] The English, however, were

---

[1] *Bagley to Winslow*, 2 *July*, 1756.   [2] *Ibid.*, 15 *July*, 1756.
[3] *Wooster to Winslow*, 2 *June*, 1756.

fast learning the art of forest war, and the partisan chief, Captain Robert Rogers, began already to be famous. On the seventeenth of June he and his band lay hidden in the bushes within the outposts of Ticonderoga, and made a close survey of the fort and surrounding camps.[1] His report was not cheering. Winslow's so-called army had now grown to nearly seven thousand men; and these, it was plain, were not too many to drive the French from their stronghold.

While Winslow pursued his preparations, tried to settle disputes of rank among the colonels of the several colonies, and strove to bring order out of the little chaos of his command, Sir William Johnson was engaged in a work for which he was admirably fitted. This was the attaching of the Five Nations to the English interest. Along with his patent of baronetcy, which reached him about this time, he received, direct from the Crown, the commission of "Colonel, Agent, and Sole Superintendent of the Six Nations and other Northern Tribes."[2] Henceforth he was independent of governors and generals, and responsible to the court alone. His task was a difficult one. The Five Nations would fain have remained neutral, and let the European rivals fight it out; but, on account of their local position, they could not. The exactions and lies of the Albany

[1] *Report of Rogers,* 19 *June,* 1756. Much abridged in his published *Journals.*

[2] *Fox to Johnson,* 13 *March,* 1756. *Papers of Sir William Johnson.*

traders, the frauds of land-speculators, the contradictory action of the different provincial governments, joined to English weakness and mismanagement in the last war, all conspired to alienate them and to aid the efforts of the French agents, who cajoled and threatened them by turns. But for Johnson these intrigues would have prevailed. He had held a series of councils with them at Fort Johnson during the winter, and not only drew from them a promise to stand by the English, but persuaded all the confederated tribes, except the Cayugas, to consent that the English should build forts near their chief towns, under the pretext of protecting them from the French.[1]

In June he went to Onondaga, well escorted, for the way was dangerous. This capital of the confederacy was under a cloud. It had just lost one Red Head, its chief sachem; and first of all it behooved the baronet to condole their affliction. The ceremony was long, with compliments, lugubrious speeches, wampum-belts, the scalp of an enemy to replace the departed, and a final glass of rum for each of the assembled mourners. The conferences lasted a fortnight; and when Johnson took his leave, the tribes stood pledged to lift the hatchet for the English.[2]

[1] *Conferences between Sir William Johnson and the Indians, December, 1755, to February, 1756,* in *N. Y. Col. Docs.,* vii. 44–74. *Account of Conferences held and Treaties made between Sir William Johnson, Bart., and the Indian Nations of North America* (London, 1756).

[2] *Minutes of Councils at Onondaga,* 19 *June to* 3 *July,* 1756, in *N. Y. Col. Docs.,* vii. 134–150.

When he returned to Fort Johnson a fever seized him, and he lay helpless for a time; then rose from his sick bed to meet another congregation of Indians. These were deputies of the Five Nations, with Mohegans from the Hudson, and Delawares and Shawanoes from the Susquehanna, whom he had persuaded to visit him in hope that he might induce them to cease from murdering the border settlers. All their tribesmen were in arms against the English; but he prevailed at last, and they accepted the war-belt at his hands. The Delawares complained that their old conquerors, the Five Nations, had forced them " to wear the petticoat; " that is, to be counted not as warriors but as women. Johnson, in presence of all the Assembly, now took off the figurative garment, and pronounced them henceforth men. A grand war-dance followed. A hundred and fifty Mohawks, Oneidas, Onondagas, Delawares, Shawanoes, and Mohegans stamped, whooped, and yelled all night.[1] In spite of Piquet, the two Joncaires, and the rest of the French agents, Johnson had achieved a success. But would the Indians keep their word? It was more than doubtful. While some of them treated with him on the Mohawk, others treated with Vaudreuil at Montreal.[2] A display of military vigor on the English side, crowned

---

[1] *Minutes of Councils at Fort Johnson, 9 July to 12 July,* in *N. Y. Col. Docs.,* vii. 152–160.

[2] *Conferences between M. de Vaudreuil and the Five Nations, 28 July to 20 August,* in *N. Y. Col. Docs.,* x. 445–453.

by some signal victory, would alone make their alliance sure.

It was not the French only who thwarted the efforts of Johnson; for while he strove to make friends of the Delawares and Shawanoes, Governor Morris of Pennsylvania declared war against them, and Governor Belcher of New Jersey followed his example; though persuaded at last to hold his hand till the baronet had tried the virtue of pacific measures.[1]

What Shirley longed for was the collecting of a body of Five Nation warriors at Oswego to aid him in his cherished enterprise against Niagara and Frontenac. The warriors had promised him to come; but there was small hope that they would do so. Meanwhile he was at Albany pursuing his preparations, posting his scanty force in the forts newly built on the Mohawk and the Great Carrying Place, and sending forward stores and provisions. Having no troops to spare for escorts, he invented a plan which, like everything he did, was bitterly criticised. He took into pay two thousand boatmen, gathered from all parts of the country, including many whalemen from the eastern coasts of New England, divided them into companies of fifty, armed each with a gun and a hatchet, and placed them under the command of Lieutenant-Colonel John

---

[1] *Johnson to Lords of Trade,* 28 *May,* 1756. *Ibid.,* 17 *July,* 1756. *Johnson to Shirley,* 24 *April,* 1756. *Colonial Records of Pa.,* vii. 75, 88, 194.

Bradstreet.[1] Thus organized, they would, he hoped,
require no escort. Bradstreet was a New England
officer who had been a captain in the last war, somewhat dogged and self-opinioned, but brave, energetic,
and well fitted for this kind of service.

In May Vaudreuil sent Coulon de Villiers with
eleven hundred soldiers, Canadians, and Indians, to
harass Oswego and cut its communications with
Albany.[2] Nevertheless Bradstreet safely conducted
a convoy of provisions and military stores to the garrison; and on the third of July set out on his return
with the empty boats. The party were pushing their
way up the river in three divisions. The first of
these, consisting of a hundred boats and three hun
dred men, with Bradstreet at their head, were about
nine miles from Oswego, when, at three in the afternoon, they received a heavy volley from the forest on
the east bank. It was fired by a part of Villiers'
command, consisting, by English accounts, of about
seven hundred men. A considerable number of the
boatmen were killed or disabled, and the others
made for the shelter of the western shore. Some
prisoners were taken in the confusion; and if the
French had been content to stop here, they might
fairly have claimed a kind of victory: but, eager to
push their advantage, they tried to cross under cover
of an island just above. Bradstreet saw the move-

1 *Shirley to Fox,* 7 *May,* 1756. *Shirley to Abercrombie,* 27 *June,*
1756. *Loudon to Fox,* 19 *August,* 1756.
2 *Détail de ce qui s'est passé en Canada, Octobre,* 1755–*Juin,* 1756

ment, and landed on the island with six or eight followers, among whom was young Captain Schuyler,
afterwards General Schuyler of the Revolution.
Their fire kept the enemy in check till others joined
them, to the number of about twenty. These a
second and a third time beat back the French, who
now gave over the attempt, and made for another
ford at some distance above. Bradstreet saw their
intention; and collecting two hundred and fifty men,
was about to advance up the west bank to oppose
them, when Dr. Kirkland, a surgeon, came to tell
him that the second division of boats had come up,
and that the men had landed. Bradstreet ordered
them to stay where they were, and defend the lower
crossing: then hastened forward; but when he
reached the upper ford, the French had passed the
river, and were ensconced in a pine swamp near the
shore. Here he attacked them; and both parties
fired at each other from behind trees for an hour,
with little effect. Bradstreet at length encouraged
his men to make a rush at the enemy, who were put
to flight and driven into the river, where many were
shot or drowned as they tried to cross. Another
party of the French had meanwhile passed by a ford
still higher up to support their comrades; but the
fight was over before they reached the spot, and they
in their turn were set upon and driven back across
the stream. Half an hour after, Captain Patten
arrived from Onondaga with the grenadiers of
Shirley's regiment; and late in the evening two

hundred men came from Oswego to reinforce the
victors. In the morning Bradstreet prepared to
follow the French to their camp, twelve miles distant; but was prevented by a heavy rain which lasted
all day. On the Monday following, he and his men
reached Albany, bringing two prisoners, eighty
French muskets, and many knapsacks picked up in
the woods. He had lost between sixty and seventy
killed, wounded, and taken.[1]

This affair was trumpeted through Canada as a
victory of the French. Their notices of it are discordant, though very brief. One of them says that
Villiers had four hundred men. Another gives him
five hundred, and a third eight hundred, against
fifteen hundred English, of whom they killed eight
hundred, or an Englishman apiece. A fourth writer
boasts that six hundred Frenchmen killed nine hundred English. A fifth contents himself with four
hundred; but thinks that forty more would have
been slain if the Indians had not fired too soon. He
says further that there were three hundred boats;
and presently forgetting himself, adds that five hundred were taken or destroyed. A sixth announces a
great capture of stores and provisions, though all the

---

[1] *Letter of J. Choate, Albany, 12 July, 1756,* in Massachusetts
Archives, lv. *Three Letters from Albany, July, August, 1756,* in *Doc.
History of N. Y.,* i. 482. *Review of Military Operations. Shirley to
Fox, 26 July, 1756. Abercrombie to Sir Charles Hardy, 11 July, 1756.*
Niles, in *Mass. Hist. Coll., Fourth Series,* v. 417. Lossing, *Life of
Schuyler,* i. 131 (1860). Mante, 60. Bradstreet's conduct on this
occasion afterwards gained for him the warm praises of Wolfe.

boats were empty. A seventh reports that the Canadians killed about three hundred, and would have killed more but for the bad quality of their tomahawks. An eighth, with rare modesty, puts the English loss at fifty or sixty. That of Villiers is given in every proportion of killed or wounded, from one up to ten. Thus was Canada roused to martial ardor, and taught to look for future triumphs cheaply bought.[1]

The success of Bradstreet silenced for a time the enemies of Shirley. His cares, however, redoubled. He was anxious for Oswego, as the two prisoners declared that the French meant to attack it, instead of waiting to be attacked from it. Nor was the news from that quarter reassuring. The engineer, Mackellar, wrote that the works were incapable of defence; and Colonel Mercer, the commandant, reported general discontent in the garrison.[2] Captain John Vicars, an invalid officer of Shirley's regiment, arrived at Albany with yet more deplorable accounts. He had passed the winter at Oswego, where he declared the dearth of food to have been such that several councils of war had been held on the question of abandoning the place from sheer starvation. More

[1] *Nouvelles du Camp établi au Portage de Chouaguen, première Relation. Ibid., Seconde Relation,* 10 *Juillet,* 1756. Bougainville, *Journal,* who gives the report as he heard it. *Lettre du R. P. Cocquard, S. J.,* 1756. *Vaudreuil au Ministre,* 10 *Juillet,* 1756. *Ursulines de Québec,* ii. 292. *N. Y. Col. Docs.,* x. 434, 467, 477, 483. Some prisoners taken in the first attack were brought to Montreal, where their presence gave countenance to these fabrications.

[2] *Mackellar to Shirley, June,* 1756. *Mercer to Shirley,* 2 *July,* 1756.

than half his regiment died of hunger or disease; and, in his own words, "had the poor fellows lived they must have eaten one another." Some of the men were lodged in barracks, though without beds, while many lay all winter in huts on the bare ground. Scurvy and dysentery made frightful havoc. "In January," says Vicars, "we were informed by the Indians that we were to be attacked. The garrison was then so weak that the strongest guard we proposed to mount was a subaltern and twenty men; but we were seldom able to mount more than sixteen or eighteen, and half of those were obliged to have sticks in their hands to support them. The men were so weak that the sentries often fell down on their posts, and lay there till the relief came and lifted them up." His own company of fifty was reduced to ten. The other regiment of the garrison, Pepperrell's, or the fifty-first, was quartered at Fort Ontario, on the other side of the river; and being better sheltered, suffered less.

The account given by Vicars of the state of the defences was scarcely more flattering. He reported that the principal fort had no cannon on the side most exposed to attack. Two pieces had been mounted on the trading-house in the centre; but as the concussion shook down stones from the wall whenever they were fired, they had since been removed. The second work, called Fort Ontario, he had not seen since it was finished, having been too ill to cross the river. Of the third, called New

Oswego, or "Fort Rascal," he testifies thus: "It never was finished, and there were no loop-holes in the stockades; so that they could not fire out of the fort but by opening the gate and firing out of that." [1]

Through the spring and early summer Shirley was gathering recruits, often of the meanest quality, and sending them to Oswego to fill out the two emaciated regiments. The place must be defended at any cost. Its fall would ruin not only the enterprise against Niagara and Frontenac, but also that against Ticonderoga and Crown Point; since, having nothing more to fear on Lake Ontario, the French could unite their whole force on Lake Champlain, whether for defence or attack.

Towards the end of June Abercrombie and Webb arrived at Albany, bringing a reinforcement of nine hundred regulars, consisting of Otway's regiment, or a part of it, and a body of Highlanders. Shirley resigned his command, and Abercrombie requested him to go to New York, wait there till Lord Loudon arrived, and lay before him the state of affairs. [2] Shirley waited till the twenty-third of July, when the earl at length appeared. He was a rough Scotch lord, hot and irascible; and the communications of his predecessor, made, no doubt, in a manner some-

[1] *Information of Captain John Vicars, of the Fiftieth (Shirley's) Regiment,* enclosed with a despatch of Lord Loudon. Vicars was a veteran British officer who left Oswego with Bradstreet on the third of July. *Shirley to Loudon, 5 September,* 1756.

[2] *Shirley to Fox,* 4 *July,* 1756.

what pompous and self-satisfied, did not please him.
"I got from Major-General Shirley," he says, "a
few papers of very little use; only he insinuated to
me that I would find everything prepared, and have
nothing to do but to pull laurels; which I understand
was his constant conversation before my arrival."[1]

Loudon sailed up the Hudson in no placid mood.
On reaching Albany he abandoned the attempt
against Niagara and Frontenac; and had resolved to
turn his whole force against Ticonderoga, when he
was met by an obstacle that both perplexed and
angered him. By a royal order lately issued, all
general and field officers with provincial commissions
were to take rank only as eldest captains when serving in conjunction with regular troops.[2] Hence the
whole provincial army, as Winslow observes, might
be put under the command of any British major.[3]
The announcement of this regulation naturally caused
great discontent. The New England officers held a
meeting, and voted with one voice that in their belief
its enforcement would break up the provincial army
and prevent the raising of another. Loudon, hearing of this, desired Winslow to meet him at Albany
for a conference on the subject. Thither Winslow
went with some of his chief officers. The earl asked
them to dinner, and there was much talk, with no
satisfactory result; whereupon, somewhat chafed, he

[1] *Loudon (to Fox?), 19 August,* 1756.

[2] *Order concerning the Rank of Provincial General and Field Officers
in North America. Given at our Court at Kensington, 12 May,* 1756.

[3] *Winslow to Shirley, 21 August,* 1756.

required Winslow to answer in writing, yes or no, whether the provincial officers would obey the commander-in-chief and act in conjunction with the regulars. Thus forced to choose between acquiescence and flat mutiny, they declared their submission to his orders, at the same time asking as a favor that they might be allowed to act independently; to which Loudon gave for the present an unwilling assent. Shirley, who, in spite of his removal from command, had the good of the service deeply at heart, was much troubled at this affair, and wrote strong letters to Winslow in the interest of harmony.[1]

Loudon next proceeded to examine the state of the provincial forces, and sent Lieutenant-Colonel Burton, of the regulars, to observe and report upon it. Winslow by this time had made a forward movement, and was now at Lake George with nearly half his command, while the rest were at Fort Edward under Lyman, or in detachments at Saratoga and the other small posts below. Burton found Winslow's men encamped with their right on what are now the grounds of Fort William Henry Hotel, and their left extending southward between the mountain in their front and the marsh in their rear. "There are here," he reports, "about twenty-five hundred men, five hundred of them sick, the greatest part of them what they call poorly; they bury from five to eight

[1] *Correspondence of Loudon, Abercrombie, and Shirley, July, August,* 1756. *Record of Meeting of Provincial Officers, July,* 1756. *Letter and Order Books of Winslow.*

daily, and officers in proportion; extremely indolent, and dirty to a degree." Then, in vernacular English, he describes the infectious condition of the fort, which was full of the sick. "Their camp," he proceeds, "is nastier than anything I could conceive; their ——, kitchens, graves, and places for slaughtering cattle all mixed through their encampment; a great waste of provisions, the men having just what they please; no great command kept up. Colonel Gridley governs the general; not in the least alert; only one advanced guard of a subaltern and twenty-four men. The cannon and stores in great confusion." Of the camp at Fort Edward he gives a better account. "It is much cleaner than at Fort William Henry, but not sufficiently so to keep the men healthy; a much better command kept up here. General Lyman very ready to order out to work and to assist the engineers with any number of men they require, and keeps a succession of scouting-parties out towards Wood Creek and South Bay." [1]

The prejudice of the regular officer may have colored the picture, but it is certain that the sanitary condition of the provincial camps was extremely bad. "A grievous sickness among the troops," writes a Massachusetts surgeon at Fort Edward; "we bury five or six a day. Not more than two-thirds of our army fit for duty. Long encampments are the bane of New England men." [2] Like all raw recruits, they

[1] *Burton to Loudon, 27 August,* 1756.

[2] *Dr. Thomas Williams to Colonel Israel Williams,* 28 *August,* 1756.

did not know how to take care of themselves; and
their officers had not the experience, knowledge, or
habit of command to enforce sanitary rules. The
same evils were found among the Canadians when
kept long in one place. Those in the camp of
Villiers are reported at this time as nearly all sick.[1]

Another penman, very different from the military
critic, was also on the spot, noting down every day
what he saw and felt. This was John Graham, minister of Suffield, in Connecticut, and now chaplain
of Lyman's regiment. His spirit, by nature far from
buoyant, was depressed by bodily ailments, and still
more by the extremely secular character of his
present surroundings. It appears by his Diary that
he left home "under great exercise of mind," and
was detained at Albany for a time, being, as he says,
taken with an ague-fit and a quinsy; but at length
he reached the camp at Fort Edward, where deep
despondency fell upon him. "Labor under great
discouragements," says the Diary, under date of July
twenty-eighth; "for find my business but mean in
the esteem of many, and think there 's not much for
a chaplain to do." Again, Tuesday, August seventeenth: "Breakfasted this morning with the General.
But a graceless meal; never a blessing asked, nor
thanks given. At the evening sacrifice a more open
scene of wickedness. The General and head officers,
with some of the regular officers, in General Lyman's
tent, within four rods of the place of public prayers.

[1] Bougainville, *Journal*.

None came to prayers; but they fixed a table without the door of the tent, where a head colonel was
posted to make punch in the sight of all, they within
drinking, talking, and laughing during the whole of
the service, to the disturbance and disaffection of
most present. This was not only a bare neglect,
but an open contempt, of the worship of God by the
heads of this army. 'Twas but last Sabbath that
General Lyman spent the time of divine service in
the afternoon in his tent, drinking in company with
Mr. Gordon, a regular officer. I have oft heard
cursing and swearing in his presence by some provincial field-officers, but never heard a reproof nor so much
as a check to them come from his mouth, though
he never uses such language himself. Lord, what
is man! Truly, the May-game of Fortune! Lord,
make me know my duty, and what I ought to do!'"

That night his sleep was broken and his soul
troubled by angry voices under his window, where
one Colonel Glasier was berating, in unhallowed
language, the captain of the guard; and here the
chaplain's Journal abruptly ends.[1]

A brother minister, bearing no likeness to the
worthy Graham, appeared on the same spot some
time after. This was Chaplain William Crawford,
of Worcester, who, having neglected to bring money
to the war, suffered much annoyance, aggravated by
what he thought a want of due consideration for his

[1] I owe to my friend George S. Hale, Esq., the opportunity of
examining the autograph Journal; it has since been printed in the
Magazine of American History for March, 1882.

person and office. His indignation finds vent in a
letter to his townsman, Timothy Paine, member of
the General Court: "No man can reasonably expect
that I can with any propriety discharge the duty of a
chaplain when I have nothing either to eat or drink,
nor any conveniency to write a line other than to sit
down upon a stump and put a piece of paper upon
my knee. As for Mr. Weld [*another chaplain*],
he is easy and silent whatever treatment he meets
with, and I suppose they thought to find me the
same easy and ductile person; but may the wide
yawning earth devour me first! The state of the
camp is just such as one at home would guess it to
be, — nothing but a hurry and confusion of vice and
wickedness, with a stygian atmosphere to breathe
in."[1] The vice and wickedness of which he complains appear to have consisted in a frequent infrac-
tion of the standing order against "Curseing and
Swareing," as well as of that which required attend-
ance on daily prayers, and enjoined "the people to
appear in a decent manner, clean and shaved," at
the two Sunday sermons.[2]

At the beginning of August Winslow wrote to the

[1] The autograph letter is in Massachusetts Archives, lvi. no. 142.
The same volume contains a letter from Colonel Frye, of Massachusetts, in which he speaks of the forlorn condition in which
Chaplain Weld reached the camp. Of Chaplain Crawford, he says
that he came decently clothed, but without bed or blanket, till he,
Frye, lent them to him, and got Captain Learned to take him into
his tent. Chaplains usually had a separate tent, or shared that of
the colonel.

[2] *Letter and Order Books of Winslow.*

heights, would guard against attack from that quarter. On a hill, a fourth of a mile beyond Old Oswego, stood the unfinished stockade called New Oswego, Fort George, or, by reason of its worthlessness, Fort Rascal. It had served as a cattle-pen before the French appeared, but was now occupied by a hundred and fifty Jersey provincials. Old Oswego with its outwork was held by Shirley's regiment, chiefly invalids and raw recruits, to whom were now joined the garrison of Fort Ontario and a number of sailors, boatmen, and laborers.

Montcalm lost no time. As soon as darkness set in he began a battery at the brink of the height on which stood the captured fort. His whole force toiled all night, digging, setting gabions, and dragging up cannon, some of which had been taken from Braddock. Before daybreak twenty heavy pieces had been brought to the spot, and nine were already in position. The work had been so rapid that the English imagined their enemies to number six thousand at least. The battery soon opened fire. Grape and round shot swept the intrenchment and crashed through the rotten masonry. The English, says a French officer, "were exposed to their shoe-buckles." Their artillery was pointed the wrong way, in expectation of an attack, not from the east, but from the west. They now made a shelter of pork-barrels, three high and three deep, planted cannon behind them, and returned the French fire with some effect.

Early in the morning Montcalm had ordered Rigaud

to cross the river with the Canadians and Indians. There was a ford three quarters of a league above the forts;[1] and here they passed over unopposed, the English not having discovered the movement.[2] The only danger was from the river. Some of the men were forced to swim, others waded to the waist, and others to the neck; but they all crossed safely, and presently showed themselves at the edge of the woods, yelling and firing their guns, too far for much execution, but not too far to discourage the garrison.

The garrison were already disheartened. Colonel Mercer, the soul of the defence, had just been cut in two by a cannon-shot while directing the gunners. Up to this time the defenders had behaved with spirit; but despair now seized them, increased by the screams and entreaties of the women, of whom there were more than a hundred in the place. There was a council of officers, and then the white flag was raised. Bougainville went to propose terms of capitulation. "The cries, threats, and hideous howlings of our Canadians and Indians," says Vaudreuil, "made them quickly decide." "This," observes the Reverend Father Claude Godefroy Cocquard, "reminds me of the fall of Jericho before the shouts of the Israelites." The English surrendered prisoners of war, to the number, according to the governor, of sixteen hundred,[3] which included the sailors, laborers,

---

[1] Bougainville, *Journal*.   [2] Pouchot, i. 76.

[3] *Vaudreuil au Ministre*, 20 *Août*, 1756. He elsewhere makes the number somewhat greater. That the garrison, exclusive of civ-

and women. The Canadians and Indians broke through all restraint, and fell to plundering. There was an opening of rum-barrels and a scene of drunkenness, in which some of the prisoners had their share; while others tried to escape in the confusion, and were tomahawked by the excited savages. Many more would have been butchered, but for the efforts of Montcalm, who by unstinted promises succeeded in appeasing his ferocious allies, whom he dared not offend. "It will cost the King," he says, "eight or ten thousand livres in presents."[1]

The loss on both sides is variously given. By the most trustworthy accounts, that of the English did not reach fifty killed, and that of the French was still less. In the forts and vessels were found above a hundred pieces of artillery, most of them swivels and other light guns, with a large quantity of powder, shot, and shell. The victors burned the forts and the vessels on the stocks, destroyed such provisions and stores as they could not carry away, and made the place a desert. The priest Piquet, who had joined the expedition, planted amid the ruin a tall

ilians, did not exceed at the utmost fourteen hundred, is shown by *Shirley to Loudon*, 5 *September*, 1756. Loudon had charged Shirley with leaving Oswego weakly garrisoned; and Shirley replies by alleging that the troops there were in number as above. It was of course his interest to make them appear as numerous as possible. In the printed *Conduct of Major-General Shirley briefly stated*, they are put at only ten hundred and fifty.

[1] Several English writers say, however, that fifteen or twenty young men were given up to the Indians to be adopted in place of warriors lately killed.

cross, graven with the words, *In hoc signo vincunt;* and near it was set a pole bearing the arms of France, with the inscription, *Manibus date lilia plenis.* Then the army decamped, loaded with prisoners and spoil, descended to Montreal, hung the captured flags in the churches, and sang Te Deum in honor of their triumph.

It was the greatest that the French arms had yet achieved in America. The defeat of Braddock was an Indian victory; this last exploit was the result of bold enterprise and skilful tactics. With its laurels came its fruits. Hated Oswego had been laid in ashes, and the would-be assailants forced to a vain and hopeless defence. France had conquered the undisputed command of Lake Ontario, and her communications with the West were safe. A small garrison at Niagara and another at Frontenac would now hold those posts against any effort that the English could make this year; and the whole French force could concentrate at Ticonderoga, repel the threatened attack, and perhaps retort it by seizing Albany. If the English, on the other side, had lost a great material advantage, they had lost no less in honor. The news of the surrender was received with indignation in England and in the colonies. Yet the behavior of the garrison was not so discreditable as it seemed. The position was indefensible, and they could have held out at best but a few days more. They yielded too soon; but unless Webb had come to their aid, which was not to be expected, they must have yielded at last.

The French had scarcely gone, when two English scouts, Thomas Harris and James Conner, came with a party of Indians to the scene of desolation. The ground was strewn with broken casks and bread sodden with rain. The remains of burnt bateaux and whaleboats were scattered along the shore. The great stone trading-house in the old fort was a smoking ruin; Fort Rascal was still burning on the neighboring hill; Fort Ontario was a mass of ashes and charred logs, and by it stood two poles on which were written words which the visitors did not understand. They went back to Fort Johnson with their story; and Oswego reverted for a time to the bears, foxes, and wolves.[1]

[1] On the capture of Oswego, the authorities examined have been very numerous, and only the best need be named. *Livre d'Ordres, Campagne de 1756*, contains all orders from headquarters. *Mémoire pour servir d'Instruction à M. le Marquis de Montcalm*, 21 *Juillet*, 1756, *signé Vaudreuil*. Bougainville, *Journal*. *Vaudreuil au Ministre*, 15 *Juin*, 1756 (designs against Oswego). *Ibid.*, 13 *Août*, 1755. *Ibid.*, 30 *Août*. Pouchot, i. 67–81. *Relation de la Prise des Forts de Chouaguen*. *Bigot au Ministre*, 3 *Septembre*, 1756. *Journal du Siége de Chouaguen*. *Précis des Événements*, 1756. *Montcalm au Ministre*, 20 *Juillet*, 1756. *Ibid.*, 28 *Août*, 1756. *Desandrouins à* ——, *même date*. *Montcalm à sa Femme*, 30 *Août*. Translations of several of the above papers, along with others less important, will be found in *N. Y. Col. Docs.*, x., and *Doc. Hist. N. Y.*, i.

State of Facts relating to the Loss of Oswego, in *London Magazine* for 1757, p. 14. *Correspondence of Shirley*. *Correspondence of Loudon*. *Littlehales to Loudon*, 30 *August*, 1756. *Hardy to Lords of Trade*, 5 *September*, 1756. *Conduct of Major-General Shirley briefly stated*. *Declaration of some Soldiers of Shirley's Regiment*, in *N. Y. Col. Docs.*, vii. 126. Letter from an officer present, in *Boston Evening Post* of 16 *May*, 1757. The published plans and drawings of Oswego at this time are very inexact.

CHAPTER XIII.

1756, 1757.

PARTISAN WAR.

FAILURE OF SHIRLEY'S PLAN. — CAUSES. — LOUDON AND SHIRLEY. — CLOSE OF THE CAMPAIGN. — THE WESTERN BORDER. — ARMSTRONG DESTROYS KITTANNING. — THE SCOUTS OF LAKE GEORGE. — WAR-PARTIES FROM TICONDEROGA. — ROBERT ROGERS. — THE RANGERS: THEIR HARDIHOOD AND DARING. — DISPUTES AS TO QUARTERS OF TROOPS. — EXPEDITION OF ROGERS. — A DESPERATE BUSH-FIGHT. — ENTERPRISE OF VAUDREUIL. — RIGAUD ATTACKS FORT WILLIAM HENRY.

SHIRLEY'S grand scheme for cutting New France in twain had come to wreck. There was an element of boyishness in him. He made bold plans without weighing too closely his means of executing them. The year's campaign would in all likelihood have succeeded if he could have acted promptly; if he had had ready to his hand a well-trained and well-officered force, furnished with material of war and means of transportation, and prepared to move as soon as the streams and lakes of New York were open, while those of Canada were still sealed with ice. But timely action was out of his power. The army that should have moved in April was not ready to move till August. Of the nine discordant semi-republics whom he asked to join in the work, three or four refused, some of the others were lukewarm, and all were slow. Even Massachusetts, usually the foremost, failed to get all her men into the field till the season was nearly ended. Having no military establishment, the colonies were forced to improvise a new army for every campaign. Each of them watched its neighbors, or, jealous lest it should do more than its just share, waited for them to begin. Each popular assembly acted under the eye of a frugal constituency, who, having little money, were as chary of it as their descendants are lavish; and most of them were shaken by internal conflicts, more absorbing than the great question on which hung the fate of the continent. Only the four New England colonies were fully earnest for the war, and one, even of these, was ready to use the crisis as a means of extorting concessions from its governor in return for grants of money and men. When the lagging contingents came together at last, under a commander whom none of them trusted, they were met by strategical difficulties which would have perplexed older soldiers and an abler general; for they were forced to act on the circumference of a vast semicircle, in a labyrinth of forests, without roads, and choked with every kind of obstruction.

Opposed to them was a trained army, well organized and commanded, focused at Montreal, and moving for attack or defence on two radiating lines, —

one towards Lake Ontario, and the other towards Lake Champlain, — supported by a martial peasantry, supplied from France with money and material, dependent on no popular vote, having no will but that of its chief, and ready on the instant to strike to right or left as the need required. It was a compact military absolutism confronting a heterogeneous group of industrial democracies, where the force of numbers was neutralized by diffusion and incoherence. A long and dismal apprenticeship waited them before they could hope for success; nor could they ever put forth their full strength without a radical change of political conditions and an awakened consciousness of common interests and a common cause. It was the sense of powerlessness arising from the want of union that, after the fall of Oswego, spread alarm through the northern and middle colonies, and drew these desponding words from William Livingston, of New Jersey: "The colonies are nearly exhausted, and their funds already anticipated by expensive unexecuted projects. Jealous are they of each other; some ill-constituted, others shaken with intestine divisions, and, if I may be allowed the expression, parsimonious even to prodigality. Our assemblies are diffident of their governors, governors despise their assemblies; and both mutually misrepresent each other to the Court of Great Britain." Military measures, he proceeds, demand secrecy and despatch; but when so many divided provinces must agree to join in them, secrecy and despatch are impossible. In conclusion he exclaims: "Canada must be demolished, — *Delenda est Carthago*, — or we are undone."[1] But Loudon was not Scipio, and cis-Atlantic Carthage was to stand for some time longer.

The earl, in search of a scapegoat for the loss of Oswego, naturally chose Shirley, attacked him savagely, told him that he was of no use in America, and ordered him to go home to England without delay.[2] Shirley, who was then in Boston, answered this indecency with dignity and effect.[3] The chief fault was with Loudon himself, whose late arrival in America had caused a change of command and of plans in the crisis of the campaign. Shirley well knew the weakness of Oswego; and in early spring had sent two engineers to make it defensible, with particular instructions to strengthen Fort Ontario.[4] But they, thinking that the chief danger lay on the west and south, turned all their attention thither, and neglected Ontario till it was too late. Shirley was about to reinforce Oswego with a strong body of troops when the arrival of Abercrombie took the control out of his hands and caused ruinous delay. He cannot, however, be acquitted of mismanagement in failing to supply the place with wholesome provisions

[1] *Review of Military Operations*, 187, 189 (Dublin, 1757).

[2] *Loudon to Shirley*, 6 *September*, 1756.

[3] The correspondence on both sides is before me, copied from the originals in the Public Record Office.

[4] "The principal thing for which I sent Mr. Mackellar to Oswego was to strengthen Fort Ontario as much as he possibly could."— *Shirley to Loudon*, 4 *September*, 1756.

in the preceding autumn, before the streams were stopped with ice. Hence came the ravages of disease and famine which, before spring, reduced the garrison to a hundred and forty effective men. Yet there can be no doubt that the change of command was a blunder. This is the view of Franklin, who knew Shirley well, and thus speaks of him: "He would in my opinion, if continued in place, have made a much better campaign than that of Loudon, which was frivolous, expensive, and disgraceful to our nation beyond conception. For though Shirley was not bred a soldier, he was sensible and sagacious in himself, and attentive to good advice from others, capable of forming judicious plans, and quick and active in carrying them into execution."[1] He sailed for England in the autumn, disappointed and poor; the bull-headed Duke of Cumberland had been deeply prejudiced against him, and it was only after long waiting that this strenuous champion of British interests was rewarded in his old age with the petty government of the Bahamas.

Loudon had now about ten thousand men at his command, though not all fit for duty. They were posted from Albany to Lake George. The earl himself was at Fort Edward, while about three thousand of the provincials still lay, under Winslow, at the lake. Montcalm faced them at Ticonderoga, with five thousand three hundred regulars and Canadians, in a position where they could defy three times their

[1] *Works of Franklin,* i. 220.

number.[1] "The sons of Belial are too strong for
me," jocosely wrote Winslow;[2] and he set himself to
intrenching his camp; then had the forest cut down
for the space of a mile from the lake to the mountains, so that the trees, lying in what he calls a
"promiscuous manner," formed an almost impene-
trable abatis. An escaped prisoner told him that the
French were coming to visit him with fourteen thousand men;[3] but Montcalm thought no more of stirring than Loudon himself; and each stood watching
the other, with the lake between them, till the season
closed.

Meanwhile the western borders were still ravaged
by the tomahawk. New York, New Jersey, Pennsylvania, Maryland, and Virginia all writhed under
the infliction. Each had made a chain of blockhouses and wooden forts to cover its frontier, and
manned them with disorderly bands, lawless, and
almost beyond control.[4] The case was at the worst
in Pennsylvania, where the tedious quarrelling of
governor and Assembly, joined to the doggedly pacific
attitude of the Quakers, made vigorous defence
impossible. Rewards were offered for prisoners and
scalps, so bountiful that the hunting of men would

[1] "Nous sommes tant à Carillon qu'aux postes avancés 5,300
hommes." — Bougainville, *Journal.*

[2] *Winslow to Loudon,* 29 *September,* 1756.

[3] *Examination of Sergeant James Archibald.*

[4] In the Public Record Office, *America and West Indies,* lxxxii.,
is a manuscript map showing the positions of such of these posts as
were north of Virginia. They are thirty-five in number, from the
head of James River to a point west of Esopus, on the Hudson.

have been a profitable vocation, but for the extreme
wariness and agility of the game.[1] Some of the forts
were well-built stockades; others were almost worthless; but the enemy rarely molested even the feeblest
of them, preferring to ravage the lonely and unpro-
tected farms. There were two or three exceptions.
A Virginian fort was attacked by a war-party under
an officer named Douville, who was killed, and his
followers were put to flight.[2] The assailants were
more fortunate at a small stockade called Fort Granville, on the Juniata. A large body of French and
Indians attacked it in August while most of the garrison were absent protecting the farmers at their
harvest; they set it on fire, and, in spite of a most
gallant resistance by the young lieutenant left in
command, took it, and killed all but one of the
defenders.[3]

What sort of resistance the Pennsylvanian borderers
would have made under political circumstances less
adverse may be inferred from an exploit of Colonel
John Armstrong, a settler of Cumberland. After
the loss of Fort Granville the governor of the province
sent him with three hundred men to attack the
Delaware town of Kittanning, a populous nest of
savages on the Alleghany, between the two French
posts of Duquesne and Venango. Here most of the

[1] *Colonial Records of Pa.*, vii. 76.

[2] *Washington to Morris, — April*, 1756.

[3] *Colonial Records of Pa.*, vii. 232, 242; *Pennsylvania Archives*,
ii. 744.

war-parties were fitted out, and the place was full of
stores and munitions furnished by the French.   Here,
too, lived the redoubted chief called Captain Jacobs,
the terror of the English border.   Armstrong set out
from Fort Shirley, the farthest outpost, on the last
of August, and, a week after, was within six miles
of the Indian town.   By rapid marching and rare
good luck, his party had escaped discovery.   It was
ten o'clock at night, with a bright moon.   The
guides were perplexed, and knew neither the exact
position of the place nor the paths that led to it.
The adventurers threaded the forest in single file,
over hills and through hollows, bewildered and
anxious, stopping to watch and listen.   At length
they heard in the distance the beating of an Indian
drum and the whooping of warriors in the war-dance.
Guided by the sounds, they cautiously moved forward, till those in the front, scrambling down a rocky
hill, found themselves on the banks of the Alleghany,
about a hundred rods below Kittanning.   The moon
was near setting; but they could dimly see the town
beyond a great intervening field of corn.   "At that
moment," says Armstrong, "an Indian whistled in a
very singular manner, about thirty perches from our
front, in the foot of the cornfield."   He thought they
were discovered; but one Baker, a soldier well versed
in Indian ways, told him that it was only some village
gallant calling to a young squaw.   The party then
crouched in the bushes, and kept silent.   The moon
sank behind the woods, and fires soon glimmered

through the field, kindled to drive off mosquitoes by some of the Indians who, as the night was warm, had come out to sleep in the open air. The eastern sky began to redden with the approach of day. Many of the party, spent with a rough march of thirty miles, had fallen asleep. They were now cautiously roused; and Armstrong ordered nearly half of them to make their way along the ridge of a bushy hill that overlooked the town, till they came opposite to it, in order to place it between two fires. Twenty minutes were allowed them for the movement; but they lost their way in the dusk, and reached their station too late. When the time had expired, Armstrong gave the signal to those left with him, who dashed into the cornfield, shooting down the astonished savages or driving them into the village, where they turned and made desperate fight.

It was a cluster of thirty log-cabins, the principal being that of the chief, Jacobs, which was loopholed for musketry, and became the centre of resistance. The fight was hot and stubborn. Armstrong ordered the town to be set on fire, which was done, though not without loss; for the Delawares at this time were commonly armed with rifles, and used them well. Armstrong himself was hit in the shoulder. As the flames rose and the smoke grew thick, a warrior in one of the houses sang his death-song, and a squaw in the same house was heard to cry and scream. Rough voices silenced her, and then the inmates burst out, but were instantly killed. The fire caught

the house of Jacobs, who, trying to escape through
an opening in the roof, was shot dead. Bands of
Indians were gathering beyond the river, firing from
the other bank, and even crossing to help their comrades; but the assailants held to their work till the
whole place was destroyed. "During the burning of
the houses," says Armstrong, "we were agreeably
entertained by the quick succession of charged guns,
gradually firing off as reached by the fire; but much
more so with the vast explosion of sundry bags and
large kegs of gunpowder, wherewith almost every
house abounded; the prisoners afterwards informing
us that the Indians had frequently said they had a
sufficient stock of ammunition for ten years' war
with the English."

These prisoners were eleven men, women, and
children, captured in the border settlements, and now
delivered by their countrymen. The day was far
spent when the party withdrew, carrying their
wounded on Indian horses, and moving perforce with
extreme slowness, though expecting an attack every
moment. None took place; and they reached the
settlements at last, having bought their success with
the loss of seventeen killed and thirteen wounded.[1]
A medal was given to each officer, not by the

---

[1] *Report of Armstrong to Governor Denny, 14 September, 1756, in
Colonial Records of Pa.*, vii. 257,— a modest, yet very minute
account. *A List of the Names of the Persons killed, wounded, and
missing in the late Expedition against the Kittanning.* Hazard, *Pennsylvania Register*, i. 366.

Quaker-ridden Assembly, but by the city council of Philadelphia.

The report of this affair made by Dumas, commandant at Fort Duquesne, is worth noting. He says that Attiqué, the French name of Kittanning, was attacked by "le Général Wachinton," with three or four hundred men on horseback; that the Indians gave way; but that five or six Frenchmen who were in the town held the English in check till the fugitives rallied; that Washington and his men then took to flight, and would have been pursued but for the loss of some barrels of gunpowder which chanced to explode during the action. Dumas adds that several large parties are now on the track of the enemy, and he hopes will cut them to pieces. He then asks for a supply of provisions and merchandise to replace those which the Indians of Attiqué had lost by a fire.[1] Like other officers of the day, he would admit nothing but successes in the department under his command.

Vaudreuil wrote singular despatches at this time to the minister at Versailles. He takes credit to himself for the number of war-parties that his officers kept always at work, and fills page after page with details of the *coups* they had struck; how one brought in two English scalps, another three, another one, and another seven. He owns that they committed frightful cruelties, mutilating and sometimes

[1] *Dumas à Vaudreuil*, 9 *Septembre*, 1756, cited in *Bigot au Ministre*, 6 *Octobre*, 1756, and in Bougainville, *Journal*.

burning their prisoners; but he expresses no regret, and probably felt none, since he declares that the object of this murderous warfare was to punish the English till they longed for peace.[1]

The waters and mountains of Lake George, and not the western borders, were the chief centre of partisan war. Ticonderoga was a hornet's nest, pouring out swarms of savages to infest the highways and byways of the wilderness. The English at Fort William Henry, having few Indians, could not retort in kind; but they kept their scouts and rangers in active movement. What they most coveted was prisoners, as sources of information. One Kennedy, a lieutenant of provincials, with five followers, white and red, made a march of rare audacity, passed all the French posts, took a scalp and two prisoners on the Richelieu, and burned a magazine of provisions between Montreal and St. John. The party were near famishing on the way back; and Kennedy was brought into Fort William Henry in a state of temporary insanity from starvation.[2] Other provincial officers, Peabody, Hazen, Waterbury, and Miller, won a certain distinction in this adventurous service, though few were so conspicuous as the blunt and sturdy Israel Putnam. Winslow writes in October that he has just returned from the best "scout" yet made, and that, being a man of strict truth, he may

[1] *Dépêches de Vaudreuil*, 1756.
[2] *Minute of Lieutenant Kennedy's Scout. Winslow to Loudon*, 20 September, 1756.

be entirely trusted.[1] Putnam had gone with six
followers down Lake George in a whaleboat to a
point on the east side, opposite the present village of
Hague, hid the boat, crossed northeasterly to Lake
Champlain, three miles from the French fort, climbed
the mountain that overlooks it, and made a complete
reconnoissance; then approached it, chased three
Frenchmen, who escaped within the lines, climbed
the mountain again, and moving westward along the
ridge, made a minute survey of every outpost between
the fort and Lake George.[2] These adventures were
not always fortunate. On the nineteenth of September Captain Hodges and fifty men were ambushed a
few miles from Fort William Henry by thrice their
number of Canadians and Indians, and only six
escaped. Thus the record stands in the *Letter Book*
of Winslow.[3] By visiting the encampments of
Ticonderoga, one may learn how the blow was
struck.

After much persuasion, much feasting, and much
consumption of tobacco and brandy, four hundred
Indians, Christians from the missions and heathen
from the far West, were persuaded to go on a grand
war-party with the Canadians. Of these last there
were a hundred, — a wild crew, bedecked and bedaubed like their Indian companions. Perière, an

[1] *Winslow to Loudon,* 16 *October,* 1756.
[2] *Report of a Scout to Ticonderoga, October,* 1756, signed **Israel
Putnam.**
[3] Compare Massachusetts Archives, lxxvi. 81.

officer of colony regulars, had nominal command of
the whole; and among the leaders of the Canadians
was the famous bush-fighter, Marin. Bougainville
was also of the party. In the evening of the sixteenth they all embarked in canoes at the French
advance-post commanded by Contrecœur, near the
present steamboat-landing, passed in the gloom under
the bare steeps of Rogers Rock, paddled a few hours,
landed on the west shore, and sent scouts to reconnoitre. These came back with their reports on the
next day, and an Indian crier called the chiefs to
council. Bougainville describes them as they stalked
gravely to the place of meeting, wrapped in colored
blankets, with lances in their hands. The accomplished young aide-de-camp studied his strange
companions with an interest not unmixed with disgust. "Of all caprice," he says, "Indian caprice is
the most capricious." They were insolent to the
French, made rules for them which they did not
observe themselves, and compelled the whole party
to move when and whither they pleased. Hiding the
canoes, and lying close in the forest by day, they all
held their nocturnal course southward, by the lofty
heights of Black Mountain, and among the islets of
the Narrows, till the eighteenth. That night the
Indian scouts reported that they had seen the fires of
an encampment on the west shore; on which the
whole party advanced to the attack, an hour before
dawn, filing silently under the dark arches of the
forest, the Indians nearly naked, and streaked with

their war-paint of vermilion and soot. When they
reached the spot, they found only the smouldering
fires of a deserted bivouac. Then there was a con-
sultation; ending, after much dispute, with the
choice by the Indians of a hundred and ten of their
most active warriors to attempt some stroke in the
neighborhood of the English fort. Marin joined
them with thirty Canadians, and they set out on
their errand; while the rest encamped to await the
result. At night the adventurers returned, raising
the death-cry and firing their guns; somewhat depressed by losses they had suffered, but boasting that
they had surprised fifty-three English, and killed or
taken all but one. It was a modest and perhaps an
involuntary exaggeration. "The very recital of the
cruelties they committed on the battlefield is horrible," writes Bougainville. "The ferocity and insolence of these black-souled barbarians makes one
shudder. It is an abominable kind of war. The air
one breathes is contagious of insensibility and hard-
ness."[1] This was but one of many such parties sent
out from Ticonderoga this year.

Early in September a band of New England rangers
came to Winslow's camp, with three prisoners taken
within the lines of Ticonderoga. Their captain was
Robert Rogers, of New Hampshire, — a strong, well-
knit figure, in dress and appearance more woodsman
than soldier, with a clear, bold eye, and features that
would have been good but for the ungainly propor-

[1] Bougainville, *Journal.*

approach; till, seeing his mistake, he called out in amazement, " *Qui êtes vous ?* " "Rogers," was the answer; and the sentinel was seized, led in hot haste to the boats, and carried to the English fort, where he gave important information.

An exploit of Rogers towards midsummer greatly perplexed the French. He embarked at the end of June with fifty men in five whaleboats, made light and strong, expressly for this service, rowed about ten miles down Lake George, landed on the east side, carried the boats six miles over a gorge of the mountains, launched them again in South Bay, and rowed down the narrow prolongation of Lake Champlain under cover of darkness. At dawn they were within six miles of Ticonderoga. They landed, hid their boats, and lay close all day. Embarking again in the evening, they rowed with muffled oars under the shadow of the eastern shore, and passed so close to the French fort that they heard the voices of the sentinels calling the watchword. In the morning they had left it five miles behind. Again they hid in the woods; and from their lurking-place saw bateaux passing, some northward, and some southward, along the narrow lake. Crown Point was ten or twelve miles farther on. They tried to pass it after nightfall, but the sky was too clear and the stars too bright; and as they lay hidden the next day, nearly a hundred boats passed before them on the way to Ticonderoga. Some other boats which appeared about noon landed near them, and they

watched the soldiers at dinner, within a musket-shot
of their lurking-place. The next night was more
favorable. They embarked at nine in the evening,
passed Crown Point unseen, and hid themselves as
before, ten miles below. It was the seventh of July.
Thirty boats and a schooner passed them, returning
towards Canada. On the next night they rowed
fifteen miles farther, and then sent men to reconnoitre, who reported a schooner at anchor about a
mile off. They were preparing to board her, when
two sloops appeared, coming up the lake at but a
short distance from the land. They gave them a
volley, and called on them to surrender; but the
crews put off in boats and made for the opposite
shore. They followed and seized them. Out of
twelve men their fire had killed three and wounded
two, one of whom, says Rogers in his report, "could
not march, therefore we put an end to him, to prevent discovery."[1] They sank the vessels, which
were laden with wine, brandy, and flour, hid their
boats on the west shore, and returned on foot with
their prisoners.[2]

Some weeks after, Rogers returned to the place
where he had left the boats, embarked in them,

[1] *Report of Rogers to Sir William Johnson, July,* 1756. This incident is suppressed in the printed *Journals,* which merely say that
the man "soon died."

[2] *Rogers, Journals,* 20. *Shirley to Cox,* 26 *July,* 1756. "This
afternoon Capt. Rogers came down with 4 scalps and 8 prisoners
which he took on Lake Champlain, between 20 and 30 miles
beyond Crown Point." — *Surgeon Williams to his Wife,* 16 *July,*
1756.

reconnoitred the lake nearly to St. John, hid them
again eight miles north of Crown Point, took three
prisoners near that post, and carried them to Fort
William Henry. In the next month the French
found several English boats in a small cove north of
Crown Point. Bougainville propounds five different
hypotheses to account for their being there; and
exploring parties were sent out in the vain attempt
to find some water passage by which they could
have reached the spot without passing under the
guns of two French forts.[1]

The French, on their side, still kept their war-
parties in motion, and Vaudreuil faithfully chronicled
in his despatches every English scalp they brought
in. He believed in Indians, and sent them to Ticonderoga in numbers that were sometimes embarrass-
ing. Even Pottawattamies from Lake Michigan were
prowling about Winslow's camp and silently killing
his sentinels with arrows, while their "medicine
men" remained at Ticonderoga practising sorcery
and divination to aid the warriors or learn how it
fared with them. Bougainville writes in his Journal
on the fifteenth of October: "Yesterday the old
Pottawattamies who have stayed here 'made medicine' to get news of their brethren. The lodge
trembled, the sorcerer sweated drops of blood, and
the devil came at last and told him that the warriors
would come back with scalps and prisoners. A
sorcerer in the medicine lodge is exactly like the

[1] Bougainville, *Journal*.

Pythoness on the tripod or the witch Canidia invoking the shades." The diviner was not wholly at fault. Three days after, the warriors came back with a prisoner.[1]

Till November, the hostile forces continued to watch each other from the opposite ends of Lake George. Loudon repeated his orders to Winslow to keep the defensive, and wrote sarcastically to the colonial minister: "I think I shall be able to prevent the provincials doing anything very rash, without their having it in their power to talk in the language of this country that they could have taken all Canada if they had not been prevented by the King's servants." Winslow tried to console himself for the failure of the campaign, and wrote in his odd English to Shirley: "Am sorry that this year's performance has not succeeded as was intended; have only to say I pushed things to the utmost of my power to have been sooner in motion, which was the only thing that should have carried us to Crown Point; and though I am sensible that we are doing our duty in acting on the defensive, yet it makes no *eclate* [*sic*], and answers to little purpose in the eyes of my constituents."

On the first of the month the French began to move off towards Canada, and before many days Ticonderoga was left in the keeping of five or six companies.[2] Winslow's men followed their example.

[1] This kind of divination was practised by Algonquin tribes from the earliest times. See "Pioneers of France in the New World," 351.

[2] Bougainville, *Journal.* Malartic, *Journal.*

Major Eyre, with four hundred regulars, took possession of Fort William Henry, and the provincials
marched for home, their ranks thinned by camp
diseases and small-pox.[1] In Canada the regulars
were quartered on the inhabitants, who took the
infliction as a matter of course. In the English
provinces the question was not so simple. Most of
the British troops were assigned to Philadelphia,
New York, and Boston; and Loudon demanded free
quarters for them, according to usage then prevailing
in England during war. Nor was the demand in
itself unreasonable, seeing that the troops were sent
over to fight the battles of the colonies. In Philadelphia lodgings were given them in the public-
houses, which, however, could not hold them all. A
long dispute followed between the governor, who
seconded Loudon's demand, and the Assembly, during which about half the soldiers lay on straw in
outhouses and sheds till near midwinter, many sick-
ening, and some dying from exposure. Loudon
grew furious, and threatened, if shelter were not
provided, to send Webb with another regiment and
billet the whole on the inhabitants; on which the
Assembly yielded, and quarters were found.[2]

In New York the privates were quartered in bar-

[1] *Letter and Order Books of Winslow. Winslow to Halifax,* 30
December, 1756.

[2] *Loudon to Denny,* 28 *October,* 1756. *Colonial Records of Pa.,* vii.
358–380. *Loudon to Pitt,* 10 *March,* 1757. *Notice of Colonel Bouquet,*
in *Pennsylvania Magazine,* iii. 124. *The Conduct of a Noble Commander in America impartially reviewed* (1758).

racks, but the officers were left to find lodging for
themselves.   Loudon demanded that provision should
be made for them also.   The city council hesitated,
afraid of incensing the people if they complied.
Cruger, the mayor, came to remonstrate. "God
damn my blood!" replied the earl; "if you do not
billet my officers upon free quarters this day, I 'll
order here all the troops in North America, and
billet them myself upon this city."   Being no respecter
of persons, at least in the provinces, he began with
Oliver Delancey, brother of the late acting governor,
and sent six soldiers to lodge under his roof.
Delancey swore at the unwelcome guests, on which
Loudon sent him six more.   A subscription was then
raised among the citizens, and the required quarters
were provided.[1]   In Boston there was for the present
less trouble.   The troops were lodged in the barracks of Castle William, and furnished with blankets,
cooking utensils, and other necessaries.[2]

Major Eyre and his soldiers, in their wilderness
exile by the borders of Lake George, whiled the winter
away with few other excitements than the evening
howl of wolves from the frozen mountains, or some
nocturnal savage shooting at a sentinel from behind
a stump on the moonlit fields of snow.   A livelier
incident at last broke the monotony of their lives.

[1] Smith, *Hist. of N. Y.*, Part II. 242. *William Corry to Johnson,*
15 *January*, 1757, in Stone, *Life of Sir William Johnson,* ii. 24, *note.*
Loudon to Hardy, 21 *November,* 1756.

[2] Massachusetts Archives, lxxvi. 153

In the middle of January Rogers came with his rangers from Fort Edward, bound on a scouting party towards Crown Point. They spent two days at Fort William Henry in making snow-shoes and other preparation, and set out on the seventeenth. Captain Spikeman was second in command, with Lieutenants Stark and Kennedy, several other subalterns, and two gentlemen volunteers enamoured of adventure. They marched down the frozen lake and encamped at the Narrows. Some of them, unaccustomed to snow-shoes, had become unfit for travel, and were sent back, thus reducing the number to seventy-four. In the morning they marched again, by icicled rocks and icebound waterfalls, mountains gray with naked woods and fir-trees bowed down with snow. On the nineteenth they reached the west shore, about four miles south of Rogers Rock, marched west of north eight miles, and bivouacked among the mountains. On the next morning they changed their course, marched east of north all day, passed Ticonderoga undiscovered, and stopped at night some five miles beyond it. The weather was changing, and rain was coming on. They scraped away the snow with their snow-shoes, piled it in a bank around them, made beds of spruce-boughs, built fires, and lay down to sleep, while the sentinels kept watch in the outer gloom. In the morning there was a drizzling rain, and the softened snow stuck to their snow-shoes. They marched eastward three miles through the dripping forest, till they reached the

banks of Lake Champlain, near what is now called
Five Mile Point, and presently saw a sledge, drawn
by horses, moving on the ice from Ticonderoga
towards Crown Point. Rogers sent Stark along the
shore to the left to head it off, while he with another
party, covered by the woods, moved in the opposite
direction to stop its retreat. He soon saw eight or
ten more sledges following the first, and sent a messenger to prevent Stark from showing himself too
soon; but Stark was already on the ice. All the
sledges turned back in hot haste. The rangers ran
in pursuit and captured three of them, with seven
men and six horses, while the rest escaped to Ticonderoga. The prisoners, being separately examined,
told an ominous tale. There were three hundred and
fifty regulars at Ticonderoga; two hundred Canadians and forty-five Indians had lately arrived there,
and more Indians were expected that evening, — all
destined to waylay the communications between the
English forts, and all prepared to march at a moment's
notice. The rangers were now in great peril. The
fugitives would give warning of their presence, and
the French and Indians, in overwhelming force,
would no doubt cut off their retreat.

Rogers at once ordered his men to return to their
last night's encampment, rekindle the fires, and dry
their guns, which were wet by the rain of the morning.
Then they marched southward in single file through
the snow-encumbered forest, Rogers and Kennedy in
the front, Spikeman in the centre, and Stark in the

whaleboats which had thus far escaped. They were only in part successful; but they fired the sloop and some buildings near it, and stood far out on the ice watching the flaming vessel, a superb bonfire amid the wilderness of snow. The spectacle cost the volunteers a fourth of their number killed and wounded.

On Wednesday morning the sun rose bright on a scene of wintry splendor, and the frozen lake was dotted with Rigaud's retreating followers toiling towards Canada on snow-shoes. Before they reached it many of them were blinded for a while by the insufferable glare, and their comrades led them homewards by the hand.[1]

[1] *Eyre to Loudon*, 24 *March*, 1757. *Ibid.*, 25 *March*, enclosed in Loudon's despatch of 25 April, 1757. *Message of Rigaud to Major Eyre*, 20 *March*, 1757. *Letter from Fort William Henry*, 26 *March*, 1757, in *Boston Gazette, No.* 106, and *Boston Evening Post, No.* 1,128. *Abstract of Letters from Albany*, in *Boston News Letter, No.* 2,860. Caleb Stark, *Memoir and Correspondence of John Stark*, 22, a curious mixture of truth and error. *Relation de la Campagne sur le Lac St. Sacrement pendant l'Hiver*, 1757. Bougainville, *Journal*. Malartic, *Journal*. *Montcalm au Ministre*, 24 *Avril*, 1757. *Montreuil au Ministre*, 23 *Avril*, 1757. *Montcalm à sa Mère*, 1 *Avril*, 1757. *Mémoires sur le Canada*, 1749–1760.

The French loss in killed and wounded is set by Montcalm at eleven. That of the English was seven, slightly wounded, chiefly in sorties. They took three prisoners. Stark was touched by a bullet, for the only time in his adventurous life.

CHAPTER XIV.

1757.

MONTCALM AND VAUDREUIL.

THE SEAT OF WAR. — SOCIAL LIFE AT MONTREAL. — FAMILIAR
CORRESPONDENCE OF MONTCALM: HIS EMPLOYMENTS; HIS IM-
PRESSIONS OF CANADA; HIS HOSPITALITIES. — MISUNDERSTAND-
INGS WITH THE GOVERNOR. — CHARACTER OF VAUDREUIL: HIS
ACCUSATIONS. — FRENCHMEN AND CANADIANS. — FOIBLES OF
MONTCALM. — THE OPENING CAMPAIGN. — DOUBTS AND SUS-
PENSE. — LOUDON'S PLAN: HIS CHARACTER. — FATAL DELAYS.
— ABORTIVE ATTEMPT AGAINST LOUISBOURG. — DISASTER TO
THE BRITISH FLEET.

SPRING came at last, and the Dutch burghers of
Albany heard, faint from the far height, the clamor
of the wild fowl, streaming in long files northward to
their summer home. As the aerial travellers winged
their way, the seat of war lay spread beneath them
like a map. First the blue Hudson, slumbering
among its forests, with the forts along its banks,
Half-Moon, Stillwater, Saratoga, and the geometric
lines and earthen mounds of Fort Edward. Then a
broad belt of dingy evergreen; and beyond, released
from wintry fetters, the glistening breast of Lake
George, with Fort William Henry at its side, amid
charred ruins and a desolation of prostrate forests.

Hence the lake stretched northward, like some broad
river, trenched between mountain ranges still leafless
and gray.   Then they looked down on Ticonderoga,
with the flag of the Bourbons, like a flickering white
speck, waving on its ramparts; and next on Crown
Point with its tower of stone.   Lake Champlain now
spread before them, widening as they flew: on the
left, the mountain wilderness of the Adirondacks,
like a stormy sea congealed; on the right, the long
procession of the Green Mountains; and, far beyond,
on the dim verge of the eastern sky, the White
Mountains throned in savage solitude.   They passed
over the bastioned square of Fort St. John, Fort
Chambly guarding the rapids of the Richelieu, and
the broad belt of the St. Lawrence, with Montreal
seated on its bank.   Here we leave them, to build
their nests and hatch their brood among the fens
of the lonely North.

Montreal, the military heart of Canada, was in the
past winter its social centre also, where were gathered
conspicuous representatives both of Old France and
of New; not men only, but women.   It was a sparkling fragment of the reign of Louis XV. dropped
into the American wilderness.   Montcalm was here
with his staff and his chief officers, now pondering
schemes of war, and now turning in thought to his
beloved Château of Candiac, his mother, children,
and wife, to whom he sent letters with every opportunity.   To his wife he writes: "Think of me affectionately; give love to my girls.   I hope next year I

may be with you all. I love you tenderly, dearest."
He says that he has sent her a packet of marten-
skins for a muff, "and another time I shall send some
to our daughter; but I should like better to bring
them myself." Of this eldest daughter he writes in
reply to a letter of domestic news from Madame de
Montcalm: "The new gown with blonde trimmings
must be becoming, for she is pretty." Again,
"There is not an hour in the day when I do not
think of you, my mother, and my children." He had
the tastes of a country gentleman, and was eager to
know all that was passing on his estate. Before
leaving home he had set up a mill to grind olives for
oil, and was well pleased to hear of its prosperity.
"It seems to be a good thing, which pleases me very
much. Bougainville and I talk a great deal about
the oil-mill." Some time after, when the King sent
him the coveted decoration of the *cordon rouge*, he
informed Madame de Montcalm of the honor done
him, and added, "But I think I am better pleased
with what you tell me of the success of my oil-mill."

To his mother he writes of his absorbing occupa-
tions, and says, "You can tell my dearest that I
have no time to occupy myself with the ladies, even
if I wished to." Nevertheless he now and then found
leisure for some little solace in his banishment; for
he writes to Bourlamaque, whom he had left at
Quebec, after a visit which he had himself made
there early in the winter: "I am glad you sometimes
speak of me to the three ladies in the Rue du Parloir;

and I am flattered by their remembrance, especially
by that of one of them, in whom I find at certain
moments too much wit and too many charms for my
tranquillity." These ladies of the Rue du Parloir
are several times mentioned in his familiar correspondence with Bourlamaque.

His station obliged him to maintain a high standard
of living, to his great financial detriment, for Canadian prices were inordinate. "I must live creditably,
and so I do; sixteen persons at table every day.
Once a fortnight I dine with the governor-general
and with the Chevalier de Lévis, who lives well too.
He has given three grand balls. As for me, up to
Lent I gave, besides dinners, great suppers, with
ladies, three times a week. They lasted till two in
the morning; and then there was dancing, to which
company came uninvited, but sure of a welcome from
those who had been at supper. It is very expensive,
not very amusing, and often tedious. At Quebec,
where we spent a month, I gave receptions or parties,
often at the Intendant's house. I like my gallant
Chevalier de Lévis very much. Bourlamaque was a
good choice; he is steady and cool, with good parts.
Bougainville has talent, a warm head, and warm
heart; he will ripen in time. Write to Madame
Cornier that I like her husband; he is perfectly well,
and as impatient for peace as I am. Love to my
daughters, and all affection and respect to my
mother. I live only in the hope of joining you all
again. Nevertheless, Montreal is as good a place as

Alais even in time of peace, and better now, because
the Government is here; for the Marquis de Vaudreuil,
like me, spent only a month at Quebec. As for
Quebec, it is as good as the best cities of France,
except ten or so. Clear sky, bright sun; neither
spring nor autumn, only summer and winter. July,
August, and September, hot as in Languedoc: winter
insupportable; one must keep always indoors. The
ladies *spirituelles*, *galantes*, *dévotes*. Gambling at
Quebec, dancing and conversation at Montreal. My
friends the Indians, who are often unbearable, and
whom I treat with perfect tranquillity and patience,
are fond of me. If I were not a sort of general,
though very subordinate to the governor, I could
gossip about the plans of the campaign, which it is
likely will begin on the tenth or fifteenth of May. I
worked at the plan of the last affair [*Rigaud's
expedition to Fort William Henry*], which might have
turned out better, though good as it was. I wanted
only eight hundred men. If I had had my way,
Monsieur de Lévis or Monsieur de Bougainville
would have had charge of it. However, the thing
was all right, and in good hands. The Governor,
who is extremely civil to me, gave it to his brother;
he thought him more used to winter marches.
Adieu, my heart; I adore and love you!"

To meet his manifold social needs, he sends to his
wife orders for prunes, olives, anchovies, muscat
wine, capers, sausages, confectionery, cloth for
liveries, and many other such items; also for scent-

bags of two kinds, and perfumed pomatum for presents; closing in postscript with an injunction not to forget a dozen pint-bottles of English lavender. Some months after, he writes to Madame de Saint-Véran: "I have got everything that was sent me from Montpellier except the sausages. I have lost a third of what was sent from Bordeaux. The English captured it on board the ship called 'La Superbe;' and I have reason to fear that everything sent from Paris is lost on board 'La Liberté.' I am running into debt here. Pshaw! I must live. I do not worry myself. Best love to you, my mother."

When Rigaud was about to march with his detachment against Fort William Henry, Montcalm went over to La Prairie to see them. "I reviewed them," he writes to Bourlamaque, "and gave the officers a dinner, which, if anybody else had given it, I should have said was a grand affair. There were two tables, for thirty-six persons in all. On Wednesday there was an Assembly at Madame Varin's; on Friday the Chevalier de Lévis gave a ball. He invited sixty-five ladies, and got only thirty, with a great crowd of men. Rooms well lighted, excellent order, excellent service, plenty of refreshments of every sort all through the night; and the company stayed till seven in the morning. As for me, I went to bed early. I had had that day eight ladies at a supper given to Madame Varin. To-morrow I shall have half-a-dozen at another supper, given to I don't know whom, but incline to think it will be La Roche

Beaucour.   The gallant Chevalier is to give us still another ball."

Lent put a check on these festivities. "To-morrow," he tells Bourlamaque, "I shall throw myself into devotion with might and main (*à corps perdu*). It will be easier for me to detach myself from the world and turn heavenward here at Montreal than it would be at Quebec." And, some time after, "Bougainville spent Monday delightfully at Isle Ste. Hélène, and Tuesday devoutly with the Sulpitian Fathers at the Mountain. I was there myself at four o'clock, and did them the civility to sup in their refectory at a quarter before six."

In May there was a complete revival of social pleasures, and Montcalm wrote to Bourlamaque: "Madame de Beaubassin's supper was very gay. There were toasts to the Rue du Parloir and to the General. To-day I must give a dinner to Madame de Saint-Ours, which will be a little more serious. Péan is gone to establish himself at La Chine, and will come back with La Barolon, who goes thither with a husband of hers, bound to the Ohio with Villejoin and Louvigny. The Chevalier de Lévis amuses himself very much here. He and his friends spend all their time with Madame de Lenisse."

Under these gayeties and gallantries there were bitter heart-burnings. Montcalm hints at some of them in a letter to Bourlamaque, written at the time of the expedition to Fort William Henry, which, in the words of Montcalm, who would have preferred another commander, the governor had ordered to march "under the banners of brother Rigaud." "After he got my letter on Sunday evening," says the disappointed general, "Monsieur de Vaudreuil sent me his secretary with the instructions he had given his brother," which he had hitherto withheld. "This gave rise after dinner to a long conversation with him; and I hope for the good of the service that his future conduct will prove the truth of his words. I spoke to him with frankness and firmness of the necessity I was under of communicating to him my reflections; but I did not name any of the persons who, to gain his good graces, busy themselves with destroying his confidence in me. I told him that he would always find me disposed to aid in measures tending to our success, even should his views, which always ought to prevail, be different from mine; but that I dared flatter myself that he would henceforward communicate his plans to me sooner; for, though his knowledge of the country gave greater weight to his opinions, he might rest satisfied that I should second him in methods and details. This explanation passed off becomingly enough, and ended with a proposal to dine on a moose's nose [*an estimed morsel*] the day after to-morrow. I burn your letters, Monsieur, and I beg you to do the same with mine, after making a note of anything you may want to keep." But Bourlamaque kept all the letters, and bound them in a volume, which still exists.[1]

[1] The preceding extracts are from *Lettres de Montcalm à Madame de Saint-Véran, sa Mère, et à Madame de Montcalm, sa Femme,* 1756,

Montcalm was not at this time fully aware of the feeling of Vaudreuil towards him. The touchy egotism of the governor and his jealous attachment to the colony led him to claim for himself and the Canadians the merit of every achievement and to deny it to the French troops and their general. Before the capture of Oswego was known, he wrote to the naval minister that Montcalm would never have dared attack that place if he had not encouraged him and answered his timid objections.[1] " I am confident that I shall reduce it," he adds; "my expedition is sure to succeed if Monsieur de Montcalm follows the directions I have given him." When the good news came he immediately wrote again, declaring that the victory was due to his brother Rigaud and the Canadians, who, he says, had been ill-used by the general, and not allowed either to enter the fort or share the plunder, any more than the Indians, who were so angry at the treatment they had met that he had great difficulty in appeasing them. He hints that the success was generally ascribed to him. " There has been a great deal of talk here; but I will not do myself the honor of repeating it to you, especially as it relates to myself. I know how to do violence to my self-love. The measures I took assured our victory, in spite of opposition. If I had been less vigilant and firm, Oswego

1757 (*Papiers de Famille*); and *Lettres de Montcalm à Bourlamaque*, 1757. See Appendix E.

[1] *Vaudreuil au Ministre de la Marine*, 13 *Août*, 1756.

Pierre François Rigaud, Marquis de Vaudreuil.

From the painting in the possession of the Countess of Clermont-Tonnerre, Château of Brugny, Marne.

MONTCALM AND WOLFE, I., 474

PIERRE RIGAUD
MARQUIS DE VAUDREUIL
GOUVERNEUR ET DIRECTEUR GÉNᵉˡ
DE LA NOUVELLE FRANCE
1698 ✕ 1760

would still be in the hands of the English.   I cannot
sufficiently congratulate myself on the zeal which my
brother and the Canadians and Indians showed on
this occasion; for without them my orders would
have been given in vain.   The hopes of His Britannic
Majesty have vanished, and will hardly revive again;
for I shall take care to crush them in the bud."[1]

The pronouns "I" and "my" recur with monotonous frequency in his correspondence.   "I have
laid waste all the British provinces."   "By promptly
uniting my forces at Carillon, I have kept General
Loudon in check, though he had at his disposal an
army of about twenty thousand men;"[2] and so without end, in all varieties of repetition.   It is no less
characteristic that he here assigns to his enemies
double their actual force.

He has the faintest of praise for the troops from
France.   "They are generally good, but thus far
they have not absolutely distinguished themselves.
I do justice to the firmness they showed at Oswego;
but it was only the colony troops, Canadians, and
Indians who attacked the forts.   Our artillery was
directed by the Chevalier Le Mercier and M. Frémont
[*colony officers*], and was served by our colony troops
and our militia.   The officers from France are more
inclined to defence than attack.   Far from spending
the least thing here, they lay by their pay.   They
saved the money allowed them for refreshments, and

---

[1] *Vaudreuil au Ministre de la Marine,* 1 *Septembre,* 1756.
[2] *Ibid.,* 6 *Novembre,* 1756.

had it in pocket at the end of the campaign. They get a profit, too, out of their provisions, by having certificates made under borrowed names, so that they can draw cash for them on their return. It is the same with the soldiers, who also sell their provisions to the King and get paid for them. In conjunction with M. Bigot, I labor to remedy all these abuses; and the rules we have established have saved the King a considerable expense. M. de Montcalm has complained very much of these rules." The intendant Bigot, who here appears as a reformer, was the centre of a monstrous system of public fraud and robbery; while the charges against the French officers are unsupported. Vaudreuil, who never loses an opportunity of disparaging them, proceeds thus: —

"The troops from France are not on very good terms with our Canadians. What can the soldiers think of them when they see their officers threaten them with sticks or swords? The Canadians are obliged to carry these gentry on their shoulders, through the cold water, over rocks that cut their feet; and if they make a false step they are abused. Can anything be harder? Finally, Monsieur de Montcalm is so quick-tempered that he goes to the length of striking the Canadians. How can he restrain his officers when he cannot restrain himself? Could any example be more contagious? This is the way our Canadians are treated. They deserve something better." He then enlarges on their zeal, hardihood, and bravery, and adds that nothing but their blind submission to his commands prevents many of them from showing resentment at the usage they had to endure. The Indians, he goes on to say, are not so gentle and yielding; and but for his brother Rigaud and himself, might have gone off in a rage. "After the campaign of Oswego they did not hesitate to tell me that they would go wherever I sent them, provided I did not put them under the orders of M. de Montcalm. They told me positively that they could not bear his quick temper. I shall always maintain the most perfect union and understanding with M. le Marquis de Montcalm, but I shall be forced to take measures which will assure to our Canadians and Indians treatment such as their zeal and services merit." [1]

To the subject of his complaints Vaudreuil used a different language; for Montcalm says, after mentioning that he had had occasion to punish some of the Canadians at Oswego: "I must do Monsieur de Vaudreuil the justice to say that he approved my proceedings." He treated the general with the blandest politeness. "He is a good-natured man," continues Montcalm, "mild, with no character of his own, surrounded by people who try to destroy all his confidence in the general of the troops from France. I am praised excessively, in order to make him jealous, excite his Canadian prejudices, and prevent

[1] *Vaudreuil au Ministre de la Marine,* 23 *Octobre,* 1756. The above extracts are somewhat condensed in the translation. See the letter in Dussieux, 279.

him from dealing with me frankly, or adopting my
views when he can help it."[1] He elsewhere complains that Vaudreuil gave to both him and Lévis
orders couched in such equivocal terms that he could
throw the blame on them in case of reverse.[2] Montcalm liked the militia no better than the governor
liked the regulars. "I have used them with good
effect, though not in places exposed to the enemy's
fire. They know neither discipline nor subordina-
tion, and think themselves in all respects the first
nation on earth." He is sure, however, that they
like him: "I have gained the utmost confidence of
the Canadians and Indians; and in the eyes of the
former, when I travel or visit their camps, I have
the air of a tribune of the people."[3] "The affection
of the Indians for me is so strong that there are
moments when it astonishes the Governor."[4] "The
Indians are delighted with me," he says in another
letter; "the Canadians are pleased with me; their
officers esteem and fear me, and would be glad if the
French troops and their general could be dispensed
with; and so should I."[5] And he writes to his
mother: "The part I have to play is unique: I am a
general-in-chief subordinated; sometimes with everything to do, and sometimes nothing; I am esteemed,
respected, beloved, envied, hated; I pass for proud,

[1] *Montcalm au Ministre de la Guerre*, 11 *Juillet*, 1757.
[2] *Ibid.*, 1 *Novembre*, 1756.
[3] *Ibid.*, 18 *Septembre*, 1757.
[4] *Ibid.*, 4 *Novembre*, 1757.
[5] *Ibid.*, 28 *Août*, 1756.

supple, stiff, yielding, polite, devout, gallant, etc.;
and I long for peace."[1]

The letters of the governor and those of the general,
it will be seen, contradict each other flatly at several
points.   Montcalm is sustained by his friend Bougainville, who says that the Indians had a great liking
for him, and that he "knew how to manage them as
well as if he had been born in their wigwams."[2]
And while Vaudreuil complains that the Canadians
are ill-used by Montcalm, Bougainville declares that
the regulars are ill-used by Vaudreuil.   "One must
be blind not to see that we are treated as the Spartans
treated the Helots."   Then he comments on the
jealous reticence of the governor.   "The Marquis de
Montcalm has not the honor of being consulted; and
it is generally through public rumor that he first
hears of Monsieur de Vaudreuil's military plans."
He calls the governor "a timid man, who can neither
make a resolution nor keep one;" and he gives another
trait of him, illustrating it, after his usual way, by
a parallel from the classics: "When V. produces an
idea he falls in love with it, as Pygmalion did with
his statue.   I can forgive Pygmalion, for what he
produced was a masterpiece."[3]

The exceeding touchiness of the governor was
sorely tried by certain indiscretions on the part of the
general, who in his rapid and vehement utterances

---

[1] *Montcalm à Madame de Saint-Véran, 23 Septembre,* 1757.

[2] *Bougainville à Saint-Laurens, 19 Août,* 1757.

[3] Bougainville, *Journal.*

sometimes forgot the rules of prudence. His anger, though not deep, was extremely impetuous; and it is said that his irritation against Vaudreuil sometimes found escape in the presence of servants and soldiers.[1] There was no lack of reporters, and the governor was told everything. The breach widened apace, and Canada divided itself into two camps: that of Vaudreuil with the colony officers, civil and military, and that of Montcalm with the officers from France. The principal exception was the Chevalier de Lévis. This brave and able commander had an easy and adaptable nature, which made him a sort of connecting link between the two parties. "One should be on good terms with everybody," was a maxim which he sometimes expressed, and on which he shaped his conduct with notable success. The intendant Bigot also, an adroit and accomplished person, had the skill to avoid breaking with either side.

But now the season of action was near, and domestic strife must give place to efforts against the common foe. "God or devil!" Montcalm wrote to Bourlamaque, "we must do something and risk a fight. If we succeed, we can, all three of us [*you*, *Lévis, and I*], ask for promotion. Burn this letter." The prospects, on the whole, were hopeful. The victory at Oswego had wrought marvels among the Indians, inspired the faithful, confirmed the wavering, and daunted the ill-disposed. The whole West

[1] *Évènements de la Guerre en Canada*, 1759, 1760.

was astir, ready to pour itself again in blood and
fire against the English border; and even the
Cherokees and Choctaws, old friends of the British
colonies, seemed on the point of turning against
them.[1] The Five Nations were half won for France.
In November a large deputation of them came to
renew the chain of friendship at Montreal. "I have
laid Oswego in ashes," said Vaudreuil; "the English
quail before me. Why do you nourish serpents in
your bosom? They mean only to enslave you." The
deputies trampled under foot the medals the English
had given them, and promised the "Devourer of
Villages," for so they styled the governor, that they
would never more lift the hatchet against his children.
The chief difficulty was to get rid of them; for,
being clothed and fed at the expense of the King,
they were in no haste to take leave; and learning
that New Year's Day was a time of visits, gifts, and
health-drinking, they declared that they would stay
to share its pleasures; which they did, to their own
satisfaction and the annoyance of those who were
forced to entertain them and their squaws.[2] An
active siding with France was to be expected only
from the western bands of the Confederacy. Neutrality alone could be hoped for from the others, who

[1] *Vaudreuil au Ministre de la Marine, 19 Avril,* 1757.

[2] *Montcalm au Ministre de la Guerre, 24 Avril,* 1757 ; *Relation de
l'Ambassade des Cinq Nations à Montreal, jointe à la lettre précédente.
Procès-verbal de différentes Entrevues entre M. de Vaudreuil et les
Députés des Nations sauvages du 13 au 30 Décembre,* 1756. Malartic,
Journal. Montcalm à Madame de Saint-Véran, 1 *Avril,* 1757.

were too near the English safely to declare against
them; while from one of the tribes, the Mohawks,
even neutrality was doubtful.

Vaudreuil, while disliking the French regulars,
felt that he could not dispense with them, and had
asked for a reinforcement. His request was granted;
and the colonial minister informed him that twenty-
four hundred men had been ordered to Canada to
strengthen the colony regulars and the battalions of
Montcalm.[1] This, according to the estimate of the
minister, would raise the regular force in Canada to
sixty-six hundred rank and file.[2] The announcement
was followed by another, less agreeable. It was to
the effect that a formidable squadron was fitting out
in British ports. Was Quebec to be attacked, or
Louisbourg? Louisbourg was beyond reach of succor from Canada; it must rely on its own strength
and on help from France. But so long as Quebec
was threatened, all the troops in the colony must be
held ready to defend it, and the hope of attacking
England in her own domains must be abandoned.
Till these doubts were solved, nothing could be
done; and hence great activity in catching prisoners
for the sake of news. A few were brought in, but
they knew no more of the matter than the French
themselves; and Vaudreuil and Montcalm rested for
a while in suspense.

[1] *Ordres du Roy et Dépêches des Ministres, Mars,* 1757.
[2] *Ministerial Minute on the Military Force in Canada,* 1757, in *N. Y.,
Col. Docs.,* x. 523.

The truth, had they known it, would have gladdened their hearts. The English preparations were aimed at Louisbourg. In the autumn before, Loudon, prejudiced against all plans of his predecessor, Shirley, proposed to the ministry a scheme of his own, involving a possible attack on Quebec, but with the reduction of Louisbourg as its immediate object, — an important object, no doubt, but one that had no direct bearing on the main question of controlling the interior of the continent. Pitt, then for a brief space at the head of the government, accepted the suggestion, and set himself to executing it; but he was hampered by opposition, and early in April was forced to resign. Then followed a contest of rival claimants to office; and the war against France was made subordinate to disputes of personal politics. Meanwhile one Florence Hensey, a spy at London, had informed the French court that a great armament was fitting out for America, though he could not tell its precise destination. Without loss of time three French squadrons were sent across the Atlantic, with orders to rendezvous at Louisbourg, the conjectured point of attack.

The English were as tardy as their enemies were prompt. Everything depended on speed; yet their fleet, under Admiral Holbourne, consisting of fifteen ships-of-the-line and three frigates, with about five thousand troops on board, did not get to sea till the fifth of May, when it made sail for Halifax, where Loudon was to meet it with additional forces.

Loudon had drawn off the best part of the troops from the northern frontier, and they were now at New York waiting for embarkation. That the design might be kept secret, he laid an embargo on colonial shipping, — a measure which exasperated the colonists without answering its purpose. Now ensued a long delay, during which the troops, the provincial levies, the transports destined to carry them, and the ships of war which were to serve as escort, all lay idle. In the interval Loudon showed great activity in writing despatches and other avocations more or less proper to a commander, being always busy, without, according to Franklin, accomplishing anything. One Innis, who had come with a message from the governor of Pennsylvania, and had waited above a fortnight for the general's reply, remarked of him that he was like St. George on a tavern sign, always on horseback, and never riding on.[1] Yet nobody longed more than he to reach the rendezvous at Halifax. He was waiting for news of Holbourne, and he waited in vain. He knew only that a French fleet had been seen off the coast strong enough to overpower his escort and sink all his transports.[2] But the season was growing late; he must act quickly if he was to act at all. He and Sir Charles Hardy agreed between

[1] *Works of Franklin*, i. 219. Franklin intimates that while Loudon was constantly writing, he rarely sent off despatches. This is a mistake; there is abundance of them, often tediously long, in the Public Record Office.

[2] *Loudon to Pitt*, 30 *May*, 1757. He had not learned Pitt's resignation.

them that the risk must be run; and on the twentieth of June the whole force put to sea. They met no enemy, and entered Halifax harbor on the thirtieth. Holbourne and his fleet had not yet appeared; but his ships soon came straggling in, and before the tenth of July all were at anchor before the town. Then there was more delay. The troops, nearly twelve thousand in all, were landed, and weeks were spent in drilling them and planting vegetables for their refreshment. Sir Charles Hay was put under arrest for saying that the nation's money was spent in sham battles and raising cabbages. Some attempts were made to learn the state of Louisbourg; and Captain Gorham, of the rangers, who reconnoitred it from a fishing vessel, brought back an imperfect report, upon which, after some hesitation, it was resolved to proceed to the attack. The troops were embarked again, and all was ready, when, on the fourth of August, a sloop came from Newfoundland, bringing letters found on board a French vessel lately captured. From these it appeared that all three of the French squadrons were united in the harbor of Louisbourg, to the number of twenty-two ships-of-the-line, besides several frigates, and that the garrison had been increased to a total force of seven thousand men, ensconced in the strongest fortress of the continent. So far as concerned the naval force, the account was true. La Motte, the French admiral, had with him a fleet carrying an aggregate of thirteen hundred and sixty cannon, anchored in a shel-

tered harbor under the guns of the town. Success
was now hopeless, and the costly enterprise was at
once abandoned. Loudon with his troops sailed back
for New York, and Admiral Holbourne, who had
been joined by four additional ships, steered for
Louisbourg, in hopes that the French fleet would
come out and fight him. He cruised off the port;
but La Motte did not accept the challenge.

The elements declared for France. A September
gale, of fury rare even on that tempestuous coast,
burst upon the British fleet. "It blew a perfect
hurricane," says the unfortunate admiral, "and drove
us right on shore." One ship was dashed on the
rocks, two leagues from Louisbourg. A shifting of
the wind in the nick of time saved the rest from total
wreck. Nine were dismasted; others threw their
cannon into the sea. Not one was left fit for immediate action; and had La Motte sailed out of Louisbourg, he would have had them all at his mercy.

Delay, the source of most of the disasters that
befell England and her colonies at this dismal epoch,
was the ruin of the Louisbourg expedition. The
greater part of La Motte's fleet reached its destination a full month before that of Holbourne. Had
the reverse taken place, the fortress must have
fallen. As it was, the ill-starred attempt, drawing
off the British forces from the frontier, where they
were needed most, did for France more than she
could have done for herself, and gave Montcalm and

Vaudreuil the opportunity to execute a scheme which they had nursed since the fall of Oswego.[1]

[1] *Despatches of Loudon, February to August,* 1757. Knox, *Campaigns in North America,* i. 6–28. Knox was in the expedition. *Review of Mr. Pitt's Administration* (London, 1763). *The Conduct of a Noble Commander in America impartially reviewed* (London, 1758). Beatson, *Naval and Military Memoirs,* ii. 49–59. *Answer to the Letter to two Great Men* (London, 1760). Entick, ii. 168, 169. *Holbourne to Loudon,* 4 *August,* 1757. *Holbourne to Pitt,* 29 *September,* 1757. *Ibid.,* 30 *September,* 1757. *Holbourne to Pownall,* 2 *November,* 1757. Mante, 86, 97. *Relation du Désastre arrivé à la Flotte Anglaise commandée par l'Amiral Holbourne.* Chevalier Johnstone, *Campaign of Louisbourg.* *London Magazine,* 1757, 514. *Gentleman's Magazine,* 1757, 463, 476. *Ibid.,* 1758, 168–173.

It has been said that Loudon was scared from his task by false reports of the strength of the French at Louisbourg. This was not the case. The *Gazette de France,* 621, says that La Motte had twenty-four ships of war. Bougainville says that as early as the ninth of June there were twenty-one ships of war, including five frigates, at Louisbourg. To this the list given by Knox closely answers.

CHAPTER XV.

1757.

FORT WILLIAM HENRY.

ANOTHER BLOW. — THE WAR-SONG. — THE ARMY AT TICON-
DEROGA. — INDIAN ALLIES. — THE WAR-FEAST. — TREATMENT
OF PRISONERS. — CANNIBALISM. — SURPRISE AND SLAUGHTER. —
THE WAR COUNCIL. — MARCH OF LÉVIS. — THE ARMY EM-
BARKS. — FORT WILLIAM HENRY. — NOCTURNAL SCENE. —
INDIAN FUNERAL. — ADVANCE UPON THE FORT. — GENERAL
WEBB: HIS DIFFICULTIES; HIS WEAKNESS. — THE SIEGE
BEGUN. — CONDUCT OF THE INDIANS. — THE INTERCEPTED
LETTER. — DESPERATE POSITION OF THE BESIEGED. — CAPITU-
LATION. — FEROCITY OF THE INDIANS. — MISSION OF BOUGAIN-
VILLE. — MURDER OF WOUNDED MEN. — A SCENE OF TERROR.
— THE MASSACRE. — EFFORTS OF MONTCALM. — THE FORT
BURNED.

"I AM going on the ninth to sing the war-song at
the Lake of Two Mountains, and on the next day at
Saut St. Louis, — a long, tiresome ceremony. On
the twelfth I am off; and I count on having news to
tell you by the end of this month or the beginning of
next." Thus Montcalm wrote to his wife from
Montreal early in July. All doubts had been solved.
Prisoners taken on the Hudson and despatches from
Versailles had made it certain that Loudon was
bound to Louisbourg, carrying with him the best of
the troops that had guarded the New York frontier.

The time was come, not only to strike the English on Lake George, but perhaps to seize Fort Edward and carry terror to Albany itself. Only one difficulty remained, the want of provisions. Agents were sent to collect corn and bacon among the inhabitants; the curés and militia captains were ordered to aid in the work; and enough was presently found to feed twelve thousand men for a month.[1]

The emissaries of the governor had been busy all winter among the tribes of the West and North; and more than a thousand savages, lured by the prospect of gifts, scalps, and plunder, were now encamped at Montreal. Many of them had never visited a French settlement before. All were eager to see Montcalm, whose exploit in taking Oswego had inflamed their imagination; and one day, on a visit of ceremony, an orator from Michilimackinac addressed the general thus: "We wanted to see this famous man who tramples the English under his feet. We thought we should find him so tall that his head would be lost in the clouds. But you are a little man, my Father. It is when we look into your eyes that we see the greatness of the pine-tree and the fire of the eagle." [2]

It remained to muster the Mission Indians settled in or near the limits of the colony; and it was to this end that Montcalm went to sing the war-song with

[1] Vaudreuil, *Lettres circulaires aux Curés et aux Capitaines de Milice des Paroisses du Gouvernement de Montreal*, 16 *Juin*, 1757.
[2] Bougainville, *Journal*.

the converts of the Two Mountains. Rigaud, Bougainville, young Longueuil, and others were of the party; and when they landed, the Indians came down to the shore, their priests at their head, and greeted the general with a volley of musketry; then received him after dark in their grand council-lodge, where the circle of wild and savage visages, half seen in the dim light of a few candles, suggested to Bougainville a midnight conclave of wizards. He acted vicariously the chief part in the ceremony. "I sang the war-song in the name of M. de Montcalm, and was much applauded. It was nothing but these words, ' Let us trample the English under our feet,' chanted over and over again, in cadence with the movements of the savages." Then came the war-feast, against which occasion Montcalm had caused three oxen to be roasted.[1] On the next day the party went to Caughnawaga, or Saut St. Louis, where the ceremony was repeated; and Bougainville, who again sang the war-song in the name of his commander, was requited by adoption into the clan of the Turtle. Three more oxen were solemnly devoured, and with one voice the warriors took up the hatchet.

Meanwhile troops, Canadians and Indians, were

[1] Bougainville describes a ceremony in the Mission Church of the Two Mountains in which warriors and squaws sang in the choir. Ninety-nine years after, in 1856, I was present at a similar ceremony on the same spot, and heard the descendants of the same warriors and squaws sing like their ancestors. Great changes have since taken place at this old mission.

moving by detachments up Lake Champlain. Fleets
of bateaux and canoes followed each other day by
day along the capricious lake, in calm or storm, sun-
shine or rain, till, towards the end of July, the whole
force was gathered at Ticonderoga, the base of the
intended movement. Bourlamaque had been there
since May with the battalions of Béarn and Royal
Roussillon, finishing the fort, sending out war-
parties, and trying to discover the force and designs
of the English at Fort William Henry.

Ticonderoga is a high rocky promontory between
Lake Champlain on the north and the mouth of the
outlet of Lake George on the south. Near its
extremity and close to the fort were still encamped
the two battalions under Bourlamaque, while bateaux
and canoes were passing incessantly up the river of
the outlet. There were scarcely two miles of navigable water, at the end of which the stream fell
foaming over a high ledge of rock that barred the
way. Here the French were building a saw-mill;
and a wide space had been cleared to form an encampment defended on all sides by an abattis, within
which stood the tents of the battalions of La Reine,
La Sarre, Languedoc, and Guienne, all commanded
by Lévis. Above the cascade the stream circled
through the forest in a series of beautiful rapids, and
from the camp of Lévis a road a mile and a half long
had been cut to the navigable water above. At the
end of this road there was another fortified camp,
formed of colony regulars, Canadians, and Indians,

under Rigaud. It was scarcely a mile farther to
Lake George, where on the western side there was
an outpost, chiefly of Canadians and Indians; while
advanced parties were stationed at Bald Mountain,
now called Rogers Rock, and elsewhere on the lake,
to watch the movements of the English. The
various encampments just mentioned were ranged
along a valley extending four miles from Lake
Champlain to Lake George, and bordered by mountains wooded to the top.

Here was gathered a martial population of eight
thousand men, including the brightest civilization
and the darkest barbarism: from the scholar-soldier
Montcalm and his no less accomplished aide-de-camp;
from Lévis, conspicuous for graces of person; from
a throng of courtly young officers, who would have
seemed out of place in that wilderness had they not
done their work so well in it; from these to the
foulest man-eating savage of the uttermost northwest.

Of Indian allies there were nearly two thousand.
One of their tribes, the Iowas, spoke a language
which no interpreter understood; and they all bivouacked where they saw fit: for no man could control
them. "I see no difference," says Bougainville, "in
the dress, ornaments, dances, and songs of the
various western nations. They go naked, excepting
a strip of cloth passed through a belt, and paint
themselves black, red, blue, and other colors. Their
heads are shaved and adorned with bunches of
feathers, and they wear rings of brass wire in their

ears. They wear beaver-skin blankets, and carry lances, bows and arrows, and quivers made of the skins of beasts. For the rest they are straight, well made, and generally very tall. Their religion is brute paganism. I will say it once for all, one must be the slave of these savages, listen to them day and night, in council and in private, whenever the fancy takes them, or whenever a dream, a fit of the vapors, or their perpetual craving for brandy, gets possession of them; besides which they are always wanting something for their equipment, arms, or toilet, and the general of the army must give written orders for the smallest trifle, — an eternal, wearisome detail, of which one has no idea in Europe."

It was not easy to keep them fed. Rations would be served to them for a week; they would consume them in three days, and come for more. On one occasion they took the matter into their own hands, and butchered and devoured eighteen head of cattle intended for the troops; nor did any officer dare oppose this "St. Bartholomew of the oxen," as Bougainville calls it. "Their paradise is to be drunk," says the young officer. Their paradise was rather a hell; for sometimes, when mad with brandy, they grappled and tore each other with their teeth like wolves. They were continually "making medicine," that is, consulting the Manitou, to whom they hung up offerings, sometimes a dead dog, and sometimes the belt-cloth which formed their only garment.

The Mission Indians were better allies than these

heathen of the West; and their priests, who followed
them to the war, had great influence over them.
They were armed with guns, which they well knew
how to use. Their dress, though savage, was generally decent, and they were not cannibals; though
in other respects they retained all their traditional
ferocity and most of their traditional habits. They
held frequent war-feasts, one of which is described
by Roubaud, Jesuit missionary of the Abenakis of
St. Francis, whose flock formed a part of the company present.

"Imagine," says the father, "a great assembly of
savages adorned with every ornament most suited to
disfigure them in European eyes, painted with vermilion, white, green, yellow, and black made of soot
and the scrapings of pots. A single savage face
combines all these different colors, methodically laid
on with the help of a little tallow, which serves for
pomatum. The head is shaved except at the top,
where there is a small tuft, to which are fastened
feathers, a few beads of wampum, or some such
trinket. Every part of the head has its ornament.
Pendants hang from the nose and also from the
ears, which are split in infancy and drawn down by
weights till they flap at last against the shoulders.
The rest of the equipment answers to this fantastic
decoration: a shirt bedaubed with vermilion, wampum collars, silver bracelets, a large knife hanging
on the breast, moose-skin moccasons, and a belt of
various colors always absurdly combined. The

sachems and war-chiefs are distinguished from the
rest: the latter by a gorget, and the former by a
medal, with the King's portrait on one side, and on
the others Mars and Bellona joining hands, with the
device, *Virtus et Honor*."

Thus attired, the company sat in two lines facing
each other, with kettles in the middle filled with
meat chopped for distribution.   To a dignified silence
succeeded songs, sung by several chiefs in succession,
and compared by the narrator to the howling of
wolves.   Then followed a speech from the chief
orator, highly commended by Roubaud, who could
not help admiring this effort of savage eloquence.
"After the harangue," he continues, "they proceeded
to nominate the chiefs who were to take command.
As soon as one was named he rose and took the head
of some animal that had been butchered for the feast.
He raised it aloft so that all the company could see
it, and cried, 'Behold the head of the enemy!'
Applause and cries of joy rose from all parts of the
assembly.   The chief, with the head in his hand,
passed down between the lines, singing his war-song,
bragging of his exploits, taunting and defying the
enemy, and glorifying himself beyond all measure.
To hear his self-laudation in these moments of martial
transport one would think him a conquering hero
ready to sweep everything before him.   As he passed
in front of the other savages, they would respond by
dull broken cries jerked up from the depths of their
stomachs, and accompanied by movements of their

bodies so odd that one must be well used to them to
keep countenance. In the course of his song the
chief would utter from time to time some grotesque
witticism; then he would stop, as if pleased with
himself, or rather to listen to the thousand confused
cries of applause that greeted his ears. He kept up
his martial promenade as long as he liked the sport;
and when he had had enough, ended by flinging
down the head of the animal with an air of contempt,
to show that his warlike appetite craved meat of
another sort." [1] Others followed with similar songs
and pantomime, and the festival was closed at last
by ladling out the meat from the kettles, and devour-
ing it.

Roubaud was one day near the fort, when he saw
the shore lined with a thousand Indians, watching
four or five English prisoners, who, with the war-
party that had captured them, were approaching in
a boat from the farther side of the water. Suddenly
the whole savage crew broke away together and ran
into the neighboring woods, whence they soon
emerged, yelling diabolically, each armed with a
club. The wretched prisoners were to be forced to
"run the gantlet," which would probably have
killed them. They were saved by the chief who
commanded the war-party, and who, on the persuasion of a French officer, claimed them as his own
and forbade the game; upon which, according to

[1] *Lettres du Père* . . . (Roubaud), *Missionnaire chez les Abenakis*, 21
Octobre, 1757, in *Lettres Édifiantes et Curieuses*, vi. 189 (1810).

rule in such cases, the rest abandoned it.   On this
same day the missionary met troops of Indians con-
ducting several bands of English prisoners along the
road that led through the forest from the camp of
Lévis.   Each of the captives was held by a cord made
fast about the neck; and the sweat was starting from
their brows in the extremity of their horror and distress.   Roubaud's tent was at this time in the camp
of the Ottawas.   He presently saw a large number
of them squatted about a fire, before which meat was
roasting on sticks stuck in the ground; and, approaching, he saw that it was the flesh of an Englishman,
other parts of which were boiling in a kettle, while
near by sat eight or ten of the prisoners, forced to
see their comrade devoured.   The horror-stricken
priest began to remonstrate; on which a young savage
fiercely replied in broken French: "You have French
taste; I have Indian. This is good meat for me;"
and the feasters pressed him to share it.

Bougainville says that this abomination could not
be prevented; which only means that if force had
been used to stop it, the Ottawas would have gone
home in a rage.   They were therefore left to finish
their meal undisturbed.   Having eaten one of their
prisoners, they began to treat the rest with the
utmost kindness, bringing them white bread, and
attending to all their wants, — a seeming change of
heart due to the fact that they were a valuable com-
modity, for which the owners hoped to get a good
price at Montreal.   Montcalm wished to send them

thither at once, to which after long debate the
Indians consented, demanding, however, a receipt in
full, and bargaining that the captives should be supplied with shoes and blankets.[1]

These unfortunates belonged to a detachment of
three hundred provincials, chiefly New Jersey men,
sent from Fort William Henry under command of
Colonel Parker to reconnoitre the French outposts.
Montcalm's scouts discovered them; on which a band
of Indians, considerably more numerous, went to
meet them under a French partisan named Corbière,
and ambushed themselves not far from Sabbath Day
Point.   Parker had rashly divided his force; and at
daybreak of the twenty-sixth of July three of his
boats fell into the snare, and were captured without
a shot.   Three others followed, in ignorance of what
had happened, and shared the fate of the first.
When the rest drew near, they were greeted by a
deadly volley from the thickets, and a swarm of
canoes darted out upon them.   The men were seized
with such a panic that some of them jumped into the
water to escape, while the Indians leaped after them
and speared them with their lances like fish.   "Terri-
fied," says Bougainville, "by the sight of these
monsters, their agility, their firing, and their yells,
they surrendered almost without resistance."   About
a hundred, however, made their escape.   The rest

---

[1] *Journal de l'Expédition contre le Fort George* [William Henry]
du 12 Juillet au 16 Août, 1757.   Bougainville, *Journal*.   *Lettre du P.
Roubaud.*

were killed or captured, and three of the bodies were eaten on the spot. The journalist adds that the victory so elated the Indians that they became insupportable; "but here in the forests of America we can no more do without them than without cavalry on the plain."[1]

Another success at about the same time did not tend to improve their manners. A hundred and fifty of them, along with a few Canadians under Marin, made a dash at Fort Edward, killed or drove in the pickets, and returned with thirty-two scalps and a prisoner. It was found, however, that the scalps were far from representing an equal number of heads, the Indians having learned the art of making two or three out of one by judicious division.[2]

Preparations were urged on with the utmost energy. Provisions, camp equipage, ammunition, cannon, and bateaux were dragged by gangs of men up the road from the camp of Lévis to the head of the rapids. The work went on through heat and rain, by day and night, till, at the end of July, all was done. Now, on the eve of departure, Montcalm, anxious for

[1] Bougainville, *Journal*. Malartic, *Journal*. Montcalm à Vaudreuil, 27 *Juillet*, 1757. *Webb to Loudon*, 1 *August*, 1757. *Webb to Delancey*, 30 *July*, 1757. *Journal de l'Expédition contre le Fort George*. *London Magazine*, 1757, 457. Niles, *French and Indian Wars*. *Boston Gazette*, 15 *August*, 1757.

[2] This affair was much exaggerated at the time. I follow Bougainville, who had the facts from Marin. According to him, the thirty-two scalps represent eleven killed; which exactly answers to the English loss as stated by Colonel Frye in a letter from Fort Edward.

harmony among his red allies, called them to a grand
council near the camp of Rigaud. Forty-one tribes
and sub-tribes, Christian and heathen, from the East
and from the West, were represented in it. Here
were the mission savages,— Iroquois of Caughnawaga,
Two Mountains, and La Présentation; Hurons of
Lorette and Detroit; Nipissings of Lake Nipissing;
Abenakis of St. Francis, Becancour, Missisqui, and
the Penobscot; Algonquins of Three Rivers and Two
Mountains; Micmacs and Malicites from Acadia: in
all, eight hundred chiefs and warriors. With these
came the heathen of the West, — Ottawas of seven
distinct bands; Ojibwas from Lake Superior, and
Mississagas from the region of Lakes Erie and
Huron; Pottawattamies and Menominies from Lake
Michigan; Sacs, Foxes, and Winnebagoes from
Wisconsin; Miamis from the prairies of Illinois, and
Iowas from the banks of the Des Moines: nine hundred and seventy-nine chiefs and warriors, men of
the forests and men of the plains, hunters of the
moose and hunters of the buffalo, bearers of steel
hatchets and stone war-clubs, of French guns and of
flint-headed arrows. All sat in silence, decked with
ceremonial paint, scalp-locks, eagle plumes, or horns
of buffalo; and the dark and wild assemblage was
edged with white uniforms of officers from France,
who came in numbers to the spectacle. Other
officers were also here, all belonging to the colony.
They had been appointed to the command of the
Indian allies, over whom, however, they had little or

no real authority. First among them was the bold and hardy Saint-Luc de la Corne, who was called general of the Indians; and under him were others, each assigned to some tribe or group of tribes, — the intrepid Marin; Charles Langlade, who had left his squaw wife at Michilimackinac to join the war; Niverville, Langis, La Plante, Hertel, Longueuil, Herbin, Lorimier, Sabrevois, and Fleurimont; men familiar from childhood with forests and savages. Each tribe had its interpreter, often as lawless as those with whom he had spent his life; and for the converted tribes there were three missionaries, — Piquet for the Iroquois, Mathevet for the Nipissings, who were half heathen, and Roubaud for the Abenakis.[1]

There was some complaint among the Indians because they were crowded upon by the officers who came as spectators. This difficulty being removed, the council opened, Montcalm having already explained his plans to the chiefs and told them the part he expected them to play.

Pennahouel, chief of the Ottawas, and senior of all the Assembly, rose and said: "My father, I, who have counted more moons than any here, thank you for the good words you have spoken. I approve

---

[1] The above is chiefly from *Tableau des Sauvages qui se trouvent à l'Armée du Marquis de Montcalm, le* 28 *Juillet,* 1757. Forty-one tribes and sub-tribes are here named, some, however, represented by only three or four warriors. Besides those set down under the head of Christians, it is stated that a few of the Ottawas of Detroit and Michilimackinac still retained the faith.

them.   Nobody ever spoke better.   It is the Manitou
of War who inspires you."

Kikensick, chief of the Nipissings, rose in behalf
of the Christian Indians, and addressed the heathen
of the west.   "Brothers, we thank you for coming
to help us defend our lands against the English.
Our cause is good.   The Master of Life is on our
side.   Can you doubt it, brothers, after the great blow
you have just struck?   It covers you with glory.
The lake, red with the blood of Corlaer [*the English*],
bears witness forever to your achievement.   We too
share your glory, and are proud of what you have
done."   Then, turning to Montcalm: "We are even
more glad than you, my father, who have crossed
the great water, not for your own sake, but to obey
the great King and defend his children.   He has
bound us all together by the most solemn of ties.
Let us take care that nothing shall separate us."

The various interpreters, each in turn, having
explained this speech to the Assembly, it was received
with ejaculations of applause; and when they had
ceased, Montcalm spoke as follows: "Children, I am
delighted to see you all joined in this good work.
So long as you remain one, the English cannot resist
you.   The great King has sent me to protect and
defend you; but above all he has charged me to
make you happy and unconquerable, by establishing
among you the union which ought to prevail among
brothers, children of one father, the great Onontio."
Then he held out a prodigious wampum belt of six

thousand beads: "Take this sacred pledge of his word. The union of the beads of which it is made is the sign of your united strength. By it I bind you all together, so that none of you can separate from the rest till the English are defeated and their fort destroyed."

Pennahouel took up the belt and said: "Behold, brothers, a circle drawn around us by the great Onontio. Let none of us go out from it; for so long as we keep in it, the Master of Life will help all our undertakings." Other chiefs spoke to the same effect, and the council closed in perfect harmony.[1] Its various members bivouacked together at the camp by the lake, and by their carelessness soon set it on fire; whence the place became known as the Burned Camp. Those from the missions confessed their sins all day; while their heathen brothers hung an old coat and a pair of leggings on a pole as tribute to the Manitou. This greatly embarrassed the three priests, who were about to say mass, but doubted whether they ought to say it in presence of a sacrifice to the devil. Hereupon they took counsel of Montcalm. "Better say it so than not at all," replied the military casuist. Brandy being prudently denied them, the allies grew restless; and the greater part paddled up the lake to a spot near the place where Parker had been defeated. Here they encamped to wait the arrival of the army, and amused themselves mean-time with killing rattlesnakes, there being a populous

[1] Bougainville, *Journal.*

"den" of those reptiles among the neighboring rocks.

Montcalm sent a circular letter to the regular officers, urging them to dispense for a while with luxuries, and even comforts. "We have but few bateaux, and these are so filled with stores that a large division of the army must go by land;" and he directed that everything not absolutely necessary should be left behind, and that a canvas shelter to every two officers should serve them for a tent, and a bearskin for a bed. "Yet I do not forbid a mattress," he adds. "Age and infirmities may make it necessary to some; but I shall not have one myself, and make no doubt that all who can, will willingly imitate me." [1]

The bateaux lay ready by the shore, but could not carry the whole force; and Lévis received orders to march by the side of the lake with twenty-five hundred men, Canadians, regulars, and Iroquois. He set out at daybreak of the thirtieth of July, his men carrying nothing but their knapsacks, blankets, and weapons. Guided by the unerring Indians, they climbed the steep gorge at the side of Rogers Rock, gained the valley beyond, and marched southward along a Mohawk trail which threaded the forest in a course parallel to the lake. The way was of the roughest; many straggled from the line, and two officers completely broke down. The first destination of the party was the mouth of Ganouskie Bay,

[1] *Circulaire du Marquis de Montcalm, 25 Juillet, 1757.*

now called Northwest Bay, where they were to wait
for Montcalm, and kindle three fires as a signal that
they had reached the rendezvous.[1]

Montcalm left a detachment to hold Ticonderoga;
and then, on the first of August, at two in the afternoon, he embarked at the Burned Camp with all his
remaining force. Including those with Lévis, the
expedition counted about seven thousand six hundred men, of whom more than sixteen hundred were
Indians.[2] At five in the afternoon they reached the
place where the Indians, having finished their rattle-
snake hunt, were smoking their pipes and waiting for
the army. The red warriors embarked, and joined
the French flotilla; and now, as evening drew near,
was seen one of those wild pageantries of war which
Lake George has often witnessed. A restless multitude of birch canoes, filled with painted savages,
glided by shores and islands, like troops of swimming
water-fowl. Two hundred and fifty bateaux came
next, moved by sail and oar, some bearing the Canadian militia, and some the battalions of Old France
in trim and gay attire: first, La Reine and Languedoc;

[1] *Guerre du Canada, par le Chevalier de Lévis.* This manuscript
of Lévis is largely in the nature of a journal.

[2] *État de l'Armée Française devant le Fort George, autrement
Guillaume-Henri, le 3 Août,* 1757. *Tableau des Sauvages qui se
trouvent à l'Armée du Marquis de Montcalm, le 28 Juillet,* 1757. This
gives a total of 1,799 Indians, of whom some afterwards left the
army. *État de l'Armée du Roi en Canada, sur le Lac St. Sacrement et
dans les Camps de Carillon, le 29 Juillet,* 1757. This gives a total of
8,019 men, of whom about four hundred were left in garrison at
Ticonderoga.

then the colony regulars; then La Sarre and Guienne; then the Canadian brigade of Courtemanche; then the cannon and mortars, each on a platform sustained by two bateaux lashed side by side, and rowed by the militia of Saint-Ours; then the battalions of Béarn and Royal Roussillon; then the Canadians of Gaspé, with the provision-bateaux and the field-hospital; and, lastly, a rear-guard of regulars closed the line. So, under the flush of sunset, they held their course along the romantic lake, to play their part in the historic drama that lends a stern enchantment to its fascinating scenery. They passed the Narrows in mist and darkness; and when, a little before dawn, they rounded the high promontory of Tongue Mountain, they saw, far on the right, three fiery sparks shining through the gloom. These were the signal-fires of Lévis, to tell them that he had reached the appointed spot.[1]

Lévis had arrived the evening before, after his hard march through the sultry midsummer forest. His men had now rested for a night, and at ten in the morning he marched again. Montcalm followed at noon, and coasted the western shore, till, towards evening, he found Lévis waiting for him by the margin of a small bay not far from the English fort, though hidden from it by a projecting point of land. Canoes and bateaux were drawn up on the beach, and the united forces made their bivouac together.

[1] The site of the present village of Bolton.

The earthen mounds of Fort William Henry still stand by the brink of Lake George; and seated at the sunset of an August day under the pines that cover them, one gazes on a scene of soft and soothing beauty, where dreamy waters reflect the glories of the mountains and the sky. As it is to-day, so it was then; all breathed repose and peace. The splash of some leaping trout, or the dipping wing of a passing swallow, alone disturbed the summer calm of that unruffled mirror.

About ten o'clock at night two boats set out from the fort to reconnoitre. They were passing a point of land on their left, two miles or more down the lake, when the men on board descried through the gloom a strange object against the bank; and they rowed towards it to learn what it might be. It was an awning over the bateaux that carried Roubaud and his brother missionaries. As the rash oarsmen drew near, the bleating of a sheep in one of the French provision-boats warned them of danger; and turning, they pulled for their lives towards the eastern shore. Instantly more than a thousand Indians threw themselves into their canoes and dashed in hot pursuit, making the lake and the mountains ring with the din of their war-whoops. The fugitives had nearly reached land when their pursuers opened fire. They replied; shot one Indian dead, and wounded another; then snatched their oars again, and gained the beach. But the whole savage crew was upon them. Several were killed, three were taken, and

the rest escaped in the dark woods.[1] The prisoners
were brought before Montcalm, and gave him valuable information of the strength and position of the
English.[2]

The Indian who was killed was a noted chief of
the Nipissings; and his tribesmen howled in grief for
their bereavement. They painted his face with vermilion, tied feathers in his hair, hung pendants in
his ears and nose, clad him in a resplendent war-
dress, put silver bracelets on his arms, hung a gorget
on his breast with a flame-colored ribbon, and seated
him in state on the top of a hillock, with his lance
in his hand, his gun in the hollow of his arm, his
tomahawk in his belt, and his kettle by his side.
Then they all crouched about him in lugubrious
silence. A funeral harangue followed; and next a
song and solemn dance to the booming of the Indian
drum. In the gray of the morning they buried him
as he sat, and placed food in the grave for his journey
to the land of souls.[3]

As the sun rose above the eastern mountains the
French camp was all astir. The column of Lévis,
with Indians to lead the way, moved through the

[1] *Lettre du Père Roubaud*, 21 *Octobre*, 1757. Roubaud, who saw
the whole, says that twelve hundred Indians joined the chase, and
that their yells were terrific.

[2] The remains of Fort William Henry are now — 1882 — crowded
between a hotel and the wharf and station of a railway. While I
write, a scheme is on foot to level the whole for other railway struc-
tures.   When I first knew the place, the ground was in much the
same state as in the time of Montcalm

[3] *Lettre du Père Roubaud.*

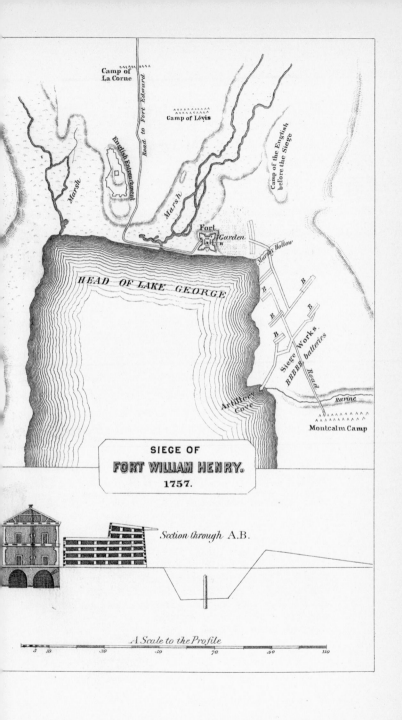

Camp of
La Corne

Camp of Lévis

Road to Fort Edward

English Entrenchment

Camp of the English
before the Siege

Marsh

Marsh

Marsh

Fort
Garden

Marsh Hollow

HEAD OF LAKE GEORGE

B

B

B

B

B

Siege Works.
B B B B B batteries

Road

Artillery
Cove

ravine

Montcalm Camp

SIEGE OF
FORT WILLIAM HENRY.
1757.

Section through A.B.

A Scale to the Profile

5   10   30   50   70   90   110

thought the attempt too hazardous. The ground where he stood was that where Dieskau had been defeated; and as the fate of his predecessor was not of flattering augury, he resolved to besiege the fort in form.

He chose for the site of his operations the ground now covered by the village of Caldwell. A little to the north of it was a ravine, beyond which he formed his main camp, while Lévis occupied a tract of dry ground beside the marsh, whence he could easily move to intercept succors from Fort Edward on the one hand, or repel a sortie from Fort William Henry on the other. A brook ran down the ravine and entered the lake at a small cove protected from the fire of the fort by a point of land; and at this place, still called Artillery Cove, Montcalm prepared to debark his cannon and mortars.

Having made his preparations, he sent Fontbrune, one of his aides-de-camp, with a letter to Monro. "I owe it to humanity," he wrote, "to summon you to surrender. At present I can restrain the savages, and make them observe the terms of a capitulation, as I might not have power to do under other circumstances; and an obstinate defence on your part could only retard the capture of the place a few days, and endanger an unfortunate garrison which cannot be relieved, in consequence of the dispositions I have made. I demand a decisive answer within an hour." Monro replied that he and his soldiers would defend themselves to the last. While the flags of truce were flying, the Indians swarmed over the fields before the fort; and when they learned the result, an Abenaki chief shouted in broken French: "You won't surrender, eh ! Fire away then, and fight your best; for if I catch you, you shall get no quarter." Monro emphasized his refusal by a general discharge of his cannon.

The trenches were opened on the night of the fourth, — a task of extreme difficulty, as the ground was covered by a profusion of half-burned stumps, roots, branches, and fallen trunks. Eight hundred men toiled till daylight with pick, spade, and axe, while the cannon from the fort flashed through the darkness, and grape and round-shot whistled and screamed over their heads. Some of the English balls reached the camp beyond the ravine, and disturbed the slumbers of the officers off duty, as they lay wrapped in their blankets and bear-skins. Before daybreak the first parallel was made; a battery was nearly finished on the left, and another was begun on the right. The men now worked under cover, safe in their burrows; one gang relieved another, and the work went on all day.

The Indians were far from doing what was expected of them. Instead of scouting in the direction of Fort Edward to learn the movements of the enemy and prevent surprise, they loitered about the camp and in the trenches, or amused themselves by firing at the fort from behind stumps and logs. Some, in imitation of the French, dug little trenches for themselves, in

which they wormed their way towards the rampart,
and now and then picked off an artillery-man, not
without loss on their own side.   On the afternoon of
the fifth, Montcalm invited them to a council, gave
them belts of wampum, and mildly remonstrated with
them.   "Why expose yourselves without necessity?
I grieve bitterly over the losses that you have met,
for the least among you is precious to me.   No doubt
it is a good thing to annoy the English; but that is
not the main point.   You ought to inform me of
everything the enemy is doing, and always keep
parties on the road between the two forts."   And he
gently hinted that their place was not in his camp,
but in that of Lévis, where missionaries were provided
for such of them as were Christians, and food and
ammunition for them all.   They promised, with
excellent docility, to do everything he wished, but
added that there was something on their hearts.
Being encouraged to relieve themselves of the burden,
they complained that they had not been consulted as
to the management of the siege, but were expected to
obey orders like slaves.   "We know more about
fighting in the woods than you," said their orator;
"ask our advice, and you will be the better for it." [1]

Montcalm assured them that if they had been
neglected, it was only through the hurry and confusion of the time; expressed high appreciation of their
talents for bush-fighting, promised them ample satisfaction, and ended by telling them that in the morn-

[1] Bougainville, *Journal*.

ing they should hear the big guns. This greatly
pleased them, for they were extremely impatient for
the artillery to begin. About sunrise the battery of
the left opened with eight heavy cannon and a mortar,
joined, on the next morning, by the battery of the
right, with eleven pieces more. The fort replied
with spirit. The cannon thundered all day, and
from a hundred peaks and crags the astonished wilderness roared back the sound. The Indians were
delighted. They wanted to point the guns; and to
humor them, they were now and then allowed to do
so. Others lay behind logs and fallen trees, and
yelled their satisfaction when they saw the splinters
fly from the wooden rampart.

Day after day the weary roar of the distant cannonade fell on the ears of Webb in his camp at Fort
Edward. "I have not yet received the least reinforcement," he writes to Loudon; "this is the disagreeable situation we are at present in. The fort, by
the heavy firing we hear from the lake, is still in our
possession; but I fear it cannot long hold out against
so warm a cannonading if I am not reinforced by a
sufficient number of militia to march to their relief."
The militia were coming; but it was impossible that
many could reach him in less than a week. Those
from New York alone were within call, and two
thousand of them arrived soon after he sent Loudon
the above letter. Then, by stripping all the forts
below, he could bring together forty-five hundred
men; while several French deserters assured him that

Montcalm had nearly twelve thousand. To advance
to the relief of Monro with a force so inferior, through
a defile of rocks, forests, and mountains, made by
nature for ambuscades, — and this too with troops
who had neither the steadiness of regulars nor the
bush-fighting skill of Indians, — was an enterprise for
firmer nerve than his.

He had already warned Monro to expect no help
from him. At midnight of the fourth, Captain
Bartman, his aide-de-camp, wrote: "The General
has ordered me to acquaint you he does not think it
prudent to attempt a junction or to assist you till
reinforced by the militia of the colonies, for the
immediate march of which repeated expresses have
been sent." The letter then declared that the French
were in complete possession of the road between the
two forts, that a prisoner just brought in reported
their force in men and cannon to be very great, and
that, unless the militia came soon, Monro had better
make what terms he could with the enemy.[1]

The chance was small that this letter would reach
its destination; and in fact the bearer was killed by
La Corne's Indians, who, in stripping the body, found
the hidden paper, and carried it to the general.
Montcalm kept it several days, till the English rampart was half battered down; and then, after salut-
ing his enemy with a volley from all his cannon, he

---

[1] Frye, in his *Journal*, gives the letter in full. A spurious translation of it is appended to a piece called *Jugement impartial sur les
Opérations militaires en Canada.*

sent it with a graceful compliment to Monro. It
was Bougainville who carried it, preceded by a
drummer and a flag. He was met at the foot of the
glacis, blindfolded, and led through the fort and
along the edge of the lake to the intrenched camp,
where Monro was at the time. "He returned many
thanks," writes the emissary in his Diary, "for the
courtesy of our nation, and protested his joy at having to do with so generous an enemy. This was his
answer to the Marquis de Montcalm. Then they led
me back, always with eyes blinded; and our batteries
began to fire again as soon as we thought that the
English grenadiers who escorted me had had time to
re-enter the fort. I hope General Webb's letter may
induce the English to surrender the sooner." [1]

By this time the sappers had worked their way to
the angle of the lake, where they were stopped by a
marshy hollow, beyond which was a tract of high
ground, reaching to the fort and serving as the
garden of the garrison.[2] Logs and fascines in large
quantities were thrown into the hollow, and hurdles
were laid over them to form a causeway for the
cannon. Then the sap was continued up the accliv-
ity beyond, a trench was opened in the garden, and a
battery begun, not two hundred and fifty yards from
the fort. The Indians, in great number, crawled
forward among the beans, maize, and cabbages, and

---

[1] Bougainville, *Journal*. *Bougainville au Ministre*, 19 *Août*, 1757.

[2] Now (1882) the site of Fort William Henry Hotel, with its
grounds. The hollow is partly filled by the main road of Caldwell.

lay there ensconced. On the night of the seventh, two men came out of the fort, apparently to reconnoitre, with a view to a sortie, when they were greeted by a general volley and a burst of yells which echoed among the mountains; followed by responsive whoops pealing through the darkness from the various camps and lurking-places of the savage warriors far and near.

The position of the besieged was now deplorable. More than three hundred of them had been killed and wounded; small-pox was raging in the fort; the place was a focus of infection, and the casemates were crowded with the sick. A sortie from the intrenched camp and another from the fort had been repulsed with loss. All their large cannon and mortars had been burst, or disabled by shot; only seven small pieces were left fit for service; [1] and the whole of Montcalm's thirty-one cannon and fifteen mortars and howitzers would soon open fire, while the walls were already breached, and an assault was imminent. Through the night of the eighth they fired briskly from all their remaining pieces. In the morning the officers held a council, and all agreed to surrender if honorable terms could be had. A white flag was raised, a drum was beat, and Lieutenant-Colonel Young, mounted on horseback, for a shot in the foot had disabled him from walking, went, followed by a few soldiers, to the tent of Montcalm.

It was agreed that the English troops should march

[1] Frye, *Journal.*

out with the honors of war, and be escorted to Fort
Edward by a detachment of French troops; that
they should not serve for eighteen months; and that
all French prisoners captured in America since the
war began should be given up within three months.
The stores, munitions, and artillery were to be the
prize of the victors, except one field-piece, which
the garrison were to retain in recognition of their
brave defence.

Before signing the capitulation Montcalm called
the Indian chiefs to council, and asked them to consent to the conditions, and promise to restrain their
young warriors from any disorder. They approved
everything and promised everything. The garrison
then evacuated the fort, and marched to join their
comrades in the intrenched camp, which was included
in the surrender. No sooner were they gone than a
crowd of Indians clambered through the embrasures
in search of rum and plunder. All the sick men
unable to leave their beds were instantly butchered.[1]
"I was witness of this spectacle," says the missionary
Roubaud; "I saw one of these barbarians come out
of the casemates with a human head in his hand,
from which the blood ran in streams, and which he
paraded as if he had got the finest prize in the world."
There was little left to plunder; and the Indians,
joined by the more lawless of the Canadians, turned
their attention to the intrenched camp, where all the
English were now collected.

[1] *Attestation of William Arbuthnot, Captain in Frye's Regiment.*

The French guard stationed there could not or would not keep out the rabble. By the advice of Montcalm the English stove their rum-barrels; but the Indians were drunk already with homicidal rage, and the glitter of their vicious eyes told of the devil within. They roamed among the tents, intrusive, insolent, their visages besmirched with war-paint; grinning like fiends as they handled, in anticipation of the knife, the long hair of cowering women, of whom, as well as of children, there were many in the camp, all crazed with fright. Since the last war the New England border population had regarded Indians with a mixture of detestation and horror. Their mysterious warfare of ambush and surprise, their midnight onslaughts, their butcheries, their burnings, and all their nameless atrocities, had been for years the theme of fireside story; and the dread they excited was deepened by the distrust and dejection of the time. The confusion in the camp lasted through the afternoon. "The Indians," says Bougainville, "wanted to plunder the chests of the English; the latter resisted; and there was fear that serious disorder would ensue. The Marquis de Montcalm ran thither immediately, and used every means to restore tranquillity: prayers, threats, caresses, interposition of the officers and interpreters who have some influence over these savages."[1] "We shall be but too happy if we can prevent a massacre. Detestable position! of which nobody who has not been in

[1] *Bougainville au Ministre, 19 Août, 1757.*

it can have any idea, and which makes victory itself a sorrow to the victors. The Marquis spared no efforts to prevent the rapacity of the savages and, I must say it, of certain persons associated with them, from resulting in something worse than plunder. At last, at nine o'clock in the evening, order seemed restored. The Marquis even induced the Indians to promise that, besides the escort agreed upon in the capitulation, two chiefs for each tribe should accompany the English on their way to Fort Edward." [1] He also ordered La Corne and the other Canadian officers attached to the Indians to see that no violence took place. He might well have done more. In view of the disorders of the afternoon, it would not have been too much if he had ordered the whole body of regular troops, whom alone he could trust for the purpose, to hold themselves ready to move to the spot in case of outbreak, and shelter their defeated foes behind a hedge of bayonets.

Bougainville was not to see what ensued; for Montcalm now sent him to Montreal, as a special messenger to carry news of the victory. He embarked at ten o'clock. Returning daylight found him far down the lake; and as he looked on its still bosom flecked with mists, and its quiet mountains sleeping under the flush of dawn, there was nothing in the wild tranquillity of the scene to suggest the tragedy which even then was beginning on the shore he had left behind.

[1] Bougainville, *Journal.*

The English in their camp had passed a troubled night, agitated by strange rumors. In the morning something like a panic seized them; for they distrusted not the Indians only, but the Canadians. In their haste to be gone they got together at daybreak, before the escort of three hundred regulars had arrived. They had their muskets, but no ammunition; and few or none of the provincials had bayonets. Early as it was, the Indians were on the alert; and, indeed, since midnight great numbers of them had been prowling about the skirts of the camp, showing, says Colonel Frye, "more than usual malice in their looks." Seventeen wounded men of his regiment lay in huts, unable to join the march. In the preceding afternoon Miles Whitworth, the regimental surgeon, had passed them over to the care of a French surgeon, according to an agreement made at the time of the surrender; but, the Frenchman being absent, the other remained with them attending to their wants. The French surgeon had caused special sentinels to be posted for their protection. These were now removed, at the moment when they were needed most; upon which, about five o'clock in the morning, the Indians entered the huts, dragged out the inmates, and tomahawked and scalped them all, before the eyes of Whitworth, and in presence of La Corne and other Canadian officers, as well as of a French guard stationed within forty feet of the spot; and, declares the surgeon under oath, "none, either officer or soldier, protected the said wounded

men." [1] The opportune butchery relieved them of a
troublesome burden.

A scene of plundering now began. The escort had
by this time arrived, and Monro complained to the
officers that the capitulation was broken; but got no
other answer than advice to give up the baggage to
the Indians in order to appease them. To this the
English at length agreed; but it only increased the
excitement of the mob. They demanded rum; and
some of the soldiers, afraid to refuse, gave it to them
from their canteens, thus adding fuel to the flame.
When, after much difficulty, the column at last got
out of the camp and began to move along the road
that crossed the rough plain between the intrenchment and the forest, the Indians crowded upon them,
impeded their march, snatched caps, coats, and
weapons from men and officers, tomahawked those
that resisted, and, seizing upon shrieking women and
children, dragged them off or murdered them on the
spot. It is said that some of the interpreters secretly
fomented the disorder. [2] Suddenly there rose the
screech of the war-whoop. At this signal of butchery, which was given by Abenaki Christians from
the mission of the Penobscot, [3] a mob of savages
rushed upon the New Hampshire men at the rear of
the column, and killed or dragged away eighty of

[1] *Affidavit of Miles Whitworth.* See Appendix F.
[2] This is stated by Pouchot and Bougainville; the latter of
whom confirms the testimony of the English witnesses, that
Canadian officers present did nothing to check the Indians.
[3] See note, end of chapter

them.[1]   A frightful tumult ensued, when Montcalm,
Lévis, Bourlamaque, and many other French officers,
who had hastened from their camp on the first news
of disturbance, threw themselves among the Indians,
and by promises and threats tried to allay their
frenzy. "Kill me, but spare the English who are
under my protection," exclaimed Montcalm. He
took from one of them a young officer whom the
savage had seized; upon which several other Indians
immediately tomahawked their prisoners, lest they
too should be taken from them. One writer says
that a French grenadier was killed and two wounded
in attempting to restore order; but the statement is
doubtful. The English seemed paralyzed, and for-
tunately did not attempt a resistance, which, without
ammunition as they were, would have ended in a
general massacre. Their broken column straggled
forward in wild disorder, amid the din of whoops and
shrieks, till they reached the French advance-guard,
which consisted of Canadians; and here they demanded protection from the officers, who refused to
give it, telling them that they must take to the
woods and shift for themselves. Frye was seized by
a number of Indians, who, brandishing spears and
tomahawks, threatened him with death and tore off
his clothing, leaving nothing but breeches, shoes,
and shirt. Repelled by the officers of the guard, he

1 Belknap, *History of New Hampshire,* says that eighty were
killed. Governor Wentworth, writing immediately after the event,
says "killed or captivated."

made for the woods. A Connecticut soldier who
was present says of him that he leaped upon an
Indian who stood in his way, disarmed and killed
him, and then escaped; but Frye himself does not
mention the incident. Captain Burke, also of the
Massachusetts regiment, was stripped, after a violent
struggle, of all his clothes; then broke loose, gained
the woods, spent the night shivering in the thick
grass of a marsh, and on the next day reached Fort
Edward. Jonathan Carver, a provincial volunteer,
declares that, when the tumult was at its height, he
saw officers of the French army walking about at a
little distance and talking with seeming unconcern.
Three or four Indians seized him, brandished their
tomahawks over his head, and tore off most of his
clothes, while he vainly claimed protection from a
sentinel, who called him an English dog, and violently
pushed him back among his tormentors. Two of
them were dragging him towards the neighboring
swamp, when an English officer, stripped of everything but his scarlet breeches, ran by. One of
Carver's captors sprang upon him, but was thrown
to the ground; whereupon the other went to the aid
of his comrade and drove his tomahawk into the back
of the Englishman. As Carver turned to run, an
English boy, about twelve years old, clung to him
and begged for help. They ran on together for a
moment, when the boy was seized, dragged from his
protector, and, as Carver judged by his shrieks,
was murdered. He himself escaped to the forest,

and after three days of famine reached Fort Edward.

The bonds of discipline seem for the time to have been completely broken; for while Montcalm and his chief officers used every effort to restore order, even at the risk of their lives, many other officers, chiefly of the militia, failed atrociously to do their duty. How many English were killed it is impossible to tell with exactness. Roubaud says that he saw forty or fifty corpses scattered about the field. Lévis says fifty; which does not include the sick and wounded before murdered in the camp and fort. It is certain that six or seven hundred persons were carried off, stripped, and otherwise maltreated. Montcalm succeeded in recovering more than four hundred of them in the course of the day; and many of the French officers did what they could to relieve their wants by buying back from their captors the clothing that had been torn from them. Many of the fugitives had taken refuge in the fort, whither Monro himself had gone to demand protection for his followers; and here Roubaud presently found a crowd of half-frenzied women, crying in anguish for husbands and children. All the refugees and redeemed prisoners were afterwards conducted to the intrenched camp, where food and shelter were provided for them and a strong guard set for their protection until the fifteenth, when they were sent under an escort to Fort Edward. Here cannon had been fired at intervals to guide those who had fled to the woods, whence they came dropping in from day to day, half dead with famine.

On the morning after the massacre the Indians decamped in a body and set out for Montreal, carrying with them their plunder and some two hundred prisoners, who, it is said, could not be got out of their hands. The soldiers were set to the work of demolishing the English fort; and the task occupied several days. The barracks were torn down, and the huge pine-logs of the rampart thrown into a heap. The dead bodies that filled the casemates were added to the mass, and fire was set to the whole. The mighty funeral pyre blazed all night. Then, on the sixteenth, the army re-embarked. The din of ten thousand combatants, the rage, the terror, the agony, were gone; and no living thing was left but the wolves that gathered from the mountains to feast upon the dead.[1]

[1] The foregoing chapter rests largely on evidence never before brought to light, including the minute *Journal* of Bougainville, — a document which can hardly be commended too much, — the correspondence of Webb, a letter of Colonel Frye, written just after the massacre, and a journal of the siege, sent by him to Governor Pownall as his official report. Extracts from these, as well as from the affidavit of Dr. Whitworth, which is also new evidence, are given in Appendix F.

The Diary of Malartic and the correspondence of Montcalm, Lévis, Vaudreuil, and Bigot, also throw light on the campaign, as well as numerous reports of the siege, official and semi-official. The long letter of the Jesuit Roubaud, printed anonymously in the *Lettres Édifiantes et Curieuses*, gives a remarkably vivid account of what he saw. He was an intelligent person, who may be trusted where he has no motive for lying. Curious particulars about him will be found in a paper called, *The deplorable Case of Mr. Roubaud,* printed in the *Historical Magazine, Second Series*, viii. 282. Compare Verreau, *Report on Canadian Archives*, 1874.

Impressions of the massacre at Fort William Henry have hitherto been derived chiefly from the narrative of Captain Jonathan Carver, in his *Travels*. He has discredited himself by his exaggeration of the number killed; but his account of what he himself saw, tallies with that of the other witnesses. He is outdone in exaggeration by an anonymous French writer of the time, who seems rather pleased at the occurrence, and affirms that all the English were killed except seven hundred, these last being captured, so that none escaped (*Nouvelles du Canada envoyées de Montréal, Août*, 1757). Carver puts killed and captured together at fifteen hundred. Vaudreuil, who always makes light of Indian barbarities, goes to the other extreme, and avers that no more than five or six were killed. Lévis and Roubaud, who saw everything, and were certain not to exaggerate the number, give the most trustworthy evidence on this point. The capitulation, having been broken by the allies of France, was declared void by the British Government.

The Signal of Butchery. Montcalm, Bougainville, and several others say that the massacre was begun by the Abenakis of Panaouski. Father Martin, in quoting the letter in which Montcalm makes this statement, inserts the word *idolâtres*, which is not in the original. Dussieux and O'Callaghan give the passage correctly. This Abenaki band, ancestors of the present Penobscots, were no idolaters, but had been converted more than half a century. In the official list of the Indian allies, they are set down among the Christians. Roubaud, who had charge of them during the expedition, speaks of these and other converts with singular candor: " Vous avez dû vous apercevoir . . . que nos sauvages, pour être Chrétiens, n'en sont pas plus irrépréhensibles dans leur conduite."

END OF VOL. I.